Empirical Models for Biblical Criticism

Empirical Models

for Biblical Criticism

Edited by
Jeffrey H. Tigay

University of Pennsylvania Press

Philadelphia

1985

Translations of biblical texts, often in modified form, are based on *The Torah, The Prophets*, and *The Writings*, copyright © 1967, 1978, and 1982 by the Jewish Publication Society of America, and are used by courtesy of the Society.

The following publishers have generously given permission to use material published previously in different form:
The Society of Biblical Literature, for excerpts from "An Empirical Basis for the Documentary Hypothesis" by Jeffrey H. Tigay, in *JBL* 94 (1975): 329–42.
E. Rubinstein's Publishing House, Jerusalem, Israel, for excerpts from "The Method of Historico-Literary Criticism Exemplified by Joshua 20" (in Hebrew) by Alexander Rofé, and "The Stylistic Criteria of Source Criticism in the Light of Ancient Near Eastern Literature" by Jeffrey H. Tigay, in *Isac Leo Seeligmann Volume* (Jerusalem: E. Rubinstein, 1983).
The Israel Society for Biblical Research, for excerpts from "II Kings 20:7 — Isaiah 38:21–22" (in Hebrew) by Yair Zakovitch, in *Beth Mikra* 17 (1972): 302–5.
The Historical Society of Israel, for excerpts from "Tendentious Chronology in the Book of Chronicles" (in Hebrew) by Mordechai Cogan, in *Zion* 45 (1980): 165–72.
Leuven University Press, for excerpts from "Some Aspects of the Textual and Literary History of the Book of Jeremiah" by Emanuel Tov, in P.-M. Bogaert, ed., *Le livre de Jérémie. Le prophète et son milieu. Les oracles et leur transmission*. Colloquium Biblicum Lovaniense XXXI, 1980. Bibliotheca Ephemeridum Theologicarum Lovaniensium, 54 (Leuven: Leuven University Press/Uitgeverij Peeters, 1981), pp. 145–67.

Library of Congress Cataloging in Publication Data
Main entry under title:

Empirical models for Biblical criticism.

  Bibliography: p.
  Includes index.
  1. Bible. O.T.—Criticism, interpretation, etc.—
Addresses, essays, lectures. I. Tigay, Jeffrey H.
BS1192.E48 1985   221.6   84-20951
ISBN 0-8122-7976-X

Printed in the United States of America

For my mother-in-law
and in memory of my father-in-law
for the obvious and more

Contents

3. The Composition of 1 Samuel 16–18 in the Light of the Septuagint Version

EMANUEL TOV

4. Joshua 20: Historico-Literary Criticism Illustrated

ALEXANDER ROFÉ

5. The Stylistic Criterion of Source Criticism in the Light of Ancient Near Eastern and Postbiblical Literature

JEFFREY H. TIGAY

ILLUSTRATIONS *following page 130*

Preface and Acknowledgements

M y interest in the subject of this volume derives ultimately from an early fascination with the documentary hypothesis. What must have piqued my imagination was the idea that scholars thought they could prove the existence of lost documents which none of them had ever seen and no known source mentioned. Though I eventually became convinced that the arguments in favor of this hypothesis are persuasive, and that the reservations of its opponents are not, I also became aware of an argument advanced by some opponents that seemed more interesting than the usual harmonizations. This was the argument that the documentary hypothesis and related critical theories about the Bible were unrealistic because no works of literature were ever created in the way these theories imagined the books of the Bible to have been.

My studies of the *Gilgamesh Epic* and of the Samaritan Pentateuch convinced me that important works of ancient literature had indeed developed in ways similar to those reconstructed by biblical critics. At the same time, other scholars had been thinking and writing along similar lines from the perspectives afforded them by other texts. It seemed to me that biblical scholars might find it useful to have a collection of such studies which would be comprehensive enough to show their cumulative effect, to discuss the approach critically, to evaluate the strengths and weaknesses of models from various proveniences, and to consider what such models might show apart from simply conforming or not conforming to current theories about the Bible. To this end, I invited four colleagues to contribute studies in their own fields (in one case a new study, in the others, revised and expanded versions of earlier articles) examining specific issues in biblical criticism in the light of such external models. Their studies, along with three of my own (also new or revised) and an introduction, form the core of the present volume. Together these studies, based on texts whose evolution can be documented by copies from several stages in the course of their development—in other words, on *empirical models*—show that many literary works from ancient Israel and cognate cultures were demonstrably produced in the way critics believe that biblical literature was produced. This point alone, however, could have been made with less effort. The aim of this book is not simply to demonstrate the validity of a particular approach to biblical literature, but to illustrate, by means of case studies, the kind of research that this approach involves. The book is not merely an argument but a casebook which aims to convey a feeling for what was likely to happen in the development of biblical texts, and to suggest how further studies of this type might be undertaken.

I am deeply grateful to my collaborators for all that they have done to make this volume possible: their responsiveness to my invitation, their patience wih my editing, and their good advice to me and to each other. It has been a privilege to work with them. In planning the volume I also benefited from the counsel of Judah Goldin, Hayim Tadmor, and the late Maurice English, and from the critiques of David N. Freedman, Thorkild Jacobsen, and Morton Smith. For references and access to unpublished material I am indebted to Michael V. Fox, Charles Kahn, Stephen A. Kaufman, Martin Ostwald, and Richard S. Ellis. The index was carefully prepared by Lee Ann Draud, and the bibliography by Jeffrey Hymowitz. At the University of Pennsylvania Press, Ingalill Hjelm, Managing Editor, and Carl E. Gross, Design and Production Manager, and their colleagues have been unstinting in their helpfulness.

The writing and publication of this book have been supported by grants from the University of Pennsylvania Research Foundation, the University's Faculty Grants and Awards Committee, and the A. M. Ellis Foundation, and by a fellowship from the American Council of Learned Societies. Much of the international collaboration that went into the volume was made possible by the University of Pennsylvania's Israel Exchange Program and its Director, Professor Norman Oler, and by the Institute of Advanced Studies at the Hebrew University and its Director, Professor Aryeh Dvoretzky. All of this support is gratefully acknowledged.

I conclude, on the eve of our twentieth wedding anniversary, with thanks to my wife, Helene, and our sons Eytan, Hillel, Chanan, and Yisrael. To them I owe an inexpressible debt, in this as in all other projects, for more than they realize.

Wynnewood, Pennsylvania
June 12, 1985

Contributors

MORDECHAI COGAN is Associate Professor of Bible and Biblical History at Ben-Gurion University of the Negev, Beer-sheba, Israel, and serves as Chairman of its Department of Bible and Ancient Near Eastern Studies.

ALEXANDER ROFÉ is Associate Professor of Bible at the Hebrew University of Jerusalem. He has been Visiting Professor at Yale University (1981) and at Ben-Gurion University of the Negev (1984).

JEFFREY H. TIGAY is A. M. Ellis Associate Professor of Hebrew and Semitic Languages and Literatures in the Department of Oriental Studies at the University of Pennsylvania and Chairman of the Graduate Group in Oriental Studies.

EMANUEL TOV is Associate Professor of Bible at the Hebrew University of Jerusalem. He also serves as co-director of the "Computer Assisted Tools for Septuagint Studies" Project and as an editor of the Hebrew University Bible Project.

YAIR ZAKOVITCH is Senior Lecturer in Bible at the Hebrew University of Jerusalem. He has been a Teaching and Research Fellow in Folklore at the University of Pennsylvania and Adjunct Professor of Bible at Dropsie University (1979–80).

Abbreviations: Terminology

Abbreviations of Scholarly Literature and Ancient Texts are at the end of this volume, pp. 257–63.

B.C.E.	Before the Common Era (same as B.C.)
C.E.	Common Era (same as A.D.)
col.	column
D	The Deuteronomic source in the Pentateuch
E	The Elohistic source in the Pentateuch
J	The Yahwistic (German "Jahvistisch") source in the Pentateuch
LB	Late Babylonian
lit.	literally
ms(s).	manuscript(s)
NB	Neo-Babylonian
OB	Old Babylonian
obv.	obverse
P	The Priestly source in the Pentateuch
rev.	reverse
sub	under the heading
var.	variant
vs.	versus

Introduction

JEFFREY H. TIGAY

The Quest for Empirical Models

S ince the seventeenth century it has become axiomatic that the contents of the Hebrew Bible have not always reached us in their original
form. The books of the Bible are products of a long evolution, in the
course of which individual traditions underwent modifications in form and
content. Many of the books are composite, combining traditions or even
documentary sources which were originally independent of each other.
Further, many are conflate, welding together two or more variant accounts
of the same subject. These conclusions were reached by scholars reading
between the lines of the Bible. No other method was available for tracing
the evolution of biblical literature. Scholars could not base their views on
direct statements in the Bible itself, for it has relatively little to say about its
own development (the case of Jeremiah 36 is a notable exception).[1] Even
less could they rely on the testimony of extrabiblical sources of the biblical
period, since none is known which refers to the Bible. Nor were actual

A draft of this Introduction was prepared at the Institute for Advanced Studies of the Hebrew
University in September 1978 and revised after a critique of Chapter 1 by my colleagues at the
Institute during a workshop held there in July 1982. I am deeply indebted to the staff of the
Institute and to my colleagues for their contributions to this study. Recent articles by two of
those colleagues (M. Tsevat, "Common Sense," and F. M. Cross, "Epic Traditions") and
further discussion with them have helped me recognize some of the issues discussed here and
to clarify my own views. I have found myself returning to these articles frequently to learn and
be challenged by them, and my debt to them is not diminished by the fact that I have taken a
different path on some of the issues.

1. Passages in the Bible which cite earlier works give no details about the nature of the
relationship and in most cases do not explicitly identify the earlier works as their sources (see
Chapter 2, n. 83).

copies of the supposed sources or earlier stages of biblical books available for consultation except in rare and late cases, such as Chronicles' sources in Samuel and Kings.[2] As a result, critics were thrown back on internal critical analysis of biblical books in their final forms. Such phenomena as anachronisms, inconsistencies, doublets, and thematic and stylistic variations within a book were considered incompatible with an early or uniform date or homogeneous authorship. They were more plausibly explained by the supposition that multiple documentary sources of differing dates and authorship had been joined together to make up the present books of the Bible.

Although the results of this approach are impressive and command the field to this day, they remain, because of the nature of the methodology involved, hypothetical (witness the term "documentary *hypothesis*").[3] The degree of subjectivity which such hypothetical procedures permit is notorious, and it is no surprise that the documentary hypothesis was subjected early to criticism which has not completely abated even today. One particular line of criticism is the object of the present inquiry. This is the argument that the results of biblical criticism, especially as represented by the documentary hypothesis, are unrealistic. The claim is that no work of literature was ever (or, at least in ancient times) produced in the way criticism supposes biblical books to have been produced. One early opponent of the documentary hypothesis, C. M. Mead, protested that "no example of such a 'crazy patchwork' can be found in all literature as the one alleged to have

2. Note the suggestion of F. M. Cross (*Ancient Library*, pp. 166–68) that the *Prayer of Nabonidus* from Qumran (4QPrNab) may reflect an early stage of the tradition underlying Daniel 4. G. Levi della Vida ("Shiloah Inscription") suggested that the *Siloam Inscription* was an excerpt from one of the sources of Kings. An exception to the general absence of known sources is the likely dependence of certain biblical texts on foreign prototypes. Such dependence is usually, though perhaps not always, indirect, and would in either case require a separate study. Skepticism about such dependence is expressed by A. R. Millard on the basis of an argument that bears on issues examined in this Introduction. With reference to the flood story Millard argues that factual and ideological differences between the Babylonian and Hebrew traditions are so great that "all who suspect or suggest borrowing by the Hebrews are compelled to admit large-scale revisions, alteration, and reinterpretation in a fashion which cannot be substantiated for any other composition from the Ancient Near East or in any other Hebrew writing" (Millard, "New Babylonian," p. 17; to Millard the true explanation for the similarities between the biblical and Mesopotamian flood stories is that both remembered similar details of the same historical event). However, equally extensive changes are observable in the evolution of the *Gilgamesh Epic*, both from one Mesopotamian version to another and from the Mesopotamian versions to the Hittite version (see below, Chapter 1 and, for further details and their implications for the issue of intercultural literary borrowing, Tigay, "Literary-Critical," pp. 22–30).

3. Carpenter and Harford-Battersby, *Hexateuch*, 1:13–14.

been discovered in the Pentateuch."[4] A later opponent of the hypothesis, M. H. Segal, asserted:

Hebrew literature, or any other literature the world over, cannot show another example of the production of a literary work by such a succession of recurring amalgamations and such a succession of compilers and redactors centuries apart, all working by one and the same method, as attributed by the [Documentary] Theory to the formation of the Pentateuch.[5]

More recently, K. A. Kitchen made a similar claim based on ancient Near Eastern literature: "Nowhere in the Ancient Orient is there anything which is definitely known to parallel the elaborate history of fragmentary composition and conflation of Hebrew literature (or marked by just such criteria) as the documentary hypothesis would postulate."[6]

The reluctance of these writers to contemplate the possibility of something unique in Israelite literary history does not commend itself. Nevertheless they correctly imply, if only negatively, that other, unimpeachable examples of the assumed methods of composition, especially from the milieu in which biblical literature developed, would enhance our confidence in the results of biblical criticism. Concrete analogues would enable the literary critic to base his work on something more than hypotheses about ancient literary techniques. They could function as models of literary development, providing the critic firsthand experience with compilers' and redactors' techniques, lending to his observations a refinement they could never have so long as they were based entirely on hypotheses devoid of external controls.[7]

Analogues were not entirely absent from the argumentation of early critics. Richard Simon (1678) held that the Torah was in part composed of historical records kept by official scribes of Moses' time; as evidence of such public record keepers he cited the Persian and Egyptian practices attested in Esther, Ezra, Josephus, and Diodorus Siculus, and the prophetic historical records and royal chronicles cited in Kings and Chronicles.

---

4. Mead, "Tatian's Diatessaron," p. 44. Mead's was the first of several sweeping and mostly unsupported generalizations made by opponents of the documentary hypothesis about what can or cannot be found elsewhere in literature (see below, quotations accompanying nn. 5, 6, 32; cf. the similar assertion about the flood story, quoted in n. 2, above).

5. Segal, *The Pentateuch*, p. 4.

6. Kitchen, *Ancient Orient*, p. 115 (the full statement is quoted below, p. 10; similarly Young, *Introduction*, p. 153; Harrison, *Introduction*, p. 517.

7. On the role of analogy in historical study, note the comment of Troeltsch: "The means by which criticism is at all possible is the application of analogy" (cited by von Rad, *Theology*, 1:107 n. 3); cf. Hirsch, *Validity*, pp. 174–77, and Albright, *Archaeology, Historical Analogy*, pp. 3–11.

Simon believed it probable that Moses himself, having witnessed the practice in his native Egypt, established it among the Hebrews early.[8] Some
fifty years later Simon was cited by Astruc as one of his authorities for the
view that Moses had employed written records in composing Genesis–
Exodus 2. Astruc himself suggested, as is well known, that Moses had
arranged about a dozen separate sources for the ancestral period in separate columns, our present Genesis being a later erroneous amalgamation of
the columns. The only analogues he could cite for this procedure were
Gospel harmonies and Origen's *Hexapla*, but these played no major role in
his argument.[9] The eighteenth and nineteenth centuries witnessed the well-
known parallel development of biblical and Homeric criticism. Although I
am not aware whether specific phenomena in the growth of Homeric literature were explicitly invoked in support of theories about the Pentateuch, it
has been shown that the methods and theories employed in each field were
soon reflected in the other, undoubtedly indicating mutual methodological
influence.[10]

Analogy began to play a more prominent, though still limited, role at
the end of the nineteenth century. Chronicles was mentioned by J. E.
Carpenter and G. Harford-Battersby as "a conspicuous instance of the free
treatment of earlier sources."[11] W. Robertson Smith made extensive use of
the Septuagint as a model of the redactional processes underlying parts of
the Bible.[12] He explained the value of the analogy as follows:

Higher criticism is often supposed to have no other basis than the subjective fancies
and arbitrary hypotheses of scholars. When critics maintain that some Old Testament writings, traditionally ascribed to a single hand, are really of composite origin,
and that many of the Hebrew books have gone through successive redactions . . . it
is often supposed that these are mere idle theories unsupported by evidence. Here it
is that the Septuagint comes to justify the critics. The variations of the Greek and

---

8. Simon, *Histoire*, book 1, chaps. 2–3, 5, 7. For Simon's guess as to Moses' sources for
Genesis, see book 1, chap. 7.

9. Astruc, *Conjectures*, pp. 6–9.

10. Cassuto, *Documentary Hypothesis*, chap. 1. Carpenter and Harford-Battersby, *Hexateuch*, 1:3, in their survey of analogues to the composition of the Hexateuch, mention the
analysis of the Iliad only as an example of critical methodology but do not include it among
compositions compared in detail. (For recent, explicit use of the Homeric analogue, see below,
n. 47.) On the classicists' side G. Murray found "the most instructive example of the growth
and change of a traditional book under ancient conditions" to be "in the Hebrew scriptures,"
and he wondered "that the comparison has not been more widely used by Greek scholars"
(Murray, *Rise*, p. 107). For a recent description of the approaches of the "analysts" and
"unitarians" in Homeric studies, see Whitman, *Homer*, chap. 1.

11. Carpenter and Harford-Battersby, *Hexateuch*, 1:11–13.

12. *OTJC*, 3d ed., pp. 90–126, the quotation is from pp. 90–91 (the same statements were
made in the first edition [1881]).

Hebrew text reveal to us a time when the functions of copyist and editor shaded into one another by imperceptible degrees. They prove that Old Testament books were subjected to such processes of successive editing as the critics maintain. . . .

Prominent among Smith's examples are the differences between the Septuagint and Masoretic texts of Jeremiah which illustrate the process of revision, and the two conflicting accounts of the story of David and Goliath in 1 Samuel 17, where the absence of the intrusive verses from manuscripts of the Septuagint shows that these represent an alternate version of the story and that the Hebrew text has combined two separate accounts of the episode.[13]

The analogies adduced on the basis of Chronicles and the Septuagint had the advantage of coming from within the literary and textual tradition of the Hebrew Bible and of being products of the same literary environment. But the paucity of examples from close at hand soon led scholars further afield. In 1890, G. F. Moore adduced the analogue of Tatian's *Diatessaron*, a harmony of the four Gospels produced around the year 170 in Syriac or Greek.[14] Unlike the harmonies cited by Astruc, which presented the complete texts of the Gospels in separate columns, the *Diatessaron* wove the four into a single running narrative, thus leading to its Syriac designation as the "Gospel of the Mixed (Gospels"; the Greek title means "[the Gospel] by means of the four").[15] By comparing the *Diatessaron* with its sources, the Gospels, Moore was able to show in it most of the redactional techniques which critics found in the Torah, a demonstration that led one observer to characterize the Torah as "the *Diatessaron* of the Old Testament."[16] It has since been cited frequently as an apt model for Pentateuchal criticism.[17]

Arabic literature (already mentioned by Moore and Robertson Smith)[18] and ancient Near Eastern literature began to figure prominently in the discussion, partly as a result of the debate about oral tradition beginning in the 1930s. The debate centered on the nature of the cultural milieu in which biblical literature was produced. H. S. Nyberg and H. Birkeland and their followers held that in the "ancient Oriental" or "Near Eastern" milieu, tradition was primarily oral, as they argued on the basis of Arabian (mostly

13. Ibid., pp. 103–6, 122–24. For a new treatment of these analogues, see below, Chapters 3 and 8.

14. Moore, "Tatian's Diatessaron," reprinted below in the Appendix.

15. Stenning, "Diatessaron," p. 452.

16. Carpenter and Harford-Battersby, *Hexateuch*, 1:11.

17. Ibid., pp. 8–11; Mowinckel, *Prophecy*, p. 20; Bentzen, *Introduction*, 2:61; de Vaux, *Bible*, p. 35.

18. Moore, "Tatian's Diatessaron," pp. 205, 211–12; *OTJC*, pp. 328–29.

Islamic) examples, so that it was wrong to treat biblical literature as essentially the product of written composition and transmission.[19] In response, S. Mowinckel, J. van der Ploeg, and G. Widengren objected to the oral traditionists' reliance on models from Islamic times to the neglect of ancient Mesopotamian, Egyptian, and Canaanite analogues which, they argued, are more relevant to conditions in ancient Israel and are all examples of written literature.[20] Furthermore, argued Widengren, written tradition did play an important role in Arabia alongside oral tradition, and it predominated in cities. Responding for the oral traditionists, I. Engnell in essence withdrew the argument from analogy (which now turned out to support the advocates of written tradition) and held that inner-biblical evidence, rather than foreign analogues, was primary and decisive in the debate and that this evidence pointed toward oral transmission. The procedure of the Chronicler and a few other writers, whose work was admittedly written, could not be extended to most other parts of biblical literature: the *Diatessaron* stems from "a different literary situation" or background than the Bible, the thrust of the Islamic evidence is moot, and it is too late for application to the Bible. The literary-critical method "reflects a modern, anachronistic *book view*, and attempts to interpret ancient biblical literature in modern categories, an *interpretatio europaeica moderna.*"[21]

The extreme position of the oral traditionists was not only incompatible with the early evidence for written alongside oral transmission of literary texts in Israel[22] but was in a sense irrelevant to the issue at hand. Since the

19. Cited by Nielsen, *Oral Tradition*, p. 13; Widengren, "Oral Tradition," pp. 203–8.

20. Mowinckel, *Prophecy*, p. 20; van der Ploeg, *RB* 54:5–41; Widengren, "Oral Tradition," p. 203; idem, *Literary*, pp. 57–61.

21. Engnell, *Rigid Scrutiny*, pp. 6–8, 11, 53–54, 163–69; idem, *Call of Isaiah*, pp. 55–60; idem, "Methodological Aspects," p. 24.

22. E.g., Exod. 17:14; 24:7; Num. 21:14; Josh. 10:13; 2 Sam. 1:18. See Widengren, *Literary*, pp. 57–68; de Vaux, *Bible*, pp. 34–36; Koch, *Growth*, pp. 82–84. The Canaanite alphabet was in use in Syria-Palestine from about the seventeenth century on (Albright, *Proto-Sinaitic*, p. 10; Cross, "Origin," pp. 10*–12*; Naveh, *Early History*, pp. 21–42). This includes the period when the Hebrews may have been living on the outskirts of Canaanite cities as seminomads (one of the proto-Canaanite inscriptions is from Shechem, a city that figures prominently in the patriarchal narratives). It is theoretically possible that some Hebrews learned to read or write in this period (literacy is not unknown among pastoral nomads living in contact with literate civilizations; see Lewis, "Literacy"), though the patriarchal narratives do not mention writing (cf. Gandz, "Oral Tradition," p. 250), and there is no reason to suppose that the Hebrew tribesmen would have found it useful to write down their traditions. References to writing among the Israelites (including the writing of historical records) appear regularly from the time of Moses and afterward (see the passages cited at the beginning of this note, as well as Josh. 18:6–9; Judg. 5:14; 8:14; 1 Sam. 10:25; see Gandz, "Oral Tradition," pp. 251–53; Koch, *Growth*, pp. 82–83; cf. Demsky, "Proto-Canaanite," pp. 23–24). The medium of literary texts and many records would have been papyrus and skin (see most recently Haran, "Scribal Workmanship," pp. 68–72; Wenamun [ca. 1090–1080 B.C.E.] refers to records written on scrolls by the ancestors of Zakarbaal of Byblos, which takes us back into the twelfth

oral traditionists stressed that their oral tradition complexes were as fixed as written texts, their critics pointed out that the process of redaction of those complexes must not have differed from processes applied to written texts and was therefore amenable to literary-critical analysis.[23] In searching for analogues to help control the analysis, the question is where appropriate analogues may be found. It goes without saying that evidence from the Bible itself about the transmission and development of Israelite literature would be of the highest value. What evidence exists will be discussed below, but there is not much. It is the very paucity of inner-biblical evidence which prompted the search for external analogues.

Quite apart from the oral tradition debate, since the 1940s scholars have begun to stress the pertinence of analogues from the ancient Near East, especially from the cuneiform literature of Mesopotamia. By the accident of discovery, the first large cache of cuneiform literature found in the nineteenth century was the library of Ashurbanipal (668–627 B.C.E.), which contained mostly the latest versions of cuneiform literary compositions. But since cuneiform literature was written on durable materials (unlike the perishable materials on which Israelite texts were written), earlier versions of these compositions also survived and were subsequently unearthed by archaeologists. It soon became possible to trace the history of some cuneiform compositions through several documented stages over a span of nearly two millennia.

The kinds of insights that ancient Near Eastern literature might offer into the development of biblical literature were illustrated by W. F. Albright in a chapter entitled "The Transmission of Written Documents,"[24] in connection with the problem of estimating the historical reliability of biblical

---

century; see *ANET*, p. 27b, and Goedicke, *Report*, pp. 76–78). The perishability of these materials in the Israelite climate explains why no literary texts from the preexilic period have been found by archaeologists (as Kitchen, *Ancient Orient*, p. 137, notes, none has been found at Byblos either). The current evidence does not imply that literacy was widespread among the early Israelites (see Warner, "Alphabet"), but this does not mean that literary texts would not have been written, only that writing them down would have had some purpose other than dissemination (such as aiding memorization or verification of the text; cf. Beck, *Greek Education*, pp. 44–45 for similar reasoning about early Greece). That most Israelites learned their historical traditions aurally is indicated by Exod. 12:26–27; 13:8, 14–15; Deut. 4:9–10; 6:6–7, 20–25; 11:19; 32:7; Josh. 4:5–7, 20–24; Judg. 6:13; Ps. 44:2; 78:1–6; cf. Gandz, "Oral Tradition," pp. 253–61. But this does not show that these traditions were written down late (thus Koch, *Growth*, p. 85), for some texts make it clear that oral teaching was sometimes accompanied by writing of the same material; see Exod. 17:14; Deut. 6:6–8; 11:19–20; and 31:19–30; compare also 17:18–19 and 27:2–3, 8, with 31:10–13; and Exod. 34:28 with 20:1 (cf. Deut. 5:19). The same is true in other cultures; see *EGE*, p. 102 n. 72; Widengren, *Literary*, p. 47; Finley, *World*, p. 36.
 23. North, "Pentateuchal Criticism," p. 78; Bentzen, *Introduction*, pp. 102–3; Eissfe¹˙ *OTI*, pp. 5–6; de Vaux, *Bible*, p. 36.
 24. Albright, *FSAC*, pp. 76–81.

literature. On the subject of literary style, Albright observed that the anonymity and stereotypicality observable in biblical literature are even more pervasive in Egyptian and cuneiform literature, where traditional, stereotypical style so predominates over personal style as to warn against "using canons of style and vocabulary too rigidly in trying to determine authorship of" biblical passages.[25] With reference to literary evolution, Albright remarked on "the tendency of ancient Oriental scribes and compilers to add rather than to subtract," in other words, the fact that literature tends in the course of time to become expanded by additions, including variants, commentaries, and glosses, rather than to become abridged. Albright argued that this tendency has implications for the method followed in the compilation of the Pentateuch and for scholars' attempts to reconstruct the original sources. It implies, he said, that whatever divergences we find between different versions of a tradition represent nearly all the variants that existed; had there been other variants they would not have been subtracted. The process of growth by addition also implies "that much of the expansion evident in legal and liturgic passages is not due to literary doublets but to the normal swelling of the text by the accretion of commentaries or of subsequent court decisions, etc."[26]

Touching on the same subject some years later, G. E. Mendenhall noted that the evaluation of the historical worth of the Pentateuchal documents has been largely hypothetical, and he suggested the study of cuneiform literary history as one possible source of criteria for evaluating the historical accuracy of written traditions:

Since some religious traditions of the ancient world can be traced over periods of many centuries, we can see how the ancient scribe conceived of his task; we can at least have preliminary insights into the circumstances under which changes in religious (or legal) traditions took place. Even here we cannot mechanically transfer into Israel all the characteristics of the Babylonian scribe, but we shall at least have some comparable material which would be far more adequate than that on which 19th-century assumptions were based.[27]

The advantage of cuneiform analogues as a corrective to the hypothetical nature of biblical literary criticism was emphasized in a programmatic study by W. W. Hallo in 1962, in which he offered the comparative method as the

one approach which seems to offer some prospect of objective, verifiable data against which to test biblical [critics'] hypotheses. . . . In the area of literary tech-

25. Ibid., p. 77.
26. Ibid., p. 80.
27. Mendenhall, "Biblical History," pp. 30–31.

niques, the evidence from the literate neighbors of ancient Israel is not only relevant to the biblical problems, but also enjoys a scholarly consensus based on a maximum of facts and a minimum of theories.

The possibility . . . presents itself of tracing the growth of a Mesopotamian literary composition through two millennia, from its first written fixation, through its creative adaptation to new forms and even new languages, to its final, orderly incorporation into an official canon. Without this basic knowledge, all higher literary criticism remains hopelessly hypothetical. With it, the foundations are laid for a comparative approach to biblical criticism.[28]

Implicit in these calls for comparative models is the recognition that their analysis might yield results at variance with certain critical hypotheses about biblical literature. Albright illustrated this point in discussing the growth in length of the various literary genres:

Following the analogies of [Mesopotamia and Egypt], as well as of Asia Minor and Greece, we should expect to have long compositions as well as short at any given period. We should, accordingly, reject the evolutionary strait jacket imposed on early literatures by H. Gunkel and some of his successors, according to which short compositions are generally earlier than long compositions in the same category.[29]

In discussing the historical reliability of the Pentateuch, M. Greenberg raised a fundamental question about some of the suppositions underlying source analysis. Two of these suppositions are: (1) "that an interruption of chronological order or a mixture of styles indicates composition—resting on the assumption that original creations in biblical times were chronologically ordered and stylistically homogeneous," and (2) "that composition implies lateness." In order to test these suppositions, Greenberg called for tapping

the materials of ancient Near Eastern literature . . . by tradition and form criticism. . . . [A] study of their literary styles and habits, especially with an eye to the differences between our expectations and their performance, would put solid ground under the feet of the man who would speak confidently about what may and may

---

28. Hallo, "New Viewpoints," pp. 12–13, 26. Hallo's study is the first known to me to have cited specific examples of phenomena in cuneiform literature that bear on questions asked by biblical literary critics. Among the phenomena discussed are authorship, creative adaptation, the use of topoi and formulas, unofficial/popular literature, and the collecting, selecting, and preserving of compositions. In several later studies, Hallo discussed Mesopotamian cultic poetry in the light of biblical-critical questions; see Hallo, "Letters," pp. 17–18. For further illustrations, see Tigay, "Literary-Critical," pp. 5–30, and idem, "On Some Aspects," pp. 372–78.

29. Albright, "Oriental Glosses," p. 163; idem, "Canaanite-Phoenician Sources," p. 4.

not be expected in a piece of ancient Near Eastern literature. . . . Until we have solid studies of the styles of ancient Near Eastern writing, how can we speak with confidence about what is in and out of order, an editorial excrescence or an original "awkwardness"—from our viewpoint—in biblical writing? Not, mind you, that one has any right automatically to equate biblical style with extrabiblical. But if the evidence goes the way I suspect it will, the same sort of verisimilitude that Mari, Nuzi, and Hammurabi have given the customs of patriarchal times is likely to be lent to the present styles of biblical writing, changing our conception of the editor's hand in creating them.[30]

One of the first to adduce specific cases allegedly discordant with current theories of biblical critics was C. H. Gordon, who argued that stylistic differences within unitary Ugaritic and Akkadian texts weakened the use of stylistic differences as a criterion for differences of authorship in the Bible.[31] The same line of reasoning was pursued vigorously by K. A. Kitchen in his broadside against the documentary hypothesis, which was partly quoted above, p. 3. He stated:

The stylistic criteria and assumed mode of composition by conflation are illusory. For the documentary theory in its many variations has throughout been elaborated *in a vacuum*, without any proper reference to other ancient Oriental literatures to find out whether they had been created in this singular manner. . . . [Failure to compare these literatures] is a most serious omission, because—in the forms actually preserved to us in the extant Old Testament—Hebrew literature shows very close external stylistic similarities to the other Ancient Oriental literatures among which (and as part of which) it grew up. Now, nowhere in the Ancient Orient is there anything which is definitely known to parallel the elaborate history of fragmentary composition and conflation of Hebrew literature (or marked by just such criteria) as the documentary hypothesis would postulate. And conversely, any attempt to apply the criteria of the documentary theorists to Ancient Oriental compositions that have known histories but exhibit the same literary phenomena results in manifest absurdities.[32]

Like Gordon, Kitchen cited specific cases to buttress his argument. In using such evidence as the basis for evaluating a specific theory about biblical literature, Gordon and Kitchen have advanced the discussion from the plane of programmatic suggestions to the practical application of the program. Below (chapter 5) we take issue with their interpretation of the evidence and their conclusions, but their studies are a salutary reminder that

30. Greenberg, "Response," pp. 41–43.
31. C. H. Gordon, *Ugaritic Literature*, pp. 6–7, 132. In *HUCA* 26 (1955): 97, Gordon added Greek evidence to the argument.
32. Kitchen, *Ancient Orient*, pp. 112–29; the quotation is from pp. 114–15 (italics in the original).

comparative models could suggest conclusions at variance with current theories of biblical criticism. Challenges such as these must be met by any scholar who wishes, as Greenberg put it, to have solid ground under his feet when he theorizes about the development of biblical literature.

Parallel to the increasing interest in ancient Near Eastern models has been a renewed interest in the evidence provided by the Septuagint and ancient biblical manuscripts, as well as a second source of extrabiblical analogues, postbiblical Jewish literature. M. Smith has observed that biblical criticism began with

methods . . . based largely, though not entirely, on subjective criteria—especially on the critic's notion of the consistency and historical reliability which might be expected of an ancient author. . . .

Ideally, the critical study of the Old Testament should have begun with the relationships between [Kings and Chronicles and the differences between the Hebrew and Septuagint texts of Jeremiah, Psalms, Proverbs, Esther, Daniel, and 1 Esdras, and between Genesis and its revision in Jubilees].[33]

What form a book had before its present form we can only guess. The most reliable guide for such guesswork is a careful study of the actual procedures of the copyists, editors, or authors—whichever one call them—of the Old Testament tradition. In the differences between [the texts listed] we have objective evidence to show the extent and nature of possible changes.[34]

A few recent studies have made reference to some of these texts for various literary-critical purposes. E. Tov described the redaction of the Masoretic edition of Jeremiah by comparing it to the shorter, earlier edition reflected in the Septuagint; unlike Robertson Smith's earlier discussion, Tov's had the advantage of being able to refer to a Hebrew manuscript from Qumran which reflects the shorter edition on which the Septuagint was based.[35] In the Greek version of Esther, E. J. Bickerman found an analogue to the way that biblical authors preserve parallel accounts of the same incidents by presenting them as different incidents.[36] P. W. Skehan described the way the text of certain passages was expanded in the Septuagint, the Samaritan

---

33. As we have seen, some of these texts were mentioned by early critics, but only to support positions already reached on other grounds. They did not serve as models for the analysis.

34. M. Smith, *Palestinian Parties*, pp. 3–5.

35. Tov, "L'incidence"; for Tov's latest treatment of the subject, see below, Chapter 8. For other parts of the LXX which have a bearing on biblical literary criticism, see Tov, *Text-Critical*, pp. 293–306.

36. Bickerman, *Studies*, pp. 264–65; idem, *Four Strange Books*, pp. 224–25, cf. 187. See below, Chapter 2, pp. 57–61.

Pentateuch, and biblical manuscripts from Qumran by the addition of matter drawn from parallel passages. He suggested that the same phenomenon underlies Exodus 36–39, which describes the building and equipping of the Tabernacle in terms that echo the divine instructions of Exodus 25–31 virtually verbatim.[37]

Among studies drawing on postbiblical literature is one by I. L. Seeligmann entitled "Aetiological Elements in Biblical Historiography." Seeligmann observed that a number of nonetiological stories from Genesis are retold in Jubilees, with supplements making etiological points. From this he inferred that the etiological element in a story can be secondary, so that the same could be true of etiological elements found in stories appearing in the Bible itself.[38] M. Weippert, in discussing the historicity of Genesis 14, responded to the view that certain archaic traits of the chapter, such as second-millennium personal names like Arioch, suggest that the chapter rests on authentic historical tradition. He pointed to the book of Judith, where there appear characters named Arpachshad and Arioch, names the author of Judith found in the Bible and regarded as exotic and archaic-sounding. This illustration of how a late author digs up ancient names to give his story an archaic flavor indicates to Weippert that "in the case of Gen. 14 . . . we cannot deduce from the ancient personal names an equal antiquity for the tradition as a whole."[39] Most recently the Qumran *Temple Scroll* has been studied by S. A. Kaufman "as a model against which to test the validity of Pentateuchal source criticism."[40]

Some recent studies have also sought analogues in Talmudic literature (roughly contemporary with the *Diatessaron*).[41] M. Greenberg invoked the

37. Skehan, "Scrolls," pp. 102–3.
38. Seeligmann, "Aetiological," pp. 151–53.
39. Weippert, *Settlement*, pp. 98–100. On the other hand, Mendenhall cited Hellenistic literature in support of a warning against hyperskepticism about biblical historical traditions. The fact that Hellenistic writings utilized very ancient traditions implies that the lateness of a text does not imply the lateness of all its contents (Mendenhall, "Biblical History," p. 31 with n. 21). This would counter Wellhausen's much-quoted dictum that from the patriarchal narratives "we attain to no historical knowledge of the patriarchs, but *only* of the time when the stories about them arose in the Israelite people" (Wellhausen, *Prolegomena*, pp. 318–19; emphasis added).
40. See below, Chapter 2, p. 83 and n. 71.
41. However, not much use has been made of Talmudic source criticism. E. Z. Melamed described some features of the Mishna which make it amenable to empirical source criticism: "Critics of the Mishna have an advantage over biblical critics. While the latter . . . analyze sources according to imaginary internal indicators and conjectures which float in the air, the former have something to rely on: firm internal indicators, the testimony of texts contemporary to the Mishna, and the testimony of sages who were close, geographically and chronologically, to the redactor and his school" (Melamed, *Introduction*, p. 24 n. 63). Some suggestions about the applicability of Mishnaic source criticism were made by D. Weiss Halivni, "Epistemological Bondage." An example of the source and redaction criticism of the Babylonian Talmud, which the biblical critic will find suggestive, is S. Friedman, *Critical Study*.

Talmudic practice of preserving variant versions of a story to help explain the similar procedure of the redactor in Exodus.[42] S. M. Paul explained the disruptive position of Exod. 22:1–2a on the basis of the Talmudic method of "footnoting."[43] J. Weingreen has argued that Deuteronomy is a "proto-Mishna," relating to Exodus through Numbers much as the Mishna relates to the written Torah.[44]

Preferences Among Models

As we can see from the above survey, interest has focused especially on three sources of analogues: inner-biblical evidence from Chronicles and from biblical manuscripts and versions; postbiblical Jewish (and some Christian) literature; and the cuneiform literature of ancient Mesopotamia. A certain amount of attention has also been directed to Arabic literature, and not only by protagonists in the oral tradition debate;[45] however, interest in Arabic analogues has been limited, perhaps as a consequence of (and for the same reasons as) the diminishing of the role of Arabic-Islamic learning in biblical studies in favor of ancient Near Eastern lore. From time to time the literary histories of more distant cultures, ranging from the classical world to Iceland, Britain, and India, have also been invoked.[46] Recently the Homeric epics, viewed as products of oral literature, have attracted renewed attention as a possible model.[47] Finally, M. Tsevat has argued that the best

42. Greenberg, *Understanding Exodus*, p. 195.

43. Paul, *Studies*, p. 110 n. 1.

44. Weingreen, *Bible*, pp. 132–54.

45. See Widengren, "Oral Tradition"; Porter, "Pre-Islamic"; Greenberg, "Response," pp. 37–38.

46. Carpenter and Harford-Battersby, *Hexateuch*, 1:2–8; Nielsen, *Oral Tradition*, pp. 47–48.

47. See Cross's suggestive "Epic Traditions" and earlier studies cited by Alster, *Dumuzi's Dream*, p. 19 n. 8, and p. 21 n. 18. As the present volume is restricted to analogues whose development can be documented, Homeric analogues have been omitted, since Homeric criticism is hypothetical in the same way that biblical criticism is (see Tsevat, "Common Sense," p. 220) and is equally in need of help from analogues (see Murray, *Rise*, pp. 93–119; Nilsson, *Homer*, pp. 184–211). (This is not to say that biblical scholarship can afford to ignore hypothetical analogues; the number of empirical analogues is not large enough to permit such a luxury.)

One aspect of the Homeric analogy, which reopens the issue of oral tradition, should be mentioned here. There has never been any doubt that there was oral tradition in Israel (see Gandz, "Oral Tradition") and that it supplied much of the information found in our texts. The oral traditionists in biblical studies have sought to go beyond this truism and demonstrate that particular texts rely on oral tradition not only for their information but also their very wording. In recent years this has been done by applying the theory of M. Parry and A. B. Lord, first developed in connection with the composition of the Homeric epics (see Lord, *Singer*). According to this theory, certain features of epic style, such as traditional themes,

models for testing critics' assumptions are modern works of literature.[48] On the relevance of such models we shall have more to say shortly, but first we

---

formulaic language, and repetitions, indicate that texts containing them in considerable density were created and transmitted orally, always with a greater or lesser degree of improvisation and variation in performance. Yet there are problems that hamper the biblicist in applying this theory to biblical literature. Even in the home field of this theory, Homeric studies, the theory is not accepted by all scholars (see Lesky, *History*, pp. 37–39). Some scholars of comparative literature question whether the use of formulas necessarily implies oral composition (cf. Stolz and Shannon, *Oral Literature*, p. x; Russo, "Composition"; Davison, "Transmission," pp. 216–17). Even if one should assume that such features could have no possible origin other than the practice of oral composition, their presence in a text is not a certain indication that *that* text was composed orally. They may indicate nothing more than that the *stylistic canons* of the literary tradition to which that text belongs were shaped (or partly shaped) in a period when literature was still created orally. They cannot prove that literature was still being composed orally when a particular text was composed. It stands to reason that a narrative style created for oral composition and delivery could survive as a norm for centuries after the transition to writing (cf. below, Chapter 1 n. 65, and see, further, Komoróczy, "Akkadian Epic Poetry," p. 63 n. 88; Zakovitch, "*For Three*," p. 9; Zwettler, *Oral Tradition*, pp. 15–19; Porter, "Pre-Islamic," p. 22; Redford, *Study*, pp. 111 [on stock expressions used by writers of Egyptian stelae]; *EGE*, pp. 102–3). Another difficulty in applying this theory to biblical literature is the fact that it depends heavily on the existence of highly trained professional or semi-professional bards who sang epic poems and who are mentioned several times in Homer, while writing is virtually absent (Kirk, *Homer*, pp. 1, 53, 83, 152; Finley, *World*, pp. 36–37; Nilsson, *Homer*, pp. 206–8). In the biblical narratives about early Hebrew and Israelite history there are no bards. Historical tradition is related by parents to children, and written records are also kept (see above, n. 22). Professional singers first appear under David and Solomon, not as traveling bards but in groups, as palace personnel (2 Sam. 19:35; 1 Kings 10:12). They were perhaps preceded by the *mošělim* poets mentioned in Num. 21:27, but the style of the poetry attributed to the singers and the *mošělim* is lyric, not epic (2 Chron. 35:25; Num. 21:27–30; cf. Ps. 68:26–27). Indeed, whether there ever was epic poetry about Israelite history is uncertain; see Chapter 1 n. 3.

48. In a provocative article, Tsevat argues that the fundamental assumptions of critics about what authors are likely or unlikely to do (e.g., authors do not contradict themselves or use different names for the same character) are based on modern Western standards, since such assumptions could not have been derived from the Bible itself; therefore it is valid to test these assumptions by seeing whether they really apply to modern Western literature (Tsevat, "Common Sense," pp. 218–19, 229). There is also an advantage in using modern examples because we are relatively well informed about their authorship and composition, which is not the case with ancient Near Eastern works (ibid., pp. 220, 225). Tsevat concludes that certain critical assumptions are proved wrong by modern works that display inconsistencies but are known to be the products of individual authors. One may grant the value of modern analogues for testing universal statements about what authors do or do not do, as well as the fact that individual authors may be inconsistent in certain situations (cf. also W. Kaufmann, *Critique*, pp. 373–78). However, the assumption that contradiction may reflect different authors is not solely a modern Western one but is found as early as the Talmud, where clauses in a mishna which are inconsistent and cannot be harmonized are attributed by some rabbis to different *tannaim* (see Samuel in *b. B. Qam.* 14a and 36b and R. Yohanan in *b. B. Meṣ.* 41a [see note of Steinsaltz, *Masseket*, ad loc.] and *Sanh.* 62b), and contradictory statements of a *tanna* are explained as reflecting different traditionists' accounts of what he said (*b. Ber.* 3a). In any

need to look more closely at scholars' reasons for preferring the nearer analogues, and at the proper role of analogues. As we have noted, inner-biblical analogues have the most direct bearing on the way literary works developed in ancient Israel. The analogues in question are the texts trans-mitted in two versions: Chronicles' revision of Samuel–Kings, certain psalms preserved in duplicate, and non-Masoretic forms of certain biblical books.[49] By comparing the different versions, we can observe the process of continuity and identify the kind of changes introduced in texts and the methods by which they were introduced. Such evidence is directly relevant to the literary growth of the compositions it comes from, but it is also valuable indirectly as an analogue that may apply to the growth of other compositions. K. Koch, in his *Growth of the Biblical Tradition*, begins a section entitled "The First Steps in an Investigation into the Background of a Text" with the observation that "a study of material with a double trans-mission will provide the experience necessary to deal with" other texts transmitted only singly.[50] The relationships between such doubly trans-mitted texts may be typical of the kind of transmission many biblical books went through.

It is this feature of double or multiple transmission which makes certain postbiblical and ancient Near Eastern compositions attractive as additional models of literary development. Given the relative paucity of evidence from within the Bible (in all its textual traditions), they are welcome additions to the body of relevant evidence. But the relevance of models from these two spheres must be carefully defined, for each has disadvantages as well as advantages.

The great advantage of models from postbiblical Jewish literature is the fact that they are part of the same Israelite literary tradition in which the Bible itself grew. Indeed, several of them are revisions of parts of the Bible (e.g., Jubilees, the *Temple Scroll*). Though many of them survived only in translations, which makes comparison with their Hebrew originals more difficult, scholars who have advocated the use of these models have implic-itly presumed that the techniques of the revisers are a continuation of techniques in use when the books of the Bible reached their present literary form. But this is not necessarily the case. Precisely when the books of the Bible reached their present literary form is a matter of conjecture, but it is fair to conclude that this occurred in most cases prior to the Hellenistic period, in some cases considerably earlier. But the postbiblical composi-tions in question (from the Apocrypha, Pseudepigrapha, and Qumran texts)

---

case, the present volume will show that we are adequately informed about the development of some ancient texts and that, in some, contradictory matter is the result of multiple authorship, that is, the combination of sources.

49. See the texts surveyed by Tov, *Text-Critical*, pp. 293–306.
50. Koch, *Growth*, p. 51; cf. Gunkel, *Legends*, pp. 99–100.

are products of the Hellenistic and Roman periods. By this time the Israelites had undergone a considerable cultural upheaval, having come under the dominion and cultural influence of the Assyrians and Babylonians, the Persians, and the Hellenistic empires. One cannot rule out the possibility that some of the techniques reflected in postbiblical literature are different from those used earlier, due either to foreign influence or late internal development.

Lateness is precisely the impediment from which ancient Near Eastern analogues do not suffer. An important part of their appeal for comparative literary criticism lies in the presumption that they stem from a milieu which is culturally and chronologically close to that in which biblical literature was produced. In its most extreme form this assumption was expressed by S. Mowinckel: analogues from these quarters are "for the mentality and literary activity of the ancient Orient . . . even primary sources compared to" the Islamic sources.[51] However, other advocates of ancient Near Eastern analogues (Mendenhall, Greenberg) cautioned against automatically transferring the evidence of Mesopotamian literature to Israel, and with good reason. No less than postbiblical literature, Mesopotamian literature may sometimes have been produced under different conditions. Although some Mesopotamian texts were perhaps composed contemporaneously with biblical literature, some of the most important ones (such as the *Gilgamesh Epic*) were first composed in the Old Babylonian period (2000–1600) and reached their classic literary form in approximately the thirteenth century. The chronological gap separating such analogues from the final redaction of the Torah ($\pm$ 500 B.C.E.) is hardly less significant than those separating that redaction from the *Diatessaron* (ca. 170 C.E.) or early Islamic historical literature (eighth to ninth centuries C.E.). Nor was ancient Mesopotamia in any period culturally identical with ancient Israel, notwithstanding the many parallels between the two civilizations that have been identified.[52] The kinds of contact Israelites had with Mesopotamia in patriarchal, monarchic, exilic, and postexilic times do not seem to have been of the sort that would familiarize Israelite writers with the techniques that their Mesopotamian counterparts used in redacting older sources. That such techniques may somehow have passed from Mesopotamia to Israel is conceivable, but hardly to be taken for granted.[53]

Therefore, neither Mesopotamian nor postbiblical analogues are perfect; neither is really a "primary source" for the techniques of Israelite writers in

51. Mowinckel, *Prophecy*, p. 20.
52. Differences between the two civilizations have been emphasized by M. Smith, "Present State," pp. 26–35, and idem, "Differences."
53. A. Lemaire summarizes similarities in the institutions responsible for the transmission of "classical" literature in Israel and elsewhere in the ancient world (Lemaire, *Écoles*, chap. 3), but these similarities do not permit us to presume a priori an identity of *techniques*.

the biblical period. Each is a step removed from biblical literature and may have been produced under different conditions. This would be a fatal flaw in the use of such analogues if we imagined that analogues can confirm any particular theory about the development of an Israelite composition. That, however, is not the function of an analogue. Even another text by the same author cannot prove how a text was produced. Analogues can only serve to show what is plausible or realistic by showing what has happened elsewhere.[54] Such a demonstration, if compatible with the evidence from within the biblical text being studied, can help critics evaluate the realism of an existing theory about the development of that text or it can suggest a new theory about it. The absence of an analogue for a particular theory is not *ipso facto* an argument against its plausibility (what is unique is not implausible), but the existence of an analogue can enhance the plausibility of a theory by showing that it is not out of line with types of literary development attested in other cases.

Keeping these considerations in mind, it remains an open question whether postbiblical and Mesopotamian analogues should be given preference above all other extrabiblical analogues. If a degree of discontinuity with biblical texts does not disqualify these analogues, is there an identifiable point at which other analogues can be ruled too distant or foreign? If we assumed that similarities in redactional techniques could only be the result of cultural contact, or if we thought that an analogue could prove a theory of development, there might be grounds for insisting on proximity or close contact. But enough similarities in techniques are known from around the world to suggest that they can arise independently as well as through cultural borrowing. Despite the doubts expressed earlier about particular theories that have been supported with Greek and Islamic analogues, it is undeniable that Greek and Islamic literary history offer some valuable and instructive parallels to the techniques underlying biblical literature.[55] The same is sometimes true of Talmudic literature and early Christian literature (the *Diatessaron*), and even literature from more distant quarters. The technique of conflating was practiced by medieval English chroniclers, who wrote accounts of Thomas à Becket's return to England by conflating and revising earlier accounts.[56] Shakespeare used Plutarch's lives of Caesar, Brutus, and Antony in a similar way in composing his

54. See Tsevat, "Common Sense"; cf. R. M. Frye's similar use of analogues from English literature, including the "disintegration" of Shakespeare, in evaluating the source criticism of the Gospels (Frye, "Synoptic Problems").
55. See nn. 45, 47. A biblical critic feels very much at home reading such works as Whitman's *Homer*. On the relevance of Greek parallels to Israelite culture in general, see the articles of M. Smith cited in n. 52.
56. Longstaff, *Evidence*, pp. 42–113. I owe this and the next reference to Frye, "Synoptic Problems," pp. 274–83, where further examples of conflation are cited.

Julius Caesar.[57] Early in the nineteenth century, Thomas Jefferson compiled *The Life and Morals of Jesus of Nazareth* by literally cutting and pasting extracts from the four Gospels to produce a single running (though selective) account.[58] In the early twentieth century the Hebrew writers H. N. Bialik and Y. H. Rawnitzki composed their anthology of aggadic literature by combination and conflation.[59] N. K. Sandars' English edition of the *Gilgamesh Epic* not only added passages from a Sumerian text about Gilgamesh that was never part of the Akkadian epic, but also interpolated passages from other epics (such as the reason for the flood, taken from *Atrahasis*).[60] As recently as 1983, D. Wolkstein and S. N. Kramer published a book of stories about the Sumerian goddess Inanna in which Wolkstein combined different Sumerian compositions (in translations by Kramer) into a single story and, in Kramer's words, "skillfully wove the texts of numerous related poems into a unifying whole."[61] No doubt one could draw up a hypothetical chain of transmission showing how such techniques could have been passed from Mesopotamia to Israel and later Near Eastern cultures, and through Anatolia to Greece and the rest of Europe down to modern times.[62] But it seems just as possible that we are dealing not—or at least not always—with techniques borrowed by one culture from another, but with common-sense techniques which developed independently among the transmitters of literary traditions when they faced similar tasks. One need merely consider the research papers of inexperienced students to realize how natural such techniques are. Until taught otherwise, schoolchildren often string together verbatim excerpts from their sources, arranging them in a somewhat coherent order. In earlier times, prior to the recognition of authors' rights over their works which eventually led to copyright laws, such practices were not limited to the inexperienced.[63]

If we are indeed dealing with widespread common-sense techniques, and if ancient Near Eastern and postbiblical Jewish analogues cannot claim exclusive validity as models for biblical literary criticism, they will nonetheless retain a preeminent position among extrabiblical models used by biblical scholars. These are the bodies of extrabiblical literature best known and most accessible on a scholarly level to students of the Hebrew Bible.

57. Dorsch, *Caesar*, pp. xii–xix.
58. Roche, *Jefferson Bible*; cf. Thomson, "Four Gospels."
59. See below, Chapter 2, pp. 87–88.
60. See Sandars, *Gilgamesh*, pp. 49–54.
61. See Wolkstein and Kramer, *Inanna*, pp. xiii–xiv, 205–7, for an account of Wolkstein's editorial procedure. For a critique of this work, see below, Summary and Conclusions, n. 7.
62. Jefferson explicitly acknowledged Gospel harmonies as analogous to, if not the source of, his idea; see Roche, *Jefferson Bible*, p. 19; cf. Sheridan, "Introduction," pp. 57–58.
63. Cf. Wilcke, "Formale Gesichtspunkte," p. 242 n. 55, 2d par.; Frye, "Synoptic Problems," p. 275.

Furthermore, it would be premature to decide that no literary techniques are shared because of cultural borrowing, and scholars will naturally feel more comfortable with analogues from cultures with known relations to biblical Israel. But so long as the main use of analogues is to show what is realistic, even distant analogues will have heuristic value if they were produced under conditions comparable to those underlying biblical literature, especially if our knowledge of how they developed is empirical rather than hypothetical.

The Present Volume

The present volume brings together a number of studies that illuminate aspects of the development of the Hebrew Bible by means of comparison with analogues. The analogues are drawn primarily, though not exclusively, from the three areas focused on above: the biblical textual tradition (Chapters 2, 3, 4, 6, 7, 8), Mesopotamian literature (Chapters 1, 5, 7), and post-biblical Jewish literature (Chapters 2, 5, 6; the Appendix is based on postbiblical Christian literature). Some of the chapters are based on single analogues and their implications for biblical criticism (Chapters 1, 3, 8) while others start from specific critical questions and seek relevant analogues (Chapters 2, 4, 5, 6, 7, Appendix). Chapters 3 and 8 do not discuss the analogical implications of the texts they study; the author of these chapters traces the development of these texts in their own right, and the studies are presented here because of my own conviction about their value as analogues (each chapter is introduced by an editor's note pointing out the bearing of that chapter on thesis of the volume as a whole).

One chapter in this volume deals with the development of a prophetic book (Chapter 8), while another studies a type of editorial technique in historical books (Chapter 7). Chapter 6 is presented as an example of a little-used approach to certain biblical narratives that is suggested by a number of analogues. Chapter 1 deals with the growth of the narrative complexes in the Pentateuch. The greatest amount of space is devoted to analogues that have a bearing on the documentary hypothesis (Chapters 2–5 and the Appendix). This is because of the seminal role played by this subject in modern biblical studies and because Pentateuchal criticism has been the focus of most controversy. It will be clear from my own chapters that I find the documentary hypothesis persuasive, but the reader is urged not to read this volume as essentially a defense of that hypothesis. The processes illustrated here do not exhaust the possibilities for explaining the development of biblical literature; they only scratch the surface. Even where a chapter lends support to a particular theory about a biblical composition, some other comparative model might lend equal plausibility to a competing theory or even suggest a new theory. Indeed, Alexander Rofé suggests in Chapter 4 that the supplementary hypothesis, rather than the documentary hypothesis, best explains the development of Joshua 20, and in Chapter 6 Yair Zakovitch offers a theory of assimilation to replace the documentary analysis of Genesis 34. But in addition to lending plausibility to particular theories, new or old, the volume is designed to give the reader experience with concrete models of literary development and to illustrate the kind of research that must go into interpreting the evidence that is available about these models. It is hoped that readers will be encouraged to seek more such models, especially for genres of biblical literature not covered in this volume. Experience with such models offers the biblical scholar what wide exposure to literature gives any student of that subject: a feeling for what happens in literature, and the sophistication to formulate literary theories and evaluate those of others in an informed and critical way.

1

The Evolution of the Pentateuchal Narratives in the Light of the Evolution of the *Gilgamesh Epic*

JEFFREY H. TIGAY

Editor's Note

The present chapter is based on the Babylonian *Gilgamesh Epic*. Because several stages in the development of this epic are documented, we can trace this development as it unfolds over a period of about 1,500 years. Many of the phenomena presumed to have taken place in the development of biblical literature demonstrably occurred in the development of *Gilgamesh*, such as the origin of the epic in unconnected tales about the hero, their collection and transformation into an integrated series of episodes illustrating themes that an author sought to highlight, and the enhancement of the series by the addition of further material originally unrelated to the hero. In the course of this development, one can see the early malleability of the materials, permitting easy integration, reinterpretation, and revision of the elements, and the increasing reluctance of later editors to tamper with their sources when adding their own contributions, so that the latest additions to the epic are less well integrated. This process, too, has been presumed by biblical critics. These and other aspects of the transmission process common to *Gilgamesh* and sources of the Torah are discussed. Although we can see now that the epic was so extensively revised that no amount of critical acumen could have led critics to reconstruct its sources and early stages as they really were, we can also see that the general outline of development presumed by M. Jastrow on the basis of nineteenth-century critical suppositions was not very wide of the mark. The larger number of inconsistencies in the Torah indicates that it was not extensively revised; that is why it is more amenable to source criticism than is *Gilgamesh*. This study thus suggests the kind of circumstances under which source criticism is most or least likely to succeed.

•   •   •   •

The Evolution of the Pentateuchal Narratives

In testing out the realism of the results achieved by the hypothetical approach to biblical criticism, it is appropriate to begin with the evolution of the Pentateuchal narratives, since it is with these that biblical criticism began.

A typical current view would summarize the evolution of the Pentateuch more or less as follows.[1] The original literary units underlying the Pentateuch were single narratives about the early Hebrew tribes and their leaders. Such narratives were for the most part created, and at first transmitted, orally,[2] some think in poetic form.[3] In the course of time, some of them were gathered together into cycles dealing with various individuals (e.g., Abraham, Jacob) or other common subjects (e.g., the Egyptian bondage, the exodus, the conquest); the cycles were later linked together

---

See p. 1 unnumbered footnote.

1. The following is based largely on Bright, *History*, pp. 67–74; Speiser, *Genesis*, pp. xx–xliii; Mowinckel, *Prophecy*, pp. 31–32; Sanders, *Torah and Canon*, pp. 1–53; Gunkel, *Legends*, pp. 37–46 (cf. Wellhausen, *Prolegomena*, pp. 296, 335); D. N. Freedman, "Pentateuch," pp. 711–17; Fohrer, *Introduction*, pp. 113–95; Eissfeldt, *OTI*, pp. 208–9, 239–41; Habel, *Literary Criticism*; and Rast, *Tradition History*.

2. See Gandz, "Oral Tradition," pp. 249–51. On oral and written tradition in Israel, see pp. 5–7, 13, including nn. 22 and 47.

3. Albright, *APB*, pp. 140–41, 145; Cassuto, *Biblical*, 2:69–109; Eissfeldt, *OTI*, pp. 132–34. I know of no reason why there should not have been epic poetry about early Israelite history, but there is no clear evidence that there was. The arguments for Israelite epic poetry about primordial times (see Cassuto, *Biblical*, loc. cit.) are much stronger than those for epic poetry about early Israelite history (ibid., 1:7–16). Arguments for the latter are based partly on the fact that the Canaanites had such epics (e.g., *Keret*), but mainly on the presence of seemingly poetic passages in the midst of the prose of Genesis and Exodus, which could be the remnants of lost epic poems on which the prose narratives were based. However, the "poetic" features in these texts may be typical of biblical Hebrew "prose" in its own right as an elevated, quasi-poetic style (see Kugel, *Idea*, chap. 2, esp. pp. 76–77). The few surviving ancient poems with historical content which are long enough to classify are lyric, not epic poems (Exod. 15:1–18; Num. 21:27–30; Judg. 5; 2 Sam. 1:19–27). Num. 21:14–15 and Josh. 10:12–13 could be excerpts from epics, but they are too brief for us to judge. For recent discussions of the question see Cross, "Epic Traditions"; Conroy, "Hebrew Epic"; Talmon, "Did There Exist."

into lengthier narrative series (e.g., the patriarchal period), and, later still, these series were linked into comprehensive historical epics (e.g., the history of Israel from the patriarchs through the death of Moses or the conquest, or later). Apparently from one such epic (Noth's "G," for *"gemeinsame Grundlage,"* "the common basis" of the attested sources)[4] there branched off separate versions which in the subsequent course of transmission developed their own unique characteristics (at least J and E and, in some views, P). By this stage the narrative was in prose. Whether G was already written is debated, but at some point the oral material was put into written form (although this did not necessarily bring the oral transmission to a halt); in the view of most critics J and E were written. By this time, certain older written documents had also been incorporated into the narratives, such as the Book of the Covenant (Exod. 21–23) and quotations from "the Book of the Wars of YHWH" (Num. 21:14). Other traditions about early Israelite history were omitted from these written sources. Some disappeared forever, while others survived, either orally or in other written forms, for centuries and in some cases were picked up in postbiblical literature.[5]

When the old narratives about early Israelite history were gathered together into a larger complex, they were organized by the itineraries and genealogical links of the patriarchs and the exodus generation and held together by the theme of the divine promise to the patriarchs of land, progeny, and protection. This promise was probably an original part of at least some of the old traditions.[6] In any case, many of the original narratives had nothing to do with this theme; each had a meaning and a function of its own. Once drawn together, however, these narratives were transformed into episodes on the way to, or threatening, the fulfillment of the promises. Literary *topoi* were pressed into service to this end: The promise was threatened by the repeated barrenness of the patriarchs' wives, and the future deliverer, Moses, was endangered and hidden in infancy and saved in a basket in a river.[7]

The smaller cycles within the larger complex also have their own subthemes. The biography of Abraham, for example, appears as a story of

---

4. Noth, *Pentateuchal Traditions*, pp. 38–41.

5. Spiegel, "Introduction," pp. xxxi–xxxviii (repr., pp. 154–61); idem, *Last Trial,* pp. 57–59; Loewenstamm, *Tradition,* pp. 4–5; Cassuto, *Biblical,* pp. 81–82.

6. See Alt, *Essays,* pp. 83–84; von Rad, *Genesis,* pp. 20–22; Noth, *Pentateuchal Traditions,* pp. 54–58; Bright, *History,* p. 101 esp. n. 74; contrast the negative views cited by Clark, "Patriarchal Traditions," pp. 136–37, and by Noth, "Noah," pp. 430–33.

7. For the motif of childlessness, cf. the Akkadian *Etana* (Speiser and Grayson, in *ANET*, p. 117), the Egyptian *Tale of the Doomed Prince* (Simpson, ed., *Literature,* pp. 85–86), the Hittite *Appu* (Friedrich, "Churritische," pp. 214–15), the Ugaritic *Aqhat* (Ginsberg, in *ANET*, p. 150), and other stories cited by Rank, *Myth,* pp. 19–21, 25, 43, 48 n. 2, 56, 57, 65. On parallels to the story of Moses see Greenberg, *Understanding Exodus,* pp. 198–99.

personal growth from loyalty to God based on an expected reward to loyalty even when that reward is threatened. This theme, too, is not present in all the individual narratives but is imparted by the literary frame (compare Gen. 12:1–4 with 22:1–3)[8] and the recurrent promises appearing in the narratives.

After developing independently for a time, the two main offshoots of G (J and E) were ultimately joined into a single running narrative, one serving as the basis of the composite, with selections from the other supplementing it. By the time they were to be joined, the texts of these versions had become largely fixed, and the redactor did not have, or at least did not take, much freedom to revise them. Rather than rewrite the sources in his own words, he strove to incorporate them essentially as he found them, using their own wording,[9] making only such modifications as were necessary for fitting the various extracts together, or for other purposes he hoped to achieve with the new version. Where the two versions still essentially duplicated each other, one version would be dropped, except for significant variants which were maintained alongside of the main version.[10] Separate versions of the same episode might be interwoven to present what was taken as a more complete account of it (e.g., the account of the flood), or left apart and treated as separate events (e.g., the wife-sister stories).[11] The editor who joined the passages added his own connective and transitional phrases and often achieved fine artistic effects simply by skillful arrangement of the material.[12] Somewhere in this lengthy process, material deemed not suitable for the traditionists' purposes was omitted. Later yet, two other elements were added to this complex. One was a body of priestly material (P), which most scholars think had already coalesced into another

8. See Sarna, *Understanding Genesis*, pp. 160–61. The opening of Genesis 22, in which Abraham is prepared to do away with his progeny, calls to mind by phraseological and stylistic echoes Gen. 12:1–3, where Abraham was motivated to abandon his home and kin by the promise of progeny. The importance of this promise in motivating Abraham is underscored by 11:30, where the only thing we are told about him, apart from the bare genealogical and geographic facts, is that his marriage was childless (and this after unbroken generations of fertile ancestors). What Abraham proves in Genesis 22 is his spiritual growth to the point of willingness to serve the Lord even without hope of reward.

9. It is this practice that left documents within the Torah which are considerably more ancient than the dates of its redactors, and left largely intact those differences in style and content by which critics have identified and disentangled the documents. Cf. Robertson Smith, *OTJC*, pp. 328–29, who notes that "it is this way of writing that makes the Bible history so vivid and interesting" and that no book written by the modern technique of digesting and rewriting the sources "could have preserved so much of the genuine life of antique times."

10. Albright, *FSAC*, p. 80, and the paraphrases of Albright by Greenberg, "Thematic," p. 154 (quoted below, Chapter 2, p. 77); idem, "Redaction," p. 243.

11. Moore, "Tatian's Diatessaron," p. 201; Driver, *ILOT*, pp. 13, 20–21; Pfeiffer, *Introduction*, pp. 282–89. (On the meaning of the wife-sister stories, see Eichler, "Please Say.")

12. Cf. Greenberg, "Thematic"; idem, "Redaction"; R. E. Friedman, "Sacred History."

version of the early history, combined with cultic and legal rules; according to this view, P was spliced into the combined JE much as the latter were joined. Others think that the priestly material was not a fully developed source document, but rather a redactional strand produced by a priestly writer or school which edited JE and supplemented it with extensive priestly lore.[13] The fourth element, D, was placed near the end of the account of the desert period. The relative order in which P and D were composed and added to JE is debated. Most scholars have considered P the latest element on both counts, while a minority view regards P as roughly contemporary with D or earlier and thinks that P and D were joined to JE simultaneously.[14]

The bearing of such a process on the historicity of the Pentateuch is beyond the bounds set for the present study. It is clear that this process provides ample opportunity for distortion. Modern historians, too, however, base their studies on a multiplicity of sources, select among them, correct them, and arrange undated events in an order based on conjecture. The results of the process are not *ipso facto* distorted, but must be tested by considerations that lie beyond the methods involved in the present study.[15] In a composition dealing with events some centuries earlier than the composition itself, the greatest allowance for distortion must be made for the creative period between the events and the earliest written record of them that source criticism can recover.[16] It is precisely this interval that the

13. Cross, *Canaanite Myth*, chap. 11.

14. See Levine, "Priestly Writers," and bibliography cited by him, and Polzin, *Late Biblical Hebrew*. For the view that P is preexilic, see Kaufmann, *Religion*, pp. 153–211; Weinfeld, "Literary Creativity," pp. 28–33; idem, "Torah," cols. 497–502; Haran, *Temples*, pp. 1–12, 140–48, and Levine's review, *JBL* 99:448–51; Haran, "Behind the Scenes"; Hurvitz, *Linguistic Study*. On the sequence of redactions, see Eissfeldt, *OTI*, pp. 239–41.

15. One point which does emerge from the present study is the fact that old elements sometimes first enter a composition in one of its later versions. Skepticism about elements that appear only in later versions of biblical traditions (e.g., in P or D but not J or E; in Chronicles but not Samuel or Kings) has been countered by the plausible observation that late writers could have had access to old material. This observation is substantiated by cases such as the late appearance in *Gilgamesh* of the flood story, probably of the twelfth tablet, and possibly of the story of Gilgamesh and the Bull of Heaven; all these elements go back to much older written texts, as we shall see below. There were many channels for ancient material to reach late writers, such as oral tradition, the continuous preservation and recopying of written texts, or even "archaeological" discoveries of old texts (for the latter see, e.g., Oppenheim, *Ancient Mesopotamia*, p. 150; Ellis, *Foundation*, pp. 13–14, 154–57; Wilson, in *ANET*, p. 495; for chance discoveries in Palestine in biblical and postbiblical times, see 2 Kings 22; Yadin, *Message*, pp. 73–78; Driver, *Judaean Scrolls*, pp. 7–15). See also below, "Miscellaneous Aspects of the Transmission Process," no. 7.

16. Gunkel, *Legends*, pp. 94–122. For the question whether early Israelite historical traditions could have been written down close to the time of the events, see Introduction, n. 22.

present study, based on the comparison of written versions of a composition, cannot deal with.[17] But it is of interest to note that many historians agree that, despite the complex process through which the Pentateuchal narratives passed, the present form of the narratives has preserved some historical memories. Even a relatively minimalist position such as B. Mazar's grants the correctness of the rough outlines of patriarchal history: origins in Mesopotamia, migration to Canaan, and descent to Egypt.[18] Others grant as well the accuracy of patriarchal names, customs, and the worship of "gods of the fathers" and ʾēls.[19]

The above summary of views concerning the evolution of the Pentateuch is far from encompassing the complete range of opinion on the question. It is highly simplified and selective (in part focusing on phenomena for which we have parallels below) and would be modified by various scholars representing different approaches to the material. Nor is it my intention to insist on any particular detail of the summary. It serves simply to illustrate the kinds of phenomena presumed by biblical literary criticism, so as to set the stage for the discussion that follows. As O. Eissfeldt observed at the end of his lengthy survey of the variety of critical theories, "The important point is indeed, in the last analysis, not this or that individual dissection of the material, but the total outlook."[20] The question I wish to explore is whether this outlook is *realistic*, not whether the very processes just summarized are demonstrably those by which the Pentateuch was produced. My question, in other words, is: Is this really the way that literature grew in the ancient Near East?

An excellent example of the evolution of a cycle of narratives is the *Gilgamesh Epic*.[21] As a hero epic, it has certain similarities to the cycles about the individual patriarchs in Genesis and about Moses in Exodus,

17. This interval can be dealt with when we have independent evidence about the event itself, in which case we can see how a writer might have refracted the original event. See Cogan, below, chapter 7, and cf. Tadmor, "History and Ideology," pp. 13–25.

18. Mazar, "Historical Background," pp. 76–77. Compare Cross, "Epic Traditions," pp. 16–17, citing as an analogy to the early Israelite traditions Nilsson's view that the outline or plot of the Homeric epics was traditional, the cycle of events with certain chief personages constituting "a premise of the epics, not their ultimate result." Note also von Rad's view of the role of the ancient historical outline as the framework within which the Yahwist organized his material (von Rad, *Problem*, chap. 1). The most negative assessments of the patriarchal traditions—those of T. L. Thompson, *Historicity*; T. L. Thompson and Irvin, "Joseph and Moses," pp. 210–12; van Seters, *Abraham*; and Clark, "Patriarchal Traditions," pp. 145–48— do not concede the historicity of this outline.

19. Bright, *History*, pp. 77–103.

20. Eissfeldt, *OTI*, p. 241.

21. See *EGE*. The development of *Gilgamesh* has been mentioned before as a possible parallel to the development of biblical literature; see Rast, *Tradition History*, pp. 5–8, and esp. the comments of von Soden, Review of Kitchen, p. 41.

though it has little in common with the contents of the rest of the Torah, which deals with the history of a national group. Without wishing to blur differences in content (or form, since *Gilgamesh* is a poem) or to claim too much on the basis of a single example, it seems nonetheless clear that the stages and processes through which this epic *demonstrably* passed are similar to some of those through which the Pentateuchal narratives are *presumed* to have passed. What is known about the evolution of the *Gilgamesh Epic* shows that some of the results of biblical criticism are at least realistic.

The *Gilgamesh Epic* and Its Historical Background

The *Gilgamesh Epic* first became known to modern scholars in the nineteenth century in copies from the library of Ashurbanipal of the seventh century B.C.E. The epic tells of a hero two-thirds divine and one-third human whose exploits included defeating a heavenly bull and visiting the survivor of the great flood. If ever there was a legendary hero whose very existence might be doubted, it was the Gilgamesh of this epic. Yet the intervening decades have brought to light considerable evidence which suggests that Gilgamesh did exist. Two historiographic texts of the twenty-first or twentieth centuries mention Gilgamesh as a king of the city Uruk (biblical Erech) during the Second Early Dynastic Period of Sumer (ca. 2700–2500) and as an approximate contemporary of two other Sumerian kings, Enmebaragesi of Kish and Mesannepadda of Ur.[22] Inscriptions of both these kings and two sons of the latter have now been discovered, confirming their existence and greatly enhancing the likelihood that Gilgamesh too was a historical person.[23] The tradition stressed in the late prologue to the epic that Gilgamesh had the wall of Uruk built is mentioned earlier in a royal inscription of ca. 1820;[24] it is made plausible, though not certain, by the fact that the wall of Uruk was built of plano-convex bricks, which are characteristic of Early Dynastic times.[25]

---

22. See the *Sumerian King List* (*SKLJ*, pp. 84–91) and the *Tummal Inscription* (Kramer, in *GSL*, pp. 59–63; Sollberger, *JCS* 16:40–47; Lambert, in *GSL*, p. 48).

23. For the inscriptions, see Edzard, in *GSL*, p. 57, and *ZA* 53:9; E. I. Gordon, *BASOR* 132:28; *SKLJ*, pp. 92–94 nn. 144–46; for discussion, see further Klein, in *Kramer AV*, pp. 273, 278–79; Kramer, in *GSL,* pp. 60–63; Lambert, in *GSL*, pp. 48–49; Hallo, *ANEH*, p. 45.

24. Inscription of An-àm, king of Uruk (ca. 1821–1817; see Falkenstein, "Inschriftenfunden," pp. 18–22); *SAKI*, p. 222, no. 2b; Edzard, *Zweite Zwischenzeit*, p. 156 n. 831; Tournay, "Inscription."

25. See Nissen, "City Wall"; Edzard. "Early Dynastic Period," p. 65.

Nonliterary texts of the twenty-sixth or twenty-fifth century through the twenty-first century indicate that Gilgamesh came to be considered a god within perhaps a century of his own lifetime if not during his life. Offerings were made to him, and he was regarded as king and judge of the netherworld, the role by which he was best known in Mesopotamian magic and religion in the first millennium. Considerable attention to Gilgamesh is attested under the third dynasty of Ur (ca. twenty-first century), some of whose kings claimed Gilgamesh as their "brother," and this interest in Gilgamesh and other kings of Uruk's first dynasty has suggested that the Ur III dynasty saw itself as the legitimate successor to Uruk.[26] It is assumed that, under the impetus of this self-understanding of the dynasty, the Sumerian narratives about Gilgamesh and other kings of Uruk, which are mostly attested in Old Babylonian copies (ca. 2000–1600), were first composed or given their present form during the Ur III period, like most of the Sumerian literary texts first attested in Old Babylonian copies.[27]

Assuming that the Sumerian texts about Gilgamesh do stem from the twenty-first century, this still leaves a gap of half a millennium between Gilgamesh's lifetime and the earliest attested narratives about him. It is generally presumed that in this period the narratives were developed and transmitted orally.[28] However, recent discoveries suggest that the oral period may have been much shorter than previously thought. Forerunners of some texts previously known only in later copies have now been found among the Old Sumerian texts from Abu-Salabikh (ca. twenty-sixth or twenty-fifth century), at least one of which is virtually identical to its later counterpart.[29] Though none of the Abu-Salabikh texts is about Gilgamesh, there is one about Lugalbanda, who is identified as Gilgamesh's father in the Sumerian Gilgamesh tales and in the Akkadian *Gilgamesh Epic.*[30] Moreover, according to G. Pettinato, two of the Sumerian tablets from Ebla, from perhaps the twenty-fifth century, are copies of a text about Gilga-

---

26. Lambert, in *GSL*, pp. 47–48; Edzard, *ZA* 53:24; Thureau-Dangin, *RA* 10:101; Sollberger, UET 8:21; Falkenstein, *ZA* 50:73–77; Hallo, *JCS* 20:136–37; Klein, in *Kramer AV*, pp. 271–92; Kramer, *JCS* 21:112ff., ll. 94, 142–43; Jacobson, *Treasures*, pp. 211–12. On Gilgamesh's role in the first millennium, see *EGE*, pp. 80–81, 186–87.

27. Matouš, *Bi.Or.* 21:5; and idem, *GSL*, p. 93; Hallo, *JCS* 20:137; Wilcke, *Lugalbandaepos*, pp. 1–4; Landsberger, in *GSL*, p. 32; Klein, in *Kramer AV*, p. 271. For a list of the Sumerian texts, see *EGE*, p. 40, and for the generally accepted view on the date of composition, see Falkenstein, *CRRAI* 2:12ff.; contrast, however, Klein, *JAOS* 91:297, and see *EGE*, p. 12 n. 40.

28. Laessøe, "Literacy," pp. 210–11; Matouš, *Bi.Or.* 21:5.

29. See Biggs, *Inscriptions*, pp. 30–33.

30. Biggs, *JCS* 20:85; idem, *Inscriptions*, p. 91, no. 327; on the interpretation of the text, see Bing, *JANES* 9:1–4, and contrast Biggs, *BA* 43:79.

mesh and the Iranian city-state Aratta.[31] Thus one cannot exclude the possibility that some of the tales about Gilgamesh in the Akkadian *Gilgamesh Epic* go back to narratives that were written down close to his own lifetime.[32]

The Original Episodes

Whatever may be the antiquity of the tales about Gilgamesh, the earliest preserved written tales about him are demonstrably separate individual tales. Given our interest in the methodology of biblical criticism, it is important to note that Morris Jastrow Jr. (1861–1922) anticipated this conclusion in studies of the *Gilgamesh Epic* published in 1898 and 1920, before the currently available evidence was discovered.[33] When the *Gilgamesh Epic* was first discovered in the nineteenth century, only the late version of the first millennium B.C.E. was found, and it was impossible to trace its development empirically by comparing this version to copies of its forerunners. The only method available at the time was the kind of critical analysis that had been developed in the study of classical and biblical literature. Apparently influenced by the results obtained in those fields, Jastrow argued that the *Gilgamesh Epic* was a composite production, combining originally unconnected tales about Gilgamesh and about Enkidu (the latter partly based on tales about the civilizing of primitive man), along with other tales originally unconnected with either of the heroes, such as the flood story in Tablet XI of the epic and the description of the netherworld in Tablet XII, which Jastrow considered a scholastic addition to the epic.[34]

---

31. See Pettinato, *Catalogo*, p. 198; in light of the description of the texts there, the description in Pettinato, *Archives*, p. 257, as "two copies of the Gilgamesh Epic" seems imprecise; cf. *EGE*, p. 16 n. 65.

32. This would tend to further undermine the view that the Sumerian texts about Gilgamesh from the Old Babylonian period are merely transcriptions of current oral poetry. See below, n. 65.

33. Jastrow, *Religion*, chap. 23; idem, *ZA* 13:288–301; idem, *YOR* 4(3):32–55; cf. also Jastrow, *AJSL* 15:193–214, and his study of *Enuma Elish*, "Composite Character."

34. Nowhere does Jastrow seek to demonstrate the original independence of elements by the kind of rigorous, detailed textual analysis common in biblical criticism. He seems rather to have assumed such independence as a possibility from the outset and to have invoked it whenever he sensed discontinuity or discrepant literary types. Note his comments in *Religion*, pp. 476 (mythological character of Enkidu ["Eabani"] episode vs. historical character of Gilgamesh stories [p. 470]), 479, 487 (superfluousness [to Jastrow] of Enkidu's death before the end of the epic), 495 (independent character of the Utnapishtim episode; cf. *ZA* 13:289: "one can remove the deluge episode from the Gilgamesh epic without disturbing the narrative of Gilgamesh's career"), 513 (Tablet XII is partly a doublet of earlier episodes, and its

In the decades following Jastrow's studies, documentary evidence of the original separateness of the tales began to appear. Later in 1898 Jastrow was able to cite the Akkadian *Atrahasis Epic* and, by 1920, the Sumerian *Deluge*, in support of his contention that the flood story was originally unrelated to Gilgamesh.[35] By 1944 the Sumerian sources of the epic were understood well enough for S. N. Kramer to point out that they were separate compositions, not a single composition; Kramer's conclusion was subsequently confirmed by L. Matouš.[36]

As of today, there are eight known Sumerian poetic compositions that focus on Gilgamesh or correspond to parts of the Akkadian *Gilgamesh Epic*.[37] (1) *Gilgamesh and the Land of the Living*[38] and (2) *Gilgamesh and the Bull of Heaven*[39] are forerunners of those parts of the epic which describe Gilgamesh's journey to the Cedar Mountain and his battle with the Bull of Heaven (*GE* III–VI). (3) *The Death of Gilgamesh*[40] contains a statement to Gilgamesh that he has been granted kingship, heroism, and the like, but not eternal life, much as Gilgamesh is told in Tablets X and XI

---

scholastic character contrasts with popular character of earlier tablets). In a few episodes, Jastrow discerned signs of compositeness: p. 481 (the description of Humbaba's home reminded Jastrow of Garden of Eden and therefore belongs with story of Enkidu, who reflects the first man, while victory over Humbaba is definitely part of Gilgamesh story), 494, 501–2, 506 (the story begins with a plan to destroy one city, Shurippak, with which the gods all agree, but then it destroys all mankind, which at least some of the gods had not intended; therefore the story combines a tradition about the destruction of Shurippak with a nature myth symbolizing the annual spring floods that inundate the entire Euphrates Valley; similarly in *ZA* 13, where Jastrow adds evidence of two different names—Utnapishtim and Atrahasis—used for the hero). In a few places Jastrow states certain critical presuppositions, such as that "when a tale associates two figures in one deed, one of them has been added" and (referring to what he thought were Enkidu's dreams about the battle with Humbaba), "the person who dreams is always the one to whom the dream applies"; these presuppositions led Jastrow in 1920 to conclude that Enkidu, not Gilgamesh, was the original hero of certain episodes (YOR 4[3], pp. 36–37). Cf. also Jastrow's "Composite Character," where the analysis of *Enuma Elish* is based mainly on the argument that the battles of Ea vs. Apsu, and Marduk vs. Tiamat, are doublets of each other. Many of Jastrow's observations seem wide of the mark today, but not his general conception of the *Gilgamesh Epic* as a story which combined various once-independent traditions and myths and which grew by accretion over the course of time (*Religion*, pp. 494, 513, 514; *ZA* 13:289–90; cf. *EGE*, p. 37).

35. Jastrow, *ZA* 13:288–301; YOR 4(3):50–51.

36. Kramer, *JAOS* 64:7–23, 83; Matouš, in *GSL*, pp. 87–88; see *EGE*, pp. 27–28.

37. The Ebla text would be a ninth, though it is conceivably but not necessarily related to one of those listed, *Gilgamesh and the Bull of Heaven*; see *EGE*, p. 16 n. 65.

38. There are several versions of *GLL*. Version A was edited by Kramer, in *JCS* 1:3–46 (trans. in *ANET*, pp. 47–50); Version B is cited there in the footnotes (see *JCS* 1:7). For additional texts and versions, see *EGE*, p. 30 n. 34, and p. 305.

39. *GBH* is available only in the out-of-date edition of Witzel; see the summaries by Kramer, *History*, pp. 190–91; Falkenstein, *RLA* 3:361 and *KLL* 3:806; see also *EGE*, pp. 24–25.

40. *DG* fragments A and B in Kramer, *BASOR* 94:2–12 (trans. in *ANET*, pp. 47–50).

of the epic.[41] (4) *The Deluge*,[42] as noted, was not connected with Gilgamesh in any way, not even, as in the epic, by being addressed to Gilgamesh. At most the Old Babylonian version of the Akkadian epic may have drawn from *The Deluge* or a related account of the flood the idea that the survivor of the flood was a source of knowledge about immortality, since *The Deluge* states that the survivor was granted "eternal life, like a god."[43] (5) The second half of *Gilgamesh, Enkidu, and the Netherworld*[44] is the source of *GE* XII, which is a literal translation of the Sumerian text in which the ghost of Enkidu describes the netherworld to Gilgamesh. In addition to contradictions between both halves of *Gilgamesh, Enkidu, and the Netherworld* and the first half of the Akkadian epic (see below, p. 42), the fact that the Akkadian is a literal translation of the Sumerian rather than a creative adaptation, like other parts of the epic, lends support to Jastrow's view that Tablet XII was not placed in the epic by the same writer who composed Tablets I–XI.[45] However, other themes from this text—the harm done to some Urukites by Gilgamesh and his *pukku* game and the citizens' resultant outcry against him, and the death of Enkidu— are echoed in earlier tablets of the epic, the *pukku* game in confused form[46] and Enkidu's death under different circumstances. These were probably drawn on by the author of the Old Babylonian version. (6) *Gilgamesh and Agga*[47] deals with a conflict between Gilgamesh and the king of the city-state Kish; it has no counterpart to speak of in the epic. (7) Another narrative about Gilgamesh, UET 6, No. 60, has not yet been edited. It is described by Kramer as a "largely unintelligible fragment . . . of what is probably a story of Gilgameš unknown hitherto."[48] (8) Finally, a hymn of Shulgi, king of Ur (2094–2047), contains two short hymns addressed by Shulgi to Gilgamesh.[49] Generically they are similar to the hymn to Gilgamesh in *GE* I, i, 27ff., but in content they have nothing in common with the hymn in the epic.[50]

41. *DG* fragment A, ll. 33–45; cf. Gilg. Me. i, 8; iii, 2–5; *GE* X, vi; XI, 197–98; see *EGE*, pp. 25–26.

42. Text and translation by Civil in Lambert-Millard, pp. 138–45, with notes on pp. 167–72; older trans. by Kramer, in *ANET*, pp. 42–44.

43. *The Deluge*, ll. 256–57 (in *ANET*, p. 44, ll. 257–58).

44. Text and translation of *GEN* by Shaffer, "Sources"; summaries by Kramer, *Sumerians*, pp. 197–205; Falkenstein, *RLA* 3:361–63; idem, "Gilgameš-Epos," p. 806.

45. See *EGE*, pp. 27, 49.

46. See ibid., pp. 26, 189–91.

47. *GA* is edited by Kramer and Jacobson in *AJA* 53:1–18; trans. by Kramer, in *ANET*, pp. 44–47.

48. Kramer, in Gadd and Kramer, UET 6/1, p. 7.

49. Klein, in *Kramer AV*, pp. 271–92.

50. *EGE*, pp. 27, 158–59.

That the Sumerian texts were not sections of a larger literary composition was shown definitively by Matouš. Matouš pointed out that most of the Sumerian texts meet one or more of three criteria which indicate their separateness: three are listed by their opening phrases (functioning as titles) as separate entries in Sumerian literary catalogs;[51] two begin with mythological introductions referring back to primordial times, a feature which typically appears at the beginning of a composition,[52] showing that neither of these was preceded by any other episode; and five end with a doxological formula which typically appears at the end of a composition,[53] showing that none of these was followed by any other episode. Since Shulgi's hymns to Gilgamesh are part of one of Shulgi's own hymns, they were clearly not part of a composition about Gilgamesh.[54] In sum, so far as is presently known, the earliest attested stage in the development of the *Gilgamesh Epic* is a number of separate (poetic) tales and hymns, a situation that is comparable to Gunkel's supposition that the narratives of Genesis began as separate tales.

As independent compositions, the Sumerian texts about Gilgamesh must have had their own meaning and function. The Akkadian epic, as we shall see, revolves around the themes of death and immortality. These themes appear in some of the Sumerian texts as well, but those texts seem to be more interested in Gilgamesh as an individual than in any message based on his life. One may guess that the function of the Sumerian compositions is indicated by their concluding hymnic doxologies. Perhaps they were sung or recited as part of the cult of Gilgamesh in the Ur III period.[55] In any case, the point to keep in mind is that they must have had a meaning and function of their own and that these were not necessarily identical to those of the Akkadian epic.

Unifying Themes in the Akkadian *Gilgamesh Epic*

In the Akkadian *Gilgamesh Epic*, several of the Sumerian tales have—to oversimplify for a moment—been welded together by means of an overall theme. The theme of the epic, as is well known, is the hero's quest for

51. *Gilgamesh and the Land of the Living*, *Gilgamesh and Agga*, and *Gilgamesh, Enkidu, and the Netherworld*. See above, n. 36.

52. *Gilgamesh, Enkidu, and the Netherworld* and *The Deluge*.

53. *Gilgamesh and the Land of the Living*, *The Death of Gilgamesh*, *Gilgamesh and Agga*, *Gilgamesh, Enkidu, and the Netherworld*, and (not known at the time Matouš wrote) UET 6, no. 60.

54. Since neither the beginning nor the end of *Gilgamesh and the Bull of Heaven* is presently known, we cannot tell whether it met any of these criteria.

55. See *EGE*, pp. 35–37. Berlin, "Ethnopoetry," pp. 17–18, suggests that the Sumerian epic tales about Uruk express nationalistic aspirations.

immortality. The episodes of the epic are arranged in a sequence that develops this theme gradually. The prologue mentions the walls of Uruk and the temple Eanna, both built by Gilgamesh. Such royal building projects, with their accompanying inscriptions, served to perpetuate the builder's name and were a conventional royal means of securing a form of immortality. After meeting Enkidu, Gilgamesh adopted another conventional method of perpetuating his name, performing a great deed, namely, defeating the terrifying Humbaba, the divinely appointed guardian of the Cedar Forest. Later in the epic, after Gilgamesh and Enkidu had slain the Bull of Heaven, Enkidu was killed by the gods for this deed. The passing of his beloved friend gave Gilgamesh a firsthand experience of death and made his own mortality palpable. Shattered and grief-stricken, he could no longer be satisfied with the conventional forms of immortality-by-reputation, but instead sought literal immortality, that is, eternal life. At first he sought to learn the secret of immortality from Utnapishtim, the survivor of the flood, who with his wife was the only mortal ever to be granted eternal life. Finally, he pinned his hopes on a plant of rejuvenation. When all these attempts failed, Gilgamesh returned to Uruk and accepted once again the conventional means by which kings can, though only indirectly, overcome death—the building of enduring structures—an achievement to which Gilgamesh called attention at the end of the eleventh tablet. The passage in which Gilgamesh calls attention to the walls (*GE* XI, 303–7) repeats a passage from the prologue (I, i, 16–21), thus framing the epic and underscoring the futility of the intervening efforts toward immortality. This was presumably once the end of the epic, but it is now followed by the twelfth tablet, in which Enkidu's ghost describes the netherworld to Gilgamesh.[56]

A comparison of the Akkadian epic to its Sumerian forerunners reveals certain features that constitute the cement unifying the episodes of the Akkadian epic around the overall theme and are either unique to the Akkadian epic or play a unique role in it. All revolve around the role of Enkidu. It seems that converting Enkidu into Gilgamesh's friend was the seminal change whereby the author of the epic lent unity to the materials he used in the epic. In the Sumerian tales, Enkidu was repeatedly described as Gilgamesh's servant. Only once or twice was he affectionately termed Gilgamesh's friend.[57] To enable Enkidu's death to shock Gilgamesh enough to set him on an obsessive quest for immortality, the Akkadian author made Enkidu into Gilgamesh's "friend," "brother," and "equal" and spoke

---

56. See *EGE*, pp. 6–7.

57. "Servant": *GLL* A, ll. 3, 8–9, 95–96, etc.; "friend": *GBH:* Zimmern, *Sumerische Kultlieder*, no. 196, rev. "II," 11; *GEN*, l. 247; see *EGE*, p. 29.

regularly of their affection.[58] Enkidu's new status as Gilgamesh's friend and equal created a need to account for Enkidu's origins, which resulted in the story of Gilgamesh's oppression of Uruk and the creation of Enkidu to stop Gilgamesh.[59] As a model for Enkidu's origins the author adopted traditions about the creation of mankind and about the animal-like, uncivilized way of life of the earliest men. The contrast between Enkidu's early way of life and the boons of human civilization he later comes to enjoy enables the writer to highlight these boons, which he presents as the only meaning in life available to mortals. In short, the epic explores the meaning of life as well as of death, and it is chiefly through changes in the role of Enkidu that the Akkadian author accomplishes this.[60]

Although the use of the themes of mortality and immortality is what gives the Akkadian epic its distinctive character in comparison with its Sumerian forerunners, these themes are by no means alien to the Sumerian tales. In *Gilgamesh and the Land of the Living*, the sight of people dying upset Gilgamesh and prompted his journey to the Cedar Mountain to establish his and the gods' names (possibly by erecting inscriptions that might keep his name alive).[61] *Gilgamesh, Enkidu, and the Netherworld* describes Enkidu's death, Gilgamesh's grief, and the condition of the dead in the netherworld.[62] *The Death of Gilgamesh* narrates how Gilgamesh was told that he could not have immortality.[63] *The Deluge* expresses the idea of a human's being granted immortality.[64] It is true that these themes did not have the same significance and were not used the same way in the Sumerian tales as in the Akkadian epic. The author of the Akkadian epic was a creative adapter of his sources, not simply a compiler. But the themes of mortality and immortality which he allowed to dominate his epic were not invented by him, and in this respect he remained true to his sources even while he transformed them.

The way the Akkadian epic unified the tales of Gilgamesh and Enkidu around a common theme bears comparison with the ways in which the narratives about early Israelite history are thought to have been integrated into a unified whole. Just as the stories of the patriarchs, for example, are held together by the divine promises, with the episodes arranged to constitute stages or obstacles on the way toward their fulfillment, or the stories of Abraham constitute stages in his personal growth, so the episodes about Gilgamesh are held together by the quest for immortality and arranged as

---

58. *GE* I, iv, 41; v, 36, 47; vi, 1, 4, 14, 19, 21; VI, 156, etc.; see *EGE*, p. 30.
59. *GE* I, ii, 8–35.
60. See *EGE*, pp. 29–30, 45–47, 192–213.
61. *GLL* A, ll. 4–7, 23–33; Kraus, *JNES* 19:127–32; see *EGE*, p. 29 n. 28.
62. *GEN*, ed. Shaffer, ll. 177–203; Kramer, *Sumerians*, pp. 203–5.
63. *DG* A, l. 35.
64. *Deluge*, ll. 256–57 (*ANET*, p. 44, ll. 257–58).

stages or obstacles in Gilgamesh's quest and in his personal growth. Just as the integrating theme of the divine promises is thought to have been original in at least some of the patriarchal traditions, so the theme of Gilgamesh's obsession with death was present in some of the Sumerian tales.

Stages in the Evolution of the *Gilgamesh Epic*

At least four different stages in the evolution of the *Gilgamesh Epic* are documented. A comparison of these stages with each other reveals a pattern of decreasing degrees of adaptation of earlier sources and versions.

1. The earliest attested written stage (apart from the reported text from Ebla) is that of the Sumerian tales presumed to date from the Ur III period (twenty-first century B.C.E.). Except for patently mythological elements, it is impossible to gauge the degree of fidelity with which these tales reflect earlier oral or written tales about Gilgamesh or the historical Gilgamesh himself, since we have no earlier texts about him (again, excluding the Ebla text) or hard facts about his life.[65]

2. The earliest known Akkadian version of the epic comes from the Old Babylonian period (ca. 2000–1600 B.C.E.).[66] Though preserved mostly in fragmentary texts, the fragments parallel or refer to the contents of most of the tablets of the late version. What is more, they all reflect the themes by which the epic was integrated: the role of Enkidu as Gilgamesh's friend, Gilgamesh's reaction to Enkidu's death, and the description of Enkidu's beginnings. We may confidently conclude, therefore, that the separate tales of Gilgamesh were first integrated into a unified epic in the Old Babylonian period and that the Old Babylonian fragments reflect the integrated version.

Precisely how the Old Babylonian version is related to the Sumerian tales is a matter of conjecture. We know that scribes in this period probably studied the Sumerian Gilgamesh texts as part of their training, since these

---

65. See *EGE*, pp. 13–16 and 34–35 for some conjectures that have been made in this regard. It has been suggested that the Sumerian texts about Gilgamesh (and other Sumerian texts from the Old Babylonian period), are merely transcriptions of oral poetry (see Limet, "Chants"; Alster, *Dumuzi's Dream*, pp. 15–27). These views are ultimately based on the oral composition theory of Parry and Lord, about which I have expressed reservations above (Introduction, n. 47). With regard to Sumerian poetry, C. Wilcke expressed similar reservations several years ago. Wilcke suggests that by the Fara Period, when works of Sumerian literature began to be written down, such stylistic features had long since become the common property of all Sumerian poets, including those who composed their works in writing. He illustrates the point with the analogy of introductory formulas in Sumerian and Akkadian letters, which were based on the oral delivery of messengers but remained in use in written letters for centuries (Wilcke, "Formale Gesichtspunkte," p. 242 n. 55).

66. On this stage, see *EGE*, pp. 39–54.

texts, including school tablets, were current in this period. But verbal similarities between the Sumerian and Akkadian versions are so few,[67] and differences in content so great, that one could conceivably argue that whoever wrote the Akkadian texts never saw the Sumerian ones, but had only heard of their themes or rough outlines. However, given the probable study of Sumerian Gilgamesh texts in scribal academies, it seems more likely that whoever first rendered the tales about Gilgamesh into Akkadian did know the Sumerian texts, but took the liberty of reworking them completely.

There is currently no way of knowing whether the Old Babylonian Akkadian rendition was the work of the author of the integrated epic, working from the Sumerian originals, or whether he worked from Akkadian paraphrases produced by one or more earlier scribes. If the latter was the case, then some of the differences in wording and content between the Sumerian and Akkadian texts—those differences which are not part of the integration process—could be the work of such earlier *paraphrasers*, rather than the *author* of the integrated epic. Other differences could be based on versions of the Sumerian tales which vary from those known to us.

Whatever may be the source of the differences, it is clear that the similarities between the Sumerian tales and their Akkadian counterparts are limited to the broad outlines of the plot, with details varying so widely that the basic relationship is sometimes difficult to recognize. For example, in the Sumerian *Gilgamesh and the Land of the Living*—the Sumerian tale most closely paralleled in the Akkadian epic—Gilgamesh decides to travel to the Cedar Mountain in order to establish his name, since he will eventually die. The proposal to battle Huwawa, the guardian of the cedars, has no place in the original plan, and Enkidu raises no objection to the plan itself. The proposal to battle Huwawa and Enkidu's objection to it appear only after the two heroes have reached the Cedar Mountain. But in the Akkadian epic the aim of killing Huwawa is an integral part of Gilgamesh's plans from the outset. It and Enkidu's warnings appear from the beginning, providing an opportunity to stress repeatedly Gilgamesh's motive of seeking to establish a reputation which will survive after his death and to magnify his achievement by having him resist several attempts at dissuasion.[68] In the Sumerian version, fifty Urukites set out with Gilgamesh and Enkidu for the Cedar Mountain; they are absent in the Akkadian version. On the other hand, the Akkadian version has Gilgamesh debate about the journey with a council of elders in Uruk, and possibly also with a group of young men; this debate is not mentioned in the Sumerian version of this tale,

---

67. Excluding *Gilgamesh, Enkidu, and the Netherworld* and its translation in *GE* XII, which was probably not part of the Old Babylonian version; see *EGE*, p. 49.
    68. *EGE*, pp. 76–78, 33.

although it has a counterpart in another of the Sumerian tales, *Gilgamesh and Agga*.[69] Other Sumerian Gilgamesh tales contributed far less to the original Akkadian epic, the relationship being limited to very general themes: Enkidu's death and Gilgamesh's grief (*Gilgamesh, Enkidu, and the Netherworld*), the denial of immortality for Gilgamesh (*The Death of Gilgamesh*), and the survivor of the flood as the source of knowledge about immortality (*The Deluge*).

The limited use of the Sumerian Gilgamesh texts implies that the author of the Akkadian epic was selective in his use of available sources. One of the Sumerian texts, *Gilgamesh and Agga*, was omitted entirely, though copies of it too are known to have been available during the Old Babylonian period.[70] This indicates that the author of the epic did not seek to preserve everything tradition had reported about Gilgamesh. How he decided what to preserve is a matter of conjecture, though it is obvious that one of his criteria must have been his subjective sense of the suitability of a tale to his own theme. *Gilgamesh and Agga* could have been omitted because its characters were exclusively human or because it culminated in Gilgamesh's recognition of Agga's authority, or because that composition had no obvious bearing on the themes of death and immortality. On the other hand, the epic's omission of the actual death of Gilgamesh forced Gilgamesh to live with the knowledge of mortality, a result that was later underscored by the late prologue, which stresses the lessons that Gilgamesh learned from his experiences.[71] One or two other Sumerian Gilgamesh texts seem to have been passed over by the author of the Old Babylonian version only to be joined to the epic later on. The story about Gilgamesh and the Bull of Heaven is not currently known to have been part of the Old Babylonian version; it is first attested in the Akkadian and Hittite fragments of the Middle Babylonian period (the fragments date to the fourteenth century B.C.E.). They could have been added to the epic in this period, though their absence from the Old Babylonian fragments may be simply an accident of discovery. On the other hand, Tablet XII, which is based on the second half of *Gilgamesh, Enkidu, and the Netherworld*, was most likely not added to the epic before the late version, and some think it was added to that version some centuries after the rest of that version was created (see below).

The Old Babylonian version not only omitted material that was present in the Sumerian tales about Gilgamesh but also added material that was not present in them. The very reference to Utnapishtim, as noted above,

69. See ibid., p. 24 n. 7.

70. Kramer, *JAOS* 64:12 and *AJA* 53:7 n. 10 (copies from Nippur); *BASOR* 88:15, l. 12, and *RA* 55:169–76, l. 12 (catalog entries from Nippur and Ur). It is not yet known whether *Gilgamesh and the Bull of Heaven* was taken up into the original, Old Babylonian, Akkadian version of the epic. On *GEN*, see above, n. 67.

71. See, further, *EGE*, p. 26 n. 16.

was based on some version of the flood story, a tale that originally had no connection with Gilgamesh.[72] The picture of Enkidu's animal-like way of life has thematic and phraseological parallels with Mesopotamian accounts of primordial man and must have been modeled on such traditions.[73] The account of Enkidu's creation, preserved fully in the late version and partially in a possibly older fragment and in the Hittite version of *Gilgamesh*, shows strong verbal and thematic similarities to stories about the creation of mankind, especially in the *Atrahasis Epic*, and must be based on some such tale, if not *Atrahasis* itself.[74] Other parts of the Old Babylonian version are indebted to various traditional speech forms and rituals. The famous *carpe diem* speech of the barmaid to Gilgamesh (Gilg. Me. iii, 6–14) has enough parallels in Egypt, Israel, and elsewhere for us to presume that it is based on popular wisdom.[75] The elders' farewell speech to Gilgamesh (Gilg. Y. vi, 31–33) seems to be based on a conventional travelers' blessing.[76] The description of the marriage scene at which Gilgamesh first encounters Enkidu (Gilg. P. v, 22–31) shares so many details with both sacred and secular marriage ceremonies that it could be based either on texts describing one or both types of ceremony or on personal observation of them.[77]

Yet another genre was drawn on to create an introduction for the Old Babylonian version. It is now known that this version began with a form of the hymn about Gilgamesh which appears in Tablet I, i, 27ff. of the late version, though apart from its opening phrase, the text of the Old Babylonian form of the hymn is missing. To the extent that we may infer its contents from the late version, the hymn appears to have been modeled on royal hymns. It was either created ad hoc for the epic or was composed independently and joined to the epic secondarily in the Old Babylonian period.[78]

3. In contrast to the freedom with which the Old Babylonian author formulated the text of the epic and modified its contents, subsequent revisions of the epic left enough similarities in outline and wording to show that the later versions are textually related to the Old Babylonian version. Though the editors of these versions made their own creative contributions to the epic both in the poetic rephrasing of older poetic passages and in the

72. See ibid., pp. 216–17.
73. See ibid., pp. 198–213.
74. See ibid., pp. 192–97.
75. See ibid., pp. 167–69.
76. See ibid., pp. 169–70.
77. See ibid., pp. 176, 182–84.
78. See ibid., pp. 150–60.

composition of new lines and sections,[79] they were clearly transmitting in revised form a text that was essentially the work of an earlier author.

When revision of the epic first began is not known. It could have begun as early as the Old Babylonian period. The earliest documented revisions come from the Middle Babylonian period (ca. 1600–1000 B.C.E.), mostly from about the fourteenth century. Since most of the fragments of this period come from outside Mesopotamia and include Hittite and Hurrian translations of the epic, it is not certain to what extent they reflect inner-Mesopotamian developments in the epic rather than foreign modifications. However, a careful comparison of the Middle Babylonian material, including the Akkadian portions, does give a general impression of what was done to the epic in this period. Differences between the Akkadian fragments suggest that they do not represent a single Middle Babylonian version, but rather two or three intermediate stages between the Old Babylonian version known to us and the late version. Comparison of all the texts (including the Hittite) shows, not unexpectedly, that the Middle Babylonian texts occupy an intermediate position between the Old Babylonian and the late versions. Some, but not all, of the changes in the forms of the characters' names known from the late version are attested in the Middle Babylonian texts (Sursunabu has become Urshanabi, "the barmaid" has become Ziduri [= Siduri], but Huwawa is not yet Humbaba). The wording of the epic has developed considerably toward its ultimate late (Standard Babylonian) form, which implies that much of the wording of the late version was formulated prior to the work of the editor who produced that version. This, plus the likelihood that the Middle Babylonian fragments represent more than one stage, indicates that the emergence of the late, Standard Babylonian text was a gradual process that took centuries, rather than something achieved all at once by the final editor.[80]

4. The latest attested stage of the Akkadian epic is the Standard Babylonian version current in the first millennium B.C.E. known from the library of Ashurbanipal (668–627) in Nineveh and from other sites in Assyria and Babylonia in manuscripts dating from the ninth or eighth century to apparently the second or first century B.C.E. It is generally assumed that this version was produced some time in the last half or quarter of the second millennium (the date conventionally given is ca. 1250), with the qualification that Tablet XII may have been added at a later date.[81]

---

79. Compare the version of Jeremiah as reflected in Edition II of that book (Tov, below, chapter 8).

80. See *EGE*, pp. 110–29.

81. See ibid., pp. 130–31. M. D. Arnaud reports the discovery at Emar, Syria, of "the oldest witness to the canonical version known to date," from about the thirteenth century. See Arnaud, "Bibliothèque."

Where the late version can be compared with those of the Middle Babylonian period, the general impression is that its editor did not reformulate the text extensively, though the degree of reformulation varies in different passages. A comparison of a sixty-line passage in a late Middle Babylonian manuscript from Ur with the same passage in the late version shows that the wording of many lines appearing in both versions is close, with lexical variants appearing approximately once every seven and a half lines. Furthermore, there are three or four additional words or phrases in the late version, and five full lines found only in the late version, two lines found only in the Middle Babylonian version, and an entire section of five lines in the Middle Babylonian version which is replaced by a sixteen-line section in the late version. In another passage, the order of lines varies between versions. The fact that the text of lines appearing in both versions is close, while at the same time other lines were added (or, in a few cases, subtracted) in the late version reminds us that the wording of verses and the addition or subtraction of verses are separate phenomena which did not necessarily develop together. It seems possible that the main body of the epic attained its final wording first, and later underwent a supplementary elaboration. Many of the additions do not give the impression of originality: They include lines synonymously parallel to those to which they are adjoined, traditional and conventional descriptions, and some material modeled on or related to other passages in the epic and contributing to the homogenized style of the late version (see below).[82]

Since the Middle Babylonian fragments are not extensively preserved, it is difficult to give a full picture of the kinds of changes made after the Middle Babylonian period. Since the Old Babylonian fragments, on the other hand, are so much more extensive, it is possible to categorize the kinds of changes that befell the epic in the long run between the earliest Akkadian version and the latest one. Only a small number of lines remained unchanged. The less extensive changes are of the following types: (1) different grammatical and lexical forms of the same word; (2) synonyms or words functioning similarly; (3) added words or phrases; (4) different formulas, such as those for introducing direct speech; (5) expansion by the addition of new lines which are synonymous or parallel to older ones; (6) contraction of parallel or synonymous lines into fewer lines; (7) reformulation of lines with negligible, partial, or complete change of meaning; and (8) textual corruption. A few of the changes in wording seem to be chronologically conditioned, with the late version adopting language which is especially prevalent in late sources. However, the number of late variants using demonstrably late language does not seem extensive, and many of

---

82. See *EGE*, pp. 119–29.

the late variants seem to employ language not less ancient than the language they replace. The changes may therefore be based largely on the subjective artistic judgment or taste of the later editors, not new linguistic developments.[83]

More extensive changes in the epic include: (1) the restructuring of sections; (2) the assimilation to each other of related passages; and (3) changes in the roles of characters. An example of the latter type is the change in the role of the sun-god, which is apparently connected to a geographic change in the epic. *In the Sumerian version* of the Cedar Mountain episode, the journey is undertaken on Gilgamesh's own initiative. He turns to the sun-god because of the latter's connection with the Cedar Mountain, which is implicitly located to the east of Sumer, as is typically the case with the Cedar Mountain connected with the sun in Sumerian texts. At first the sun-god seems to have reservations about Gilgamesh's plan, but he ultimately agrees (see *GLL* A, ll. 1–35). *In the Old Babylonian Akkadian version* the Cedar Mountain is explicitly located in the northwest, in or near Lebanon (Gilg. O. I., ll. 13–14),[84] a change presumably influenced by the western orientation of the West Semitic dynasties which came to dominate Mesopotamia in the Old Babylonian period. With the Cedar Mountain no longer located in the east, the original reason for turning to the sun-god was also eliminated, and a new rationale was called for. This rationale seems to be related to the sun-god's role as banisher of baneful (especially black-magical) forces, for in this version the vanquishing of Huwawa was part of Gilgamesh's original intention for the journey, and in so doing Gilgamesh explicitly intended to banish from the land "what is baneful." *The late version* seems to have drawn the logical inference from this rationale: it has Ninsun accuse the sun-god of inspiring Gilgamesh to undertake the journey (*GE* III, ii, 10ff.). Thus it seems that a historical stimulus followed by theological reflection combined to transform the role of the sun-god from at best endorsement of Gilgamesh's journey, if not opposition to it, to inspiration of the journey.[85]

In addition to these changes, three major additions appear in the epic after the Old Babylonian version known to us; these are first attested in manuscripts of the late version. (1) The prologue (*GE* I, i, 1–26) describes the subject of the epic and stresses, rather than Gilgamesh's heroic deeds, the wisdom that he obtained from his experiences. The Old Babylonian version had apparently opened with the hymn that begins in line 27, the opening phrase of which is cited (as a title) in the colophon of a tablet of the Old Babylonian version. The hymn cited Gilgamesh's heroic qualities.

83. See ibid., pp. 55–72. [Cf. below, Chapter 4, n. 29.]
84. Grayson in *ANET*, p. 504.
85. See *EGE*, pp. 76–81.

The new prologue thus gives a different, more intellectual emphasis to the epic.[86] (2) The flood story in Tablet XI. Although Gilgamesh traveled to Utnapishtim already in the Old Babylonian version, and presumably reached him, this does not necessarily imply that in the Old Babylonian version Utnapishtim recounted the entire flood story. In the Old Babylonian period there is no textual evidence for the presence of the story in the epic and there is reason to believe that it was not added to the epic until the late version. In the account of Gilgamesh's meeting with Utnapishtim (*GE* X, iv–vi and XI), two different formulas are used for introducing speeches. Outside Utnapishtim's narration of the flood story, the formula is consistently "A said to him/her, to B," a formula used only in *Gilgamesh*, but in the Old Babylonian as well as the late version. However, within the flood story itself, a different formula is consistently used, one found only in late texts (including the late version of *Atrahasis*): "A opened his mouth to speak, saying to B." The different formulas clearly reflect the different sources of the material: on the one hand, the meeting with Utnapishtim, taken from earlier versions of *Gilgamesh*, and on the other hand, Utnapishtim's flood narrative, which is known to derive from *Atrahasis* (see below, Chapter 5, pp. 159–61). That the flood narrative uses a late formula implies that the flood story was joined to the rest of the Utnapishtim pericope only in the late version, for it shows that the flood story underwent a particular modernization which the rest of this pericope escaped. It is scarcely plausible that *after* the flood story was added to this pericope, only the flood portion of the pericope had its speech introductions modernized, while the rest of the pericope did not. We must therefore infer that prior to the late version of *Gilgamesh* the flood narrative was not part of the Utnapishtim pericope and that it was taken into the epic from a *late* version of *Atrahasis*, one dating from a time when the late formula was in vogue. The rest of the Utnapishtim pericope, on the other hand, must have reached its present form apart from the flood story.[87] (3) Tablet XII. The opinion that Tablet XII was not part of the Old Babylonian version cannot at present be proved. The only way it could be proved would be if we had a relatively complete text of the entire Old Babylonian version, which had a final colophon and lacked the contents of Tablet XII. Therefore, the opinion depends on arguments from content and style similar to arguments followed in biblical criticism: the tablet contradicts the rest of the epic by having Enkidu still alive at its beginning and in describing Enkidu as Gilgamesh's servant, and it is, unlike the rest of the Old Babylonian version, a literal translation from the Sumerian rather than a creative adaptation.[88]

86. Ibid., pp. 104–5, 138, 140–60.
87. See ibid., pp. 233–34. For other vocabulary and stylistic differences between the components of the Utnapishtim pericope, see below, chapter 5, pp. 162–67.
88. See ibid., pp. 5, 26–27, 138.

With the formulation of the late version, the process of development we have been tracing came largely to an end, and the text approached stability, though even then its stability was not absolute. Although the late version is the most fully preserved and is attested in the largest number of manuscripts (8 to 12 manuscripts in the case of *GE* XI), only a few lines are not verbally identical in all of them.[89] A preliminary review of the manuscripts shows about 100 true variants among about 1,600 fully or partly preserved lines in the late version, or one per sixteen lines.[90] Most of these are of the least extensive types; more than a quarter, for example, involve simply the presence or absence of the copula or the use of different particles and prepositions (mostly synonymous). Some variants are synonyms or words of similar meaning. In one five-line section the variation is simply between third person and first person. There are, in addition, pluses and minuses of about five single words, four or five phrases, five lines, and possibly one section. In number and character these differences are so minimal that they indicate we are dealing with a single version and several slightly variant witnesses thereto. The late version was nearly a *textus receptus* or "authorized version" in wording and content, and different copies or editions differed from each other almost exclusively in matters of orthography, grammar, and format.[91]

---

89. This excludes grammatical and orthographic variants, which continued to abound.

90. Variants due to scribal error are omitted. In tablets from which a large number of exemplars is available, the number is naturally higher, but it does not reach a ratio of 1 to 10.

91. See *EGE*, pp. 127, 130–38. This conclusion is not affected by the comments of J. G. Westenholz in her review of *EGE* (*JAOS* 104:370–72). The reviewer attributes to me a "hypothesis of one *textus receptus*" and a single recension of the epic in the first millennium, says that the book "ignores differences among the later [i.e., first millennium] manuscripts," and proceeds to dispute this picture. In fact, I state that there was a single *version* of the epic in the first millennium (I define the terms version and recension in *EGE*, p. 3 n. 1) and that it became *nearly* a *textus receptus*, and I devote an entire chapter (6) to differences among its manuscripts. None of the variants in previously known manuscripts cited in the review is substantial enough to indicate a different *version*. Nor does the new manuscript of *GE* V (published by von Weiher in *Baghdader Mitteilungen* 11 (1980):90–105) "prove beyond doubt the existence of a second recension" as the reviewer claims and von Weiher assumes, though this is possible. Tablet V is the most poorly preserved tablet of the epic, and because the new manuscript does not contain any of the previously known lines of that tablet, a textual comparison is impossible. We do not know whether its contents were *never* present in the previously known tablets (in which case it represents a second version) or whether its contents simply belong in the many large gaps in the previously known tablets. The fact that the new tablet begins differently than the previously known Tablet V is no impediment to the latter possibility. Different editions of the epic may have had different numbers of verses on the tablets, so that certain scenes may have appeared at different spots on the tablets, as Kinnier Wilson has argued for the Nineveh copies of Tablets IV and V (see *GSL*, pp. 103–11, esp. p. 105). In this case the new tablet would represent a different *edition* of the epic (for the term, again see *EGE*, p. 3 n. 1).

The textual stability of this version, though not absolute, was strong enough to withstand modification in response to later religious developments. Toward the end of the second millennium, Marduk and Ashur were "exalted" to national and cosmic status. These deities had played no role in Old Babylonian myths and epics, and no role was given them even in the post–Old Babylonian versions of those myths and epics. The late version of *Atrahasis* does not introduce them into its account of the creation of man, even though the late[92] myth *Enuma Elish* makes Marduk the creator,[93] and some (not all) manuscripts of *Enuma Elish* from Assur make Ashur its hero.[94] Similarly, the late manuscripts of *Anzû* have Ninurta, not Ashur or Marduk, as the hero.[95] It is not that late theologians failed to credit Marduk with the defeat of Anzû: A hymn of Ashurbanipal celebrates him as "the one who crushed the skull of Anzû," but contemporary copies of the *Anzû* myth were not altered in accordance with this declaration.[96]

Lambert has argued that Marduk did not rise to his later preeminence until toward the end of the second millennium.[97] Ashur apparently first began his rise to superlocal prominence around the thirteenth century.[98] These approximate dates are well in accord with a date in the last half or quarter of the second millennium for the late versions of *Gilgamesh* and other Akkadian literary texts of Old Babylonian origin. In other words, these texts reached their final form before Marduk and Ashur were considered important enough to be given a place in them. Once they had been given their classical late formulations, they were not subject to further theological revision.[99]

The gradual progression of the transmission process, as we can trace it in the evolution of the *Gilgamesh Epic*, from free adaptation of sources to

---

92. On the date of *Enuma Elish*, see Lambert, "Reign"; Hallo and van Dijk, *Exaltation*, pp. 66–67; Grayson, in *ANET*, p. 501; cf. Schott, MVAG 30(2):123; Jacobson, *Treasures*, p. 167; contrast van Dijk, *MIO* 12:57–74; cf. Yadin, *IEJ* 21:82–85; Grafman, *IEJ* 22:47–49.

93. See *En.El.* VI–VII (Speiser and Grayson, in *ANET*, pp. 67–72, 501–3).

94. Labat, *Le poème*, p. 22; see his notes on *En.El.* I, 81–82; III, 10; for further details, see *EGE*, p. 108 n. 95.

95. See Speiser and Grayson, in *ANET*, pp. 111 n. 12, 113, 514–17; Hallo and Moran, "First Tablet."

96. See Speiser and Grayson, in *ANET*, p. 113, end.

97. Lambert, "Reign."

98. Edzard, "Mythologie," p. 43.

99. *EGE*, pp. 108–9. An interesting theological development is reflected in the version of the flood story in *GE* XI. When this version is compared with that in the Old Babylonian *Atrahasis*, one can see that all references to divine hunger and thirst during the flood have been carefully excised from the text in *Gilgamesh*. Even the celebrated passage about the flies gathering around the sacrificer (*GE* XI, 161) is now seen to soften the "anthropomorphism" of its source, for in *Atrahasis* (III, v, 35) they had gathered around the sacrifice itself, in

minimal adaptation resembles a process that has been postulated in the evolution of the Pentateuchal narratives. As described by M. Greenberg, "plasticity and integrative capability are characteristic of early stages of transmission; rigidity and unassimilability, characteristic of the quasi-canonical status of the material in the time of the redaction."[100] The text of the *Gilgamesh Epic* never became quite as rigid as biblical criticism presumes the text of the Pentateuchal sources became just before they were combined. But this is a slight difference in degree, not in kind. The principle described by Greenberg is borne out by *Gilgamesh* when one considers the practical consequences Greenberg ascribes to this principle: "The less integrated the disturbance is into its context, the later it may be assumed to have been combined. . . . The grossest disturbances are thus to be ascribed to the last redactional stage of combination, while lesser disturbances belong to earlier development of the tradition complexes."[101] Within those parts of *Gilgamesh* known to have been part of the Old Babylonian version, no significant inconsistencies are discernible.[102] The flood story, on the other hand, which was added to the epic in its late version, contains a number of stylistic inconsistencies with the rest of the Utnapishtim pericope in which it is located: it uses a different formula for introducing speeches, as we have seen; it terms Utnapishtim's wife his "woman" (*sinništu*), whereas the rest of the pericope calls her his "spouse" (*marḫītu*); and it has a much less homogenized, repetitious style (identical commands and executions, etc.) than does the rest of the pericope.[103] Since we know that the flood story

---

Gilgamesh only around the one who offered the sacrifice. See *EGE*, pp. 226–29. (For a more complicated theological development, in which the text of the epic seems to have lagged behind theological developments by several centuries [perhaps due to polemical motives], see *EGE*, pp. 76–81.)

Comparable religious/theological differences between different versions of biblical traditions are seen in comparing such passages as 2 Sam. 5:21 with 1 Chron. 14:12 and are frequently predicated of the Pentateuchal sources; see, e.g., Driver, *ILOT*, pp. 120–21, 128–29, 140–41; Weinfeld, *Deuteronomy*, part 2.

100. Greenberg, "Redaction," p. 245.

101. Ibid. This observation is important as an answer to one of the strongest arguments of Cassuto against source criticism (Cassuto, *Documentary Hypothesis*, pp. 66–67). Since source criticism assumes that a contradiction or an inconsistency points to divergent authorship, because a single writer is not likely to have contradicted himself or been inconsistent, Cassuto claimed that criticism had merely transferred the problem from the author to the redactor. In his view, a redactor was no more likely to have tolerated such disturbances than an author would have been. The principle discussed here indicates that a redactor *would* have tolerated such disturbances more than an author, because the redactor worked with materials that were no longer felt to be subject to extensive revision. Inconsistencies which are demonstrably the result of editorial activity will be observed frequently below.

102. For some minor differences, note the inconsistencies between the introductory hymn and other parts of the epic discussed in *EGE*, pp. 157–58, and the different speech introduction formulas in different Old Babylonian tablets of *Gilgamesh*, discussed in *EGE*, p. 44.

103. See below, Chapter 5.

was borrowed from another source—*Atrahasis*—we know that the differences reflect different sources; indeed, in the flood story itself Utnapishtim is once called Atrahasis. Here, however, our point is that these inconsistencies coincide with the lateness of the addition of this element to the epic. It is not that no attempt was made to integrate the flood narrative into the rest of the epic.[104] The name Utnapishtim was not invented by the editor of the late version; it appears already in the Old Babylonian version, but the editor's decision to use this name in place of Atrahasis may have been because the meaning of "Utnapishtim" ("He found(?) life") fit the theme of the epic and Utnapishtim's role in it. The replacement of *Atrahasis'* third-person narrative with the first-person form of *GE* XI was necessary so that Gilgamesh could hear about the flood from Utnapishtim, as the plot of the epic requires. The god Shamash is given a role in the narrative (*GE* XI, 86); he had played no real role in the *Atrahasis* flood story but was important in *Gilgamesh* (Gilg. Y. v, 37; *GE* III, ii, 8ff.; etc.). Two scenes in the flood story begin with one of the epic's frequently used formulas: "With the first glow of dawn" (*GE* XI, 48, 96); this phrase does not appear in *Atrahasis*, and it may be unique to *Gilgamesh* (see *GE* VIII, i, 1; ii, 23; etc.).[105] These features, which may have resulted from an attempt to integrate the flood story with the rest of the epic, are nonetheless superficial. The differences that remain are themselves not serious and may not even have been noticed by the editor or his readers. Still, their presence in the epic is due not simply to their unobtrusiveness but to the fact that at the time when the flood story was added to the epic its text was no longer being revised very much. That even blatant contradictions would also have been tolerated at this stage seems indicated by the presence in the epic of Tablet XII, which opens with Enkidu still alive, though in Tablet VII he had died. However, since we cannot presently document the lateness of this tablet in the epic, it remains theoretically possible that this contradiction was introduced into the epic much earlier. If so, the fact that it was introduced without being harmonized with the rest of the epic would make it an exception to the pattern being discussed.

Miscellaneous Aspects of the Transmission Process

In the preceding summary of stages in the evolution of the epic, the reader will have noticed many phenomena presumed to have taken place in the development of biblical literature. Here I would like to call attention to

104. See *EGE*, pp. 229–31.
105. See ibid., p. 9 n. 25; p. 231 n. 49.

a few of those, and add some others, which seem most important or suggestive.

1. Components of a text stemming from different sources often differ from each other in vocabulary and style (above, pp. 42, 45). This subject is discussed below, Chapter 5, where it is also noted that a text produced by conflation can still possess artistic unity.

2. Different accounts of a subject sometimes use different names for the same character. One may compare the double names of such biblical characters a Jacob/Israel and Gideon/Jerubaal. In the case of *GE* XI, there is no evidence (as Jastrow thought) that the names Utnapishtim and Atrahasis come directly from the editor's combining two versions of the flood story, each using one name. The process is a bit more complex. The Old Babylonian version of *Gilgamesh* had used the name Utnapishtim. It presumably owed this name somehow to an earlier account of the flood but did not itself tell that story, as we have noted. The late version of the epic appropriated the story itself from the *Atrahasis Epic* but replaced the name Atrahasis with Utnapishtim in all but one line (XI, 187). Why the editor's revision was incomplete—whether this was intentional or accidental—we can only guess, but in any case he left a trace of the two separate traditions underlying his text.[106]

3. Another case of incomplete revision appears in *GE* XI, 37. As we noted, the editor of the *Gilgamesh Epic* reformulated the third person narrative of *Atrahasis* to first person format of *GE* XI. However, a trace of the third-person formulation remains in XI, 37. "(Ea) said to his servant, me" (*izakkara ana ardišu jâtu*). Apparently the line originally read "(Ea) said to his servant," as in the Old Babylonian version of *Atrahasis* (I, 373; III, i, 16). The editor of *GE* XI added "me" in line with his first-person style, but did not drop "his servant." Whether this was intentional or neglectful we cannot say. While "his servant" was now redundant, the resulting noun plus appositional pronoun was not ungrammatical or contrary to accepted style.[107] Still, in other passages that must originally have been formulated in the third person (XI, 190–92, whose counterparts in *Atrahasis* are now lost), the editor of *GE* XI did not leave traces of the original wording.[108]

---

106. Cf. ibid., pp. 217 n. 11, 229–30.

107. See *GAG*, sec. 134b; Hecker, *Untersuchungen*, p. 128 n. 1; *LH* prologue, i, 27–31; *GE* XI, 194.

108. Another third-person reference to Utnapishtim is *GE* XI, 161, where he calls himself "the one who offered the sacrifice" (*bēl niqî*), replacing "the sacrifice" (*niqî*) in OB Atr. III, v, 35. For the reason behind this reformulation, see n. 99, above. It does not seem likely that the editor of *GE* would have created this third-person formulation; more likely, he found it in a now-lost intermediate version of *Atrahasis*. For another reading that escaped editing, see *EGE*, p. 89, on *GE* I, vi, 13.

4. Resumptive repetition (*Wiederaufnahme*) is a literary device whereby an editor, after an interpolation, returns to the point of interruption and before continuing repeats part of what immediately preceded the interpolation. It has been observed as a source-critical indicator in the Bible[109] and appears in Gilgamesh as well. In the Old Babylonian passage Gilg. Y. vi, 19–43, the elders of Uruk bless Gilgamesh and advise him to rely on Enkidu and be attentive to Shamash and Lugalbanda; following this, Enkidu addresses Gilgamesh (from col. vi, 44 into a break in the tablet). The late version of this passage begins similarly with a group (the elders?) advising Gilgamesh to rely on Enkidu and charging Enkidu to bring Gilgamesh back safely (*GE* III, i, 1–12). Following this, the late version inserts more than four columns of new material before Enkidu's address to Gilgamesh (*GE* III, vi, 12ff.). But before continuing with Enkidu's speech, the late version presents another passage in which a group (seemingly the elders[110]) repeats the elders' earlier advice to Gilgamesh that he rely on Enkidu, and then charges Enkidu to bring Gilgamesh back safely (*GE* III, vi, ?–8)—in other words, a resumptive repetition. Another case involves Enkidu's warnings to Gilgamesh about Huwawa/Humbaba. In the Old Babylonian version, one of those warnings ends with the declaration: "To safeguar[d the Cedar Forest], a sevenfold terror [Enlil gave him]" (Gilg. Y. iv, 1–2). The text then continues with Gilgamesh's reply (Gilg. Y. iv, 3ff.). An earlier warning had included this description of Huwawa:

> At sixty leagues the forest is encompassed;
> [Who is there th]at would go down into its midst?
> [Huwa]wa—his roaring is the flood-storm,
> His mouth is fire,
> His breath is death!
>
> (Gilg. Y. iii, 14–24)

In the late version there is a fragment of Enkidu's warning which incorporates (in textually corrupt form) parts of both these warnings. It opens with a counterpart of Gilg. Y. iv, 1–2, then presents a counterpart of Gilg. Y. iii, 16–20 (with differing line order), and then repeats the counterpart of iv, 1–2 before continuing with Gilgamesh's reply, as in iv, 3ff. The text reads as follows:

To safeguard the Cedar [Fores]t,
As a terror to mortals has Enlil appointed him.

---

109. But also as an author's device; cf. below, Chapter 2, n. 46.
110. See *EGE*, p. 75 n. 6.

Humbaba—his roaring is the flood-storm, his mouth is fire, his breath is death!
He can hear (at a distance of) sixty leagues rustling in the forest; who is there that
would go down to his forest?
To safeguard the cedar(s), as a terror to mortals has Enlil appointed him.
Weakness seizes him who goes down to his forest.
Gilgamesh [said] to him, [to] Enkidu. . . .

$$(GE \text{ II, v, } 1-7)^{111}$$

5. The geographic background of episodes sometimes changes in the course of transmission. The shift of the location of the Cedar Mountain from the east to the northwest recalls Noth's view that the Jacob-Esau stories were originally located in northern Israel and Gilead, with Esau being transferred to Edom only later.[112] Similarly, in Gilgamesh (*GE* XI, 140–44) the landing place of the ark after the flood is Mount Niṣir, east of the Tigris, but in Gen. 8:4 and later traditions it is farther north, in Urartu/Armenia.[113]

6. The transmission of material is selective, as indicated by the complete or partial omission in the Akkadian epic of tales known from the Sumerian texts (*Gilgamesh and Agga, The Death of Gilgamesh*). In the Bible the omission of certain tales is indicated by brief references which seem to presuppose knowledge of them, such as references to Enoch and the Canaanite Daniel (Gen. 5:22–24; Ezek. 14:14, 20; 28:3).[114]

7. Pertinent early tales not originally included in a text sometimes survive for centuries and are retrieved in a later stage of tradition. Assuming that the contents of *Gilgamesh, Enkidu, and the Netherworld* (*GE* XII) and possibly of *Gilgamesh and the Bull of Heaven* (*GE* VI) entered the epic only after the original Old Babylonian version, this in a way parallels the survival into Second Temple and rabbinic times of certain materials absent from the Torah but thought to be ancient (e.g., traditions about YHWH's defeat of the primordial sea, about the Akedah, and about the exodus).[115]

---

111. For the first example, see *EGE*, p. 75; for the second, see ibid., p. 95. For further examples, see below, Chapters 2 and 8.

112. Noth, *Pentateuchal Traditions*, pp. 94–96. Gunkel, on the other hand, thought the identification with Edom original and the location in the north of certain episodes with Esau secondary (Gunkel, *Legends*, pp. 96–97).

113. Cf. Heidel, *Gilgamesh Epic*, pp. 250–51. On differences between Mesopotamian and foreign versions of a story, see above, Introduction, n. 2.

114. Cf. Cassuto, "*ḥᵃnôk*"; Spiegel, "Noah, Daniel, and Job"; Noth, "Noah, Daniel und Hiob."

115. See above, n. 5.

Conservative Elements in the Transmission

Considering the liberties the Old Babylonian author took with the Sumerian sources (or their Akkadian paraphrases) and the fact that few lines of the Old Babylonian version were left unchanged by the time of the late version, one may well wonder whether anything in the final version of the epic preserves recognizable features of the earliest forms of the traditions about Gilgamesh or about the historical Gilgamesh himself. There does seem to be an ancient residue preserved in the final form of the epic. Some of its elements may be identified as follows:

1. From the earliest known Akkadian version of the epic the late version has preserved the general drift of many verses in the epic, though often in revised wording; the basic plot and sequence of events in the epic; and its basic message.

2. From the Sumerian tales about Gilgamesh the late version has preserved the concern with death and desire for immortality reflected in several of them, although it has given these themes a new significance. The general plot of two tales has also been preserved (*Gilgamesh and the Land of the Living* and *Gilgamesh and the Bull of Heaven*), although in the best preserved of these (the first) it is clear that the sequence of individual scenes within the tale was not preserved in the late version and that the characters' motives were not preserved completely unchanged. Half of a third text (*Gilgamesh, Enkidu, and the Netherworld*) was preserved in literal translation.

3. Of the historical Gilgamesh it is possible that a few details have been preserved. The likelihood that Gilgamesh actually existed and the plausibility of the tradition that he built the wall of Uruk were discussed above (p. 27). Jacobsen has argued that Gilgamesh's name is of a type which was well attested in Early Dynastic times but disappeared later.[116] Hence his name—though perhaps in a slightly modified form—seems authentic. Certain social institutions reflected in the epic—the sacred marriage ceremony, the political authority of the assembly of elders—could reflect Early Dynastic times,[117] but since the sacred marriage was also practiced long after the Early Dynastic period, and the elders' political authority may have been known after this period,[118] we cannot rule out the possibility that these institutions were first associated with Gilgamesh by later traditionists.

---

116. *SKLJ*, pp. 187–90; see also Lambert, in *GSL*, p. 49. On changing onomastic fashions in Early Dynastic Sumer, see Hallo, "Date."

117. See Renger, "Heilige Hochzeit"; Cooper, "Heilige Hochzeit"; Jacobsen, "Primitive Democracy."

118. See Renger, "Heilige Hochzeit," p. 258; Cooper, "Heilige Hochzeit," p. 266; Jacobsen, "Primitive Democracy," p. 165.

In any case, the extensive and reflective modifications we have seen to characterize the transmission of the epic down to the first millennium B.C.E. indicate that the epic is less a record of Gilgamesh and his times than a record of the impact his life made on later writers and what they thought it might mean to their audiences—a point sometimes made about the narratives concerning early Israelite history too.[119]

We should not overestimate the conclusions one can draw for biblical studies from the evolution of the *Gilgamesh Epic*. The form and content of the epic and the social setting of its transmission differed widely from those of biblical literature. The chief value of such data for biblical studies lies in their heuristic value in helping test the appropriateness of a certain method of analysis that has characterized biblical criticism for the past couple of centuries. The present study partially vindicates the theoretical approach by which Jastrow recognized the diversity of the sources, some about Gilgamesh and some not, which underlay the *Gilgamesh Epic*, and succeeded in identifying some of them in a general way. Of course, Jastrow could hardly give a precise, detailed description of the sources, since they were not then available. Now that we have so many more texts of the epic and its sources, we can see how extensively the late version, and even the much earlier Old Babylonian version, differ from the Sumerian sources, and how much room there would be for error in trying to reconstruct those sources from texts of the Akkadian epic alone. For the source critic this is sobering, but it seems doubtful that this conclusion is applicable in the same degree to the Torah. Indeed, the extensive revision characterizing the evolution of the *Gilgamesh Epic* explains why it contains so few inconsistencies in comparison with the Torah, and this suggests what the Torah might have looked like had it undergone similarly extensive reformulation in the course of its compilation and transmission. The number of inconsistencies left in the Torah suggests that it was not extensively reformulated and encourages the belief that its sources can be unraveled to a much greater extent than those of *Gilgamesh* could have been.[120]

In the final analysis, the theoretical approach did not lead Jastrow very wide of the mark in his general conception of the elements the epic was composed from. As Eissfeldt, quoted above, remarked: "The important point is . . . not this or that individual dissection of the material, but the total outlook." The present study has shown that even some of the specific phenomena and processes postulated by biblical critics did indeed characterize literary development and transmission in the ancient Near East.[121]

119. E.g., Greenberg, *Understanding Exodus*, pp. 193–96.

120. See, further, Chapter 2, n. 71.

121. The development of the *Gilgamesh Epic* did not demonstrably involve the conflation of two versions of the same story. For this phenomenon, so prominent in Pentateuchal criticism, see below, Chapters 2 and 3.

Conceivably, other empirical models yet to be compared with biblical texts might show that competing theories about the evolution of biblical literature are equally realistic. In any case, one may hope that the knowledge gained about literary history in cases where the evolution of a composition can be studied empirically, coupled with a fuller knowledge of ancient history in general, will enable us to use the theoretical approach in a more sophisticated and realistic way, for we will never be able to do without the theoretical approach in biblical studies.

2

Conflation as a
Redactional Technique

JEFFREY H. TIGAY

Editor's Note

One important aspect of biblical criticism not paralleled in the evolution of the *Gilgamesh Epic* is the theory, best known from the documentary hypothesis, that many biblical texts are not only *composite* but *conflate*. That is, they are composed of two (or more) variant versions of the same event, spliced or woven together by a redactor. Skeptics have considered this approach especially vulnerable, arguing that such a phenomenon is unheard of in the history of literature. The present chapter shows that conflation is a well-attested practice of redactors from ancient times down to our own day. Examples are brought from the Qumran scrolls, the Samaritan Pentateuch, the Septuagint, postbiblical Jewish literature, and modern works. The ancient examples display the kinds of inconsistencies which critics take as signs of conflation; they confirm that such phenomena do sometimes result from the conflation of sources. By enabling us to compare conflate texts with their sources, these examples also reveal the techniques and aims of the redactors. The chapter concludes with citations from the writings of two modern redactors, H. N. Bialik and Y. J. Rawnitzki, who describe their own assumptions and procedures in terms that are strikingly similar to those which critics have used in describing the work of ancient redactors.

•   •   •   •

Parts of this chapter were originally published in *JBL* 94:329–42 and revised in *Beth Mikra* 22:348–61. They are reprinted here with permission.

Conflation in Pentateuchal Criticism

One of the most important techniques of redaction posited by Penta-teuchal criticism is the combination of different texts—often variants of one and the same text or tradition—into a single text, that is, *conflation*. In the simplest form, a redactor might simply place two versions of an event side by side, treating the second as an amplification of the first (such as the accounts of creation in Gen. 1:1–2:4a[P] and 2:4b–24[J]), or he might keep the accounts separate and treat them as different events (such as the wife-sister stories, Gen. 12:10–20[J]; 20[E]; 26:6–11[J]). In other circumstances the redactor would insert one version of an event into another (e.g., Abram's migration, with Gen. 12:1–4a[J] inserted between Gen. 11:31–32 and 12:4b–5[P]),[1] or would fully interweave two versions, suggesting that their conflicting details represent different stages of a process or different aspects of an event[2] (e.g., the J and P accounts of the flood in Gen. 6:5–8:17). The procedure of the Pentateuchal redactor has been character-ized by M. Greenberg as follows:

[He] seems to have been intent on forging a continuous narrative. He therefore incorporated significant, complementary variants side by side, attempting to elabo-rate a single, reasonably effective narrative out of them. At times we suspect he may have regarded the result as a restoration of the true complexity of the event—a complexity dissolved into its elements among the various traditions he received.[3]

It is this aspect of Pentateuchal criticism which a number of its critics have found hard to believe is realistic, as we have seen.[4] But conflation is in fact a well-attested technique in Hebrew and related literature from antiq-uity down to modern times. Although G. F. Moore's analogy from the *Diatessaron* was resisted by some on the ground of its lateness, we shall see in this and the next chapter that the technique of conflation is attested much earlier.

1. For the logic of the redactor's arrangement, see Friedman, "Sacred History," pp. 29–30.
2. See Chapter 1, nn. 9 and 10.
3. Greenberg, *Understanding Exodus*, p. 196. This aspect of redaction is described by Friedman as "mechanical," by which he means that the order in which the redactor arranges details is dictated by the contents of the elements: certain elements are presupposed by others and must therefore precede them, etc. (Friedman, "Sacred History," pp. 28–34; note that Friedman does not use "mechanical" pejoratively). Cf. the description of Tatian's work in the *Diatessaron* by Abd-Isho bar Berika (d. 1318): "he preserved with all care the accurate order of the sayings and deeds" of Jesus (Stenning, "Diatessaron," p. 454), a description that may capture what Tatian himself thought he was doing. Both Friedman and Greenberg show that the redactors are sometimes motivated by literary and theological considerations as well as mechanical ones; see Friedman, "Sacred History"; Greenberg, *Understanding Exodus*; idem, "Thematic Unity"; idem, "Redaction."
4. See Introduction, pp. 2–3.

Conflation is most familiar as a phenomenon in textual history, where a scribe, confronted with variant readings, refuses to choose one over the other but presents them both (usually producing a redundant text). A number of redundant biblical passages are presumed to have come about in this way, and the process is demonstrably present in biblical manuscripts and translations.[5] In principle, the "scribal" preservation of double readings does not differ from the "redactorial" practice of presenting two variant accounts of the same theme or event.[6] In cuneiform literature the practice can be seen in an inscription of Ashurbanipal in which two versions of the mission of an envoy to Ashurbanipal have been preserved side by side (see below, Chapter 5, pp. 154–55).[7] The practice is well attested in biblical manuscripts and translations, and in postbiblical Jewish literature. We shall examine several cases in this chapter.

Texts of the Sabbath Command

The Qumran manuscript 4QDeut[n] presents a composite version of the motive clause for the Sabbath command, adding the version found in Exod. 20:11 (citing the creation) after that found in Deut. 5:15 (citing the exodus). The same combination appears in the Codex Vaticanus of the LXX (LXX[B]), where the passage from Exodus is added in Deut. 5:14.[8] Note the redundancy produced by the conflation (the passage from Exodus is italicized):

4QDeut[n] 5:12–15[9]

[12]Observe the Sabbath day, to keep it holy, as the Lord your God commanded you. [13]Six days you shall labor and do all your work; [14]but on the seventh day, the

5. Perles, *Analekten*, p. 82; idem, *Analekten*, N.F., pp. 109–12; Gordis, *Biblical Text*, pp. liv–lvi, 41–43; Talmon, "Double Readings"; idem, "Synonymous Readings"; idem, "Conflate Readings"; Janzen, "Double Readings." Talmon's articles include many examples from the ancient translations, as do the following: Swete, *Introduction*, pp. 375, 480; Driver, *Samuel*, pp. lv–lvii; Komlosh, *Bible*, pp. 154–55, 365–66, 377; Weiss, *Aramaic Targum*, pp. 191–92, 288–93; Shinan, *Aggadah*, pp. 202–5; for further bibliography, see Talmon, "Conflate Readings," bibliography, and Tov, *Text-Critical*, pp. 189–90 n. 6. For Sumero-Akkadian examples, see Kutscher, *Angry Sea*, pp. 121, 132, 138–39, 141–42; Krecher, "Glossen," pp. 435–36. For an Egyptian example, see Gilula, "Smiting," p. 94.

6. Cf. Seeligmann, Review of Elliger, *Studien*, p. 39, col. 2; Talmon, "Conflate Readings," p. 132, sec. 8.

7. For a possibly conflate cuneiform creation story, see *EGE*, p. 104 n. 79.

8. Skehan, "Scrolls," p. 102.

9. Text in Cross, *Scrolls*, plate 19 (where the old siglum 4QDeut[m] is used); trans. based on pp. 31–32 there. Note also the phylactery text 8Q3, where Deut. 5:1–14 is followed by Exod. 20:11 (DJD 3, p. 154, fig. 10).

Sabbath to the Lord your God, you shall do no work in it, you, your son, your daughter, your manservant, your ox, or your ass, or your cattle, the sojourners who are within your gates, that your manservant and your maidservant may rest as well as you. [15]You shall remember that you were a servant in the land of Egypt and the Lord your God brought you out thence with a mighty hand and an outstretched arm; therefore the Lord your God commanded you to observe the Sabbath day to keep it holy; *for in six days the Lord made the heaven and earth, the sea and all that is in them; and He rested on the seventh day. Therefore the Lord blessed the Sabbath day to keep it holy.*

LXX^B, Deut. 5:12–15[10]

[12]Observe the Sabbath day, to keep it holy, as the Lord your God commanded you. [13]Six days you shall labor and do all your work; [14]but on the seventh day is the Sabbath of the Lord your God; you shall do no work in it, you, and your son, and your daughter, your manservant and your maidservant, your ox, and your ass, and all your cattle, the sojourner who dwells among you, *for in six days the Lord made the heaven and earth and the sea and all that is in them*; that your manservant and your maidservant and your cattle may rest as well as you. [15]You shall remember that you were a slave in the land of Egypt, and the Lord your God brought you out thence with a mighty hand and a raised arm; therefore the Lord commanded you to observe the Sabbath day and keep it holy.

Of the two texts,[11] that from Qumran has the longer interpolation from Exodus, and the redundancy is blatant. Two clauses, each beginning with "therefore," explain the sanctity of the Sabbath in different ways. On the face of it a fine distinction could be drawn between the two clauses: the first explains why God commanded *Israel* to observe the Sabbath and keep it holy, while the second explains why God *himself* blessed the day to keep it holy. Possibly the interpolator made such a distinction in his own mind. But such a distinction would be forced. The presence of "to make it holy" in both clauses indicates that they explain the same thing, and it would be difficult to show that, in the context of the Decalogue, God's blessing the

10. Rahlfs, *Septuaginta*, 1:295, last note.
11. Since Exod. 20:11 is inserted in different verses in the two texts, 4QDeut^n clearly does not reflect the Hebrew *Vorlage* of Vaticanus. The latter interrupts the Deuteronomic version of the command by inserting Exod. 20:11a_1 in Deut. 5:14 after "the stranger within your gates," which is precisely where it appears in Exodus 20; this has the effect of making the reference to creation precede the reference to the exodus, as it should historically, but it creates a non sequitur (see below). The Qumran text adds Exod. 20:11 at the end of Deuteronomy's Sabbath command, thus preserving the unity of the Deuteronomic version and avoiding separation of the logically connected references to letting servants rest and to Israel's past servitude in verses 14 and 15.

day means something other than commanding Israel to observe it. We have here two different views of the reason for the sanctity of the Sabbath, the kind of inconsistency which figures prominently in source-criticism.[12] In LXX[B] the interpolation from Exod. 20:11 omits the first clause, which begins with "therefore," and thereby eliminates the explicit clash of competing explanations of the sanctity of the Sabbath. But the inconsistency is not fully eliminated: the remaining part of the interpolation still explains the command to observe the Sabbath on the basis of creation, while verse 15 explains it by the exodus. What is more, in LXX[B] the location of the interpolation is awkward, interrupting the natural continuity between those who are to refrain from work and the explanation that the command is for the benefit of some of them. The resulting sequence—the Lord created everything in six days so that your servants, etc., may rest—is a non sequitur. Indeed, God's six days of creating would seem to justify man's weekday labors better than his Sabbath rest. In any case, here too is the kind of awkwardness with which critical analysis begins.[13] In both cases it seems likely that, even without knowledge of the Masoretic Text of Exodus and Deuteronomy, the redundancy and awkwardness of the passages from Exodus in these manuscripts would have led critics to recognize them as interpolations from elsewhere.

A Doublet in the Septuagint of Esther

A narrative doublet resulting from conflation is found in the LXX of Esther, in one of the six additional passages not found in the Hebrew text. One of these describes an incident that duplicates another found later in both the Hebrew and LXX, at 2:21–23. In the LXX these are presented as two separate episodes. Their similarities are such that source criticism of the LXX would recognize them as two variants of the same episode even if we did not have documentary evidence to that effect. Translations of the two episodes, along with a translation of the Hebrew text of the second, are on the following pages.

The two episodes differ from each other in the following details (only the relevant ones are noted): in A:12 the conspirators are named, while in 2:21 they are not; in A:13 Mordecai personally informs the king of the plot, while in 2:22 he reports through Esther; and in A:16 the king rewards Mordecai for his actions, while he was not rewarded for the incident in

---

12. See, e.g., Driver, *ILOT*, pp. 8–9, for double explanations of one phenomenon.
13. See, e.g., Eissfeldt, *OTI*, pp. 187–88.

LXX Est. Addition A:12–16[14]

¹²And Mordecai was resting
in the court
with Gabatha and Tharra,
two of the king's eunuchs
who guarded the court,
¹³and he overheard their discussion and investigated
their concerns, and learned
that they were preparing to
lay hands on King Artaxerxes.

So he
informed the king about it.

¹⁴The king then interrogated
the two eunuchs,
and when they had confessed,
they were led off (to execution).
¹⁵The king wrote these matters
down as a record,

LXX Est. 2:21–23[15]

²¹And two of the king's eunuchs,
the chiefs of the body-guard,
became angry because Mordecai
was promoted,

and they sought
to kill King Artaxerxes.
²²The matter, however, became
known to Mordecai, and he made
it known to Esther, and she
reported the matter of the
conspiracy to the king.
²³And the king interrogated
the two eunuchs,

and hanged them.
And the king gave orders to
make an entry as a record
in the royal archives
about Mordecai's benefac-
tion, as a commendation.

Hebrew Est. 2:21–23

²¹At that time, when Mordecai
was sitting in the King's Gate,
Bigtan and Teresh,
two of the king's eunuchs
who guarded the threshhold,
became angry

and they sought
to kill King Ahasueros.
²²The matter, however, became
known to Mordecai, and he told
Queen Esther, and Esther
informed the king in Mordecai's name.
²³The matter was investigated

and confirmed,
and the two (conspirators)
were impaled on stakes,
and (the affair) was
recorded
in the daily record
in the king's presence.

and Mordecai wrote about this matter. [16]The king ordered Mordecai to serve in the court, and bestowed gifts upon him for this.

14. Text in Rahlfs, *Septuaginta*, 1:952; trans. based on C. A. Moore, *Additions*, p. 174 (modified for greater literalness).

15. Text in Rahlfs, *Septuaginta*, 1:956.

2:21–23 (see 6:2–3). In the context of the LXX these differences do not make the episodes contradictory because they are placed at different points in the story and appear as two different incidents, between which differences are to be expected. The one detail that would have made the episodes mutually exclusive is the names of the eunuchs in 2:21. We know from the Hebrew text of 2:21 and 6:2 that these were Bigtan and Teresh, the same two who were executed after the incident in A:12–16.[16] This confirms that the two episodes were originally variants of one and the same episode. However, the other differences between the two versions must have convinced the Greek translator (or the redactor of his Hebrew *Vorlage*) that these were separate incidents.[17] He must have inferred from this that the conspirators in 2:21–23 could not have been Bigtan and Teresh[18] and eliminated their names there. Since 6:2–3 indicated that Mordecai still remained unrewarded for the incident in 2:21–23, the incident for which he *was* rewarded must have been earlier; accordingly, that incident was moved up to an earlier location. The redactor of this version thus did a satisfactory job of smoothing out discrepancies within his material.[19] However, the surviving similarities would have led a critic to classify the two stories as variants of each other, much as the wife-sister stories or the accounts of Hagar's flight/expulsion in Genesis are classified.[20] Indeed, in the "Lucianic" revision of the LXX of Esther the entire incident in 2:21–23 is omitted,

---

16. Their names are still recognizable in the corrupt Greek forms Gabatha (metathesized form of Bagatha, cf. 1:10) and Tharra.

17. Bickerman's comments on the doublets are worth quoting: "Why, then, two parallel stories in the Greek Esther? When an ancient author, particularly an Oriental historian, had before him two or more variants of the same story, he rarely ventured to make a choice. He rather supposed that the different versions were narrations of different events, and tried to co-ordinate the variants to the best of his knowledge and ability. Everybody knows how the same incidents are reported twice or three times in mutually exclusive parallel narratives in the historical parts of Scripture. In the Hellenistic East, Jews told various stories with considerable difference in detail about Queen Esther and the vizir Mordecai. A mural in the Synagogue at Dura-Europos shows the king and Esther together in a scene that seems to be unknown in the extant written sources. The author of the Hebrew Book of Esther collected and edited only a part of this lore. Lysimachus [the Greek translator], however, also heard another version of the conspiracy of eunuchs. It seems that a dream led Mordecai to discover the criminal plot [see A:1–17]. Conspiracies hatched by royal eunuchs being no rare occurrence in the East, Lysimachus conjectured that his hero had saved the king twice. Accordingly, he re-arranged his sources." (Bickerman, *Four Strange Books*, pp. 224–25)

18. Or, that they were two other eunuchs with the same names, which would confuse his readers.

19. Moore, *Additions*, p. 168.

20. Skinner, *Genesis*, pp. 285, 325, on the Hagar stories, and pp. 315, 364–65, on the wife-sister stories; more generally Gunkel, *Legends*, pp. 99–100; Eissfeldt, *OTI*, pp. 186–87; Driver, *ILOT*, pp. 8, 9, etc. (see his Index s.v. "Double narratives"); Cassuto, *Documentary Hypothesis*, chaps. 6–7.

along with a number of other details of the Hebrew text which are paralleled in the LXX's additions.[21] This implies that 2:21-23 was already recognized in antiquity as a doublet of A:12-16, just as the other dropped details were recognized as repetitions of matters covered in the additions.

Our ability to check the redactor's sources shows us more than the fact that his text is composite. When we can compare the combined form with the original, uncombined forms, we can see what changes, if any, the redactor made to effect the join and accommodate the texts to each other. The ideal situation is represented in the case of the Qumran and Codex Vaticanus texts of the Sabbath command, where we have the uncombined source texts in the Masoretic Text of Exodus and Deuteronomy as well as the combined forms in the Qumran and Greek manuscripts. We can see that both manuscripts left the text of Deuteronomy essentially intact, and that Vaticanus included less of the Exodus version than 4QDeut[n] did and thereby avoided an explicit clash of motive clauses, but at the price of a non sequitur in the text. The evidence for the story of the eunuchs' conspiracy in the Septuagint of Esther is not quite as clear. There only one of the components is known to us in its original form (2:21-23, known from the Masoretic Text), while the version in Addition A:12-16 is known to us only in the form in which it is found in the Septuagint of Esther. While a comparison of the Septuagint's 2:21-23 with its Hebrew original enabled us to see that the Septuagint dropped the names of the conspirators in order to avoid an out-and-out conflict with A:12-16, we cannot tell whether the latter was incorporated intact or also underwent adjustment.

The Samaritan Pentateuch: Jethro's Advice to Moses

Another case where we have both sources of a conflate text is in the Samaritan Pentateuch.[22] The Samaritan version of the Torah is part of a group of expansive, synthesizing manuscripts classified by P. Kahle and others as vulgar or popular[23] and by F. M. Cross as Palestinian.[24] These

---

21. See Tov, "The 'Lucianic' Text," pp. 11-12.

22. For characterizations of the Samaritan Pentateuch, see Waltke, "Samaritan Pentateuch"; Weiss, *Studies*, pp. 63-189; Purvis, *EM* 8:173-77.

23. Kahle, "Untersuchungen," pp. 5-12; idem, *Cairo Geniza*, pp. 147-48; Gaster, *Samaritans*, pp. 123-28; Gerleman, *Synoptic Studies*, pp. 3-8; Talmon, "Samaritan Pentateuch"; Greenberg, "Stabilization." For these designations, note the reference to "village people" in the ʿĀrûk passage cited by Greenberg, "Stabilization," p. 159, and to hedyôṭôt, "common folk," in b. Sanh. 21b, cited by Talmon, "Samaritan Pentateuch," pp. 149-50. The designations are rejected by Cross, followed by Purvis; see the next note.

24. Purvis, *Samaritan Pentateuch*, pp. 69-87; Cross, "Evolution," and his earlier studies cited by Purvis, pp. 79-80; see also the very useful study of Waltke, "Samaritan Pentateuch"

manuscripts, well attested at Qumran and best exemplified in the Samaritan Pentateuch, are characterized by expansion of the basic text with variant readings or with material imported from related passages elsewhere in Scripture,[25] in other words, by "double" or "conflate" readings such as those mentioned above.

In Pentateuchal manuscripts a number of the expansions involve material from Deuteronomy, since Deuteronomy contains variant accounts of several earlier narratives. Because of its full preservation, the Samaritan Torah is the best witness to such synthesizing, and it will serve as the basis of the following discussion. However, the practice is not exclusively Samaritan.[26] The Samaritan Pentateuch itself is not an exclusively Samaritan text, apart from a few sectarian additions and changes; rather, it is essentially an early Hebrew text-type which is sometimes reflected in early manuscripts of the Mishna,[27] a decidedly non-Samaritan composition, as well as in the proto-Samaritan manuscripts from Qumran.[28] These characteristics are

---

(reference courtesy of Edward M. Curtis). A brief demurrer to the geographic classification was registered by Skehan, "Two Books," p. 77 with n. 2; a comprehensive survey and critique are presented by Talmon, "Old Testament Text," esp. pp. 193–99.

25. Cf. Skehan, "Scrolls." On p. 102 Skehan notes the exegetical character of such synoptic additions, "explaining the Bible by the Bible, within the Bible itself." Similarly, A. Toeg noted the exegetical character of the conflate Samaritan version of the Sinai theophany (see below) by comparing it to a medieval Karaite commentary: "The interpretation is identical; only the exegetical technique differs, owing to the [intervening] santification of the wording of the text" (Toeg, *Lawgiving*, pp. 44–46; reference courtesy of Professors J. Licht and S. E. Loewenstamm). Likewise Rashi, in his commentary at Num. 13:1 (in *MG*), refers to Deut. 1:22, whereas SP inserts Deut. 1:20–23, slightly modified, into the text right before Num. 13:1. The same point is made in Talmudic sources with reference to the Samaritan plus "near Shechem" in Deut. 11:30; in *y. Soṭa* 7:3, 21c, and parallels it is observed that what the Samaritans make explicit in the text itself the Jews do externally by exegesis (see E. S. Rosenthal, *Lěšônôt*, pp. 319–20 n. 186 [reference courtesy of Professor Shamma Friedman]).

26. Kahle, "Untersuchungen," pp. 7–12; idem, *Cairo Geniza*, pp. 144–48.

27. Weiss, *Studies*, pp. 206–9.

28. Skehan, "Scrolls," pp. 101–3. 4QpaleoEx^m (Skehan, "Exodus") preserves a bit of the conflate text, and Skehan showed that the size of the lacuna in the ms. leaves no doubt that the rest of the interpolation from Deuteronomy was present ("Qumran," pp. 22–23; cf. idem, "Exodus," p. 187). Elsewhere Skehan pointed out that the conflate text is reflected in 4Q175 ("Testimonia") as well ("Period," p. 435; cf. idem, "Exodus," p. 187; 4Q175 was edited by Allegro, "Further," pp. 182–87). The same is true of 4Q158, frag. 6, though it is debated whether this is part of a proto-Samaritan biblical ms. (Weiss, *Studies*, pp. 209 n. 17, 330–31) or a paraphrase (Allegro, DJD 5, p. 3; Tov, "Harmonizations," pp. 16–18); the term "paraphrase" is questioned by Strugnell, "Notes," p. 168). (M. Baillet, "Texte samaritaine," suggested that the "proto-Samaritan" mss. are actually Samaritan, but the absence of the Samaritan tenth commandment—the most distinctive Samaritan feature—from 4QpaleoEx^m [see below, n. 42] argues against this view). F. M. Cross kindly informed me that the unpublished 4QEx^a has all the pluses from Deuteronomy that the Samaritan Exodus has, as well as affinities with the LXX (cf. the fragment transliterated in Cross, *Ancient Library*, pp. 184–85 n. 31). On 4QNum^b, see ibid., p. 186.

well known but have not been brought to bear on the documentary hypothesis.[29]

In a number of pericopes the Samaritan presents a conflate text. This conflateness is secondary compared with the shortness of the Masoretic Text.[30] Apart from the question of precise recensional relationships,[31] the "conservative, often pristine"[32] Masoretic Text reflects a stage anterior to the expansion which produced the Samaritan. Therefore, by a comparison of the Masoretic and Samaritan texts of these pericopes, we can disentangle the component parts of the latter and view the methods by which they were combined, just as G. F. Moore did with the *Diatessaron* and the Gospels. In following this procedure below, we will for convenience refer somewhat anachronistically to the Masoretic Text as the source of the Samaritan, though in fact in its present form the Masoretic Text merely reflects that source.

An example that shows the harmonistic purpose of conflation is found in the story of Jethro's advice to Moses as it is presented in the Samaritan's Exodus 18 and the proto-Samaritan Exodus manuscript from Qumran.[33] On the following pages is the text of the Samaritan version, in the center column, flanked by the "sources" of that version: the Masoretic Exodus (left-hand column, in Roman type) and the Masoretic Deuteronomy (right-hand column, in italics); the components of the Samaritan text are printed in typefaces corresponding to their sources. Material found in neither source, and thus inferably by the redactor, is underlined. To facilitate comparison with the Masoretic Text, verses in the Samaritan are given the same numbers as their MT counterparts, and the interpolated verses are designated by letters added to the number of the verse they follow (thus: 24, 24a, 24b, etc.). As we can see, the Masoretic text of Exodus 18 has Moses institute Israel's judicial administration at Jethro's suggestion, which is addressed to Moses (Exod. 18:19–24). Deuteronomy, however, speaks

---

29. That a "pleonasm" similar to the Samaritan's may underlie parts of the MT has been alluded to before: König, "Samaritan Pentateuch," p. 70b; Skehan, "Scrolls," p. 103 (cf. Levine, "Descriptive," though Levine and Skehan posit different orders of development); regarding Jeremiah, see Cross, "Contribution," p. 82, and Tov, below, Chapter 8, pp. 229–30, 233. On Num. 21:33–35 (called to my attention by A. Rofé) see Gray, *Numbers*, p. 306. That inferences have not been drawn from the synthetic techniques for the documentary hypothesis is probably due to preoccupation with the Samaritan and Qumran biblical manuscripts as aids in text criticism, which is generally kept separate from literary criticism; cf. the opening paragraph of Roberts, *O.T. Text*, p. 1.

30. Cf. Cross, "Contribution," p. 86, and Talmon, "O.T. Text," pp. 194–96.

31. Note the remark of Kahle, "Untersuchungen," p. 7, par. 3: the Urtext presupposed by the Samaritan is not to be confused with the Jewish *textus receptus*.

32. Cross, "Contribution," p. 86.

33. For the proto-Samaritan text see Skehen, "Qumran," p. 22, on col. 26; for the Masoretic and Samaritan texts, see Appendix A to this chapter.

Samaritan Exodus 18

[21]"You shall seek out for yourself from among all the people capable men who fear God, trustworthy men who spurn ill-gotten gain; and set these over them as chiefs of thousands, chiefs of hundreds, chiefs of fifties and chiefs of tens. [22]Let them exercise authority over the people at all times; let them bring every major matter to you, but decide every minor matter themselves. Make it easier for yourself, and let them share the burden with you. [23]If you do this—and God so commands you—you will be able to bear up; and all these people will go home content." [24]Moses heeded his father-in-law and did all that he had said. [24a]*Mo-*

Masoretic Exodus 18

[21]"You shall seek out for yourself from among all the people capable men who fear God, trustworthy men who spurn ill-gotten gain; and set these over them as chiefs of thousands, chiefs of hundreds, chiefs of fifties and chiefs of tens. [22]Let them exercise authority over the people at all times; let them bring every major matter to you, but decide every minor matter themselves. Make it easier for yourself, and let them share the burden with you. [23]If you do this—and God so commands you—you will be able to bear up; and all these people will go home content." [24]Moses heeded his father-in-law and did all that he had said.

9 I said to you at that time, "I cannot bear the burden of you alone. 10 The Lord your God has multiplied you until you are today as numerous as the stars in the sky. 11 May the Lord, the God of your fathers, increase your numbers a thousandfold, and bless you as He promised you. 12 How can I alone bear the trouble of you, and the burden, and the bickering! 13 Pick from each of your tribes men who are wise, discerning, and experienced, and I will appoint them as your heads." 14 You answered me and said, "What you propose to do is good." 15 So I took your tribal leaders, wise and experienced men, and I appointed them heads over you: chiefs of thousands, chiefs of hundreds, chiefs of fifties, and chiefs of tens, and

ses said to the people, "I myself cannot bear the burden of you alone. 24b The Lord your God has multiplied you until you are today as numerous as the stars in the sky. 24c May the Lord, the God of your fathers, increase your numbers a thousandfold, and bless you as He promised you. 24d How can I alone bear the trouble of you, and the burden, and the bickering! 24e Pick from each of your tribes men who are wise, discerning, and experienced, and I will appoint them as your heads." 24f They answered and said, "What you propose to do is good." 24g So he took their tribal leaders, wise and experienced men, and he appointed them heads over them: chiefs of thousands, chiefs of fifties, and chiefs of tens, and

25 Moses chose capable men out of all Israel, and appointed them heads over the people: chiefs of thousands, chiefs of hundreds, chiefs of fifties, and chiefs of tens.

officials for your tribes.
[16] I charged your magistrates
at that time as follows:
"Hear out your
fellow men, and decide justly
between any man and a fellow
Israelite or a stranger. [17] You
shall not be partial in judg-
ment; hear out high and low
alike. Fear no man, for judg-
ment is God's. And any matter
that is too difficult for you,
you shall bring to me and I
will hear it." [18] Thus I com-
manded you at that time about the
various things that you should
do.

officials for their tribes.
[24h] He charged their magistrates
as follows:

"Hear out your
fellow men, and decide justly
between any man and a fellow
Israelite or a stranger. [24i] You
shall not be partial in judg-
ment; hear out high and low
alike. Fear no man, for judg-
ment is God's. And any matter
that is too difficult for you,
you shall bring near to me and I
will hear it. [24j] Thus He com-
manded them   about the
various things that they should
do. [26] And they would exercise
authority over the people at all
times: the major matters
they would bring to Moses, and
all the minor matters they
would decide themselves. [27] Then
Moses bade his father-in-law
farewell, and he went his way
to his own land.

[26] And they   exercised
authority over the people at all
times: the difficult matters
they would bring to Moses, and
all the minor matters they
would decide themselves. [27] Then
Moses bade his father-in-law
farewell, and he went his way
to his own land.

only of Moses' initiative, addressed to the people (Deut. 1:9–18). The Samaritan Exodus resolves this by arranging the conflicting details in sequence. First come Jethro's advice and Moses' compliance, from Exodus; then, from Deuteronomy, Moses broaches the idea to the people, the people approve, Moses appoints the chiefs and charges them. All this is absent from the Masoretic Exodus save the appointment, which comes about halfway through the Deuteronomic insert; rather than interrupt the insert momentarily for the sake of a variant which offers nothing substantially different from Deuteronomy's description, the Samaritan preserves Deuteronomy's version and drops that of Exodus. The hand of the redactor is visible in the change from first and second person, which befits the insert's Deuteronomic home, to third person where necessary, as suits the narrative context of its new home in the Samaritan Exodus; and in the dropping of Deuteronomy's *bāʿēt hahîʾ*, which fits Deuteronomy's retrospective stance but not Exodus.

How much of this could have been recognized by source criticism if the Masoretic Exodus and Deuteronomy were not available to guide the analysis? Clearly, some omissions, such as "at that time," and changes such as that from first to third person, would have eluded detection, and the stance of Deuteronomy as a retrospective speech by Moses could not have been surmised from this pericope. On the whole, however, the Samaritan pericope is full of signs of compositeness which would have led critics to unravel its components rather accurately. The analysis would have begun with inconsistencies between the proposal and its execution. Jethro advises *Moses* to seek out men "from among all the people" (18:21, from Exodus), but in complying Moses asks *the people* to do the choosing (24e, from Deuteronomy). He then takes (on the people's recommendation?) not men "from among all the people" but "the tribal leaders" (24g, from Deuteronomy). Jethro recommends "capable men who fear God, trustworthy men who spurn ill-gotten gain" (21, from Exodus), but Moses asks for and appoints "wise, discerning, and experienced men" (24e and 24g, from Deuteronomy).[34] Jethro speaks only of "chiefs of thousands, hundreds, fifties, and tens" (21, from Exodus), but Moses adds "magistrates" (*šōṭĕrîm*, 24g, from Deuteronomy). These inconsistencies would have suggested that Jethro's proposal and Moses' execution of it are from different sources. Vocabulary differences would have supported the suggestion and carried it further: Jethro had used the verb "bring" (*yĕbîʾûn*, 22, from Exodus) with major matters, but Moses used "bring near" (*taqrîbûn*, 24i, from Deuteronomy); Jethro had differentiated between major and minor matters (*gādôl, qāṭôn*, 22, from Exodus), whereas Moses spoke only of any

---

34. On these differences between Exodus and Deuteronomy, see Weinfeld, *Deuteronomy*, pp. 244–45. *yĕdūʿîm* is a *pāʿûl* active participle; see *GKC* sec. 50f; Hoffman, *Sēfer Dĕvārîm*, 1:31; E. Y. Kutscher, *Language*, p. 268; Yalon, *Pirqê Lāšôn*, pp. 323–24.

matter that is "too difficult" (*yiqšeh mi-*, 24i, from Deuteronomy). The reversion to "bring," "major," and "minor" in verse 26 would have indicated that the redactor had now returned to the first source.[35] Harmonistic exegesis might regard such variation as an attempt to avoid monotony. The redactor may have told himself the same, and there is no denying that the differences have such an effect and that Hebrew writers sometimes strove for variety.[36] But having seen the sources of the Samaritan pericope, we know that in this case the variation stems from differences between the sources.

The particular vocabulary differences we have mentioned are not characteristic of the sources in which they appear in this case[37] and would not have enabled critics to assign the components of this pericope to the larger literary entities to which they belong, that is, Exodus and Deuteronomy. But other terms, phrases, and themes in verses 24a–24j are characteristic of Deuteronomy, and assuming that much of Deuteronomy had been reconstructed by critics, these would have facilitated its identification as the source of those verses. These include: "YHWH the God of your fathers" (24c), "as He promised you" (24c), the long form *ʾêkâ* for "how" (24d),[38] the intellectual qualifications for judges (24e and 24g),[39] and the idiom *hikkîr pānîm* for judicial partiality (24i).[40]

The Samaritan Pentateuch: The Theophany at Mount Sinai

The best-known composite pericope in the Samaritan Torah is the theophany at Mount Sinai in Exodus 20. In the Samaritan and in the

---

35. This verse might have been misleading, since it would suggest that verse 26 in the source read "major," whereas in the MT of Exodus it reads "difficult." The reading in the Samaritan is probably a harmonization to verse 22, abetted by the awkwardness of the contrast "difficult . . . minor" in the MT of verse 26 (see Weiss, *Studies*, p. 151). Conceivably this harmonization was already made in the *Vorlage* on which the Samaritan version was based.

36. Note, e.g., the different vocabulary of the suggestion and execution in Exod. 18:21–22 and 24–25: "seek out . . . set . . . major" (*teḥ͑zeh . . . wĕśamtā . . . haggādōl*) vs. "chose . . . appointed . . . difficult" (*wayyibḥar . . . wayyittēn . . . haqqāšeh*). For another example, see Kaufman, "Temple Scroll," p. 41 and n. 33.

37. Thus *hēbîʾ* is used not only in Exodus (18:22) but also in Deuteronomy (e.g., 7:26; 12:6, 11; 23:19; 26:10; 29:26), and *hiqrîb* is used in a judicial context not only in Deuteronomy (1:7), but also in Num. 27:5.

38. On these three items, see Driver, *Deuteronomy*, pp. lxxx–lxxxi, nos. 16, 29, 19; on the second, see, further, Milgrom, "Profane Slaughter."

39. Compare Deut. 16:19 to Exod. 23:8, and see Weinfeld, *Deuteronomy*, pp. 244–47.

40. Cf. Deut. 16:19; Driver, *Deuteronomy*, pp. 18, 201; Weinfeld, *Deuteronomy*, p. 245.

proto-Samaritan biblical fragments and reflexes from Qumran, the variant account of Deuteronomy 5, supplemented by Deuteronomy 18, is fully spliced into the Exodus version.[41] The Qumran attestations show that the expansion is not an exclusively Samaritan feature. Only the law of the altar on Mount Gerizim, imported from Deuteronomy 11 and 27, which the Samaritan treats as the tenth commandment, is absent at Qumran and appears to be an exclusively Samaritan item.[42] On the following pages are the texts of the Samaritan version and its "sources," presented in the same format we followed for Exod. 18:21–27 above: the Masoretic Exodus is on the left in Roman type, the Masoretic Deuteronomy 5 is on the right in italics, and the Masoretic Deuteronomy 18 is also on the right, in boldface.[43] Material presumably by the redactor is underlined.

Just as we suppose with texts built up from J, E, and P, one finds the Samaritan Exodus here flitting back and forth between the Masoretic Exodus and Deuteronomy, adding or dropping a phrase or detail here and there in an attempt to merge and reconcile the conflicting accounts. Immediately after the Masoretic Decalogue (Exod. 20:2–17),[44] the Samaritan adds its own tenth commandment (vv. 17a–h), to which we shall return below. Following this the Samaritan text returns to where it left off in the Masoretic Exodus, whose description of the people's fright at the theophany is slightly reworded to avoid the awkward "seeing" the sounds and perhaps to avoid separating the sounds of the *šôpār* from the other sounds (v. 18).[45] The text then introduces the people's plea to Moses, but suddenly shifts after the first three words of verse 19 to Deuteronomy's version of that plea, after which it places the shorter Exodus version of the same as its conclusion (the second half of Exod. 20:19). The Masoretic Exodus is followed through Moses' response to the people, his approach to God, and the introduction to God's speech (beginning of v. 22). But before Exodus' version of God's speech (remainder of v. 22 through v. 26, concerning the altar, etc.), the text shifts to Deuteronomy 5's very different divine speech, into which is inserted Deuteronomy 18's promise of a future prophet, which promise Deuteronomy 18:16 stated was indeed first voiced on this occasion. After this interpolation the divine speech of Deuteronomy 5 is concluded from the point of interruption, and the text then returns to where it left off in Exodus 20. Exodus' introduction to its divine speech (beginning

41. See n. 28; cf. Kahle, *Cairo Geniza*, pp. 144–45; Gaster, *Samaritans*, p. 128.
42. Skehan, "Qumran," pp. 22–23, shows that the Samaritan tenth commandment could not have been present in 4QpaleoEx^m; the same is true of 4Q158, nos. 7–8.
43. For the Hebrew texts, see Appendix B to this chapter.
44. The Samaritan Exodus Decalogue begins by adding, from Deut. 5:21, the neighbor's field to the list of items not to be coveted (see below; so LXX and some Hebrew mss.).
45. Weiss, *Studies*, pp. 119–21.

Masoretic Exodus 20

18All the people saw the thunderclaps and the torches, the sound of the horn and the mountain smoking, and when all the people saw it, they fell back and stood at a distance. 19And they said to Moses:

Samaritan Exodus 20

18All the people heard the thunderclaps and the sound of the horn, and saw the torches and the mountain smoking, and when all the people saw it, they fell back and stood at a distance. 19And they said to Moses: 19a*The Lord our God has just shown us His presence and His greatness, and we have heard His voice from out of the fire; we have seen this day that man may live, though God has spoken to him.* 19b*Let us not die, then, for this great fire will consume us; if we hear the voice of the Lord our God any longer, we shall die.* 19c*For what mortal ever heard the voice of the living God speak out of*

Masoretic Deuteronomy

5:22*The Lord spoke those words—those and no more—to your whole congregation at the mountain, with a mighty voice out of the fire, the cloud, and the thick cloud. He inscribed them on two tablets of stone, which He gave to me.* 23*When you heard the voice out of the darkness, while the mountain was ablaze with fire, you came up to me, all your tribal heads and elders,*

24*and said:*

"*The Lord our God has just shown us His presence and His greatness, and we have heard His voice from out of the fire; we have seen this day that man may live, though God has spoken to him.* 25*Let us not die, then, for this great fire will consume us; if we hear the voice of the Lord our God any longer, we shall die.* 26*For what mortal ever heard the voice of the living God speak out of*

the fire, as we did, and lived?
19d You go closer and hear all
that the Lord our God says;
then you speak to us everything
that the Lord our God tells you,
and we will listen and obey.

"You speak with us

and we will listen,

but let not God speak to us,
lest we die." 20 Moses answered
the people: "Be not afraid, for
The God has come only in order
to test you, and in order that
the fear of Him may be ever with
you, so that you do not go
astray." 21 So the people remained
at a distance, while Moses approached the thick cloud where The
God was.

22 The Lord said to Moses:

---

the fire, as we did, and lived?
19d You go closer and hear all
that the Lord our God says;
then you speak to us everything
that the Lord our God tells you,
and we will listen and obey,
19e but let not The God speak to us,
lest we die." 20 Moses answered
the people: "Be not afraid, for
The God has come only in order
to test you, and in order that
the fear of Him may be ever with
you, so that you do not go
astray." 21 So the people remained
at a distance, while Moses approached the thick cloud where The
God was.

22 The Lord spoke to Moses,
saying: 22a "*I have heard the sound*
of this people's words which
they spoke to you; they did
well to speak thus. 22b *May*
they always be of such a mind,
to revere Me and follow all My
commandments, that it may go
well with them and with their

---

the fire, as we did, and lived?
27 You go closer and hear all
that the Lord our God says;
then you speak to us everything
that the Lord our God tells you,
and we will listen and obey.

28 The Lord heard the
sound of your words
as you spoke to me,
and the Lord said to me:
"I have heard the sound
of this people's words which
they spoke to you; they did
well to speak thus. 29 *May*
they always be of such a mind,
to revere Me and follow all My
commandments, that it may go
well with them and with their

children forever. [18:18]I will raise up a prophet for them from among their own people, like yourself: I will put My words in his mouth and he will speak to them all that I command him; [19]and if anybody fails to heed the words he speaks in My name, I Myself will call him to account. [20]But any prophet who presumes to speak in My name an oracle which I did not command him to utter, or who speaks in the name of other gods—that prophet shall die. [21]And should you ask yourself: 'How can we recognize an oracle which the Lord did not utter?'—[22]if the prophet speaks in the name of the Lord and the word does not come true, that word was not spoken by the Lord; the prophet has uttered it presumptuously: do not stand in dread of him. [5:30]*Go, say to them, 'Return to your tents.'* [31]*But you remain here with Me, and I will speak to you the whole instruction—*

children forever. [22]I will raise up a prophet for them from among their own people, like yourself: I will put My words in his mouth and he will speak to them all that I command him; [22d]and if anybody fails to heed the words he speaks in My name, I Myself will call him to account. [22e]But any prophet who presumes to speak in My name an oracle which I did not command him to utter, or who speaks in the name of other gods—that prophet shall die. [22f]And should you ask yourself: "How can we recognize an oracle which the Lord did not utter?"—[22g]if the prophet speaks in the name of the Lord and the word does not come true, that word was not spoken by the Lord; the prophet has uttered it presumptuously: do not stand in dread of him. [22h]*Go, say to them, 'Return to your tents.'* [22i]*But you remain here with Me, and I will speak to you the whole instruction—*

"Thus shall you say to the Israelites: 'You yourselves saw that I spoke to you from the very heavens: [23]With Me, therefore, you shall not make any gods of silver, nor shall you make for yourselves any gods of gold. [24]Make for Me an altar of earth and sacrifice on it your burnt offerings and your sacrifices of well-being, from your sheep and your oxen; in every place where I shall cause My name to be mentioned, I will come to you and bless you. [25]And if you make for Me an altar of stones, do not build it of hewn stones; for by wielding your tool upon them you have profaned them. [26]Do not ascend My altar by steps, that your nakedness may not be exposed upon it.'"

the laws and the norms—which you will teach them, for them to observe in the land that I am giving them to possess." [22]The Lord spoke to Moses, saying: "Speak to the Israelites: 'You yourselves saw that I spoke to you from the very heavens: [23]With Me, therefore, you shall not make any gods of silver, nor shall you make for yourselves any gods of gold. [24]Make for Me an altar of earth and sacrifice on it your burnt offerings and your sacrifices of well-being, your sheep and your oxen; in the place where I have caused My name to be mentioned, there I will come to you and bless you. [25]And if you make for Me an altar of stones, do not build it of hewn stones; for by wielding your tool upon them you have profaned them. [26]Do not ascend My altar by steps, that your nakedness may not be exposed upon it.'"

the laws and the norms—which you will teach them, for them to observe in the land that I am giving them to possess."

of v. 22) is repeated (resumptive repetition),[46] and the speech itself now appears as the conclusion of a long speech.

This pericope does not display the same kind of obvious inconsistencies we observed in the Jethro pericope, for the Exodus and Deuteronomy accounts of the Sinai theophany were very similar in the first place.[47] But a degree of unevenness which could have attracted the attention of the source critic is still visible. In the description of the theophany in 19:16–19 and 20:18, fire had been only one among several phenomena accompanying God's appearance; the narrator's description in 20:18 of what frightened the people mentioned fire only in the form of torches, and it gave them no more conspicuous a place than the thunderclaps (*qōlôt*, plural), the ram's horn, and the smoking mountain. But in the people's speech in 19a–c it is only the fire and God's voice (*qôl*, singular) within it which terrify the people. These differences are by no means irreconcilable, since fire is the most dangerous phenomenon mentioned in the earlier passages, and 19:18 did say that God had come down in fire. But as an introduction to 19a–c, 18 is at least partly pointless. Not one of the items listed in verse 18 is identical to one in 19a–c. Only if one allows that verse 18's torches are 19b's "great fire," and that 18's thunderclaps (*qōlôt*) are 19a–c's "voice of God" (*qôl YHWH/ᵉlōhîm*) could one produce a partial congruence between the introduction and the speech, and even then the sequence would be: when the people heard A, B, C, and D, they were frightened and said "we are afraid of C′ and A′." Furthermore, after the stress on God speaking from within the fire, one is unprepared for verse 21's reference to "the thick cloud (*ᶜᵃrāpel*) where God was." This reference seems more in keeping with 19:16, which refers to a "heavy cloud" (*ᶜānān kābēd*). The critic might thus have come to the working hypothesis that 19:16–19 and 20:18 and 21 represent one strand in the text, and 20:19a–c another. The hypothesis

---

46. In other words, a composite of Deut. 5:28–29 + 18:18–22 + 5:30–31 is interpolated in Exod. 20:22–26; following the interpolation, Exodus resumes by first repeating the last sentence before the interpolation. The repetition is clearly the interpolator's creation, for the MT (which reads *wayyōᵓmer* for the Samaritan's *wayyĕdabbēr*) has the sentence only once. For the redactorial technique of resumptive repetition (or *Wiederaufnahme*), see above, pp. 48–49; Seeligmann, "Hebräische Erzählung," pp. 314–24; Talmon and Fishbane, "Aspects," pp. 35–38. For Akkadian examples, see *GE* III, i, 1–10, and iii, ?–11; II, v, 1–2 and 5 (see *EGE*, pp. 75–76, 95), and *VTE*, sec. 4 (Reiner, in *ANET*, p. 535a; see Frankena, "Vassal Treaties," pp. 128, 132–33). For the technique as an author's device, see Rashi at Exod. 6:29 and 30 and cf. the resumptions after digressions in Erman, *Literature*, p. 32, par. 1 end and p. 33, par. 1 end; cf. p. 29; and the *Odyssey*, book 19:393–466. Cf. also the looser recapitulations noted by J. Licht in 1QS: "Analysis," pp. 92–93, 94–95.

47. See Driver, *Deuteronomy*, pp. xiv–xix for the dependence of Deuteronomy on JE. A closer affinity with E has been stressed by some; see Wright, "Deuteronomy. Introduction," pp. 319–20; Weinfeld, *Deuteronomy*, p. 34; Haran, "Methodological Observations," p. 139, considers D dependent on E alone, not JE.

would have been nudged forward by some observations about verses 19e–21. Verse 19e is mildly redundant, since it merely makes explicit the request that God not speak to the people, a request implicit in 19b and 19d. There is nothing inherently unacceptable about the people's request being made explicit, given their anxiety. But this mild redundancy goes along with a sudden shift in the terms for God. In 19a–d the people had called him "YHWH our God,"[48] but in 19e–21 they, Moses, and the narrator refer only to "The God" (*hā ᵊᵉlōhîm*). The shift is particularly noticeable in 19e, where it comes in midsentence: "You go close and hear all that YHWH our God tells you . . . but let not The God speak with us. . . ." Based on these different terms for God, the working hypothesis would have identified verses 19a–d as one unit and 19e–21 as another. The shift back to YHWH in verse 22 would then have suggested that the text had again changed sources, but this would have been misleading because for this redactor the proximate source of verse 22 was the same as that of 19e–21 (Exodus). Verses 22c–g would most likely have been recognized as out of place: God has approved the people's request that Moses serve as intermediary but then digresses to speak of future intermediaries, their authentication, and what will happen to those who disobey them, before getting to the point of what Moses should do. The digression interrupts the natural connection of verses 22a–b and 22h–i and produces a glaring non sequitur in which instructions on how to respond to a future false prophet (v. 22g) are followed by instructions on how Moses is to proceed immediately (v. 22h). The recognition of 22c–g as belonging to another context would have been substantiated by a shift in the audience in 22f–g, where Moses addresses future generations of Israelites who will encounter his successor prophets; this audience is appropriate in a passage from Deuteronomy, Moses' farewell speech, but not in the theophany narrative of Exodus, where that generation is unborn and Moses is not the speaker. The original unit would thus have been identified as verses 22–22b and 22h–i, with verses 22c–g recognized as an interpolation of uncertain provenance. That the unit ends with 22i would have been recognized from 22j, where God is introduced; since God has been speaking since verse 22, the introduction is superfluous in the present context. Thus it would have been recognized that verses 22j ff. were taken from a context in which God had not just been speaking.

How much of this unevenness would really have been recognized without the benefit of the Masoretic Exodus and Deuteronomy is difficult to

---

48. If "God" (*ᵊᵉlōhîm*) is taken as referring to YHWH in the second half of verse 19a and in verse 19c, this would still be different from "The God" (*hā ᵊᵉlōhîm*) in verses 19e–21. Possibly, however, the people are referring to any god(s) (as in the similar context of Deut. 4:7, 33–34), their point being that nobody has ever heard a god speaking and lived, but they have just learned it is possible.

say. Many of the incongruities noted above could have been rationalized and the exercise dismissed as hypercritical. As noted, the unevenness is certainly not as blatant as in the Samaritan Jethro pericope. It is quite possible that critics would have regarded the Sinai pericope as one of those which show some signs of composition but are difficult to unravel due to great similarity between the original sources, and/or skillful blending by the redactor, a situation which in the Masoretic Torah is found especially in passages from JE.[49] Assuming that some degree of compositeness was recognized, it would have been possible to recognize several details characteristic of Deuteronomy in one of the main strands: "YHWH our God"[50] and "from the midst of the fire"[51] (vv. 19a–c), God's "greatness" (*gōdel*, v. 19a),[52] "to fear" (*lĕyir²â*) Him,[53] "that it may be well for them,"[54] and "all the days"[55] (v. 22b); and, in the digression: "from the midst of" (*miqqereb*) their brethren (v. 22c),[56] "presume" (*hēzîd*, v. 22e),[57] and "dread" (*gûr*, v. 22g).[58] On the other hand, verses 22j–26 would not have been recognized as coming from a non-Deuteronomic source. Although this is clear in the Masoretic Text, where verse 24 permits sacrifice "in every place where I shall cause/allow my name to be invoked," contrasting with Deuteronomy's restriction of sacrifice to a single site (Deut. 12), the Samaritan (not proto-Samaritan) revision of this verse completely hides this fact (see below).

The redaction of the Jethro and Sinai pericopes in the Samaritan Pentateuch is as fine an example as one could wish of scissors-and-paste composition, a "patchwork." But the patchwork is not "crazy." The main task of the redactor in these pericopes was to reconcile dissimilar accounts of the same events. By interweaving their details in sequence, he facilitated their harmonious coexistence. He accommodated their differing details by having them refer to different moments of those events. He has also drawn in material (vv. 22c–22g) from outside the parallel accounts which purported to belong to the theophany pericope. This illustration of the redactor's procedure, in sum, supports Greenberg's characterization of the (Masoretic) Pentateuchal redactor's method, cited above (p. 54).

As instructive as his inclusions from Deuteronomy are the redactor's omissions. He was essentially interested in filling in speeches in places

49. See, e.g., Gunkel, *Legends*, pp. 125–26.
50. See Driver, *Deuteronomy*, pp. lxxix–lxxx, no. 15.
51. Ibid., no. 69 (cf. Weinfeld, *Deuteronomy*, pp. 206–8).
52. Driver, *Deuteronomy*, no. 26 (contrast Weinfeld, *Deuteronomy*, pp. 1–2, 329, no. 16).
53. Driver, no. 45 (cf. Weinfeld, pp. 332–33, nos. 3–3b).
54. Driver, no. 42 (cf. Weinfeld, p. 345, no. 4).
55. Driver, no. 41 (cf. Weinfeld, p. 333, no. 3b).
56. Driver, no. 58 (contrast Weinfeld, pp. 1–2).
57. Driver, p. lxxxiv (list of unusual words).
58. Ibid.

where they purported to have been uttered, and in reconciling conflicting versions of speeches by treating them as parts of a sequence rather than variants.[59] He had little interest in nonverbal action. In this, his aims differ from those attributed to the redactor of the Torah. But in handling the speeches his methods are the same as those attributed to the latter. His omissions are minimal and insubstantial. Clearly, he aimed to use as much of his source material as possible, and he incorporated every significant detail of his parallel sources. In the Jethro pericope, he brought in everything Deuteronomy had to offer save the phrase "at that time," which was unnecessary now that the story had been brought back to its contextually proper place in Exodus; he preserved everything from the Masoretic Exodus except a verse covered by the Deuteronomic insert. In the Sinai pericope, what he dropped from one source was either covered in the parallel source, unnecessary, or out of place in the theophany scene. A good example is Deut. 5:22. The first half of this verse reads: "The Lord spoke those words—those and no more—to your whole congregation at the mountain, with a mighty voice out of the fire and dense clouds." Since the redactor preserved Exod. 20:18, which includes most of this information, the Deuteronomy version could be dispensed with. The second part of Deut. 5:22 reads: "He inscribed them on two tablets of stone, which He gave to me." Since this refers to a later event (see Exod. 24:12, 18; 32:15–16; Deut. 9:9–10), it is out of place in the theophany pericope. This is typical of the redactor's omissions: what he drops is either substantially covered in parallel material which he preserves, or dispensable on other grounds. This procedure comports with a tendency which has been observed in the redaction of the Pentateuch. Building on an observation of Albright's, Greenberg concludes: "What has not been preserved of a given source may the more confidently be supposed to have differed from our text only insubstantially."[60] In the cases we have examined, this observation is borne out.

---

59. This interest is also seen in other passages where the Samaritan has filled in gaps by adding speeches where later passages say they belong. For example, in Gen. 31:11–13 Jacob refers to an oracle he had previously received from an angel. The MT had not mentioned this oracle, but the Samaritan supplies it in Genesis 30 after verse 36, with wording based on 31:11–13 (for lists of such synoptic additions in SP, see Purvis, *Samaritan Pentateuch*, pp. 71–72; Gray, *Numbers*, p. xl). In the present examples, however, the Deuteronomic material that goes with these pericopes in Exodus is not simply absent from Exodus, needing merely to be added at the appropriate place. Rather, something else is already there in its place, so that a redactor needs not only to add what is missing but to adjust the two versions to facilitate their coexistence.

60. Greenberg, "Thematic Unity," p. 154; cf. idem, "Redaction," p. 243. Greenberg cites Albright, *FSAC*, p. 46 (2d ed., p. 80); cf. Dillmann, *Genesis* (Eng. trans.), p. 249; Bright, *History*, pp. 71–72.

The redactor's aim of full utilization of his source material was not fully compatible with the aim of reconciling inconsistencies. In the examples surveyed so far in this chapter, different redactors have resolved this problem in different ways. The editor of the Codex Vaticanus text of the Decalogue dropped "Therefore the Lord your God blessed the Sabbath day . . ." and avoided an explicit clash with another motive clause. The editor of the Septuagint Esther dropped the names of the eunuchs in Est. 2:21–23 and avoided conflict with A:12–16. To these editors, clearly, consistency was more important than full utilization of source material. To the redactor whose work underlies the Samaritan Pentateuch, the aim of full utilization overrode the demands of consistency. The result, as we have seen, is a text that displays, albeit in relatively minor forms, just such internal discrepancies as are at the core of Pentateuchal source criticism. That Pentateuchal source criticism would have arisen, let alone triumphed, had all internal discrepancies been as minor as these seems unlikely. However, the material used by the redactors who produced the Pentateuch seems to have been much more discrepant, and the result was a text with greater inconsistencies and therefore more amenable to critical unraveling.[61]

The Samaritan Pentateuch: The Tenth Commandment

The conflate accounts of the Jethro and theophany episodes are, as mentioned, already present in the proto-Samaritan Exodus manuscripts from Qumran. There is nothing sectarian about these accounts or the redactional techniques by which they were composed.[62] Only the Samaritan tenth commandment (Exod. 20:17a–h) and certain related tendentious features are exclusively Samaritan characteristics. That commandment has been shown by Skehan to have been absent from the Qumran manuscript, since there is insufficient space for it.[63] In other words, the Samaritan tenth commandment represents a tendentious supplement beyond the stage of redaction represented in the proto-Samaritan recension from Qumran. On the following pages, in the center column, is a translation of the commandment (preceded by the ninth), flanked by its sources. Roman type is used for material from the Masoretic Exodus 20, italics for material from the Masoretic Deuteronomy 11, boldface for material from the Masoretic Deuteronomy 27, and underlining for redactional material.

61. See further n. 71, and Chapter 1, p. 51, Chapter 5, p. 172.
62. See above, n. 26.
63. See above, n. 42. For the Hebrew texts of this commandment and its sources, see Appendix C to this chapter.

Masoretic Deuteronomy 27

²And as soon as you cross the Jordan into the land which the Lord your God is giving you, you shall set up large stones and coat them with plaster. ³And you shall inscribe upon them all the words of this teaching when you cross over, so that you may invade the land which the Lord your God is giving you, a land oozing milk and honey, as the Lord, the God of your fathers, promised you. ⁴And, upon crossing the Jordan, you shall set up these stones, about which I charge you this day, on Mount Ebal, and coat them with plaster. ⁵And you shall build an altar there to the Lord your God, an

Samaritan Exodus 20

¹⁷You shall not covet your neighbor's house; you shall not covet your neighbor's wife, his field, his male or his female slave, his ox or his ass, or anything that is your neighbor's. ¹⁷ᵃ*And when the Lord your God brings you into the land of the Canaanites which you are about to invade and occupy,* ¹⁷ᵇYou shall set up large stones and coat them with plaster. ¹⁷ᶜAnd you shall inscribe upon the stones all the words of this teaching.

¹⁷ᵈAnd, upon crossing the Jordan, you shall set up these stones, about which I charge you this day, on Mount Gerizim.
¹⁷ᵉAnd you shall build an altar there to the Lord your God, an

Masoretic Deuteronomy 11

²⁹And when the Lord your God brings you into the land which you are about to invade and occupy, you shall pronounce the blessing at Mount Gerizim and the curse at Mount Ebal.

altar of stones. Do not wield an iron tool over them; 17ᵗYou must build the altar of the Lord your God of unhewn stones. You shall offer on it burnt offerings to the Lord your God, 17ᵍand you shall sacrifice sacrifices of well-being and eat them there, rejoicing before the Lord your God. 17ʰ*That mountain is across the Jordan, beyond the west road which is in the land of the Canaanites who dwell in the Arabah—near Gilgal, by the terebinth of Mora, near Shechem.*

altar of stones. Do not wield an iron tool over them; ⁶You must build the altar of the Lord your God of unhewn stones. You shall offer on it burnt offerings to the Lord your God, ⁷and you shall sacrifice sacrifices of well-being and eat them there, rejoicing before the Lord your God. ⁸And on those stones you shall inscribe every word of this teaching most distinctly.

³⁰Both are across the Jordan, beyond the west road which is in the land of the Canaanites who dwell in the Arabah—near Gilgal, by the terebinths of Moreh.

Unlike the Jethro and Sinai pericopes, the Samaritan tenth commandment is not a conflation of variant accounts of the same thing. It is rather a pastiche or mosaic. It consists of verses and partial verses from Deuteronomy 11 and 27, originally dealing with the same place (Shechem) but with different subjects, brought together here to create something new. Since the author of this pastiche was not trying to preserve and reconcile variants of the same text, he took greater liberty in dropping parts of his sources and using only what suited his purposes. Nonetheless, even this tendentious supplement is composed in almost every detail, save the presumed change from Ebal to Gerizim,[64] of elements already present in the Masoretic Torah and thus admittedly divine. Nor is the interpolation of this commandment at the end of the Decalogue without logic, for this law about an altar of uncut stone is thereby brought into the same context as Exodus' law, which includes an altar of uncut stone (Exod. 20:25). In this way the Samaritan interpolator endowed his religion's central dogma with Sinaitic, Decalogue authority.[65] In order to accommodate this interpolation and his dogma, it was necessary to emend verse 24b: the Masoretic "in every place where I cause/allow my name to be mentioned," which contemplates several places as yet unnamed, becomes "in the place where I have caused/allowed my name to be mentioned [*ʾzkrty*, a hybrid form],[66] there I will come and bless you," referring to the just-named site of Gerizim (and not the as-yet-unnamed Jerusalem).

What is noteworthy about the interpolator's technique is that actual changes in substance are remarkably few. On the whole he accomplished his tendentious purpose with material already present somewhere in his sources. Nonetheless, the interpolation creates a telltale inconsistency in the pericope. It requires the construction of a *stone* altar on Mount Gerizim for the purpose of sacrificing whole and peace offerings. But the reworded altar law of verse 24 (see above) requires construction of an *earthen* altar in the same place for that purpose; permission to build a *stone* altar is merely a concession (v. 25). The interpolator, who was willing to drop half-verses in his own interpolation, could not remove conflicting verses in the original text. But the point of the interpolation was so important for him that he was willing to live with the inconsistency, which he presumably rationalized in some way. For us it is another example of how interpolations can

---

64. There is no need to go into this ancient debate here (cf. Josephus, *Ant.* 13.3, 4, secs. 74–79). The Jewish claim that the text originally read "Mount Ebal" has wide support (e.g., Kahle, "Untersuchungen," p. 7; Kaufmann, *Joshua*, 2d ed., p. 130), but it is not unanimously accepted (see, e.g., Pfeiffer, *Introduction*, pp. 101–2; Eissfeldt, *OTI*, p. 216 n. 9, but contrast p. 695; Tov, *RB*, 78:374, 376; Purvis, *EM* 8:175).

65. Cf. Greenberg, "Decalogue," col. 1438.

66. See Weiss, *Studies*, pp. 201–2.

cause inconsistencies. Furthermore, since the interpolation was the latest element added to the text, its inconsistency within its context further illustrates the point that the grossest disturbances in a composite text are those added in the latest redactional stage, when the traditional materials have lost plasticity.[67]

We are thus able to document three stages in the evolution of the Jethro and theophany pericopes: (1) a first stage, represented by the Masoretic Torah, in which the Exodus and Deuteronomy versions were separate; (2) a second stage, represented by the proto-Samaritan Qumran manuscripts, which combined the two versions; and (3) a third stage, represented by the Samaritan Torah, in which the conflate narrative has been tendentiously interpolated and revised. The second stage in particular answers the query which prompted this study. Obviously there are differences between the proto-Samaritan redactor's interests, the state of his source material and his freedom of operation and what is presumed in the case of the Pentateuch. The proto-Samaritan redactor encountered variant accounts scattered about the Torah in already fixed places, and these included variant speeches which all purported to have been uttered on the same occasions. He could combine a variant from one locus with its counterpart elsewhere in the Torah, but could not then drop it from the former locus to avoid redundancy. As a result, material added to Exodus from Deuteronomy was simultaneously preserved in Deuteronomy. Even though his sources were continuous documents, the proto-Samaritan redactor appears as an interpolator who supplemented one basic text from another rather than giving equal play to both sources or creating a totally new account. The compiler of the Pentateuch is credited with somewhat greater freedom in this regard. It is not in these respects that the redaction of the proto-Samaritan Torah and the composition of the Pentateuch are analogous, but in the very fact of combining and in the techniques and goals of combining.

In the cases of the Samaritan Pentateuch, including the proto-Samaritan manuscripts, and the manuscripts of the Decalogue in Deuteronomy, we have both sources of the conflate passages in their independent forms. In the case of the Septuagint of Esther, we have one source in its original form (Est. 2:21–23 in the MT), and the other only in the form in which it appears in the conflate text, from which we must infer what the original form was.[68] In all these cases we find that the non-Masoretic versions

67. See above, Chapter 1, pp. 44–46. Another contextual inconsistency in the interpolation is the very notion that the promised land will be entered by crossing the Jordan (v. 17d) and the location of Mount Gerizim as across the Jordan (v. 17h). At Mount Sinai, where the Samaritan Pentateuch has this commandment given, the Israelites had no idea that they would be entering the land from the east.

68. The same is true of version 2 of the MT narrative in 1 Samuel 17–18; see below, Chapter 3.

represent a stage in the process of composition beyond the point at which the Masoretic Text was frozen.[69] Elsewhere the reverse is true and the Septuagint reflects an earlier stage in the development of the text, with the Masoretic Text representing a further development.[70] In either case, the examples illustrate the process of composition by conflation. They show that inconsistencies, vocabulary variation, and similar phenomena considered to be source-critical clues do sometimes result from conflation. They demonstrate that the documentary hypothesis presumes a method of composition which was demonstrably employed in ancient Israel and by Jewish editors at a time close to that in which most of the biblical books attained their present form. The examples reviewed here are cases of conflation unfolding before our very eyes.

Conflation in Postbiblical Literature

Hebrew and other author-editors continued to create texts by conflation from late antiquity down to modern times. One of the techniques by which the Qumran *Temple Scroll* was created is the conflation of passages from different contexts in the Torah dealing with the same or related topics (mostly legal), although on the whole the *Temple Scroll* is much more independent of its sources than the Torah is presumed to be.[71] Rabbinic

69. See Tov, *Text-Critical*, pp. 293–94. Another case is the account of the rise of Jeroboam in the LXX, which contains both a version of the MT's account in 1 Kings 11:26–12:24 and a second account not found in the MT, though resembling it in many details (12:24a–z in Rahlfs's edition, 1:661–64; a translation is printed in *The Septuagint Version*, pp. 465–67). The result is a version of 1 Kings in which Jeroboam is introduced twice (11:26–28 and 12:24b); his conflict with Solomon and flight to Egypt are reported twice (11:27, 40, and 12:24b end, 25); two prophecies are addressed to him, and in each a garment is torn into twelve pieces, symbolizing the twelve tribes of Israel (11:29–39 and 12:24o); Solomon's death, Rehoboam's succession, and Jeroboam's return from Egypt are reported twice (11:4–44 and 12:24a, 24d–f); there are two accounts of the abortive negotiations at Shechem and the revolt of the north (12:1–20 and 24p–t) and of Shemaiah's prophecy forbidding the south to oppose the secession (12:22–24 and 24y–z), etc. Opinions differ regarding the origins of these two versions, their relationship to the MT, and their historical value. These questions do not concern us directly. For our purposes, what is important is that two different versions of the story reached the LXX and both were incorporated in it, with no apparent attempt to integrate them. Because of difficulties of interpretation and a complicated textual tradition, however, the work of redaction that went into the LXX here is difficult to reconstruct. See the bibliography given by Tov, *Text-Critical*, pp. 303–4.

70. See below, Chapters 3–4.

71. The similarity of some of the editorial techniques used by the author of the scroll to those presumed to have been used in the redaction of the Pentateuch can be inferred from Yadin's analysis of the scroll's sources (Yadin, *Temple Scroll* 1:38–60 [col. 3 of chart], 60–65) and has been noted by several scholars (Levine, "Temple Scroll," p. 20; Brin, "Bible," p. 224;

literature, too, often presents texts from separate sources fused together in a single passage.[72]

In addition to legal texts, a number of liturgical texts were produced by conflation. The *Passover Haggadah* contains two different introductions to a homiletic commentary on Deut. 26:5–8. The Mishna requires that the

---

Licht, "Torah," cols. 485–86; Kaufman, "Temple Scroll"). The most extensive comparison of the methods of the author of the scroll to those presumed in biblical criticism is that of S. Kaufman, who concludes that the scroll "demonstrat[es] the feasibility of the documentary hypothesis" and its general conception of how the Torah was composed, but that it also shows that for the critic to analyze "verses and paragraphs composed of two, three, or more texts" accurately without knowing their sources in advance would be nearly impossible. In the latter conclusion, Kaufman comes down on the negative side of a question that has been considered several times in this and the preceding chapter, and supports the doubts expressed even by advocates of the documentary hypothesis that one could successfully unravel texts as composite as the more extreme source critics have posited (cf. Y. Kaufmann, *Tôlĕdôt* 1:19, *Religion*, p. 136). But the fact that some of the analogues we have studied in this chapter seem as if they could have been analyzed without the critic knowing their sources in advance, while the *Temple Scroll* does not, suggests that different analogues are applicable to different parts of the Torah. In Chapter 1 we expressed doubt that the sources of the *Gilgamesh Epic* could have been accurately reconstructed from the texts of its Akkadian versions (p. 51). This doubt was based on the fact that the epic was extensively revised from version to version. Extensive rewriting by the author of the *Temple Scroll* is what would make its analysis, too, so difficult if we did not have its sources. Kaufman shows that the scroll is sometimes extremely conflate and that its author has taken great liberties in rephrasing and modifying his sources, and has added much material of his own (see also Tov, "Temple Scroll"). Further, rather than preserve contradictions between the sources, the scroll at least sometimes simply omits contradictory matter (see Yadin, *Temple Scroll*, pp. 79 and 81 with n. 11). In the Samaritan Pentateuch, on the other hand, the redactor preserved the wording of his sources essentially as he found it, modifying only slightly; this is what would have made critical analysis of the Samaritan Pentateuch much easier. (Only the Samaritan tenth commandment—a tendentious, sectarian passage like the *Temple Scroll*—reflects a freer use of the sources, but even that passage does not approach the degree of freedom reflected in the *Temple Scroll*.) To the extent that the *Temple Scroll* is analogous to Pentateuchal narratives (see S. Kaufman, "Temple Scroll," p. 32), I would argue that the analogy applies basically to those pericopes in the Torah which critics have found difficult to analyze thoroughly, and it would support the assumption that the difficulty is sometimes due to extensive rewriting by the redactor (cf. Pfeiffer, *Introduction*, p. 283; others attribute the difficulty to original similarities between the sources [cf. ibid., pp. 13, 19, 117, 126] a view which could also find support in the *Temple Scroll*; cf. the passage discussed by Kaufman, "Temple Scroll," p. 36 n. 22). That the analogy would not apply to pericopes which display considerable inconsistencies of style and content is clear from the fact that the *Temple Scroll* is relatively free of such inconsistencies, and this would support the assumption that inconsistencies in the Torah are due to original differences between the sources and the redactor's refraining from rewriting, as in the case of the Samaritan Pentateuch. The upshot is that different analogues apply to different passages in the Torah and that different passages have to be explained by different critical theories, for which reason we need to consider numerous analogues (cf. the observations of Rofé, below, Chapter 4, pp. 143–44).

72. See Epstein, *Māvôʾ*, 2:797–803, 1214; idem, *Prolegomena*, pp. 234–40; Lieberman, *Hellenism*, p. 99.

commentary be preceded by a narrative which "begins with the degradation and ends with the glory" (*m. Pes.* 10:4). In the view of the sage Samuel (Babylonia, third century C.E.) the account of the degradation is to begin with "We were slaves to Pharaoh in Egypt (Deut. 6:21)," whereas the sage Rav (also third-century Babylonia) held that the account was to begin with "At first our ancestors were idol-worshippers" (*b. Pes.* 116a). The early post-Talmudic authorities ruled that "we practice in accordance with both (views)" and "we recite them both," and since that time the *Passover Haggadah* has included both introductions.[73] The principle "we recite them both"—which could well serve as a redactor's motto—was invoked to resolve several other disagreements over the wording of liturgical texts. The Talmud records several discussions in which different rabbis propose different formulations for blessings to be recited on certain occasions, and the final ruling is "therefore we shall recite both/all (the formulations)"; accordingly, it is the conflate forms which are found in the traditional Jewish prayerbook.[74]

What makes these conflate texts frustrating for the historical-critical scholar (though not necessarily for their intended users) is the fact that the variants are not explicitly identified as such in the texts. When G. F. Moore first adduced the analogy of the *Diatessaron*, he mentioned in passing Ibn Hisham's *Life of Mohammed* as a similarly composite work.[75] Moore's interlocutor, C. M. Mead, sought to turn this example against the analogy by pointing out that Ibn Hisham does precisely what the redactor of the Torah does not do: he names the authorities from whom each tradition or variant has come.[76] In fact, manuscripts of the *Diatessaron*—at least some of the Arabic ones—also identify the sources of each excerpt with sigla standing for the four Gospels.[77] Mead insisted that if the Pentateuch were really conflate, the redactor could have done something similar or, if he did not know the authors of his sources, "he could have indicated that his sources, though anonymous, were various, and he could have kept them separate and distinguishable if he had wished to do so." In fact, however, it

---

73. See Glatzer, *Haggadah*, pp. 22–23, 28–29; Kasher, *Haggadah Shelemah*, pp. 17–30; E. D. Goldschmidt, *Haggadah*, pp. 13–19.

74. See Goldschmidt, *Maḥᵃzôr*, 1:15–16; Heinemann, *Studies*, p. 56, citing, e.g., *b. Ber.* 11b, 12b, 59a; *Meg.* 21b; *Soṭa* 40a. Goldschmidt describes a "general tendency . . . not to choose one version from among those transmitted, but to join two parallel texts to each other and to recite one after the other"; Heinemann speaks similarly. Goldschmidt notes that in addition to the conflation of variants into a single text, parallel versions were sometimes kept separate and used on different occasions; see also Ehrman, *Talmud*, p. 238.

75. Moore, "Tatian's Diatessaron," pp. 205, 212 (below, pp. 247, 252–53).

76. Mead, "Tatian's Diatessaron," p. 51; cf. Moore, "Tatian's Diatessaron," p. 212; Widengren, "Oral Tradition," pp. 236–41.

77. Moore, "Tatian's Diatessaron," p. 211.

appears that the redactor probably could not or would not have done so.[78] It was not until the Roman period that Jewish scribes developed or adopted a technique for explicitly designating variants as such.[79] In biblical manuscripts this did not happen until the Middle Ages, when the *kĕtîb-qĕrê* system was adopted for this purpose.[80] The very fact that earlier biblical manuscripts could only record alternate readings side by side, sometimes sacrificing intelligibility in so doing,[81] indicates the absence of a system in the period of the redactor.[82] The failure of the redactor to indicate that he was drawing on different sources is therefore a reflection of the state of ancient Hebrew scribal practice. It is not an essential difference between the redactor of the Torah and later editors of conflate texts who name their sources and indicate their variety.[83]

78. See ibid., pp. 211–12, for reasons (including the normal anonymity of Israelite historiography; cf. below, n. 83) why the redactor had no need to do so; Mead's objections ("Tatian's Diatessaron," pp. 51–52) are not persuasive.

79. In Qumran biblical commentaries, second and third interpretations are introduced with *wĕ^cal*, "and (its interpretation is also) about" and *wĕkēn*, "and likewise (1QpHab I, 3, 5). In rabbinic literature, variant traditions are introduced by such phrases as *ʾîkâ dĕʾāmrê*, "there are those who say" (*b. Ḥul.* 3b), while alternative interpretations are introduced by *dābār ʾaḥēr* (*Lev. R.* 1:2, pp. 6, 9), or by the names of their proponents (*Gen. R.* 3:1, pp. 18–19), or both. Medieval manuscripts of the targums introduce variant readings with abbreviations for *lîšānāʾ ʾaḥ^arînâ*, "another wording," *nûshāʾ ʾaḥ^arînâ*, "another reading," and the like (see Weiss, *Aramaic Targum*, p. 288), while some manuscripts of the Mishna place variant readings between colons (Epstein, *Māvôʾ*, p. 1212; on the Talmud, see idem, *Prolegomena*, pp. 137–44). Akkadian scribes had developed methods for indicating variants already in the second millennium B.C.E.: they could either be introduced with *šanîš*, "secondly, alternatively," and the like (see *AHw*, p. 1164, s.v. *šanîš* II; Lambert, "Birdcall," p. 110; idem, "Theology," pp. 55–56) or marked off by a siglum which scholars call a "Glossenkeil" (Krecher, "Glossen").

80. Gordis, *Biblical Text*, pp. xxiii–xxiv, 41–43.

81. See above, n. 5, on conflate readings.

82. Unsatisfactory as this situation was, it should occasion no surprise, since even in late antiquity the technology of writing still lacked many aids for readers that we take for granted, such as punctuation, sentence dividers, parentheses, special layout for poetry, etc. A similar situation obtained in classical literature; see Reynolds and Wilson, *Scribes*, pp. 4–15. Somewhat reminiscent of the introduction of undesignated variants in a way that interrupts the flow of the text is the introduction of parenthetic and background material with similar disregard for its intrusive effect; see Paul, *Studies*, p. 110 n. 1 (where the second reference to Weiss, *Sources and Traditions*, should read p. 524 n. 1), and Sarna, "Anticipatory."

83. Biblical writers and editors did cite the sources of some lyric poems (Josh. 10:13; 2 Sam. 1:18) and the authors of some psalms and proverbs (2 Sam. 23:1; Ps. 90:1; Prov. 1:1; 25:1; 30:1; 31:1; etc.), but for whatever reason, not the sources of narrative texts. (The various royal chronicles and prophetic writings cited in Kings and Chronicles may have served as sources of information for those books, but the text does not identify them as such, but as places where further information is found. The "Book of Adam's Line" [Gen. 5:1] is cited as a title of what follows, not an external source, although that's what it may be). The incorporation of one text in another with minimal change and without attribution is typical. Note the chapters shared by Kings and Isaiah, Kings and Jeremiah, Ezra and Nehemiah (see Bendavid, *Parallels*, pp. 144–51, 158–67), and the wholesale incorporation of parts of Samuel and Kings in Chronicles (see ibid., passim).

A Modern Example: *Sēfer hā-ʾAggādâ*

The Jewish liturgical texts and Arabic historical texts such as *The Life of Mohammed*[84] show the continued use of conflation in the Middle Ages. The practice has in fact been followed in modern times as well.[85] In the years 1908–11, H. N. Bialik and Y. H. Rawnitzki published their classic anthology of rabbinic aggadic lore, *Sēfer hā-ʾAggādâ*. In presenting tales about biblical and postbiblical characters, the editors often "joined different excerpts from different sources (and sometimes from parallels of the same aggadah) into a single unit."[86] Where it met their criteria the editors would give preference to the version of an aggadah found in the Babylonian Talmud, replacing or supplementing it with extracts from other sources as they saw fit. At times they interrupted one source in midsentence with an extract from elsewhere, and sometimes they virtually created a new aggadah without adding a single passage or word that was not found in one or another of their sources. In analyzing the work of Bialik and Rawnitzki, J. Heinemann concluded:

> The editors were really confident that they had not presented to their readers anything but what they had found in their sources. . . . [They] were of the opinion that they had not created an aggadah of their own, but that they had succeeded in "restoring the crown to its former glory" and in rediscovering an original and authentic aggadah which had been cut up, its fragments preserved in different sources.[87]

Like the examples we have been studying, the methods of Bialik and Rawnitzki can be inferred from a comparison of their work with their sources. But the critic of *Sēfer hā-ʾAggādâ* has an additional source of information at his disposal: Bialik and Rawnitzki's own introduction to their work and other essays of theirs. According to an essay quoted by Heinemann, Bialik believed that the aggadah once really included "large units, extensive in scope, of epic tales" which are now lost.[88] In their introduction, Bialik and Rawnitzki indicate that one of the factors which made their anthology necessary is the fact that "nowadays . . . not everybody is able to join scraps and patches into a complete cloak, or fragments of

---

84. For others see Widengren, "Oral Tradition," pp. 231–43.
85. For modern non-Hebrew writers, see Introduction, p. 18.
86. Heinemann, "On Bialik's Method," p. 89; see also Halevy, "Composition."
87. Heinemann, "On Bialik's Method," p. 91; cf. Greenberg's description of the Pentateuchal redactor, above, p. 54.
88. Heinemann, "On Bialik's Method," p. 84.

broken stones into an edifice."[89] The main task the editors assigned themselves was to gather the material in "an arrangement which is construc-
tive . . . [i.e.,] whatever involves the joining of links into chapters, and
chapters into a single body with a complete form, whatever includes inner
harmony and unity among the parts, whatever makes it possible to understand the whole from its parts"[90] and presents everything in its proper
place.[91]

Aggadah is sometimes impoverished in one place and rich in another; likewise,
many aggadot are related in a number of places in different versions, some incomplete, some excessive, and the like. In such cases the editors tried to choose the
most complete and lovely of the versions, and also, where necessary and where it
would provide a remedy, to combine a number of versions with each other and
blend them together, or to join scattered fragments of a single aggadah into something complete. The editors believe that in a popular book this does no violence to
the essence of the aggadah. On the contrary, if this is done properly and with the
appropriate caution, sometimes this "restores the crown to its former glory" since,
as is known, the aggadot have been considerably confused and mixed up by scribes
and copyists. . . .[92]

Convinced that the original style and language of the aggadot was an
expression of the spirit of the Jewish people, the editors strove to preserve
these wherever possible, so that the reader would have direct contact with
the material, not an adaptation of it. This aim did not forbid the editors
from correcting readings on the basis of the sources and "restrained conjecture" when necessary, or from rephrasing indelicate expressions in view of
the book's popular audience, but on the whole they were convinced that
they had not added "a pennysworth of cosmetics of their own" or changed
anything of the original form of the aggadah.[93]

There is much in the form of aggadic literature and the approach of
Bialik and Rawnitzki which differs from what is observable in the analogues

---

89. Bialik and Rawnitzki, *Sēfer*, p. ii (in the 1960 edition the front matter is unpaginated; I
have numbered the pages of the introduction starting with i). The aim of piecing the legends
together to aid the many who cannot rummage through the sources and reconstruct the
sequence of the narratives on their own bespeaks the popular character of *Sēfer hā-ʾAggādâ*.
The *Diatessaron*, the Samaritan Pentateuch, and the Hebrew *Vorlage* of the LXX have also
been described as popular for similar reasons; see Stenning, "Diatessaron," p. 456a; Gaster,
Samaritans, pp. 124–29.
90. Bialik and Rawnitzki, *Sēfer*, p. v.
91. Ibid., p. iv.
92. Ibid., p. iii.
93. Ibid., pp. iii, v, and passim.

we have reviewed in this chapter and from what is presumed about biblical literature and its redactors. Furthermore, as a modern work, *Sēfer hā-ʾAggādâ* cannot be accorded much weight in confirming the methods of ancient redactors. But composition by conflation was not an exclusively ancient procedure, and the writings of Bialik and Rawnitzki are a piquant testimony to redactors' own understanding of their aims and methods. They add color to what critics have inferred from the Bible and to what we have inferred from its ancient analogues. The latter, to repeat what we have said above, constitute cases of composition by conflation unfolding before our very eyes, and they confirm that the method was demonstrably employed at a time close to that in which most of the biblical books were still being formed. They show that the kinds of inconsistencies and vocabulary variations observable in the Torah do sometimes result from the conflation of sources.

Appendix A.
Samaritan Exodus 18:21–27 and Sources

Different typefaces are used for material from the Masoretic Exodus and from the Masoretic Deuteronomy; underlining indicates redactional material. The Masoretic Text is from BHS; the Samaritan text is from the edition of A. and R. Sadaqa, with verses numbered as explained above, p. 63.

Masoretic Deuteronomy 1

Samaritan Deuteronomy 1

Samaritan Exodus 18

Masoretic Exodus 18

נאך הרמנו.

בזאת ההוא את כל הרהובים
אלי ואנכיהן. [18]ואנכיהן ההוא
הברו נאך אלהו איכם אכם הרמנו
נאך כי הרהובה לכלהו כלו הברו
ברכו הרהמנו קך הרוני ברברכו
לכן הרהני אכם קקך נאך תקף.[17]
קך נאך תקך נאך תקך תכך.
אכם כל נכום לאסומהו ארכך
[18]ואנכיהן את אסומהו בזאת הרמנו אכם
לאכך אראוהו ואנהלהו לאבכמהם.
נאסהם לאכך כאנהו לאכך הרהמהם.
ואנך נכום לראומהו אלכמהם אלך
אבוהכם אראמהו הככמהו ברכהו
לכמהם. [15]ואנהלהו את לראך
הראובהו אוה הרהך נאך בכהך
ואנאמהם בלראמהם. [11]הראהך אכם

ההוא בכבך כל את אך אראהו.
כאסומהו הם. [27]לכעכמהו ברמם אכם
קבראהו את כמהו לכך הרהך בכבם
את הברם בככך כל את הרהך בכמהו
נאך ליההם. [29]לאסומהו

— — — אך כל הרהובים

בזאת ההוא את כל הרהובים
אלי ואנכיהן. [24]ואנכיהן ההוא
הברו נאך אלהו איכם אכם הרמנו
נאך כי הרהובה לכלהו כלו הברו
ברכו הרהמנו קך הרוני ברברכו
לכן [24]הרהני אכם קקך נאך תקף.
קך נאך תקך נאך תקך תכך.
אכם כל נכום לאסומהו [24]ארכך
לכך נאך אכך אסומהו לאבכמהם.
נאסהם לאכך כאנהו לאכך הרהמהם.
ואנך נכום לראומהו אלכמהם אלך
אבוהכם אראמהו הככמהו ברכהו
לכמהם. [24]ואנהלהו את לראך
הראובהו אוה הרהך נאך בכהך
ואנאמהם בלראמהם. [24]הראהך אכם — — —

ההוא בכבך כל את אך אראהו.
כאסומהו הם. [27]לכעכמהו ברמם אכם
קבראהו את כמהו לכך הרהך בכבם
את הברם בככך כל את הרהך בכמהו
נאך ליההם. [29]לאסומהו

לאכך אראוהו.
אבכמהם אלך אראמהו הככמהו
לכך נאך אראמהו קך הרהך בכבם
אבכם הרך ברכך יאכאך
[25]לאסומהו בכמם

Appendix B.
Samaritan Exodus 20:18–26 and Sources

Different typefaces are used for material from the Masoretic Exodus, the Masoretic Deuteronomy 5 and from the Masoretic Deuteronomy 18; underlining indicates redactional material.

Masoretic Exodus 20	Samaritan Exodus 20	Masoretic Deuteronomy	Samaritan Deuteronomy
		את הדברים האלה דבר ה' אל כל $^{5:22}$	

[28]וישמע ה׳ את קול דבריכם
בדברכם אלי ויאמר ה׳ אלי שמעתי
את קול דברי העם הזה אשר דברו
אליך היטיבו כל אשר דברו. [29]מי
יתן והיה לבבם זה להם ליראה אתי
ולשמר את כל מצותי כל הימים למען
ייטב להם ולבניהם לעלם.
[18:18]נביא אקים להם מקרב אחיהם כמוך
ונתתי דברי בפיו ודבר אליהם את כל
אשר אצונו. [19]והיה האיש אשר לא
ישמע אל דברי אשר ידבר בשמי אנכי
אדרש מעמו. [20]אך הנביא אשר יזיד
לדבר דבר בשמי את אשר לא צויתיו
לדבר ואשר ידבר בשם אלהים אחרים
ומת הנביא ההוא. [21]וכי תאמר
בלבבך איכה נדע את הדבר אשר לא
דברו ה׳. [22]אשר ידבר הנביא בשם
ה׳ ולא יהיה הדבר ולא יבוא הוא
הדבר אשר לא דברו ה׳ בזדון דברו
הנביא לא תגור ממנו. [5:30]לך אמר
להם שובו לכם לאהליכם. [31]ואתה

נמות. [20]ויאמר משה אל העם אל
תיראו כי לבעבור נסות אתכם בא
האלהים ובעבור תהיה יראתו על
פניכם לבלתי תחטאו. [21]ויעמד העם
מרחק ומשה נגש אל הערפל אשר שם
האלהים.

[22]וידבר ה׳ אל משה לאמר. [22a]שמעתי
את קול דברי העם הזה אשר דברו
אליך היטיבו כל אשר דברו. [22b]מי
יתן והיה לבבם זה להם ליראה אתי
ולשמר את מצותי כל הימים למען
ייטב להם ולבניהם לעולם.
[22c]נביא אקים להם מקרב אחיהם כמוך
ונתתי דברי בפיו ודבר אליהם את כל
אשר אצונו. [22d]והיה האיש אשר לא
ישמע אל דבריו אשר ידבר בשמי אנכי
אדרש מעמו. [22e]אך הנביא אשר יזיד
לדבר דבר בשמי את אשר לא צויתיו
לדבר ואשר ידבר בשם אלהים אחרים
ומת הנביא ההוא. [22f]וכי תאמר
בלבבך איך נודע את הדבר אשר לא
דברו ה׳. [22g]אשר ידבר הנביא בשם
ה׳ לא יהיה הדבר ולא יבוא הוא
הדבר אשר לא דברו ה׳ בזדון דברו
הנביא לא תגור ממנו. [22h]לך אמר
להם שובו לכם לאהליכם. [22i]ואתה

נמות. [20]ויאמר משה אל העם אל
תיראו כי לבעבור נסות אתכם בא
האלהים ובעבור תהיה יראתו על
פניכם לבלתי תחטאו. [21]ויעמד העם
מרחק ומשה נגש אל הערפל אשר שם
האלהים.

[22]ויאמר ה׳ אל משה

אל תראוני שחורה אני[26]
שאני כי, שזפתני השמש בני אמי
נחרו־בי שמוני נטרה את־הכרמים
כרמי שלי לא נטרתי. אמ[25]
הגידה לי שאהבה נפשי איכה תרעה
איכה תרביץ בצהרים שלמה אהיה
כעטיה על עדרי חבריך[24]
אם־לא תדעי לך היפה בנשים
צאי־לך בעקבי הצאן ורעי את־גדיתיך
על משכנות הרעים אמרה[23]
לססתי ברכבי פרעה דמיתיך רעיתי
<u>נאוו לחייך בתרים[22]</u> צוארך בחרוזים

אל תראוני שחורה אני.
שאני כי, שזפתני השמש בני אמי
נחרו־בי שמוני נטרה את־הכרמים
כרמי שלי לא נטרתי

Appendix C.

Samaritan Ninth and Tenth Commandments (Exodus 20:17ff.) and Sources

Different typefaces are used for material from the Masoretic Exodus, the Masoretic Deuteronomy 11, and from the Masoretic Deuteronomy 27; underlining indicates redactional material.

Masoretic Deuteronomy 27

Samaritan Exodus 20

Masoretic Deuteronomy 11

Masoretic Deuteronomy 27

3

The Composition of 1 Samuel 16–18 in the Light of the Septuagint Version

EMANUEL TOV

Editor's Note

Another example of conflation is found in the account of David's battle with Goliath and its aftermath in 1 Samuel 17–18. The text of this account in the Masoretic Text is nearly twice as long as that found in the Septuagint. The version of the events found in the Septuagint constitutes a complete, though more compact, account, while the extra forty-nine verses found only in the Hebrew text amount to another version of the same events. These two versions differed from each other in a number of details, and redundancies and inconsistencies found in the version presented in 1 Samuel 17–18 are actually due to its combining the two shorter versions. A comparison of the conflate version with its sources enables us to see what the redactor did or did not do in order to smooth out inconsistencies.

Unlike the examples of the proto-Samaritan and Samaritan versions of the Torah cited in Chapter 2, where the conflate text was later than, and based on, the (proto-)Masoretic Text, in the present case the Masoretic Text is the conflate one and the Septuagint reflects the earlier stage. This is what was presumed by W. Robertson Smith, who cited the story of David and Goliath in the nineteenth century as an example of conflation which supported the position of Pentateuchal criticism. At the time it was simply taken for granted that the shorter Septuagint text reflected a more original form of the Hebrew text of this episode. Today scholars realize that the

Septuagint sometimes reflects a revision or abridgement of the Hebrew text and that its priority cannot be taken for granted. Hence, before the Septuagint can be used for reconstructing the development of the Masoretic version of an episode, one must be sure that it reflects its Hebrew prototype reliably. Here Emanuel Tov demonstrates that the Greek translator of 1 Samuel 17–18 rendered his prototype relatively literally and that he is therefore unlikely to have abridged it. The short text that he produced must therefore reflect a short Hebrew prototype from which he worked. Only after this has been determined is it possible to treat the Septuagint's short version of the story as a reflection of one of the sources used by the editor of the Masoretic version.

•   •   •   •

The Two Versions of the David and Goliath Story

In 1 Samuel 16–18—the story of the encounter of David and Goliath and its aftermath—the Greek version in the LXX differs greatly from the Hebrew Masoretic Text.[1] In particular, the LXX presents a short version of the story, lacking thirty-nine of the eighty-eight verses of these chapters.[2]

1. In the following pages, the term "LXX" refers to the "Old Greek" (abbreviated OG), or the original Greek translation of the Bible, contained in mss. Vaticanus (B) and Venetus (V), and in minuscules a, n, v, y, b$_2$. This text was subsequently revised toward the Masoretic Text in the Hexapla and other revisions.

The oldest attestation of the short text of the LXX is in Hippolytus's *Sermo* (2d century C.E.) in its omission of 1 Sam. 17:55–58. See the edition of G. Garitte, *Traités.*

The earliest witness of the long Masoretic Text is a small fragment from Qumran, 1Q7, published by Barthélemy, DJD 1, p. 64 (1 Sam. 18:17–18, lacking in the LXX).

The latter two details are culled from Lust, "Story." Lust's article, as well as monographs by D. W. Gooding and D. Barthélemy and the present author were originally written independently of each other on the same topic. The authors subsequently exchanged views on each others' manuscripts but agreed not to revise their own articles in the light of the others'. Therefore, except for this note, the present article does not refer to these contributions.

2. The following verses are lacking in the OG: 17:12–31, 41, 48b, 50, 55–58; 18:1–6a, 10–11, 12b, 17–19, 21b, 29b–30. These amount to 44 percent of the verses found in the MT of these chapters. We should note that whereas the OG version contained in mss. B, etc., omits these verses, mss. A, etc., do provide a Greek translation of them. However, the vocabulary of that translation has been recognized as Hexaplaric; see Peters, *Beiträge,* pp. 37–38; Wellhausen, *Text,* p. 104; Driver, *Notes,* p. 140; and Johnson, *Hexaplarische,* pp. 118–23 (Johnson shows that mss. Acx, etc., also reflect a Hexaplaric text elsewhere in 1 Sam.). The origin of the Hexaplaric pluses in 1 Sam. 17–18 is probably *kaige*-Theodotion; see Johnson, ibid., p. 123. Another detail in codex A also betrays its secondary nature. In the OG, 17:11 is immediately followed by 17:32, which begins *kai eîpen Daueid,* "And David said." 17:12, however, begins in the Hebrew *wĕdāwid (ben),* "And David (was the son of . . .)." But instead of rendering the latter phrase in Greek (*kai Daueid*), codex A begins verse 12 with *kai eîpen*

In other words, the Masoretic Text has 80 percent more verses than does the LXX. The background of the minuses[3] of the LXX has often been treated in scholarship. The most extensive discussions are found in the works of Wellhausen, Peters, Stoebe, and McCarter. These analyses focus on the larger minuses of the LXX, thus neglecting three other aspects of the LXX translation of 1 Samuel 16–18 without which that translation cannot be evaluated well:

1. In addition to the large minuses, the LXX lacks twenty-four shorter elements in these chapters, ranging from one to five words (see Appendix A to this chapter).

2. The LXX reflects several variant readings (see Appendix B).

3. More important, the LXX reflects about seventeen pluses, ranging from single words to complete sentences (see Appendix C).

In view of these elements, the picture would be distorted by limiting discussion to the large minuses. Any explanation of the origin of the text tradition reflected in the LXX must consider *all* aspects of the relation between the Masoretic and LXX versions of these chapters.

Approaches to the Origin of the Short Version

The opinions expressed about the origin of the LXX's short version of 1 Samuel 16–18 can be divided into two groups. Some scholars ascribed the divergencies between the two texts to the Greek translator, who was said to have omitted 44 percent of the text because of exegetical motives, namely, to create a smoother story by omitting conflicting details.[4] This tendency has been called *harmonization*, even though the term normally refers to making two *different* texts agree. These scholars focused on the

---

Daueid and then continues with the remainder of the verse, yielding a passage that makes little sense in the context: *kaì eîpen Daueid hyiòs anthrṓpou ephrathaíou hoûtos ek Bethleem Iouda kaì ónoma autǭ Iessai,* "And said David, son of an Ephrathite man, this one was of Bethlehem Judah and his name was Jesse. . . ." In fact, the phrase at the beginning of verse 12 is simply the beginning of verse 32, from the LXX. It stands to reason that the person responsible for this reading was copying from the LXX and intending to insert a translation of verses 12–32 from another manuscript, but when he finished copying verse 11, he inadvertently continued into the next verse (v. 32) for three more words before remembering to insert the translation of verses 12ff.; having just copied the name of David (from v. 32), he then continued from the word following "David" in the translation of verse 12.

3. The terms *plus* and *minus* are used here in their text-critical sense to refer to items present or absent in one text as compared to another.

4. Thus Kuenen, *Historisch-kritische Einleitung*, 1/2: 61; Budde, *Richter und Samuel*, p. 212; Schmid, *Septuagintageschichtliche Studien* (cited from Johnson, *Hexaplarische*, p. 118); Barthélemy, "Qualité," pp. 1–44, esp. 17–20.

large minuses, usually disregarding the pluses in the translation, and if they did discuss the pluses (as did Barthélemy, for example), they also regarded them as exegetical. According to the other, diametrically opposed view, the LXX was based on a short *Hebrew* text which lacked what the Greek text lacks.[5] This shorter Hebrew text was usually considered to reflect an earlier stage of the literary development of the story, one which preceded the Masoretic Text (though one scholar, Kuenen, regarded it as an abridgement [in Hebrew] of the forerunner of the Masoretic Text).

On the basis of what type of arguments have scholars decided in favor of one of the two views?[6] With all due respect to the scholarship of the past, it seems that no solid arguments for any one view have so far been presented. Those scholars who suggested that the translator abridged the Masoretic Text were probably influenced by the lack of supporting evidence for the alternative explanation. Writing before the discovery of the Qumran scrolls, they were not aware of Hebrew texts which departed as much from the Masoretic Text as the reconstructed short *Vorlage* of the LXX would. They therefore assumed that the shorter text was produced by the Greek translator. This view was probably based more on this negative evidence and scholars' intuition than on positive evidence that the translator omitted large sections of the story because they contained conflicting details. The alternative view, likewise, was based mainly on intuition and a negative judgment concerning the abridgement theory; some of its exponents stressed that the translator was not likely to omit such large sections and that he therefore probably found a short Hebrew text in front of him.

Methodology

Since to date scholars have accepted a certain view mainly by ruling out the alternative one, we should ask whether there exists any positive evidence in favor of either view. As noted above, previous attempts to explain the origin of the short version have focused on its large minuses, neglecting

---

5. See Thenius, *Bücher Samuels*, p. 67 (where earlier adherents of this view are cited); Peters, *Beiträge*, pp. 30–62; Wellhausen, *Text*, p. 105 (however, in his later work Wellhausen's attitude toward the short text is not clear; see *Composition*, [3d ed.], p. 247); H. P. Smith, *Samuel*, p. 150; Steuernagel, *Lehrbuch*, p. 317; Habel, *Literary Criticism*, pp. 10–11; Woods, *Light*; Stoebe, *VT* 4: 397–413; Johnson, *Hexaplarische*; McCarter, *I Samuel*. For a suggested reconstruction of the original short Hebrew text of the story, more or less identical with the Hebrew text underlying the LXX, see Peters, *Beiträge*.

6. We cannot think of any compromise between these two views, for it is not realistic to assume that some of the large minuses were due to the translator, while others were already in his Hebrew parent text.

its shorter minuses, its pluses in comparison with the Masoretic Text, and its other variant readings. The point of departure for a new analysis must be the recognition that the translation of 1 Samuel 17–18 has to be studied as a whole and that any solution suggested should take all the characteristics of the translation into account, not only minuses (the content of which provides no clues for a solution) but also pluses and variant readings. In short, only a study of *translation technique* in the broad sense of the term can bring us closer to a solution.

The idea behind this approach is the conviction that each translation is internally consistent at least with regard to its general approach to the source text, to which it is either faithful or not. If the translator did omit 44 percent of the text, he must have approached that text freely, and this *free approach* should also be visible in other details. If, on the other hand, there are indications that the translation is *literal*, that the translator approached the source text with care and introduced but little exegesis of his own, it is not likely that he would have omitted large sections because of exegetical (e.g., harmonistic) motives; in that case, the short text of the LXX would more likely reflect a short Hebrew text. These suppositions reflect a logical inference from the act of translating, but they can also be supported by some evidence from the translations themselves. Known Greek translators who took care to represent the Hebrew source text exactly showed their careful approach in all details, that is, they introduced as little exegesis as possible in the translation equivalents and produced a literal translation which was quantitatively equal to the Hebrew source text (that is, without additions and omissions). This applies to the so-called revisers of the LXX (except for "Lucian") and, within the canon of the LXX, to the sections ascribed to *kaige*-Theodotion (2 Kings and the second part of 2 Samuel), to Ecclesiastes, Psalms, and, to a lesser degree, many other units as well. By the same token, free translators show their approach to the text in all details of their translation, that is, in their word choices and in free additions and omissions as well as in exegetical alterations of various types. This applies to the translations of Isaiah and Daniel and, to a greater extent, Job, where large sections of the Masoretic Text have been omitted from the translation.

It is against the background of these characteristics of the translation techniques of the other books of the LXX that the translation of 1 Samuel 17–18 must be examined. This is no easy task, since the two chapters are part of a much larger unit[7] whose translation technique can be examined

---

7. The larger unit comprises at least 1 Samuel 1–31, but probably also 2 Sam. 1:1–11:1: thus modern scholarship in the wake of Barthélemy, *Devanciers*, pp. 36ff. According to Shenkel, *Chronology*, pp. 117–20, this unit ends at 2 Sam. 10:1; according to Kelly, *Septuagint Translators*, it ends in 2 Samuel 5.

much more easily than that of two chapters alone. However, since these chapters contain unusually large minuses and some scholars might therefore claim that they reflect a separate translation unit, they must be singled out for this analysis.

The Texts

A full reconstruction of the Hebrew text underlying the LXX would unnecessarily complicate the present study (for an attempt, see Peters, cited in n. 5). For our purposes it will be sufficient to present a translation of the Masoretic Text of 1 Sam. 16:17–18:30, indicating where the LXX differs from it.[8] The narrative shared by LXX and the Masoretic Text is printed in Roman type. Points at which the LXX shows minor deviations from the Masoretic Text, where the LXX probably reflects different readings (see Appendix B), are indicated by underlining. Elements which are absent in the LXX (small minuses) are indicated by parentheses (see Appendix A). Small pluses of the LXX are not indicated here (see Appendix C), nor are exegetical renderings reflecting the translator's exegesis. Portions of the narrative found only in the Masoretic Text are printed in italics.

16:17So Saul said to his courtiers, "Find me someone who can play well and bring him to me." 18One of the attendants spoke up, "I have observed a son of Jesse the Bethlehemite who is skilled in music; he is a stalwart fellow and a warrior, sensible in speech, and handsome in appearance, and the Lord is with him." 19Whereupon Saul sent messengers to Jesse to say, "Send me your son David, who is with the flock." 20Jesse took an ass laden with bread, a skin of wine, and a kid, and sent them to Saul by his son David. 21So David came to Saul and entered his service; Saul took a strong liking to him and made him one of his arms-bearers. 22Saul sent word to Jesse, "Let David remain in my service, for I am pleased with him." 23Whenever the [evil] spirit of God came upon Saul, David would take the lyre and play it; Saul would find relief and feel better, and the evil spirit would leave him.

17:1The Philistines assembled their forces for battle; they massed at Socoh of Judah, and encamped at Ephes-dammim, between Socoh and Azekah. 2Saul and the men of Israel massed and encamped in the valley of Elah. They drew up their

---

8. The translation follows NJV, with minor adjustments; words in square brackets are explanatory additions of the NJV translators. For the text of the LXX we follow codex B, the best representative of the Old Greek translation (see n. 1). An English translation of the LXX is found in the anonymous *The Septuagint Version*, pp. 378–81; the Hexaplaric translation of the missing verses, found in mss. A, etc., is found in the appendix to the same volume, second and third pages following p. 1130.

line of battle against the Philistines, [3]with the Philistines stationed on one hill and Israel stationed on the opposite hill; the ravine was between them. [4]A champion of the Philistine forces stepped forward; his name was Goliath of Gath, and he was six cubits and a span tall. [5]He had a (bronze) helmet on his head, and wore a breastplate of scale armor, a bronze breastplate weighing five thousand shekels. [6]He had bronze greaves on his legs and a bronze javelin slung from his shoulders. [7]The shaft of his spear was like a weaver's bar, and the iron head of his spear weighed six hundred shekels; and the shield-bearer marched in front of him.

[8]He stopped and called out to the ranks of Israel and he said to them, "Why should you come out to engage in battle? I am the Philistine champion, and you are Saul's servants. Choose one of your men and let him come down against me. [9]If he bests me in combat and kills me, we will become your slaves; but if I best (him) and kill him, you shall be our slaves and serve us." [10]And the Philistine ended, "I herewith defy the ranks of Israel. Get me a man and let's fight it out!" [11]When Saul and all Israel heard these words of the Philistine, they were dismayed and terror stricken.

[12]*David was the son of a certain Ephrathite of Bethlehem in Judah whose name was Jesse. He had eight sons, and in the days of Saul the man was already old, advanced in years.* [13]*The three oldest sons of Jesse had left and gone with Saul to the war. The names of his three sons who had gone to the war were Eliab the firstborn, the next Abinadab, and the third Shammah;* [14]*and David was the youngest. The three oldest had followed Saul,* [15]*and David would go back and forth from attending on Saul to shepherd his father's flock at Bethlehem.*

[16]*The Philistine stepped forward morning and evening and took his stand for forty days.*

[17]*Jesse said to his son David, "Take an ephah of this parched corn and these ten loaves of bread for your brothers in camp.* [18]*Take these ten cheeses to the captain of their thousand. Find out how your brothers are and bring some token from them."* [19]*Saul and the brothers and all the men of Israel were in the valley of Elah, in the war against the Philistines.*

[20]*Early next morning, David left someone in charge of the flock, took [the provisions], and set out, as his father Jesse had instructed him. He reached the barricade as the army was going out to the battle lines shouting the war cry.* [21]*Israel and the Philistines drew up their battle lines opposite each other.* [22]*David left his baggage with the man in charge of the baggage and ran toward the battle line and went to greet his brothers.* [23]*While he was talking to them, the champion, whose name was Goliath, the Philistine of Gath, stepped forward from the Philistine ranks and spoke the same words as before; and David heard him.*

[24]*When the men of Israel saw the man, they fled in terror.* [25]*And the men of Israel were saying, "Do you see that man coming out? He comes out to defy Israel! The man who kills him will be rewarded by the king with great riches; he will also give him his daughter in marriage and grant exemption to his father's house in Israel."* [26]*David asked the men standing near him, "What will be done for the man*

who kills that Philistine and removes the disgrace from Israel? Who is that uncircumcised Philistine that he dares defy the ranks of the living God?" [27] *The troops told him in the same words what would be done for the man who killed him.*

[28] *When Eliab, his oldest brother, heard him speaking to the men, Eliab became angry with David and said, "Why did you come down here, and with whom did you leave those few sheep in the wilderness? I know your impudence and your impertinence: you came down to watch the fighting!"* [29] *But David replied, "What have I done now? I was only asking!"* [30] *And he turned away from him toward someone else; he asked the same question, and the troops gave him the same answer as before.* [31] *The things David said were overheard and were reported to Saul, who had him brought over.*

[32]David said to Saul, "Let no <u>man</u>'s courage fail him. Your servant will go and fight (that) Philistine!" [33]But Saul said to David, "You cannot go to that Philistine and fight him; you are only a boy, and he has been a warrior from his youth!" [34]David replied to Saul, "Your servant has been tending his father's sheep, and if a lion or <u>a bear</u> came and carried off an animal from the flock, [35]I would go after it and fight it and rescue it from its mouth. And if it attacked me, I would seize it <u>by the beard</u> and strike it down and kill it. [36]Your servant has killed both lion and bear; and (that) uncircumcised Philistine shall end up like one of them, for he has defied the ranks of the living God. [37]The Lord," (David went on,) "who saved me from lion and bear will also save me from that Philistine." "Then go," Saul said to David, "<u>and may the Lord be with you!</u>"

[38]Saul clothed David in his own garment; <u>he placed</u> a bronze helmet on his head (and fastened a breastplate on him). [39]David girded his sword over his garment. <u>Then he tried</u> to walk; but he was not used to it. And David said to Saul, "I cannot walk in these, <u>for I am not used to them</u>." So he (David) took them off. [40]He took his stick, picked a few smooth stones from the wadi, put them in the pocket of his shepherd's bag and, sling in hand, he went toward the Philistine.

[41] *The Philistine, meanwhile, was coming closer to David, preceded by his shield-bearer.* [42](And the Philistine looked) and he saw David; he scorned him, for he was but a boy, ruddy and <u>handsome</u>. [43]And the Philistine called out to David, "Am I a dog that you come against me with <u>sticks</u>?" The Philistine cursed David by his gods; [44]and the Philistine said to David, "Come here, and I will give your flesh to the birds of the sky and the beasts of the field."

[45]David replied to the Philistine, "You come against me with sword and spear and javelin; but I come against you in the name of the Lord of Hosts, the God of the ranks of Israel, whom you have defied. [46]This (very) day the Lord <u>will deliver you</u> into my hands. I will kill you and cut off your head; and I will give <u>the carcasses</u> of the Philistine camp to the birds of the sky and the beasts of the earth. All the earth <u>shall know</u> that there is a God in Israel. [47]And this whole assembly shall know that the Lord can give victory without sword or spear. For the battle is the Lord's, and He will deliver you into our hands."

[48]When the Philistine <u>began to</u> come (and advance) toward David, *David quickly ran up to the battle line to face the Philistine.* [49]David put his hand into the

bag; he took out a stone and slung it. It struck the Philistine in the forehead; the stone sank into his forehead, and he fell face down on the ground. ⁵⁰*Thus David bested the Philistine with sling and stone; he struck him down and killed him. David had no sword.* ⁵¹So David ran up and stood over the Philistine, grasped his sword (and pulled it from its sheath); and (with it) he dispatched him and cut off his head.

When the Philistines saw that their warrior was dead, they ran. ⁵²The men of Israel and Judah rose up with a war cry and they pursued the Philistines all the way to Gai and up to the gates of Ekron; the Philistines fell mortally wounded along the road to Shaarim up to Gath and Ekron. ⁵³Then the Israelites returned from chasing the Philistines and looted their camp.

⁵⁴David took the head of the Philistine and brought it to Jerusalem; and he put his weapons in his own tent.

⁵⁵*When Saul saw David going out to assault the Philistine, he asked his army commander Abner, "Whose son is that boy, Abner?" And Abner replied, "By your life, Your Majesty, I do not know."* ⁵⁶*"Then find out whose son that young fellow is," the king ordered.* ⁵⁷*So when David returned after killing the Philistine, Abner took him and brought him to Saul, with the head of the Philistine still in his hand.* ⁵⁸*Saul said to him, "Whose son are you, my boy?" And David answered, "The son of your servant Jesse the Bethlehemite."*

¹⁸:¹When he finished speaking with Saul, Jonathan's soul became bound up with the soul of David; Jonathan loved David as himself. ²Saul took him [into his service] that day and would not let him return to his father's house.—³Jonathan and David made a pact, because he loved him as himself. ⁴Jonathan took off the cloak and tunic he was wearing and gave them to David, together with his sword, bow, and belt. ⁵David went out, and he was successful in every mission on which Saul sent him, and Saul put him in command of all the soldiers; this pleased all the troops and Saul's courtiers as well. ⁶When they came home [and] David returned from killing the Philistine, the women of all the towns of Israel came out (singing and dancing to greet King Saul) with timbrels, shouting, and sistrums. ⁷The women sang as they danced, and they chanted: Saul has slain his thousands; David, his tens of thousands! ⁸(Saul was much distressed) and greatly vexed about the matter. For he said, "To David they have given tens of thousands, and to me they have given thousands. (All that he lacks is the kingship!)" ⁹From that day on Saul kept a jealous eye on David. ¹⁰*The next day an evil spirit of God gripped Saul and he began to rave in the house, while David was playing [the lyre], as he did daily. Saul had a spear in his hand,* ¹¹*and Saul threw the spear, thinking to pin David to the wall. But David eluded him twice.* ¹²Saul was afraid of David, *for the Lord was with him and had turned away from Saul.* ¹³So Saul removed him from his presence and appointed him chief of a thousand, to march at the head of the troops. ¹⁴David was successful in all his undertakings, for the Lord was with him; ¹⁵and when Saul saw that he was successful, he dreaded him. ¹⁶All Israel and Judah loved David, for he marched at their head.

¹⁷*Saul said to David, "Here is my older daughter Merab, I will give her to you*

in marriage; in return, you be my warrior and fight the battles of the Lord." Saul *thought: "Let not my hand strike him; let the hand of the Philistines strike him."* [18]*David replied to Saul, "Who am I and what is my life—my father's family in Israel—that I should become Your Majesty's son-in-law?"* [19]*But at the time that Merab, daughter of Saul, should have been given to David, she was given in marriage to Adriel the Meholathite.* [20]Now Michal, daughter of Saul, had fallen in love with David; and when this was reported to Saul, it (the matter) was pleasing for him. [21]Saul thought: "I will give her to him, and she can serve as a snare for him, so that the Philistines may kill <u>him</u>." *So Saul said to David, "You can become my son-in-law even now through the second one."* [22]And Saul instructed his courtiers to say to David privately, "The king is fond of you and all his courtiers like you. So <u>why not</u> become the king's son-in-law?" [23]When the king's courtiers repeated these words to David, David replied, "Do you think that becoming the son-in-law of a king is a small matter, when I am but a poor man of no consequence?" [24]Saul's courtiers reported to him (saying), "This is what David answered." [25]And Saul said, "Say this to David: 'The king desires no other bride price <u>than</u> the foreskins of a hundred Philistines, as vengeance on the king's enemies.'"—Saul intended to bring about <u>David's</u> death at the hands of the Philistines.—[26]When his courtiers told this to David, David was pleased with the idea of becoming the king's son-in-law. (Before the time had expired,) [27]David went out with his men and killed <u>two</u> hundred Philistines, (David) brought their foreskins (and they were counted out) for the king, that he might become the king's son-in-law. He (Saul) then gave him his daughter Michal in marriage. [28]When Saul saw (and knew) the Lord was with David and that <u>Michal daughter of Saul</u> loved him, [29]and he (Saul) grew still more afraid of David; *and Saul was David's enemy ever after.*

[30]*The Philistine chiefs marched out to battle; and every time they marched out, David was more successful than all the other officers of Saul. His reputation soared.*

The LXX Translator's Technique: Relatively Literal

In the following discussion, five aspects of the LXX translation are analyzed: (1) linguistic versus exegetical renderings of individual elements in the text; (2) adherence to the word order of the Hebrew text; (3) quantitative representation; (4) consistency in translation equivalents; and (5) Hebraisms in the translation. These five aspects of translation technique are suitable for testing the relative degree of literalism or freedom with which the translator approached the Hebrew text. The analysis shows that the translator of 1 Samuel 17–18 remained relatively faithful to the Hebrew text, and it is therefore unlikely that he would have omitted 44 percent of that text. In other words, the Greek translation was based on a short Hebrew text containing only that part of the story presently found in the LXX (as well as in the corresponding verses in the Masoretic Text); the remaining material, now found *only* in the Masoretic Text, had not been added to that short text.

LINGUISTIC VERSUS EXEGETICAL RENDERINGS[9]

Technically a distinction between "linguistic" and "exegetical" renderings is a bit misleading, in that this terminology implies that linguistic renderings are not exegetical. Actually, even a linguistic rendering reflects exegesis, though of a strictly technical type. By linguistic exegesis we mean the grammatical identification of all words (especially forms of verbs and nouns) in the source text as well as their semantic interpretation. Often, however, translations go beyond linguistic exegesis, deviating from the literal sense of a given word, phrase, or sentence. Such deviations may add elements to the source text or omit elements from the text, as well as introduce changes into the text. Most exegetical elements, however, are reflected in the lexical choices of the translators. The choice between different equivalents of the same word is influenced by the immediate context or by the conceptual world of the translators. We thus distinguish between renderings of the latter type, calling them *exegetical*, and of the former type, calling them *linguistic*.

It is exegetical renderings which point to a translator's approaching the text with freedom. Linguistic renderings do not, for they are inherent in the very nature of translation and can hardly be avoided. It is important to note, however, that linguistic renderings are not limited to what we would consider linguistically correct renderings. Many translators rendered all occurrences of a given Hebrew word, element (e.g., preposition), root, or construction as far as possible by the same Greek equivalent, often disregarding the context in which the item in question appears. Such consistent representations became stereotyped. Once the initial lexical choice of a certain equivalent had been made, either by the translator or by his predecessors in the tradition of translation, it was used wherever possible. For example, when the translator of 1 Samuel 17–18 decided to render Hebrew *kîdôn* with Greek *aspís* ("shield"; modern translations: "javelin"),[10] he was reflecting a certain lexical-exegetical tradition with regard to the meaning of this word, but no specific contextual exegesis (which would have been denoted by an asterisk in our appendices). Likewise, the rendering of (*ʾîš*) *habbēnayim* (17:4) as *dynatós* ("mighty") is probably an etymological translation deriving the Hebrew word from *bānâ*, "build," and taking the phrase to mean "a well-built person";[11] for the translation equivalent,

---

9. For the theoretical background of this and the following paragraphs see Tov, *Text-Critical*, pp. 50ff.

10. The different translation equivalents of *kîdôn* in the LXX reflect the translators' uncertainty with regard to its meaning. For a discussion, see Zipor, *Ancient Versions*, pp. 196–206.

11. As in *b. Soṭa*, p. 42b: "What is the meaning of *bēnayim*? Said Rab: that he was built (*mĕbûneh*) without blemish. Samuel said: He was the middle one (*bênônî*) of his brothers. A student of the school of Rabbi Shela said: That he was built like a building (*binyān*)."

compare the rendering of *mĕbînîm* (*kĕtîb*: *mĕbûnîm*) in 2 Chron. 35:3 as *toîs dynatoîs* "who were capable" (modern translations: "who taught"). Even in cases such as this, where the modern scholar might disagree with the ancient translator's rendering, from the point of view of the ancient translator's methodology such renderings may still constitute linguistic exegesis. Admittedly, however, it is sometimes difficult to determine where linguistic exegesis ends and contextual exegesis starts.

A second problem in this regard is created by the nature of the Greek language, which requires certain deviations from Hebrew syntax and thus makes a stereotyped rendering of the Hebrew seemingly impossible. However, as much as possible literal translators did represent each element of the Hebrew with its stereotyped Greek equivalent, even when such a rendering would create a Hebraism[12] in the Greek language. Since renderings of this type do exist within the LXX, we may legitimately search for nonstereotyped renderings, even when a stereotyped rendering would have created a Hebraism, and consider them cases of free translation. For example, the translation of 1 Sam. 17:9 has been adapted to the rules of the Greek language: the Hebrew *ʾim yûkal lĕhillāḥēm ʾittî wĕhikkānî* says literally, "if he shall be able to fight with me and he shall smite me," whereas the Greek *kaì eàn dynēthę̂ pròs emè polemḗsai kài eàn patáxę̄ me* says literally, "and if he shall be able against me to fight and *if* he shall smite me." In the continuation of that verse, the Hebrew *ʾim . . . wihĕyîtem* says literally, "but if . . . *and* (i.e., then) you shall be . . . ," whereas the Greek *eàn dè . . . ésesthe* says literally, "but if . . . *you shall be. . . .*" In the first case the translator avoided a stereotyped rendering of *wĕ-* as *kaì* by adding *eàn*, "if"; in the second case he did so by not translating *wĕ-* (*wi-*) at all.

The following list contains examples of contextual-exegetical renderings (in some cases the possibility of a variant reading [indicated by !] is not excluded):

17:2	ואיש ישראל	καὶ οἱ ἄνδρες Ισραηλ
	and the men (lit. *man*) of Israel	and the *men* (pl.) of Israel
17:2	בעמק האלה ויערכו	! ἐν τῇ κοιλάδι. αὐτοὶ παρατάσσονται
	in the valley of Elah	in the valley.
	and they drew up battle lines	They drew up battle lines
17:2	(ויערכו) מלחמה	παρατάσσονται εἰς πολεμόν
	(they drew up) battle lines	they drew up a line for battle
17:3	עמדים	ἵσταται
	were stationed (pl.)	*was* stationed (sg.)

---

12. By "Hebraisms" we refer to Greek words, phrases, or constructions which transfer certain characteristic Hebrew elements into Greek in disregard of Greek idiom (Tov, *Text-Critical*, p. 56).

17:5 (ומשקל) השריון	καὶ ὁ σταθμὸς τοῦ θώρακος αὐτοῦ
(and the weight of) *the* breastplate	and the weight of *his* breastplate
17:7 ולהבת חניתו	καὶ ἡ λογχὴ αὐτοῦ
and the *head of his spear*	and his *spear-head* (one word)
17:7 הצנה	τὰ ὅπλα αὐτοῦ
the shield	*his* shield
17:8 לערך מלחמה	παρατάξασθαι πολέμῳ
to *draw up* battle lines	to arrange *yourself for* battle
17:8 הפלשתי	ἀλλόφυλος
the Philistine	(an [no article]) alien
17:9 (אם יוכל) להלחם אתי	καὶ ἐὰν δυνηθῇ πρὸς ἐμὲ πολεμῆσαι
(if he is able) *to fight with me*	if he is able *with me to fight*
17:9 והכני	καὶ ἐὰν πατάξῃ με
and smites me	and *if* he smites me
17:9 ואם אני אוכל לו	! ἐὰν δὲ ἐγὼ δυνηθῶ
lit., but if I am able *to him*	but if I am able
17:9 והייתם	ἔσεσθε
and you will be	you will be
17:34 ובא	καὶ ὅταν ἤρχετο
and there came	and *when* there came
17:35 ויקם	καὶ εἰ ἐπανίστατο
and he rose up	and *if* he rose up
17:35 והכתיו והמיתיו	καὶ ἐπάταξα καὶ ἐθανάτωσα αὐτόν
and I struck *him* and killed him	and I struck and killed him
17:42 ואדמני	καὶ αὐτὸς πυρράκης
and ruddy	! and *he (was)* ruddy
17:46 יש אלהים לישראל	! ἔστιν θεὸς ἐν Ισραηλ
there is a God *to* Israel	! there is a God *in* Israel
17:47 וידעו (כל הקהל הזה)	! καὶ γνώσεται
and *they* shall know	! and *he* shall know
18:14 לכל דרכיו	! ἐν πάσαις ταῖς ὁδοῖς αὐτοῦ
lit., *to* all his ways	! *in* all his ways
18:20 ויגדו	! καὶ ἀπηγγέλη
and *they* (pl.) reported	and *it was* reported
18:23 ונקלה	καὶ οὐχὶ ἔνδοξος
and unimportant	and *not* important

In analyzing chapters 17–18 we are interested in forming a judgment on the amount of (contextual) exegetical renderings the translation contains. From the above list it is apparent that it contains only a very limited amount of such exegesis (at most twenty-two examples, from seventeen of the forty-nine verses present in the LXX version), especially if one takes into consideration the possibility that some (about nine) of the deviations listed may reflect variant readings. Unfortunately we must be content with this generalized statement, for ideally the amount of contextual exegesis in a unit should be measured statistically and then compared with that in other translation units, but no absolute figures are available for these units.

WORD ORDER

With the exception of 17:9, *yûkal lĕhillāḥēm ʾittî* ("shall be able to fight with me") vs. *dynēthē̃ pròs emè polemẽsai* ("is able against me to fight"), the translator kept the exact word order of the Masoretic Text. (The differences in word order in 17:38 and 18:7, 22(twice) probably derived from a different Hebrew text.)

QUANTITATIVE REPRESENTATION

Partly as a result of the tendency toward stereotyping, literal translators did their utmost to represent each individual element in the Masoretic Text by one equivalent element in the translation. Free translators, on the other hand, felt free to add clarifying elements or not to represent elements which, in their view, were expressed by other words in the translation. They often compressed two or more elements of the Hebrew text into one, and expanded one element into two or more, in accordance with their literary tastes and the nature of the Greek language. The quantitative relationship between the source text and the translation can be expressed statistically. The more literal translators aimed at a one-to-one representation of words in the Masoretic Text, whereas free translators did not.

The LXX translation of 1 Samuel 17–18 usually follows a system of precise quantitative adherence to the Hebrew. Some exceptions, which partially overlap with the list of exegetical elements in the translation (above, pp. 108–9), are listed here:

17:7	*haṣṣinnâ*, the-shield	*tà hópla autoũ, his* shield
17:9	*wĕhikkānî*, and-strikes-me	*kaì eàn patáxę̄ me*, and *if* he strikes me
17:7	*wĕlahebet ḥᵃnîtô*, and the head of his spear	*kaì hē lógchē autoũ*, and the spear-head of his
17:9	*wihĕyîtem, and* you will be	*ésesthe*, you will be
17:34	*ûbāʾ*, and there came	*kai hótan ḗrcheto*, and *when* there came
17:35	*wayyāqom*, and he rose up	*kaì ei epanístato*, and *if* he rose up
18:23	*wĕniqleh*, and unimportant	*kaì ouchì éndoxos*, and not important

CONSISTENCY IN TRANSLATION EQUIVALENTS

As noted above, many translators rendered all occurrences of a given Hebrew word, element (e.g., preposition), root, or construction as far as possible by the same Greek equivalent, often disregarding the context and the effect of this type of translation on the quality of the translation. There are two aspects to such consistency: (a) *internal* consistency in the choice of translation equivalents within a certain textual unit and (b) the translator's adherence to the *general vocabulary of the LXX*. No firm data for the comparison of 1 Samuel 17–18 with other translation units are available, so we must content ourselves with mere impressions. It seems that in the matter of consistency 1 Samuel 17–18 reflects a type of translation which holds the middle ground between literal and free translations. The following examples illustrate both types of consistency.

INTERNAL CONSISTENCY

Most translation equivalents in 1 Samuel 17–18 are internally consistent, that is, the translator used the same equivalent for words which occur in more than one place. For examples, note the following and those listed in the section below, pp. 112–13.

אסף	συνάγω	collect	17:1,1,2
מחנה	παρεμβολή	camp	17:2,46
חנה	παρεμβάλλω	encamp	17:1,2
ערך	παρατάσσω	draw up battle lines	17:2,8
ק/כובע	περικεφαλαία	helmet	17:5,38
מערכ(ו)ת	παράταξις	ranks	17:8,10,36,45 (also 17:4)
חרף	ὠνειδίζω	defy	17:10,33,45
ירא	φοβέομαι	fear	17:11; 18:9,12
כלי	κάδιον	wallet	17:40,49
ישר	εὐθύνω	be set right	18:20,26

Lack of consistency is visible in the following equivalents:

עבד	δοῦλος	slave	17:9,9,32,34
	παῖς	servant	18:22,22,23,23,24
הציל	ἐκσπάω	rescue	17:35
	ἐξαιρέω		17:36
מקל	βακτηρία	stick	17:40

ῥάβδος   17:43
(the differentiation may be intentional as Goliath calls David's βακτηρι
[staff] a mere ῥάβδος [stick])
הכה   πατάσσω   strike   17:9,35,35,49; 18:6,27
             τύπτω   17:36
             ἀποκτείνω   17:46

ADHERENCE TO THE GENERAL VOCABULARY OF THE LXX

The basis for the vocabulary of the LXX was established by the translators of the Pentateuch. The translators who came after them and worked
on the later books often adhered to this vocabulary, certainly the more
literal ones. This is particularly noticeable in the cases of δεῦρο and εἴσοδος
(see immediately) because they are words that would not usually be chosen
as equivalents for the Hebrew words with which they are here matched.
The examples mentioned in the preceding section as well as the following
ones reflect this approach:

בין	ἀνὰ μέσον	between	passim
עמק	κοιλάς	valley	17:2
שריון	θώραξ	breastplate	17:5,5
צנה	ὅπλα	shield	17:7
איש מלחמה	ἀνὴρ πολεμιστής	man of war	17:33
ערל	ἀπερίτμητος	uncircumcised	17:36
לכה	δεῦρο	(Heb.) Go! (Greek) Come!	17:44
קהל	ἐκκλησία	assembly	17:47
הריע	ἀλαλάζω	cry out	17:52
בואך	εἴσοδος	"all the way to"	17:52
מוקש	σκάνδαλον	snare	18:21
התחתן	ἐπιγαμβρεύω	become related by marriage	18:22,22,23,26,27
צוה	ἐντέλλομαι	command	18:22
ערלה	ἀκροβυστία	foreskin	18:25,27
אהב	ἀγαπάω	love	18:16,20,22,26,28
הגיד	ἀπαγγέλλω	report	18:20,24

Unusual word choices, not (or rarely) used elsewhere in the LXX, are
found in the following:

| רגלים | σκέλη | legs (usually:
πόδες) | 17:6 |

הלך לפני	προπορεύομαι	walk in front (usually two words)	17:7
לחם	μονομαχέομαι	fight (usually: πολεμέω as in vv. 32,33)	17:10
יחד	ἀμφότεροι	together (usually: ἅμα)	17:10

The main conclusion with regard to the translation equivalents used in 1 Samuel 17–18 is that they reflect a rather consistently Septuagintal type of translation.

HEBRAISMS IN THE TRANSLATION[13]

On the basis of the above data, the translation technique of 1 Samuel 17–18 may be described as relatively literal. A similar conclusion has been reached by others with regard to 1 Samuel as a whole.[14] Special mention should be made of R. Sollamo's thorough investigation of one aspect of the translation technique of the LXX which yielded the conclusion that 1 Samuel belongs to the most literal units of the whole LXX.[15] On the basis of a similar study by I. Soisalon-Soininen, 1 Samuel may be characterized as relatively literal.[16] The following data support this characterization.

13. See n. 12.
14. Thus Thenius, *Bücher Samuels*, pp. xxvff.; Woods, *Light*, p. 21; Driver, *Judaean Scrolls*, pp. lix–lxii, with many examples. Likewise Kelly (cited in n. 7), p. 24 (". . . which aim at literalism to a greater extent than the majority of the Septuagint books"), though the greater part of Kelly's dissertation discusses the translator's exegetical deviations. The predominantly exegetical character of the translation is maintained by Gehman, "Exegetical Methods," pp. 292–96. In this short article, Gehman provides examples of various exegetical renderings subdivided into six groups: (1) theological changes; (2) toning down of offensive expressions; (3) maintaining of royal dignity; (4) maintaining of human dignity; (5) free approach to content; and (6) contextual exegesis. In our view, however, this collection of examples is not convincing. The issue is not *whether* there are exegetical renderings in the LXX of 1 Samuel— the existence of some of these is apparent—but *how many* are found in that translation unit when compared with its literal renderings. It is clear, we claim, that exegetical renderings are much less frequent than literal renderings.
A second point which must be raised against Gehman's article, as well as that of his student Kelly, is that many (most?) of the examples can also be explained as reflecting variant readings. The decision whether a particular deviation of the LXX from the MT reflects the translator's exegesis or a variant reading can be made only on the basis of an investigation of the translation technique used in a particular unit or in the whole book.
15. Sollamo, *Renderings*, esp. pp. 280ff.
16. Soisalon-Soininen, *Infinitive*, esp. pp. 169ff.

THE PRESENCE OF HEBRAISMS IN THE TRANSLATION OF 1 SAMUEL 17-18

Numerous Hebraisms appearing in the translation illustrate the translator's literalism. In the following these are underlined.

17:1   ויחנו בין שוכה ובין עזקה
and encamped between Socoh and between Azekah
καὶ παρεμβάλλουσιν ἀνὰ μέσον Σουχωθ καὶ ἀνὰ μέσον Αζηκα

17:4   ויצא איש הבנים . . . גלית שמו
and a champion stepped forward . . . Goliath (was) his name
καὶ ἐξῆλθεν ἀνὴρ δυνατὸς . . . Γολιαθ ὄνομα αὐτοῦ

17:5   ושריון קשקשים הוא לבוש
and with armor of scales he was dressed
καὶ θώρακα ἁλυσιδωτὸν αὐτὸς ἐνδεδυκώς

17:9   אם יוכל . . . והיינו
if he is able . . . then (lit. and) we will become
καὶ ἐὰν δυνηθῇ . . . καὶ ἐσόμεθα

17:32   אל יפל לב אדם עליו
Let no man's heart fall upon him
μὴ δὴ συμπεσέτω καρδία τοῦ κυρίου μου ἐπ' αὐτόν (reflecting variant
אל נא יפל לב אדני עליו, Let not, I pray, my lord's heart fall upon him

17:33   ללכת . . . להלחם
to go . . . to fight
πορευθῆναι . . . τοῦ πολεμεῖν

17:40   וישם אתם בכלי הרעים אשר לו
and he put them in the shepherd's bag which he had
καὶ ἔθετο αὐτοὺς ἐν τῷ καδίῳ τῷ ποιμενικῷ τῷ ὄντι αὐτῷ

17:42   נער ואדמני עם יפה מראה
he was a boy, ruddy with beauty of appearance
αὐτὸς ἦν παιδάριον καὶ αὐτὸς πυρράκης μετὰ κάλλους ὀφθαλμῶν (perhaps
reflecting variant עם יפה עינים, with beauty of eyes)

17:43   אתה בא אלי במקלות
you come against me with (lit. in) sticks
σὺ ἔρχῃ ἐπ' ἐμὲ ἐν ῥάβδῳ (reflecting variant במקל, with a stick)
For similar use of ἐν, see vv. 43b, 45, 47; 18:6.

18:8   וירע בעיניו הדבר הזה
and this matter (word) was evil in his eyes
καὶ πονηρὸν ἐφάνη τὸ ῥῆμα ἐν ὀφθαλμοῖς Σαουλ περὶ τοῦ λόγου τούτου
and the word was evil in the eyes of Saul concerning this word
For similar constructions, see 18:20, 23, 26.

18:12   וירא שאול מלפני דוד
lit., Saul was afraid from the face of David
καὶ ἐφοβήθη Σαουλ ἀπὸ προσώπου Δαυειδ

18:22 חפץ בך המלך
the king is fond of (lit. in) you
ὁ βασιλεὺς θέλει ἐν σοι (cf. also v. 25)

18:27 יולך הוא ואנשיו
and he went out, he and his men
καὶ ἐπορεύθη αὐτὸς καὶ οἱ ἄνδρες αὐτοῦ

18:27 ויך בפלשתים
lit., and smote in the Philistines
καὶ ἐπάταξεν ἐν τοῖς ἀλλοφύλοις

HEBRAISMS IN THE PLUSES IN THE TRANSLATION

Hebraisms in the pluses (that is, in the material not found in the Masoretic Text) underscore the translator's adherence to his parent text:

17:8   *ex enantías hēmōn = liqrā'tēnu*, to meet us
17:36 *ouchì poreúsomai kaì patáxō autòn kaì aphelō̃ sḗmeron óneidos*
       = *haʾlô' 'ēlēk wĕhikkētîw wahaʾsirôtî hayyôm ḥerpâ*, shall I not go
       and smite him and remove today disgrace
17:48 *eis synántēsin Daueid = liqra't dāwid*, to meet David.

Note further the use of *légōn* (= *lē'mōr*) in a plus in 18:22.

Further Arguments Against Abridgement in the LXX

In our view the above-mentioned data show that the translator remained, as a rule, loyal to his parent text, and it is therefore not likely that he would have omitted 44 percent of the text. As in all arguments, this is subjective reasoning, but under the circumstances we consider this the most feasible argument, since it is based on the internal consistency of the translator's approach to his text. We therefore assume that the translator worked from a text which was much shorter than the Masoretic Text.

This working hypothesis is supported by three further arguments:

1. Confidence in the reliability of the LXX of Samuel has been enhanced in recent years by the finds of Hebrew scrolls of Samuel in Qumran Cave 4. These scrolls contain many readings which had been reconstructed previously from the LXX (either the mainstream or the Lucianic group of mss.).[17] This situation thus gives the LXX more credibility in those chapters

---

17. For the material, see the articles in Tov, ed., *Texts of Samuel.*

of which no ancient Hebrew manuscripts have been found. At the same time, it must be admitted that the differences between the Masoretic Text and the reconstructed parent text of the LXX are larger in 1 Samuel 17–18 than in any other section of the book;[18] nor do any of the Qumran scrolls differ as much from the Masoretic Text. The only parallels showing similarly extensive divergence from the Masoretic Text which come to mind are the large plus of 4QSam[a] before the beginning of 1 Samuel 11 (five lines) and the beginning of the second column of the same scroll (1 Sam. 2:13ff.), which differs considerably from the Masoretic Text.[19]

2. Our working hypothesis, that the short version of the story found in the LXX is based on a short Hebrew original, is more acceptable if the alternative view, that it is an abridgement by the Greek translator, cannot be sustained. And indeed, in our view there are no cogent reasons for assuming a large-scale shortening of the original text by the translator. One might suppose, for example, that the translator omitted a substantial portion of the narrative in order to shorten the lengthy stories. But the argument from translation technique militates against this supposition too: The translator has not shown himself willing to take such liberties with his source elsewhere. Furthermore, the presence of pluses in the translation also gainsays such an assumption.

3. The motive usually given to explain why the translator would have abridged is that he recognized difficulties in certain passages, which he therefore omitted. Two examples of such difficulties are the following:

• In 17:55–58, Saul and Abner express ignorance of David when they see him approaching Goliath, and Saul asks to have David introduced to him. This contradicts the scene preceding the battle, where Saul and David have a lengthy discussion about David's confronting Goliath (17:31–39), and the earlier story of David's being introduced to Saul as a skillful harper and being made his armor bearer, where it is even said that Saul "loved" David (16:17–23). It is often claimed that the translator omitted 17:55–58 to eliminate this contradiction of the earlier scenes.

• In 18:17–19, Saul offers David his eldest daughter, Merab, while verses 20–26 tell about David's marriage to Michal, "daughter of Saul" (vv. 20, 27). The tension between these passages is apparent (despite the harmonizing remark of v. 21b), and this may have prompted the translator to omit the first section (vv. 17–19), which is now lacking in the LXX. See further below, p. 123.

---

18. Elsewhere in 1 Samuel the LXX lacks individual phrases or clauses, but nowhere does it lack so many as in chapters 17–18. For some examples, see 1:9; 4:17; 6:4, 11; 10:16; 12:13; 21:10; 23:23; 26:4; 30:7b; 31:6. For a discussion, see Méritan, *La version grecque*, pp. 139–48.

19. See Cross, "Ammonite Oppression"; idem, "New Qumran Fragment."

That a translator omitted complete sections from his parent text to avoid inconsistencies *is* a legitimate assumption, albeit a very difficult one. It presupposes not only that the translator allowed himself considerable liberty in his translation, but also that he was a sophisticated reader, almost a critical scholar. I wonder whether there are any parallels for such a presumed action within the realm of the Greek translations of the Bible. Scores of contradictory passages have been left everywhere else in the translation, including the LXX of Samuel (see below, p. 118). Not only is the mere fact of the omission surprising, so is the assumed reason for that omission, which ascribes to the translator the mind of an attentive critic.

More important, while a harmonizing omission by the translator in the above two examples is, in view of their contents, at least plausible, such an assumption is much more difficult, if not impossible, in the case of the other minuses in the LXX. In 18:1–4 we are informed of the covenant of love between David and Jonathan; why should that section be omitted? And why should verses 5–6a, which merely introduce the next section, be omitted? True, 18:1–6a too contains a detail which could be read as inconsistent with the earlier narrative: In 18:2 Saul installs David in his court, even though he had already been installed there in 16:22. But should we expect the translator to be sensitive to such details? And even if we should, why would the translator omit six and a half verses because of one detail (18:2)? Would it not have been easier and more responsible merely to change a detail (e.g., in 17:15) or to omit a smaller part of the section in question? Did the translator omit 18:10–11 (Saul's attempt to spear David) because it is repeated in 19:9–10? Or did he consider this section inconsistent with Saul's feelings of love for David? The latter possibility is unlikely, because the translation also lacks 18:2a, which mentions Saul's love.

The same type of questions may be asked regarding the translator's supposed omission of 17:12–31, the largest of the minuses of the LXX in 1 Samuel 17–18. This section contains several elements that contradict the preceding or following account (see below, pp. 121–22), but all these contradictions are relatively minor, and we do not know whether the translator would have sensed them. But even if he would have, would a translator omit a complete section of twenty verses because of difficulties regarding *some* of the verses in that section?

Apart from these questions, two other considerations show the inadequacy of harmonization as an explanation for the minuses in the LXX of 1 Samuel 17–18. First, several of the minuses show no inconsistency with the remaining text, and there would have been no reason to omit them on that score (17:41, 48b, 50; 18:12b, 29b–30). And second, not all difficulties have been removed from the version found in the LXX: 17:33, in which David is called a mere lad, unqualified to fight Goliath, remains, despite its apparent inconsistency with 16:18, where he is called a man of valor and a man of war (see n. 25).

In sum, we cannot think of any motive which would convincingly explain an abridgement of the text. Only in a few cases can one point to possible reasons for a stylistic or exegetical abridgement of individual passages, and these are not sufficient to establish a case for extensive abridgement. These considerations also militate against the likelihood that the short text was the result of abridgement by a Hebrew scribe (rather than the Greek translator), as suggested by A. Kuenen. Such a theory would encounter the same objections as those just discussed, as well as another: It is highly unlikely that the Hebrew text would be revised only in chapters 17–18 and not in other chapters in 1 Samuel which contain obvious contradictions and doublets of stories (e.g., the different traditions concerning the origin of the monarchy in 1 Sam. 8:1–22; 10:17–27 // 9:1–10:16; the parallel stories about David and Saul in 1 Sam. 19:11–17 // 19:18–24 // 20:1–42; 1 Sam. 24 // 1 Sam. 26).

The Two Versions Underlying 1 Samuel 17–18

What emerges from the preceding discussion is that the short version of 1 Samuel 17–18 reflected in the LXX was not an abridgement, either by the Greek translator or by a Hebrew scribe, of the long version found in the Masoretic Text. It is rather an independent and coherent version of the events. In what follows we analyze the nature of this version and its counterpart in the passages absent from the LXX and found only in the Masoretic Text. In so doing, we turn from the realm of textual criticism to that of literary criticism and exegesis.

The argument up to this point implies that the short version underlying the LXX reflects an early stage of chapters 17–18 (continuing chap. 16 [see n. 20]) and that the long version found in the Masoretic Text represents a later, expanded stage. Since the long version contains additional information (traditions) about the encounter of David and Goliath, parallel to that in the short version, the additional material in the long version constitutes a separate version of the story. We shall refer to the short text underlying the LXX (and parts of the Masoretic Text) as *version 1* and the additions found only in the Masoretic Text as *version 2*.[20] The Masoretic Text thus

20. Version 1 is taken as reflecting the main story of 1 Samuel (i.e., it follows chap. 16 and continues with chap. 19), since version 2 has been superimposed on it and inserted in it. This is merely a logical inference from the relationship between versions 1 and 2, but considering the contents of both versions, it is not impossible that version 2 also reflects the framework of 1 Samuel (note, e.g., the depiction of David as a shepherd boy in version 2 and in 16:11, 19).

contains both versions 1 and 2.[21] In a way, this situation resembles that in Jeremiah where a short *edition* of the book is contained in the LXX and a Qumran scroll (4QJer[b]) and a long one is contained in the Masoretic Text.[22]

For a more detailed analysis we present a summary of the contents of the two versions, disregarding small pluses and minuses.[23]

	Version 1 (LXX and MT)	*Version 2 (MT only)*
16:17–23	David is introduced to Saul as a skillful harper and he is made his armor bearer.	
17:1–11	Attack by the Philistines. Goliath suggests a duel with one of the Israelites.	
17:12–31		David is sent by his father to bring food to his brothers at the front. He hears Goliath and desires to meet him in a duel.
17:32–39	David volunteers to fight with Goliath.	
17:40–54	The duel. After Goliath's miraculous fall, the Philistines flee.	Short account of the duel (vv. 41, 48b, 50)
17:55–58		Saul asks who David is. David is introduced to Saul by Abner.
18:1–4		David and Jonathan make a covenant.
18:5–6a		David is appointed as an officer in Saul's army.
18:6b–9	Saul's jealousy of David.	
18:10–11		Saul attempts in vain to kill David.
18:12–16	David's successes.	
18:17–19		Saul offers David his eldest daughter, Merab.
18:20–27	Saul offers David his daughter Michal.	
19:29b–30		Saul's love for David. David's successes.

21. This terminology is appropriate for the two versions of the encounter of David and Goliath (chap. 17) and for the two versions of Saul's offer of marriage (18:17–19, 20–27), but not for other details in version 2, which do not provide alternative material to version 1 but rather simple expansions with no counterparts in version 1. Since, however, the majority of the pluses of the MT do add parallel material, it is best to use the term *versions*.

22. For a summary of the problems see below, chapter 8.

23. Most commentaries merely remark on the relation between the two versions of the story of David and Goliath, but McCarter (*I Samuel*) presents the two versions as two

The parallels between the two versions of the events are that in each David is introduced to Saul (16:17–23 [part of an earlier section of version 1] and 17:55–58) and that in each David is made an officer in Saul's army (18:5, 13). Furthermore, in each version Saul offers David one of his daughters (both termed "daughter of Saul": 18:19, 20), without the text's making any cross reference to the offer of the other daughter (18:17–19, 20–27 [see, however, below, p. 123 on 18:21b]). At the same time, it must be noted that the two versions are not *fully* parallel, as they often contain different elements. Version 1 is much more extensive than version 2, as is obvious from a comparison of the two accounts of the duel. Version 1 presents a continuous[24] and internally consistent story,[25] and if version 2 were not known, we would not have lacked any information in chapters 17 and 18 which is crucial to the understanding of version 1.[26] Whether or not version 2 once existed in a fuller form, from which the present form was excerpted, cannot be known.

The two versions underlying chapters 17–18 contain only partial parallels, and because there is not sufficient evidence for contrasting the two stories, it is not clear whether the duplication should be connected with other duplications in Samuel. Even though several parallel versions of events have been detected elsewhere in Samuel, it is hard to know whether the two versions of the encounter of David and Goliath should be connected with these other duplicate strands of tradition.

From the point of view of literary history, we consider version 1 to be more original than version 2, since the latter has been added to it (or, rather, inserted in it). However this does not imply that the *content* of version 1 is more authentic than that of version 2. For example, we do not express any opinion on the type of description of David's person which is

---

independent units ("David and the Philistine Champion I, II"), translating and commenting on them separately.

24. 17:32 links immediately with 17:11, not with 17:31 (ʿālayw "because of him," in verse 32 probably refers to Goliath, and Goliath has not been mentioned in the verses which immediately precede verse 32 in the MT, but he is mentioned in verse 11 [alternatively, ʿālayw means "upon himself"]). In the other instances too the verse in the MT which immediately precedes the minus has its natural continuation in the verse following the minus.

25. A slight problem, however, is created by a comparison of 16:18 and 17:33. In the first verse, David is described as gibbôr ḥayil wĕʾîš milḥāmâ, "a man of valor and a man of war," while in the second Saul advises David not to fight because he is a mere naʿar, "lad." The tension between these two verses may be misleading. It is possible that the phrase in 16:18 is an exaggeration by one of Saul's men; possibly he means to say that David has the right traits for a warrior. Likewise, Saul's statement in 17:33 could be exaggerated (cf. the use of naʿar in 1 Kings 3:7).

26. One difficulty, however, is created by the covenant of friendship between David and Jonathan mentioned in 18:1–4 (version 2) and subsequently referred to in 20:8. If, however, we assume that the redactor who joined versions 1 and 2, the latter including 18:1–4, then wrote or rewrote 20:8, the problem is solved.

found in the different versions. It is hard to know whether "David the harper and the armor bearer" (version 1) is more original in the history of the tradition than "David the shepherd" (version 2, but also 1 Sam. 16:11, 19). The later tradition depicts David as both a musician and a shepherd (see, e.g., Psalm 151 in 11QPs^{a27} and in the LXX).

Version 1 in chapter 17 thus should not be preferred to version 2 from the point of view of its contents. In chapter 18, at times version 1 is preferable to version 2, and at times the mere editorial juxtaposition of versions 1 and 2 creates contextual problems that render the isolated reading of *either* version 1 or 2 desirable. This refers especially to the two versions of Saul's offer of a daughter to David in marriage (18:17–19 [version 2], 20–27 [version 1]) and to Saul's attempt to kill David (vv. 10–11 [version 2]). All exegetes agree that Saul's attempt to kill David is not in place in this chapter (it is repeated by an identical section in 19:9–10). In fact, the sequence of events in the short version 1 is more logical than that in the combined text of versions 1 and 2. In version 1, Saul is at first envious of David (vv. 8–9), then suspicious (v. 12) and frightened because of David's successes (vv. 13–15); subsequently he wants to have David killed by the Philistines, and when this stratagem does not succeed, he attempts to kill him himself (19:9–10). In the combined Masoretic version, the progressive intensification of Saul's response is undercut by Saul's premature attempt in 18:10–11.

The Composition of the Masoretic Version of 1 Samuel 16–18

From the above discussion it is clear that the Masoretic version of 1 Samuel 16–18 was created by the juxtaposition of two separate accounts of the events, the complete version 1 and the partial (or partially preserved) version 2.

Since both versions cover some of the same events, but with differing details, the conflate Masoretic version which was produced by the join contains several inconsistencies:

1. The most conspicuous difficulty, as explained above, is that after David had been introduced to Saul and had become his armor bearer (16:17–23, from version 1), he is absent from the battlefront and occupied as a shepherd with his father's flock and is still unknown to Saul who, when David arrives, has to ask Abner who he is (17:55–58, from version 2). Note that Saul asks in general terms about "the lad" (17:55, 56).

---

27. Published by Sanders in *Psalms Scroll*.

2. In 17:12 (the first sentence of version 2), David and Jesse are introduced to the reader, but they were already known from chapter 16 (version 1).

3. If indeed Eliab was present at the time of David's anointing (16:13, from version 1), it is hard to understand why he should utter such harsh words to David (17:28, from version 2). Admittedly, if the issue is judged only on a psychological level, it is understandable that the oldest brother might be jealous or anxious about the safety of his youngest brother.

4. David is depicted in different ways in the composite narrative. In 16:21 he is Saul's armor bearer (from version 1), and in that capacity he fights Goliath. In 17:12–31 and 55–58 (from version 2) he is an unknown shepherd boy who happens to be on the spot visiting his brothers when Goliath challenges the Israelites to a duel.

5. In 18:13 (from version 1) David is made an officer in Saul's army, though he was already made an officer in 18:5 (from version 2). This inconsistency holds as long as the two appointments are not taken as referring to *different* positions.

6. According to 17:25ff. (from version 2), whoever defeats Goliath is to be given the king's daughter in marriage. 18:20ff. (from version 1) seem unaware of this promise, since Saul has to look for pretexts that would convince David to marry his daughter, while David says that he is unworthy.

7. According to 18:20–27 (from version 1), Saul offers David Michal, "daughter of Saul," but in verses 17–19 (from version 2), Saul offered David his eldest daughter, Merab, also termed "daughter of Saul," in accordance with his earlier promise to marry his daughter to whoever defeats Goliath (17:25, likewise from version 2).

The fact that the redactor who combined versions 1 and 2 created a text displaying such inconsistencies is precisely what is supposed to have happened in other cases throughout the Bible where texts underwent conflation, expansion, and interpolation. Why the redactor created this conflate version, despite its inconsistencies, is a matter of conjecture. It stands to reason that he wanted to preserve certain traditions and details that were not included in version 1, which formed the framework of his story. Presumably the redactor derived most of version 2 from a written source. It is hard to determine why he added 17:12–31 and 55–58 (the main body of version 2). Possibly he simply liked the story; possibly he wanted to convey a certain idea it expresses, namely, that God can bring victory to his people even through initially unimportant figures (in this version David was unknown before the battle). Other additions may reflect the editor's own ideas.[28] In verse 50, for example, he stressed that David did not need a sword in order to defeat the Philistine.

---

28. For further speculations on the different tendencies visible in the two versions, see esp. Peters, *Beiträge*, p. 57; de Vries, "David's Victory"; Jason, "Story of David and Goliath." According to the latter, version 1 reflects a "romantic epic" and version 2 a "heroic epic."

Still, the redactor did not necessarily ignore all the inconsistencies created by his juxtaposition of the two versions. There are a few details in the text which have the effect of smoothing out certain of the inconsistencies. If we did not have the evidence of the LXX that the narrative is indeed composite, we might take such details as evidence for its original unity, but since that is ruled out, these details have plausibly been taken as belonging to neither version but rather as composed by the redactor for the purpose of smoothing out the inconsistencies. Here are some examples:[29]

• *hazzeh*, lit. "this one," in 17:12: *wĕdāwid ben ʾîš ʾeprātî hazzeh mibbêt leḥem*, "David was the son of an Ephrathite man, this one, from Bethlehem." Since David's father[30] had already been introduced in chapter 16, his introduction in 17:12 would have seemed repetitious and oblivious of the earlier introduction, as we have noted. The ungrammatical use of the demonstrative particle in this verse suggests that it was added by the redactor to remove the impression of obliviousness (proper Hebrew usage would have been *hā ʾîš hā ʾeprātî hazzeh*, "this Ephrathite man"; the formulation *ʾîš ʾeprātî*, "an Ephrathite man," is correct only without *hazzeh*). In context the particle must mean "the aforementioned," as Jerome understood it (*de quo supra dictum est*).[31]

• 17:15, *wĕdāwid hōlēk wāšāb mēʿal šāʾûl lirʿôt ʾet ṣōʾn ʾābîw bēt lāḥem*, "David would go back and forth from attending on Saul to shepherd his father's flock at Bethlehem." Since David had already left him and become Saul's armor bearer (16:17–23, from version 1), the fact that he was still with Jesse when Saul and the army were at the front (17:12–20, from version 2) would have seemed inconsistent. 17:15 smoothes out the inconsistency by indicating that David alternated his time between home and Saul's court.

• 1 Sam. 18:21b "you can become my son-in-law even now through the second one" (NJV), added in version 2, may be in the nature of a cross-reference to the mentioning of the other daughter (Michal) in version 1 (see above, p. 116).

The present study shows that the Masoretic version of 1 Samuel 16–18 combines two originally separate versions of the narrative. These versions sometimes told of the same incidents, though not always with identical details; at other times they told of different incidents. As a result, when the two versions were combined, the combined text displayed a certain amount of redundancy and inconsistency. In a few places the redactor added notes

---

29. For the technique and one additional example from Samuel and one from Genesis, see Seeligmann, "Hebräische Erzählung," esp. pp. 312–14.

30. Even if *hazzeh* refers to David (thus Qimḥi), it would still be considered an editorial or scribal addition.

31. Alternatively, *hazzeh* is a corruption of *hāyāh* (interchange of *zayin* and *yod*).

in an attempt to smooth over these difficulties; in other places he made no such attempt.

If the above analysis is correct, the results are of major importance for our understanding not only of 1 Samuel 16–18, but of other sections of Samuel too, and in a way of the whole of biblical literature. For in this case we are able to document the existence of two layers of one story, while in other cases the assumption of different layers is merely an abstract possibility.

Appendix A.
Shorter Minuses in the LXX of 1 Samuel 17–18

The items missing in the LXX are those enclosed in parentheses.

17:5	וכובע (נחשת)	and a (bronze) helmet
17:9	ואם אני אוכל (לו)	but if I am able (to him)
17:33	הפלשתי (הזה)	(this) Philistine
17:36	הפלשתי הערל (הזה)	(this) uncircumcised Philistine
17:37	(ויאמר דוד)	(and David said)
17:38	(וילבש אתו שריון)	(and dressed him in a breastplate)
17:39	ויסירם (דוד) מעליו	and (David) [he] took them off of him
17:42	(ויבט הפלשתי)	(when the Philistine looked)
17:46	היום (הזה)	(this) [to-]day
17:48	וילך (ויקרב)	and went (and drew close)
17:51	ויקח את חרבו	and he took his sword
	(וישלפה מתערה)	(and pulled it from its sheath)
17:51	ויכרת (בה)	and he cut off (with it)
18:6	(לשיר והמחלות לקראת שאול המלך)	(singing and dancing towards king Saul)
18:7	הנשים (המשחקות)	the (dancing) women
18:8	(ויחר לשאול מאד)	(and Saul was greatly angered)
18:8	(ועוד לו אך המלוכה)	(and all that he lacks is the kingship)
18:20	וישר (הדבר) בעיניו	and (the matter) was pleasing in his eyes
18:24	ויגדו עבדי שאול לו (לאמר)	Saul's servants reported to him (saying)
18:26	(ולא מלאו הימים)	(Before the days were fulfilled)
18:27	ויבא (דוד)	and (David) [he] brought
18:27	ויתן לו (שאול)	and (Saul) [he] gave him
18:27	(וימלאום) למלך	(and they were counted out) for the king
18:28	וירא שאול (וידע)	and Saul saw (and knew)
18:29	ויאסף (שאול) לרא	And (Saul) [he] became more afraid

Appendix B.
Variant Readings Reflected in the LXX of 1 Samuel 17–18

Appendix B.
Variant Readings Reflected in the LXX of 1 Samuel 17–18

As noted above, recognition of these variants is necessarily subjective. The LXX and MT readings are presented in parallel columns, with tentative retroversions of the variants reflected in LXX added in an additional column. Deviations that may be due to translation technique are indicated with an asterisk.

	LXX	MT	Retroverted variant
17:2	*ἐν τῇ κοιλάδι. αὐτοὶ παρατάσσονται in the valley. They drew up battle lines	בעמק האלה ויערכו in the valley of Elah and drew up battle lines	בעמק אלה...
17:4	ἐκ τῆς παρατάξεως from the battle line	מהמחנות from the camps	מהמערכה
17:4	(ὕψος αὐτοῦ) τεσσάρων (πήχεων) (his height was) four (cubits)	(גבהו) שש (זרת) (his height was) six (cubits)	ארבע
17:7	καὶ ὁ κοντός and the (wooden) pole	וחץ and the shaft	ועץ
17:8	Ἑβραῖοι Hebrews	עבדים servants	עברים
17:9	καὶ ἐάν and if	אם if	ואם
17:32	τοῦ κυρίου μου my lord	אדם man	אדני
17:34	καὶ ἡ ἄρκος and a bear	ואת הדוב and the bear (acc.)	ודוב והארי
17:35	τοῦ φάρυγγος αὐτοῦ of his throat	בזקנו of his beard	בגרונו

Verse	Greek (LXX)	English	Hebrew (MT)	English	Hebrew
17:36	καὶ τὸν ἄρκον (ἔτυπτεν ὁ δοῦλος σου) καὶ τὸν λέοντα	both bear (has your servant killed) and lion	גם הדב (אֵת) גם הארי (אֵת) הכה (עבדך)	both lion and bear (has your servant killed)	גם הדב (את) גם הארי (את) הכה
17:37	καὶ ἔσται κύριος	may be the Lord (with you)	יהי 'ה	may the Lord be (with you)	תהיה 'ה
17:38	καὶ (περικεφαλαίαν)	and (a helmet)	ויתן קובע	and placed a helmet	ויבלבל
17:39	καὶ ἐκοπίασεν	and he was unable	ויאל	and he tried	ויאל
17:39	ἅπαξ καὶ δίς	once and twice	כי לא נסה	for he was not used to them	?
17:40	εἰς συλλογήν	into (his) bag	ובילקוט	and into (his) bag	ובילקוט
17:42	κάλλους ὀφθαλμῶν	beauty of eyes	יפה מראה	handsome of appearance	יפה עינים
17:43	ἐν ῥάβδῳ	with a stick	במקלות	with sticks	במקלך
17:46	καὶ ἀποκλείσει σε	and he will deliver you	יסגרך	he will deliver you	יסגרך
17:46	τὰ κῶλα σου καὶ τὰ κῶλα	your carcasses and the carcasses	פגר	the carcasses	פגרי
17:47	*καὶ γνώσεται	and it will know	וידעו (כל הקהל הזה)	and they will know (all this assembly)	וירע
17:48	καὶ ἀνέστη	and he went up	ויקם	and it happened that he went up	ויקם
17:51	ἐπ' αὐτόν	over him	אל הפלשתי	to/over the Philistine	עלי/אל
17:52	Γεθ	Geth	גיא	Gai	גי
17:52	ὀπίσω αὐτῶν	after them	את הפלשתים (וירדפו)	(and they pursued) the Philistines	אחרים

Verse	Greek	English	Hebrew	English
17:52	Ασκαλῶνος	Ashkelon	אקרון	Ekron
17:53	ἄνδρες Ισραηλ	men of Israel	איש ישראל	(cf. v. 2)
				?
			בני ישראל	sons of Israel
18:6	αἱ χορεύουσαι	the dancers	הנשים	the women
				?
18:8	ἐν ὀφθαλμοῖς Σαουλ	in the eyes of Saul	בעיניו	in his eyes
18:8	περὶ τοῦ λόγου	about the matter	הדבר	the matter
18:14	*ἐν πάσαις ταῖς ὁδοῖς αὐτοῦ	in all his undertakings	לכל דרכו	to all his undertakings
18:16	πρὸ προσώπου τοῦ λαοῦ	before the people	לפניהם	before them
18:21	ἐπὶ Σαουλ	against Saul	בו	against him
18:22	καὶ σύ	and you	ועתה	and now
18:25	ἀλλ᾽ ἤ	other than	כי	than
18:25	αὐτὸν ἐμβαλεῖν	to cast him	להפיל את דוד	to cast David
18:27	ἕκατον	one hundred	מאתים	two hundred
18:28	καὶ πᾶς	and all	ומיכל	and Michal
18:28	Ισραηλ	Israel	בת שאול	the daughter of Saul
18:28	ἠγάπα αὐτόν	he loved him	אהבתהו	she loved him

Appendix C.
Pluses in the LXX of 1 Samuel 17–18

With due caution, the majority of the pluses can be retroverted into Hebrew; they are the elements after the plus sign or in between two plus signs in the following list. What stands outside these signs is present in the MT.

	LXX	*Retroverted variant*
17:5	χαλκοῦ + καὶ σιδήρου	נחשת + וברזל
	brass + and iron	
17:8	πολεμῷ + ἐξ ἐναντίας ἡμῶν	מלחמה + לקראתנו
	battle + toward us	
17:32	μὴ + δὴ + συμπεσέτω	אל + נא + יפל
	let not + I pray + fall	
17:36	+ οὐχὶ πορεύσομαι καὶ πατάξω αὐτὸν	+ הלוא אלך והכתיו
	καὶ ἀφέλω σήμερον ὄνειδος	והסרותי היום חרפה
	ἐξ Ισραηλ διότι τίς	מעל ישראל כי מי
	ὁ ἀπερίτμητος οὗτος +	הערל הזה +
	+ shall I not go and smite him and remove today disgrace from Israel, for who is this uncircumcised +	
17:37	τοῦ ἀλλοφύλου + τοῦ ἀπεριτμήτου + τούτου	הפלשתי + הערל + הזה
	this + uncircumcised + Philistine	
17:40	πρὸς + τὸν ἄνδρα + τὸν ἀλλόφυλον	אל + האיש + הפלשתי
	to + the man + the Philistine	
17:42	καὶ εἶδεν + Γολιαθ	ויראה + גלית
	and saw + Goliath (subject)	
17:43	+ καὶ λίθοις καὶ εἶπεν Δαυειδ	+ ואבנים ויאמר דוד
	οὐχί ἀλλ' ἢ χείρω κυνός . . . +	לא כי אם . . . +
	+ and stones and David said, No, but rather . . . +	
17:46	καὶ ἀποκλείσει σε κύριος + σήμερον	ויסגרך ה' + היום
	and the Lord will deliver you + today	
17:47	καὶ παραδώσει + κύριος	ונתן + ה'
	and will give + the Lord (subject)	
17:49	λίθον + ἕνα	אבן + אחת
	stone + one	
17:49	καὶ διέδυ ὁ λίθος	ותטבע האבן
	+ διὰ τῆς περικεφαλαίας +	+ בעד הכובע +
	εἰς τὸ μέτωπον αὐτοῦ	במצחו
	and the stone penetrated + through the helmet + into his forehead	
18:6	+ εἰς συνάντησιν Δαυειδ +	+ לקראת דוד +
	+ towards David +	
18:22	+ λέγων +	+ לאמר +
	+ saying +	

18:22 λαλήσατε + ὑμεῖς   דברו + אתם
       speak + you (pl., subject pronoun)

18:24 κατὰ τὰ ῥήματα ταῦτα + ἃ + ἐλάλησεν   כדברים האלה + אשר + דבר
       according to these things + which + he spoke

18:27 τὴν Μελχολ θυγατέρα αὐτοῦ + αὐτῷ +   את מיכל בתו + לו +
       his daughter Michal + to him +

Part of the reverse and edge of CBS 7111, the "Pennsylvania Tablet" of the Old Babylonian version of *Gilgamesh* (Gilg. P.). The colophon at the end identifies this as "Tablet 2 of (the text beginning with) *šūtur eli*, ('Surpassing . . .')," which is the beginning of line 27 of the Standard Babylonian version of the epic. See pp. 38, 41–42.

Exodus 20 in the Samaritan Pentateuch. In this chapter parallel passages from Deuteronomy 5 and 18 are spliced into the text at the appropriate points. See pp. 61–83. The photo is from a modern Samaritan Torah scroll, Samaritan MS. 76 in the library of Dropsie College, Philadelphia.

(Published by courtesy of Dropsie College. Photography by the Department of Biomedical Communications, University of Pennsylvania School of Medicine.)

1 Samuel 17:44–18:22 in the Septuagint, Codex Vaticanus (LXX^B). In this version almost half of the verses of 1 Samuel 17–18 are absent, reflecting the Hebrew text of the story prior to the addition of those verses. See chapter 3.

(Photo reproduced from p. 333 of *Bibliorum SS. Graecorum Codex Vaticanus 1209 [Cod. B] denovo phototypice expressus jussa et cura praesidium Bybliothecae Vaticanae, Pars Prima, Testamentum Vetus*. Vol. 1. Mediolani: Ulricum Hoepli, 1905. Photography by the Department of Biomedical Communications, University of Pennsylvania School of Medicine.)

Joshua 19:49–21:12 in the Septuagint, Codex Vaticanus (LXX[B]). In this version chapter 20 lacks the Deuteronomistic verses 4, 5, and most of 6, and reflects the Hebrew text of Joshua 20 prior to the addition of those verses. See chapter 4.

(Photo reproduced from ibid., p. 263. Photography by the Department of Biomedical Communications, University of Pennsylvania School of Medicine.)

Columns 10–12 of CBS 13981, a manuscript of the *Sumerian King List*. The number of cities listed in the summary at the end of the tablet indicates that even when complete this tablet lacked the antediluvian section of the text. See pp. 158–59.

(Copyright University Museum, Philadelphia; published with permission.)

Column 32 of the "Great Isaiah Scroll" from Qumran cave 1 (1QIs^a) showing Isaiah
38:8–40:2. Beginning in the fourteenth line and extending downward in the left-hand
margin is Isaiah 38:21–22, added by a later hand. See pp. 181–85.

(Photograph by Dr. John C. Trever, copyright 1970; published with permission.)

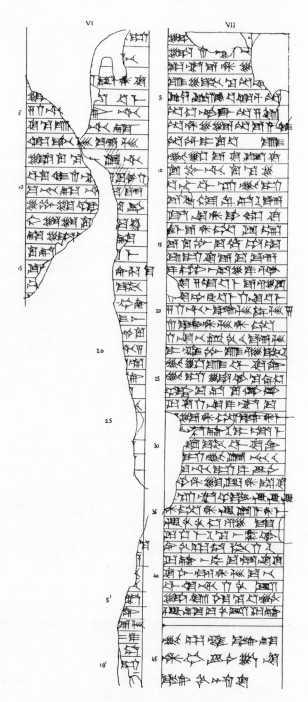

Two columns of BM 78223, from recension A of Esarhaddon's *Babylon Inscription*. Although the text tells of activities from relatively late in Esarhaddon's reign, the colophon dates the text to his accession year, obviously a pseudo-date. See pp. 199–201.

(Reproduced by permission of the Trustees of the British Museum from Th. G. Pinches, *Cuneiform Texts from Babylonian Tablets in the British Museum*. Part 44. London: Trustees of the British Museum, 1963, plate III.)

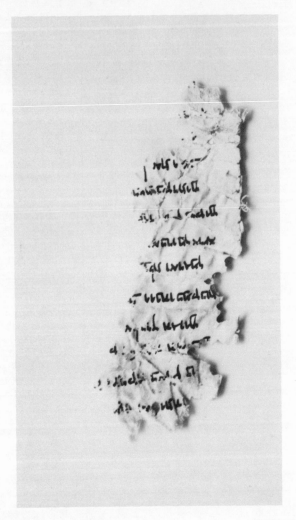

A fragment of 4QJer[b], showing parts of Jeremiah 9:22–10:18. The text presents a short version of Jeremiah 10 comparable to that underlying the Septuagint. Both 4QJer[b] and the LXX reflect an edition of Jeremiah earlier than that presented by the Masoretic Text. See chapter 8.

(Photograph courtesy of Prof. Frank M. Cross, Jr.; copyright Department of Museums and Antiquities, State of Israel.)

4

Joshua 20: Historico-Literary Criticism Illustrated

ALEXANDER ROFÉ

Editor's Note

In addition to conflation, in which two preexistent versions of a text are joined, criticism often presumes that a single source text has been supplemented by a later writer. In the present chapter, Alexander Rofé argues that this is how the Masoretic Text of Joshua 20 developed. Here too, just as in the David and Goliath story, the Septuagint reflects a shorter version of the text which is more plausibly explained as original and not due to abridgement. Linguistically and conceptually the short version agrees with the Priestly source in the Torah, while the additional matter found only in the Masoretic Text agrees with Deuteronomy. However, the additional verses in this chapter do not add up to a second complete account of the events, and Rofé therefore argues that these verses could never have existed independently of the version underlying the Septuagint. They must be understood as an addition written expressly to supplement the earlier version. Rofé shows that the linguistic and conceptual inconsistencies in the chapter reflect differences between the two strata, thus validating the critical methods which take such differences as source-critical clues.

•   •   •   •

This chapter is an expanded and revised version of an article which appeared in Hebrew in the *Isac Leo Seeligmann Volume*, vol. 1, ed. Y. Zakovitch and A. Rofé (Jerusalem: Rubinstein, 1983), pp. 137–50. Material from that article is reprinted here with permission.

Historico-Literary Criticism

. Historico-literary criticism studies the Hebrew Bible to ascertain its literary history and to extract from it data for a description of Israelite history and religion. Its point of departure, Scripture in its present form, displays tensions that are especially noticeable in the Torah and the Former Prophets. On the one hand, these works portray, in living color, events that occurred at the dawn of Israelite civilization, as if their authors were contemporaries of the events described. On the other hand, these works were transmitted to us by the Jewish community of the Persian and Hellenistic eras. Thus, hundreds of years separate the events from the canonization of the books which describe them; the place and date of authorship of most of these books is indeterminate, with possibilities ranging over hundreds of years, from the era of Israelite origins through the end of the Persian period. Therefore it becomes difficult to appraise the historical value of these sources. The historian of ancient Israel must make the resolution of this question his foremost aim; the tool which comes to hand is historico-literary criticism.

How does this method serve the historian? First, it concerns itself with the *unity* of the text under consideration. Many biblical passages display unity of both style and content, and so may be assumed to have been written by one author. On other occasions one finds passages replete with repetitions, contradictions, and inconsistencies, which indicate their composite nature. This should not come as a surprise if one remembers that biblical books were formed over the course of many generations and that their final texts were established only as the result of an arduous process whose end coincided more or less with the end of the Second Commonwealth. Keeping this developmental process in mind, one may proceed to an appraisal of the nature of the composition. Is it a combination of various oral traditions? a redaction of several documents? an accumulation of layers of revisions and recensions? Does it incorporate the marginal notes of late scribes? Does it reflect some other form of authorship? Possibly what we see in our text is a complex case involving some or all of these phenomena; for example, a later editor may have revised a written document while making use of oral traditions preserved in his circle.[1] Other combinations are also possible; for example, oral traditions may have been used in the composition of documents which in turn were expanded through additions and reedited, all followed by corruption of the text and ancient attempts at its restoration.[2]

---

1. A good example of this may be found in the story of Sennacherib's campaign against Jerusalem in 2 Kings 18:17–19:35; see my treatment in *Prophetical Stories*, pp. 78–83.

2. Here too I will allow myself the liberty of referring the reader to my study *The Book of Balaam.*

The second concern of historico-literary criticism is the *origin* of the text under study: when and where was it composed? In answering these questions, no small role is played by stylistic determinations. Elements of style enabled biblical scholars to identify various schools of biblical authors, for example, the later Ephraimite historiographer (E^2),[3] the Deuteronomic-Deuteronomistic school and its various stages, and the Priestly school. For each of these groups, dates indicating their origins and *floruits* have been assigned: the end of the Northern Kingdom in the late eighth century B.C.E.; the end of the Kingdom of Judah in the seventh to sixth centuries; and the Babylonian Exile, Restoration, and foundation of the Second Temple, respectively. These are instructive examples of how biblical criticism processes the data available in order to determine the distance between the story and its teller. But the study of biblical origins does not stop at dating; it goes on to ask to which *literary genre* a particular text belongs and what its purpose was. For example, in studying a narrative text, historico-literary criticism will attempt to determine whether it is a folktale, a novel, a history, or a parable. Thus the question of origins also includes determination of the social milieu in which a work grew, and its function within that group.

The third stage of criticism is the distillation and evaluation of the *historical evidence* provided by the text. Having previously established the place of a biblical text in the history of biblical literature, one moves to its utilization for writing Israelite national and religious history. It is important to stress that no source is completely devoid of historical worth. If it cannot reliably tell us about the period it purports to describe, it can always reveal something about the author, his period and institutions, his legal views, and/or his spiritual life. Source-criticism and intelligent appraisal guide us in the proper use of these ancient materials.

From time to time, however, doubts have been raised regarding the historico-literary method. Some of the doubts may be attributed to various kinds of apologists, overt or covert, conscious or unconscious.[4] But even groups who are not to be suspected of apologetics often take a skeptical or even derisive attitude toward historico-literary criticism. Such attitudes are often encountered among scholars in the cognate disciplines, such as archaeologists, historians of the Near East, Semitic philologists, and literary critics. One source of doubt is the lack of consensus among biblical critics. It is difficult to find two biblical scholars who agree on critical method and its proper application. Might this not indicate that the discipline lacks

3. Compare Burney, *Judges*, pp. xli–l. Scholars should carefully note Burney's contribution, made sixty-five years ago, before accepting Martin Noth's Deuteronomistic theory wholesale.

4. An interesting example of modern Jewish apologetic trends can be found in a work of one of the great contemporary Hebrew writers, S. Y. Agnon; see his *Šîrâ*, p. 142.

scientific grounding? Exceptional skepticism has been displayed toward the analytic aspect of biblical criticism, in which the unity of a passage is investigated and layers of authorship, revision, and editing are postulated. In this process, say criticism's critics, one unfounded assumption leads to the next with no objective control.[5] There is no proof that any of the proposed layers of development ever existed independently, at any stage in the history of biblical literature. Biblical criticism, says this approach, is merely an exercise in speculation, a pilpulistic conceit, a new scholasticism. There is a trend in some quarters toward a total abandonment of historico-literary criticism, toward an "as-is" reading of the Bible, and toward a literary perspective that views biblical pericopes, even whole books, as hermetic units formed by single authors.[6] Similarly, there are those who utilize the biblical texts as sources for historical information without inquiring as to their authorship, date of composition, form or type, or ideological and theological intent.[7] The appraisal of the historical worth of a passage, left to the historian, is guided by his views regarding the degree of authenticity of the passage and its correlation with ancient Near Eastern sources.

Yet those who so readily dispense with historico-literary criticism have not taken account of the substantial evidence for the legitimacy of the method and its conclusions.[8] Such evidence has long been known and can be found in works written in the previous century. Yet critics, for reasons that we shall see, preferred not to make use of this evidence, and as a result the opponents of biblical criticism were not required to deal with it. Recent attempts to undermine biblical criticism require that the method and the evidence for it be subjected to investigation. I would like to present one such piece of evidence for the historico-literary method, which I believe may be found in the account of the cities of refuge in Joshua 20.

Analysis of Joshua 20

The content of Joshua 20 is quite clear. God commands Joshua to appoint cities of refuge for unintentional manslayers, as he had already commanded Moses (vv. 1–3), and he details the procedures to be followed

5. Yeivin, "Additional Notes," pp. 183–87, esp. p. 186.

6. Compare the observation of Alter, p. 20.

7. This trend is reflected in the uncritical use of Chronicles as a reliable source for early monarchic times. Of course, one must be careful to avoid the alternative pitfall: blind acceptance of the verdicts of criticism without checking their accuracy for the passage under consideration.

8. Cf. Tigay, "Empirical Basis" [revised version above, Chapter 2—Ed.].

with such killers (vv. 4–6). Joshua fulfills the commandment: three cities are appointed on the west bank of the Jordan (v. 7), and three on the east bank (v. 8). A brief recapitulation concludes the passage (v. 9).

Joshua's actions are, as noted, the fulfillment of God's command to Moses. Here, however, a minor problem arises. We read about the cities of refuge both in Num. 35:9–34 and in Deut. 4:41–43 and 19:1–13. In Numbers we are told that all six cities are to be appointed simultaneously, after the crossing of the Jordan (35:10, 13, 14), while Deuteronomy tells us that Moses himself appointed the three cities east of the Jordan (4:41–43), leaving appointment of the three remaining cities to the conquerors of Canaan (19:1–7); a third triad of cities of refuge is to be appointed upon expansion of the borders of the land in the future (19:8–9).[9] Which of these two prescriptions is followed by Joshua 20? The LXX[B] version of Josh. 20:7–8 uses singular verbs: "he provided ... he assigned" (*diésteilen ... édōken*), indicating that the action is attributed to Joshua, in accordance with the account in Numbers 35. On the other hand, the Masoretic Text is indeterminate: "so they consecrated ... they assigned" (*wayyaqdîšû ... nātěnû*, pl.), which could be taken to imply that the action was half Joshua's (v. 7) and half Moses' (v. 8). The verse as it appears in the Masoretic Text is amenable to the prescription of either Numbers or Deuteronomy.

A more serious difficulty is encountered in considering the flow of verses 4–6. Verse 4 describes how the accidental manslayer states his case before the elders of the city of refuge and is admitted to the city, which implies that he is recognized as an accidental manslayer. But in verse 6 the manslayer is to live in the city "until he can stand trial before the assembly" (v. 6a$_2$). This means that his case has not yet been heard! Theoretically one might harmonize the two verses by saying that verse 4 describes a preliminary investigation, conducted quickly because of the manslayer's urgent need for immediate refuge, while verse 6a$_2$ is talking about a regular trial.[10] But this solution founders on verse 5; that verse, the direct continuation of verse 4, states: "They shall not hand the manslayer over to him [the blood

---

9. So, *y. Mak.* 2:7, pp. 31d–32a: "Moses set aside three cities in Transjordan. When they entered the land they set aside an additional three, and in the future they will set aside yet another three, as it is written: 'Three ... three ... three'—nine altogether." Cf. *t. Mak.* 3:10. We cannot go into the internal history of the laws of asylum in Deuteronomy at this point, but it is worth noting that both the law of Deut. 19:1–7, which commands the separation of cities as if it were a new issue, and the continuation in verses 8–9, which says that in the future three cities are to be added to the original three, know nothing of Deut. 4:41–43. The explanation given in *y. Makkot*, in which the total number of cities is nine, does not reflect the simple contextual meaning of these verses.

10. Note the remarks of Hertzberg, *Josua, Richter, Ruth*, p. 115; Kaufmann, *Joshua* (1959 ed.), p. 230; Kiel, *Joshua*, ad loc. For a slightly different interpretation, see Dinur, "The Religious Character of the Cities of Refuge," p. 140b.

avenger], since he [the manslayer] killed the other person without intent," indicating that the trial has already been conducted by the elders (v. 4) and the killing has been ruled accidental. What room is there for an additional trial before the assembly, as called for by verse 6a₂?

Verse 6 itself is also not without difficulties. It says: "He shall live in that city until he can stand trial before the assembly, until the death of the high priest who is in office at that time." The juxtaposition of the two clauses beginning with "until" (i.e., 6a₂ and 6a₃) is awkward. One expects a connecting sentence to the effect that when the manslayer stands trial, *if he is found by the assembly to have acted accidentally, he is to be admitted to the city of refuge and remain there* until the death of the high priest.[11] Lacking such a connective, we must say that these two clauses are contradictory: one clause has the manslayer live in the city of refuge until he can be tried (v. 6a₂), while the other has him live there "until the death of the high priest" (6a₃); only the latter reads smoothly after verses 4–5, according to which the manslayer already stood trial immediately upon his arrival. It is the former clause (v. 6a₂), calling for a redundant second trial, which brings verses 4–5 and 6 into conflict, as well as making verse 6 internally inconsistent.

Rather than attempt to reconcile these contradictions, historico-literary criticism takes its cue from them to infer that this passage is composed of materials written by two different authors. According to one of them, the manslayer stood trial before the city elders immediately upon his arrival. If his innocence was upheld, he resided in the city until the death of the high priest (vv. 4, 5, 6a₁, 6a₃, and 6b). The other author pictured the manslayer as residing in the city of refuge for some time before standing trial before the assembly (v. 6a₂). The collation of these two opinions in one passage led to the contradiction which we witness in our text.

The Authors of Joshua 20

In the next stage of inquiry, the critic attempts to identify these two authors. He tries to accomplish this through a stylistic and ideational comparison of the text under study with previously identified sources in the Hexateuch. In the case of Joshua 20 the task is simplified by the existence of detailed laws governing manslaughter and refuge in both Num. 35:9–34 (P) and in Deut. 4:41–43 and 19:1–13 (D). Such a comparison yields the following results:

---

11. See Kimḥi's comment in *MG* ad loc., esp. his conclusion: "The verse is elliptical"; cf. NJV.

1 "The Lord spoke to Joshua, saying." A formula typical of P; compare, e.g., Num. 35:9, and many others.[12]

2a "Speak to the Israelites, saying." Also a P formula, especially common after the previous introduction; compare, e.g., Lev. 4:2; 7:23, 29; 12:2; 23:24, 34, etc.

2b "Assign the cities of refuge—about which I commanded you through Moses." P; the term "city of refuge" appears only there (Num. 35:11, 12, 13, 14, 15, 26, 27 bis, 32). Also typical of P is the combination "assign (*tēn*) cities" (Num. 35:12, 13), while D prefers "set aside" (*tabdîl*) cities" (Deut. 4:41; 19:7).

3a "to which a manslayer who kills a person by mistake may flee." P; cf. Num. 35:11, 15, almost word-for-word the same as our passage. The phrase "by mistake" (*bišĕgāgâ*) does not appear in D.

"unintentionally." This term (*bibĕlî dā ͨat*) appears only in D, never in P. Cf. Deut. 4:42; 19:4.

3b "They shall serve you as a refuge from the avenger of blood." P; cf. Num. 35:12 and see above regarding the phrase "city of refuge."

4a "He shall flee to one of these cities." D; similar phrasing is found in Deut. 4:42; 19:5, 11, but not in Num. 35:9–34.

"present himself at the entrance to the city gate." D; The "entrance to the city gate" is found in Josh. 8:29 in the description of the conquest of Ai, which belongs to the Deuteronomistic history of the conquest. The Deuteronomistic character of that story is also supported by the details of the judgment carried out against the king of Ai: his being hung on a tree and buried at dusk, in accordance with Deut. 21:22–23.[13]

"and plead his case before the elders of that city." D; "city elders" as a judicial body play a role in Deut. 19:12; 21:3, 4, 6, 19–20; 22:15–18; 25:7–9. P, on the other hand, knows only of the "elders of the assembly" (Lev. 4:15).

4b "and they shall admit him (*wĕ ᵓāsĕpû ᵓōtô*) into the city (*hā ͨîrâ*)." This phrase does not appear in either Pentateuchal discussion of the cities of refuge. A similar phrase, however, may be found in Deut. 22:2, a commandment regarding one's temporary responsibility for a found article: "You shall bring it (*wa ᵓªsaptô*) into your house." The accidental manslayer is temporarily admitted into the city of refuge—a sign of D.

"and give him a place in which to live among them." This phrase is similarly lacking from the Pentateuchal sections treating of the

---

12. Cf. Carpenter and Harford-Battersby, *Composition*, p. 219.

13. For the dependency of Josh. 8:29 on Deuteronomy, see Seeligmann, "Aetiological Elements."

laws of the cities of refuge. However, the phrases "to live among them" (*wĕyāšab ᶜimmām*) and "they shall not hand the manslayer over (*yasgîrû*) to him" are reminiscent of the language used in another Deuteronomic law: "You shall not turn over (*tasgîr*) to his master a slave who seeks refuge with you from his master. He shall live with you (*ᶜimmĕkā yēšēb*) in any place he may choose . . ." (Deut. 23:16–17). Therefore this section may also be assigned to D.

5a   "Should the blood avenger pursue him." D; cf. Deut. 19:6. Such phrasing does not appear in P.

"they shall not hand the manslayer over to him." D; see above on verse 4b.

5b   "since he killed the other person without intent." D; cf. Deut. 4:42; 19:4. P, on the other hand, uses the term "by mistake" (*bišĕgāgâ*) and does not use the term "the other person" (*rēᶜēhû*, lit. "his friend") in this law.

"and had not been his enemy in the past." D; cf. Deut. 4:42; 19:4, 6; and also Deut. 19:11.

6   The style of this verse is difficult to categorize. While illustrating the limitations of stylistic comparisons, it might be instructive about the history of the formation of the section incorporating verses 4–6.

"He shall live (*wĕyāšab*) in that city." Closer to P; cf. Num. 35:25: "And the assembly shall restore him to the city of refuge to which he fled, and there he shall live (*wĕyāšab*) . . ." and 35:28: "For he must live (*yēšēb* inside his city of refuge. . . ." But no conclusions may be drawn from the use of such commonplace terminology. What is significant is that D speaks of the cities as *refuges*; only P regards them as places of *dwelling*, residence therein until a certain time being a requirement for which no compensatory payment may be made.[14]

"until he can stand trial before the assembly." P; cf. Num. 35:12. The trial before the assembly is also described in verse 25 there.

"until the death of the high priest who is in office at that time." While the death of the high priest as a date of release for the accidental manslayer is found only in P (Num. 35:25, 28, 32), the tag "who is in office at that time" for various future national officials is quite characteristic of D; cf. Deut. 17:9; 19:17; 26:3.

"Thereafter, the manslayer may go back to his home in his own town." Here too, comparison with the sources yields no clear-cut identification. In P: "The manslayer may return to his *landholding* (*ᵓereṣ ᵓᵃḥūzātô*, Num. 35:28)." This term is not employed arbitrarily; P stresses that the blood shed by the manslayer defiles the land (35:32–34). On the other hand, it is D which calls the point of departure of the

14. Cf. David, "Bestimmungen."

manslayer "his town" (Deut. 19:12), and the phrase "go back to his home" is used by D in the laws regarding those exempt from army service (Deut. 20:5–8).

"to the town from which he fled." This phrase gives no indication of its origin. As was noted, the term "town" as the point of departure of the manslayer is more characteristic of D.

7   "So they consecrated (*wayyaqdišû*). This term is nowhere else used of the cities of refuge. It seems an inappropriate term, given its usual biblical meaning,[15] even taking into account the scriptural propensity for paronomasia (*wayyaqdišû ʾet qedeš*).[16] The Septuagint translates with *diastellō*, which is used several times for the word *hibdîl*, including the law about the cities of refuge in Deut. 19:2, 7. However, it is also found as the translation of *wĕhiqrîtem* in P's version of this law in Num. 35:11. The Targum here gives *wĕzamînû*, which is used to translate the verb *qrh* in *hiphʿîl* in Gen. 24:12; 27:20; and Num. 35:11. It seems that the Septuagint and the Targum had a different reading before them in our verse, probably *wayyaqrû* or *wayyaqreh*, which corresponds to the term used by P in Num. 35:11.[17] A similar corruption, *qrh > qdh > qdš*, also occurred in Nehemiah.[18] The rest of the verse has no distinguishing features, but Kedesh, Shechem, and Hebron as cities of refuge are also found in the next chapter (Josh. 21:13, 21, 32), which stylistic and substantive considerations identify as belonging to P.

8   Even though in content this verse closely resembles Deut. 4:43, it also belongs to P, for stylistic reasons: use of the verb "to assign" (*ntn*) in the context of cities of refuge; the word *maṭṭeh* for tribe, rather than *šēbeṭ*; "across the Jordan, east of Jericho"; and the listing of these cities in Josh. 21:27, 36 (LXX), 38 (*BHS*; the verse is numbered as 36 in other editions, such as *MG* and Letteris).

9   The entire verse is couched in the style of P except for the expression *ʿārê hammûʿādâ*, a hapax legomenon. The Septuagint offers *hai póleis*

---

15. The verb *qdš* is applied to the following objects: the altar, the tabernacle and its utensils, the priestly offerings, and the head of the Nazirite. It is not applied to the Levitical cities or elsewhere to the cities of refuge. Only in Neh. 12:47 do people consecrate (*maqdišîm*) offerings to the Levites.

16. See Ehrlich, *Miqra ki-Pheschutô*, 2, ad loc.

17. Cf. Hollenberg, *Charakter*, ad loc.

18. Neh. 3:1 reads: "And they built the Sheep Gate, they consecrated it (*qiddĕšûhû*) and set up its doors." We do not elsewhere find consecration of the city boundaries during the biblical era. Indeed, regarding the Fish Gate and of the Old Gate it is said that "they laid its beams (*qērûhû*) and set up its doors" (vv. 3, 6). About the Fountain Gate it is said that "he built it and roofed it (*wîyṭalĕlennû*) and set up its doors" (v. 15). I am satisfied that in verse 1 *qērûhû* is to be read (twice): the *resh* was read as a *dalet*, and then a *shin* was added to the otherwise incomprehensible word.

hai epíklētoi. Seemingly *epíklētoi,* "called, named," is a translation not of *mûʿādâ* but of a word whose root is *qrʾ* or *qrh* mistaken for *qrʾ.* Since the law in Num. 35:11 begins with the word *wĕhiqrîtem,* and since this was the word used in verse 7 according to the Greek and Aramaic versions, it is plausible that the *Vorlage* of verse 9 read *ʾēlleh heʿārîm hammûqrôt,* "these are the cities provided," or the like. The fact that the Greek translator did not take this verb as a derivative of *qrh,* but rather translated as if he had before him the passive participle of *qrʾ,* frees him of the suspicion of having been influenced by Num. 35:11 or by the assumed text of Josh. 20:7. The upshot of this is that verse 9 too is deeply imprinted with the style of the P document.

This survey shows that verses 1–3 (except for the expression *bibĕlî dāʿat,* "unintentionally" in v. 3) and verses 7–9 bear the imprint of P. On the other hand, verses 4–5 are characteristically D. Regarding verse 6, the situation is complex. "Until he can stand trial before the assembly" is P. The rest of the verse is closer to the style of D, even though it is aware of P concepts, such as the date of the death of the high priest being a determining factor.

Therefore, the two authors whose writings compose this section may be identified with certainty. The author who thinks the manslayer should await trial by the assembly is of the Priestly school. Opposed to him stands the author who thinks the manslayer is to be judged by the elders of the city of refuge before entering the city and is to reside in the city until the death of the high priest; this author is a member of the Deuteronomistic school. It is also possible to say something about the relationship of each of these elements. The ground story came from P, as the P elements here add up to a complete story. D appears here merely as supplementing the existing P text, since the D elements neither add up to a complete story nor look as if they have been taken from one. D also may be seen as having known and borrowed from Numbers 35. The Deuteronomistic addition uses the date "until the death of the high priest," while adapting it by attaching to it the phrase "who is in office at that time."

What was the goal of the Deuteronomistic author in writing his additions to this Priestly passage? It seems that his intention was to clarify the question of who decides to admit the manslayer to the city of refuge. He would not assign this task to P's "assembly" (*ʿēdâ*), which was a pan-Israelite court (Josh. 20:6a₂ and 9, in accordance with Num. 35:12, 24, 25). As for the elders of the killer's home town, who are mentioned in Deut. 19:12, their action was limited to intentional homicide. Thus in the legislation of D nobody competent to decide on the admission of the accidental manslayer was mentioned. The Deuteronomistic writer in Joshua 20 filled in this lacuna by having the ostensibly accidental manslayer who sought admission to a city of refuge appear before the elders of *that* city at the city gate and explain his case. Once convinced of his innocence, the elders allow him to enter the city. This author, who quotes freely from the laws in D yet strives to complement them by his own reasoning, represents a late stage in the history of the Deuteronomistic school. He is also aware of the death of the high priest, a feature of P (Num. 35:25, 28, 32). Since he knows both D and P, he must be dated at a rather late period, toward the end of the period of the collation and closing of the canonical Torah.

The Septuagint of Joshua 20

This analysis, if presented to an audience of noncritics, is sure to arouse skepticism and disbelief. How is it possible to offer such a detailed breakdown of who wrote what when, down to the last word? And this while the whole argument is based on one small contradiction, which certainly could be harmonized with a little intelligent effort![19] But most important, is not the entire analysis grounded in a modern secular "Western" system of logic, whose principles of order and noncontradiction might be foreign to the biblical mind? How can one ignore the special nature of biblical literature, its sacred character and Oriental origins?

Here I will not attempt to deal with these general questions. Elsewhere, I have shown how the kind of difficulties to which the critic is sensitive were noticed and dealt with by a biblical author living in the Persian period.[20] This demonstrates that the basic principles of logic which animate modern critical studies were employed in biblical times as well.

Relevant to our case, however, is an ancient witness that confirms the correctness of the above analysis—the Septuagint, Codex Vaticanus (LXX[B]), of Joshua 20. Translated into English, the presumed Hebrew *Vorlage* of the Septuagint reads as follows:

[1]The Lord said to Joshua: [2]Speak to the Israelites: "Assign the cities of refuge— about which I commanded you through Moses—[3]a refuge to the manslayer who kills a person unintentionally; and the cities shall be to you a refuge; and the slayer shall not be put to death by the avenger of blood [6a2]until he can stand trial before the assembly." [7]And he provided Cades in Galilee in the Mount of Nephthali, and Sychem in the Mount of Ephraim, and the city of Arboc, this is Chebron, in the Mountain of Juda. [8]And beyond Jordan he assigned Bosor in the wilderness in the

---

19. Cf. the comments of Hertzberg, Kaufmann, and Kiel, cited in n. 10.

20. E.g., the reworking of 2 Samuel 24 by the author of 1 Chronicles 21, who worked before the composition of the book of Chronicles itself. See my comments in *Belief in Angels*, pp. 184–203.

plain, out of the tribe of Ruben, and Aremoth in Galaad out of the tribe of Gad, and Gaulon in the country of Basan out of the tribe of Manasse. [9]These were the cities provided for the Israelites, and for aliens residing among them, that every one who killed a person unintentionally should flee there, that he should not die by the hand of the blood avenger until he could stand trial by the assembly.

It is certainly difficult to reconstruct the exact Hebrew *Vorlage* of the Septuagint here. It seems almost certain, for reasons noted above, that in verse 7 *wayyaqreh*, "he provided," appeared in the *Vorlage* instead of *wayyaqdišû*, "they consecrated" of the Masoretic Text. Less definite is the reconstruction of verse 9 to read *he ʿārîm hammūqrôt*, "the cities provided," instead of *ʿārê hammû ʿādâ*, "the appointed cities," of the Masoretic Text. And it is impossible to guess what word was being translated in verse 3 by *phygadeutêrion*, which generally stands for *miqlāṭ*, "refuge." Does the use of this word indicate that a different text was read, or did the translator merely paraphrase "may flee there" (*lānûs šammâ*)? Similarly, the rest of verse 3 in the Septuagint: "And the cities shall be to you a refuge and the slayer shall not be put to death by the blood avenger" suggests that its *Vorlage* was longer than the Masoretic Text. Apparently the Deuteronomistic author of verses 4–6 deleted the original end of verse 3, replacing it with his own detailed description in verse 5.

Aside from these points, however, the glaring omission of verses 4, 5, and most of 6 in the Greek version can be explained in only one way. These verses were not translated because they did not appear in the Septuagint's *Vorlage*. It would be illogical to say that these verses were left out for exegetical-harmonistic reasons, that is, in order to avoid the contradiction in verses 4–6 noted above. If this were the motivation of the translator, he would have translated verses 4–6 as they appeared and omitted only the contradictory "until he can stand trial before the assembly" when he reached it in verse 6.[21] Furthermore, precisely those elements lacking in the Septuagint were the ones shown above to bear the Deuteronomistic stamp.[22] If we should say that the Greek translator, or the editor of his Hebrew *Vorlage*, intentionally omitted them, we would be forced to conclude that in third-century B.C.E. Alexandria the documentary hypothesis was applied in order to distinguish between P and D elements on stylistic grounds! As this is hardly conceivable, we must conclude that the section

21. Contra Dillmann, *Numeri, Deuteronomium, und Josua*, ad loc., and David, "Bestimmungen," p. 46.
22. This includes "He shall live there . . . until the death of the high priest who is in office at that time" in verse 6, since "who is in office at that time" betrays this author's affinity with the Deuteronomistic school (see the comment on v. 6, above). As we have noted, this author also knows of the Priestly law.

of the Masoretic Text not translated in the Septuagint was not omitted but was never present to begin with.[23] Thus, the conclusions drawn from application of historico-literary criticism are fully corroborated: the contradiction in the chapter resulted from the fusion of two sources. In this case D expanded a story originally written by P.[24]

That LXX[B] faithfully reflects the original P story is further corroborated by consideration of verses 7–8: "He provided . . . he assigned," in the singular; the subject is Joshua. This ties in well with the law of P in Num. 35:9–34, which states that the cities of refuge are to be assigned *after* entering the land. The Masoretic Text, on the other hand, which reads "They consecrated . . . they assigned," yields no definite subject, and so no specific time when the assignment was carried out. This accords well with Deut. 4:41–43, which has Moses play a role in choosing the cities of refuge. In this matter too, the Masoretic Text of Joshua 20 shows signs of the editorial work of a Deuteronomist.

The Septuagint has provided us with strong evidence in favor of the critical method as applied above. The concern with irregularities and contradictions is thus shown to be legitimate, as are the conclusions drawn from them regarding distinct legal and literary strata. Also confirmed are the use of stylistic features for the identification of the various schools of authorship represented in this passage, and the conclusion that the core of the story was written by the Priestly school, while Deuteronomistic writers are responsible for later additions.

Relevance for the Documentary Hypothesis

Does the Septuagint version of Joshua 20 prove the validity of the documentary hypothesis? In my opinion, only partially. It proves the validity of its methods: the examination of stylistic phenomena, especially vocabulary, in assigning biblical writers to various schools. In any event, the stylistic differences between P and D are borne out by this case. On the other

23. The suggestion that the Septuagint in many cases reflects a shorter and more original version of Joshua than the MT was raised by Holmes, *Joshua*; cf. my comments in "End of Joshua."

24. It is impossible to claim with certainty that *akousíōs* in verse 3 of the LXX reflects P's term "by mistake" (*bišĕgāgâ*) and not D's "unintentionally" (*bibĕlî dāᶜat*; see comment on v. 3). Usually this word translates *bišĕgāgâ*, but in Deut. 19:4 Codex Alexandrinus uses it for *bibĕlî daᶜat*. It is possible that the Greek translator used one word to render the two expressions, similar in meaning, in our verse 3; for this practice, see Tov, *Text-Critical*, pp. 85–86. Only in the light of conclusions drawn below may we maintain that here the Deuteronomistic term did not appear in the Septuagint *Vorlage*.

hand, evidence may not be had from Joshua 20 for the specific explanation offered by the documentary hypothesis regarding the formation of complex passages in biblical literature. According to the documentary hypothesis, there originally existed independent and discrete documents, which were gathered and assembled by a later editor. What we see in Joshua 20 reflects a different process. There was only one independent document, whose existence is witnessed by the Septuagint. The element identified as D in this chapter never was an independent document; it was merely an expansion of verse 3, intended to explain how the cities of refuge admit the accidental manslayer. In this respect, Joshua 20 actually supports the supplementary hypothesis, which prefers to see the formation of biblical literature as a gradual developmental process: layer on layer, stratum on stratum, continuing until the works reached their canonical form.

It could be that this is why biblical critics of the past century, despite their awareness of the evidence that could be adduced from Joshua 20, preferred to ignore it. Since most of them adhered to the documentary hypothesis, our case did not meet their needs.

Comparison of the versions of Joshua 20 provides support for the supplementary hypothesis from another angle as well. Reading the underlying Priestly story as preserved in the Septuagint, we find to our surprise that the sole purpose of the cities of refuge is to protect the accidental manslayer "from the blood avenger until he can stand trial before the assembly" (vv. 3, 6, 7). Only the later Deuteronomistic author knows of the second role of the cities of refuge—that of a place of detention for the manslayer beginning after the trial and ending with the death of the high priest, an enforced exile (*gālût*) as described in rabbinic literature. We must conclude that the ancient Priestly law of the cities of refuge, with which the author of the primary element of Joshua 20 was familiar, considered them to be only a haven for the manslayer awaiting trial. Indeed, if in light of this conclusion we examine the Priestly law in Num. 35:9–34, we find that only from verse 25 onward is detention in the cities of refuge mentioned. On the other hand, a concluding formula stylistically typical of P is found in verse 15: ". . . to the Israelites, and the resident aliens among them for refuge, so that anyone who kills a person unintentionally may flee there." It appears that the original law of the cities of refuge, in Num. 35:9–15, was expanded first by a series of distinctions between intentional and accidental manslaughter (vv. 16–24) and then by a law which changed the cities of refuge into cities of detention. In this respect, Joshua 20 makes an important contribution to the recognition of stages of development in the Priestly law.[25]

---

25. The consequences of this realization for the history of asylum in biblical law are of utmost importance, but they cannot be fully developed in this context. I plan to deal with the issue at another time.

Our case causes difficulties for the generally accepted Graf-Wellhausen school's dating of the Pentateuchal sources. According to this school, D was composed in the seventh century B.C.E., and in its wake the Deuteronomistic school flourished in the sixth century; P, on the other hand, was written at the end of the sixth century through the fifth century and brought the Torah to a close. Joshua 20, however, provides us with a different picture. It is the Deuteronomistic stratum which came latest, indeed, so late that it was not in the *Vorlage* of the Greek translator in the third century B.C.E. This does not mean that it was written after the Greek translation was done;[26] that would be an extreme conclusion. What can be deduced is that the Deuteronomistic stratum was composed too late to be introduced into all manuscripts, and therefore happened not to appear in the *Vorlage* of the Septuagint. We may posit that this stratum did not greatly predate the Greek translation, that is, that it was written sometime during the fourth century. This conclusion accords well with the date we suggested earlier on the basis of the examination of the content of the stratum. Thus, it appears that the Deuteronomistic school flourished for almost three hundred years, from the mid-seventh to the fourth centuries B.C.E. During part of this time, if not all of it, it coexisted with the Priestly school. The P and D schools with their output of various literary layers were to a certain extent contemporary. As we noted above, such a conclusion is not to the liking of those who assign P an absolutely later date than D.[27]

On the other hand, Joshua 20 provides evidence for a different trend in biblical scholarship, that of form criticism, which maintains that most of the various literary forms represented in the Bible were formed in different circles—those of singers, prophets, sages, priests, and others—in certain societal situations, preserve their discrete original forms, and may therefore be extracted from surrounding materials. There is a certain degree of arbitrariness in this assumption, for it chooses to ignore the fact that biblical literature was not a product of a primitive culture but rather the inheritor of a rich tradition of antecedent literatures, Canaanite and Israelite,[28] and as such the product of the influence and mutual enrichment of many creative circles over many generations. Yet the distinctions made by form criticism are borne out in the case of Joshua 20. Two forms may be discerned in our text: a descriptive legal text (vv. 1–3, 7–9) which tells of the fulfillment of a commandment from the Torah, and a prescriptive legal text (vv. 4–6). The prescriptive text seems somewhat out of place, because the introduction to the story includes a command to carry out a law *already*

26. As was opined by Wellhausen, *Composition* (4th ed.), p. 132; G. A. Cooke, *Joshua,* ad loc.

27. Compare the remarks made by Kuenen, *Historico-Critical Inquiry,* p. 131.

28. Cf. Cassuto, "Biblical and Canaanite Literature," in *Biblical and Oriental Studies,* 2:16–59.

given (v. 2: "about which I commanded you through Moses"). In form criticism this variance of forms would be used to isolate the individual elements of this passage, an approach that could be confirmed here by the textual evidence of the Septuagint.

Clarification of the literary form of any passage involves the identification of its aim. The aim of the author who inserted a legal dictum into the story is clear: he was a jurist trying to make a new legal point. As our examination of the content of the legal passage has shown, he wanted to stress that the accidental manslayer needed to stand trial before the elders of the city of refuge and after the trial the city was to become a place of detention for him. The author phrased his innovation in the familiar language of the sources, imitating ancient usage rather than writing in his own Second Commonwealth Hebrew; thus he was successful in hiding his origins and date.[29] The archaic appearance is enhanced by the use of the term "the elders of the city," which is characteristic of the most ancient strata of Deuteronomy.

The legal innovation of the Deuteronomistic writer should not be viewed as the beginning of Halachic legal activity, for two reasons. First, his innovation never caught on in the course of the development of Halacha. In rabbinic sources the manslayer is judged by a court of his own city, who bring him back from the city of refuge for this purpose (*m. Mak.* 2:6). The elders of the city of refuge play no role in the judicial proceedings,[30] and their only role is to qualify the city to be a place of refuge.[31] On the stylistic plane, Halacha does not attempt to imitate biblical diction. It uses contemporary language with its own distinctive terminology, unlike the epigonic author of Josh. 20:4–6. It is interesting to note that legal terminology attempting to imitate a biblical model does appear elsewhere from the middle of the Second Temple period on—in the book of Jubilees and in Qumran literature.

This, in my opinion, is the contribution made by biblical criticism to the understanding of this short passage. Historical criticism may detract from Joshua's legendary reputation as the leader who fulfilled the precepts of the

29. Phenomena such as these detract from the value of linguistic considerations in the dating of biblical passages. [Cf. pp. 40–41, comments accompanying n. 83.—Ed.]

30. Possibly the extension of the innovation of Josh. 20:4–6 is to be found in the statement of R. Judah Ha-Nasi in a *baraita* which reads: "Rabbi says: 'They would exile themselves, under the misconception that cities of refuge admit both accidental and willful manslayers; they know not that in case of accident they admit, but in case of willful (slaying) they do not admit" (*b. Mak.* 10b). I am indebted to Dr. David Rosenthal for exploring this passage with me.

31. "R. Eleazar said: 'A city, the majority of whose population are manslayers, does not admit (accidental manslayers), as it is written: "And plead *his* case before the elders of the city," not that his case and theirs be the same.' And R. Eleazar said: 'A city without elders does not admit, as elders are required, and here they are lacking, etc.'" (*b. Mak.* 10b).

Torah of Moses, or as a direct recipient of new Torah laws from God,[32] but it compensates by providing added insight into the spiritual and literary creativity of the Jewish community at the end of the Persian period. Through the critical method we have identified a legislator-author who examined a legal question and incorporated his opinion in the text of an ancient scroll.

Thus far we have concentrated in verses 4–6. Nothing has yet been said about the story comprising the balance of the chapter, which is its core, except to note its Priestly origin. I believe that we may be able to establish the date of authorship of this story, which determines its place in the history of biblical law. In order to achieve this dating, however, one should undertake a thorough examination of all the biblical laws of asylum, which is beyond the scope of this chapter. Suffice it to stress that there are two passages, one about the cities of refuge (Josh. 20) and one about the Levitical cities (Josh. 21:1–40), which portray Joshua as faithfully carrying out the laws of Numbers 35. Both these passages are located *after* the conclusion of the story of the distribution of the land (Josh. 19:49–51). They appear in the book as *additions*. An ancient scribe was aware of this incongruity; therefore, after the section dealing with the Levitical cities he added a second concluding passage, LXX Josh. 21:42a–c, based on MT Josh. 19:49–50. The secondary character of Josh. 20:1–21:40 suggests that their origin is rather late.[33] Those scholars who regard these chapters as ancient and reliable, reflecting the era of the conquest or the early monarchy[34] must deal with this fact.

The study of Joshua 20 involves the entire array of critical questions and methods: the composite nature of biblical texts, the identification of their components on the basis of the documentary hypothesis, the conflict between the documentary and supplementary hypothesis, gathering data in order to date a particular verse, application of form-critical analysis, the redaction-history of biblical books, and above all the decisive evidence provided by the Septuagint, wherein text criticism and higher criticism blend into each other. Although many of our conclusions differ from those reached by earlier critics, they validate the methods of source criticism. By following those methods we were able to reconstruct a process of literary development which is substantially confirmed by a comparison of the Septuagint and the Masoretic Text.

---

32. This portrait, already found in the biblical account of Joshua (e.g., Josh. 8:30–35), is the dominant one in rabbinic thought. See, e.g., *b. Erub.* 63b = *b. Sanh.* 44a–b, regarding Joshua who walks, or spends the night, in the depths of the Halacha.

33. See Rofé, "End of Joshua," pp. 34–35.

34. Cf. Kallai, *The Tribes of Israel*, pp. 379–403, with reference to earlier literature; Wright and Boling, *Joshua*, p. 473; Milgrom, "Sancta."

5

The Stylistic Criterion of Source Criticism in the Light of Ancient Near Eastern and Postbiblical Literature

JEFFREY H. TIGAY

Editor's Note

One of the main criteria used by source criticism in the analysis of a text is differences in vocabulary, formulas, and other aspects of style between different parts of the text. Harmonizers have argued that such differences are not the accidental by-product of the diversity of sources but the result of authors' choices, either to express different shades of meaning, to avoid monotony, or to achieve some other literary aim. Analogies from other literatures have been adduced to buttress this claim: texts of allegedly undisputed unity are said to display similar variation which no one would think of explaining by source criticism. We have already begun to see evidence that points in the opposite direction. In Chapter 2 some stylistic differences between the components of the Samaritan version in Exodus were

An earlier version of this chapter is scheduled for publication in *Isac Leo Seeligmann Volume*, non-Hebrew section, ed. Y. Zakovitch and A. Rofé (Jerusalem: Rubinstein, in press). Material from that version is reprinted here with permission. Parts of this chapter were also published in *EGE*, chapter 12, and are reprinted here with permission. Part of the research underlying this chapter was conducted at the Hebrew University during the academic year 1975–76 with the support of a fellowship from the American Council of Learned Societies and grants from the University of Pennsylvania and its Israel Exchange Program. All this aid is gratefully acknowledged.

noted, and in Chapter 4 consistent stylistic differences between the components of Joshua 20 were pointed out. In the present chapter, several further texts, including some of those cited by opponents of criticism, are shown to combine originally separate components and to display stylistic differences which correspond to the characteristics of their original sources. The survival of such differences depends on the degree to which the original wording of texts has remained untouched in the course of redaction and transmission. Even texts that have undergone considerable revision, however, still display some of the original differences between their components. Sometimes the differences are not consistent features of the larger literary works from which the sources of an episode are drawn but typify these works only in particular pericopes. In such cases those characteristics may help analyze a text into its components but not help identify the larger sources from which the components come. But even in such cases the analogues confirm that stylistic characteristics used judiciously in conjunction with each other or with other signs of compositeness are valid clues in source criticism.

•　　•　　•　　•

The Stylistic Criterion

In Chapters 1, 2, and 4, we referred a number of times to stylistic and vocabulary differences between the individual components of composite and conflate texts. Because of the utility of such differences in source criticism, this subject deserves further attention.

Although the most persuasive arguments in source criticism are those based on the presence of factual inconsistencies and doublets within a text, these—especially the first—are usually not pervasive enough to guide the analysis of an entire text. Most often it is the more pervasive clues of vocabulary, formulas, and style, often subsumed under the general rubric of "style," which serve as the main guide in analyzing any particular composition. Once the inconsistencies and duplications have provided the initial hint that a text is composite, the stylistic features associated with them are then identified throughout the rest of the text and assist in connecting the remaining verses with one or another of the doublets or inconsistent statements. Unless the stylistic phenomena are very distinctive (such as the differing names of God in Genesis or certain characteristics of P and D), they usually cannot stand by themselves as decisive evidence of compositeness.[1]

---

1. Noth, *Pentateuchal Traditions*, p. 21.

They must either be associated with inconsistencies or doublets or fall into clear patterns of distribution which cannot be explained plausibly as the result of an author's random variation of style (for example, in the flood story, *maḥâ* "blot out," and *kol hayyĕqûm*, "all existence," are regularly used in paragraphs where God is called YHWH [Gen. 6:7; 7:4], while *šiḥēt* / *hišḥît* "destroy," and *kol bāśār*, "all flesh," are regularly used where he is called *ʾelōhîm* [6:12, 13, 17, 19; 7:16; 8:17; 9:11, 15–17]).

Basic to the use of the stylistic criterion is the assumption that redactors whose works show stylistic unevenness did not freely rewrite their sources but strove to incorporate them essentially as they found them, making only such modifications as they considered necessary for their purposes.[2] Since the message a redactor wished to convey was usually not impaired by differences in vocabulary, formulas, and style, these were normally left untouched. It was the clue of differing divine names in Genesis which led to the pioneering analyses of Witter and Astruc, and Eichhorn put the documentary hypothesis on a solid footing by showing that each of the doublets in Genesis was marked off from its counterpart by distinctive terminology, formulas, and literary character.[3] These elements continue to play a central role in biblical source criticism to the present.[4]

Opponents of the documentary hypothesis have denied that such differences in style and content really point to divergent authorship. Instead, they argue, these differences either correspond to differences in subject matter or reflect subtle distinctions intentionally drawn by the author or intentional variation for the sake of avoiding monotony.[5] Some scholars have sought to buttress this argument with the claim that other ancient texts of unquestioned unity display similar differences, thereby ruling out multiple authorship as an explanation of the differences. Thus C. Gordon argued that the use of several names for the same character in one and the same Ugaritic text drastically weakened the use of variant names as a criterion for differences of authorship.[6] He argued further that differences in literary style in the same composition can also be found in Ugaritic and Akkadian sources and that these differences were due to changes of topic rather than disparate authorship. Thus the poetry of the prologue and epilogue of the *Laws of Hammurapi* alongside the prose of the laws showed

---

2. Moore, "Tatian's Diatessaron," p. 201 (below, p. 244).

3. Eichhorn, *Einleitung*, part 2, pp. 264–84, secs. 418–21.

4. Cf. Fretheim, "Source Criticism," *IDBS*, p. 839. For a recent example, cf. the comment of Weinfeld, *Deuteronomy*, p. vii end; contrast Rofé in *Qiryat Sefer* 48:875, col. 2 = *Christian News from Israel* 24:209.

5. See Cassuto, *Documentary Hypothesis*, as well as his commentaries on Genesis and Exodus; Martin, *Stylistic Criteria*.

6. Gordon, *Ugaritic Literature*, p. 6. In *HUCA* 26:97 Gordon added Greek evidence to the argument.

that the dichotomy of poetry and prose cannot be taken as a sign of divergent authorship in the book of Job, with its prose framework and poetic dialogues.[7] Gordon stated clearly the axiom from which this inference proceeded: "No one questions that Hammurabi's Code is a single composition."[8] This assumption, that with ancient Near Eastern compositions we have hit a sort of literary bedrock, was applied wholesale by K. A. Kitchen in his critique of the documentary hypothesis.[9] Kitchen held, as we noted in the Introduction, that "any attempt to apply the criteria of the documentary theorists to Ancient Oriental compositions that have known histories but exhibit the same literary phenomena results in manifest absurdities." What Kitchen means by "compositions that have known histories" usually refers to "monumental Near Eastern texts that had *no* prehistory of hands and redactors."[10] He cites several texts, mostly Egyptian stelas, which use two or more terms for the same thing, to prove his point.

Gordon's argument was not part of an onslaught against source criticism, as was Kitchen's, but rather a warning to apply its criteria in a more sophisticated way.[11] However, the arguments of both scholars have much in common, including the following points, to which we would take exception.

First, in singling out the stylistic criterion for discussion, Gordon and Kitchen write as if isolated vocabulary differences or stylistic differences *alone* normally guided the analysis of a text. As noted above, however, it is the conjunction of these differences with other criteria which is especially telling in source criticism. It is not the dichotomy of prose and poetry which leads scholars to posit that the framework and body of Job are from different hands, but primarily the inconsistencies between those two parts of the book; the stylistic difference plays merely a supporting role in the argument.[12] It is not the mere alternation of divine names and other synonyms which indicates that the biblical flood story is conflate; it is that so many incidents are related twice, that the doublets are sometimes inconsistent, and that the different divine names and other terms regularly line up with one or the other of the doublets—all these add up to a case for conflation. None of the texts adduced by Gordon and Kitchen displays such a combination of criteria (or at least none is shown by them to do so). Hence none is truly analogous to the biblical texts which critics consider

---

7. Gordon, *Ugaritic Literature*, p. 132.
8. Ibid., pp. 6–7.
9. Kitchen, *Ancient Orient*, pp. 112–29. The quotation which follows is from pp. 114–15 (italics in the original).
10. Ibid., p. 117 (italics in the original); similarly, pp. 121, 125, 126.
11. Gordon, *Ugaritic Literature*, p. 7.
12. See Pope, *Job*, pp. xxiii–xxiv.

composite, and none can serve as a control against which to test the methods of biblical criticism. Only texts that display such *combinations* of evidence can serve this purpose.

Second, most of the examples cited by Gordon and Kitchen are royal inscriptions, monuments, and epics, all of which are written in a poetic or quasi-poetic style, whereas the subject of Pentateuchal criticism is prose texts. Poetry, particularly parallelistic poetry, values variety of expression, especially multiple designations of the gods.[13] What Gordon and Kitchen infer from these texts—that compositions by single authors can use varied terminology—is both correct and beside the point, for what is normal and desirable in poetry does not demonstrate what we may expect in prose, even if biblical prose shares *some* features with poetry.[14] In poetry and in "elevated prose" the variant terms may appear in an order which is determined by poetic canons (e.g., A words precede B words),[15] but apart from that the distribution of the variants throughout a poetic text is usually random and independent of the distribution of other variants in the same text. This is not the phenomenon that confronts us in Pentateuchal criticism. In the Torah, as we have noted, the variants appear in consistent patterns in conjunction with other variants and other source-critical criteria. On this score too, then, the poetic texts cited by Gordon and Kitchen are not really analogous to the biblical texts in question.

Third, both Gordon and Kitchen share the assumption that the compositions they cite as analogues are unities whose texts cannot be subdivided into separate sources. Although each acknowledges in passing that any text may have "diverse antecedents"[16] or "sources of information and inspiration,"[17] neither of them really considers the possibility that his analogues have any *textual* prehistory.

That ancient Near Eastern compositions—at least those from Mesopotamia—do have textual prehistories is recognized by most scholars who have called for a comparative approach to biblical criticism (see the Introduction, pp. 7–10), and this is abundantly clear from the evolution of the *Gilgamesh Epic* (Chapter 1).[18] In the present chapter we shall review a

13. See Redford, *Joseph*, p. 111 and n. 1 there. The large number of designations for a deity that can appear in poetic texts is graphically illustrated in D. N. Freedman, *Pottery*, chap. 3, esp. the charts on pp. 127–29.

14. See Kugel, *Idea*, chap. 1.

15. See Boling, "'Synonymous' Parallelism," pp. 223–24, citing M. Held. The sequence of these words is less rigidly fixed in Hebrew than in Ugaritic (ibid.).

16. Gordon, *Ugaritic Literature*, p. 6.

17. Kitchen, *Ancient Orient*, p. 113; cf. p. 134.

18. There is little evidence available for reconstructing the evolution of the Ugaritic myths and epics, but given the likelihood that some of them are several centuries older than the fourteenth-thirteenth century copies found at Ras Shamra, the possibility of textual

number of compositions, including some cited by Gordon and Kitchen, where stylistic differences are demonstrably the result of the fusion of different sources and occur either in patterns or in conjunction with other signs of compositeness.

An Assyrian Royal Inscription

We begin with an Assyrian royal inscription (Ashurbanipal's *Prism A*) from which Kitchen drew one of his examples. Kitchen characterizes the example as the "free use of the practically synonymous terms" *rakbû*, "rider," and *mār-šipri*, "messenger," and cites this as an example of how a single author may use different words in his composition to describe the same thing.[19] Upon examination, however, the passage in question turns out not only to contain variant terms but to be a doublet. The text describes the dispatch of an envoy from Gyges, king of Lydia, as follows:

On the (very) day he (Gyges) had this dream, he sent his rider (*rakbû*) to inquire of my well-being.
Through his messenger (*mār-šipri*), he sent to relate to me the dream that he had.[20]

The passage tells of the sending of the envoy twice, each sentence describing the mission differently and using a different term for the envoy. Of course one might harmonize the two sentences as describing two aspects of the envoy's mission, though this would not explain why the verb "he sent" had to be repeated and the envoy mentioned a second time and with a different word (why not simply, "On the day he had this dream he sent his rider to inquire of my well-being and to relate to me the dream that he had"?). The harmonizer might credit this repetition to the quasi-poetic style of the inscription, or perhaps take the passage as referring to two separate envoys with different tasks. But in this case such explanations are undercut by the fact that the passage is demonstrably the result of the fusion of two earlier versions of the same episode. M. Cogan and H. Tadmor have studied the literary antecedents of this inscription and concluded that this passage was modeled on two earlier prisms (E_1 and E_2), both of which they have pieced together from fragments.[21] The first of

---

development must be reckoned with. The fact that a few passages are attested in different versions seems to substantiate such a process. See Rosenthal, "Parallelstellen"; Cassuto, *Goddess*, pp. 54, 101–6; de Moor, "Studies."

19. Kitchen, *Ancient Orient*, p. 124.
20. Cogan and Tadmor, "Gyges," p. 75.
21. Ibid.; see esp. pp. 68, 72, 74, 77–78.

these, E$_1$, relates how Gyges dispatched a rider to inquire of Ashurbanipal's well-being ([*rak*]*bûšu it*[. . .] *ana ša$^{?}$al šul*[*me*]*ya*), while E$_2$ (which is preserved only fragmentarily) refers to a messenger (LÚ A.[KIN] = *mār šipri*) and his assignment, "to see . . ." (*ana a-mar* [. . .]; perhaps restore [*pa-ni-ia*], i.e., "to see [my face]," "to visit [me]"). *Prism A* preserved (and perhaps partly reformulated) both versions of the mission, and in so doing created a *doublet* with *vocabulary variation*. These two features *together* would have led the source critic to suspect conflation here.

The *Laws of Hammurapi*

Our next example is the *Laws of Hammurapi*, a collection (not a "code") of laws appearing on a stele and several clay tablets of the reknowned Old Babylonian king (1792–1750).[22] The prologue to the laws, describing the events leading up to the gods' call of Hammurapi to be king and to establish justice, lists several of Hammurapi's achievements, culminating in his promulgation of the laws. Its style is poetic, as is that of the epilogue, in which Hammurapi calls on citizens who feel they have been wronged to consult his law stele and invokes curses on anybody who should change or remove his reliefs. The laws themselves are written in an academic, prosaic style.

Gordon argued, as we have seen, that "since no one questions that Hammurabi's Code is a single composition," the different syles do not reflect disparate authorship.[23] However, scholars have speculated about the possibly different backgrounds of the laws and most or all of the prologue, and the style of the prologue has played an important role in the speculation. The argument has not been based on style alone, but on a combination of style and content. In their study of the *Laws*, G. R. Driver and J. C. Miles noted that only a few passages in the prologue are directly relevant to the laws and that those passages are free of the archaic style of the rest of the prologue. The rest of the prologue contains archaisms and phrases drawn from Hammurapi's historical inscriptions. From this Driver and Miles concluded "that these portions of the prologue, which together constitute the bulk of it, were not entirely an original composition but a compilation consisting largely of matter common to Hammu-rabi's laudatory inscriptions."[24] This conjuncture did not require the inference that the

22. For opinions about the function of Hammurapi's and other kings' law collections, see the survey of Paul, *Studies*, pp. 23–26.
23. Gordon, *Ugaritic Literature*, p. 132.
24. Driver and Miles, *Babylonian Laws*, 1:40–41.

laws were originally published without the prologue. The point was rather that when the stela containing the laws was prepared, some of Hammurapi's own historical inscriptions were drawn on to provide material for the prologue.

The prefacing of the laws with a historical prologue describing the background of the ruler's reforms would have been in keeping with a literary tradition going all the way back to the "Reform Texts" of Urukagina of Lagash[25] (twenty-fourth century). But although the combination of laws and historical prologue was traditional, the specific content of the prologues was based on events in the reign of each king. It is theoretically possible than when royal scribes composed a king's law corpus, they simply incorporated *en bloc* an already existing historical inscription of that king, adding a few passages to emphasize his mandate to establish justice and to serve as a transition to the laws.

There is, in fact, some evidence for the separateness of the laws and the prologue, though not all scholars agree that this separateness is original. Although Hammurapi's stele and one Old Babylonian tablet copy of the *Laws*[26] contained both the prologue and the laws, at least one Old Babylonian copy lacked the prologue. This copy, of late Old Babylonian date, begins with the laws, and its colophon indicates that it was the first tablet of the text to which it belonged (the text is entitled ṣinda[*t Ḥammurapi*], "the decrees of Hammurapi").[27] From this fact J. J. Finkelstein inferred that "from an early date, perhaps contemporaneously with Hammurapi himself, the laws circulated as a text without the prologue."[28] A version of Hammurapi's laws without a prologue would not be anomalous. Several other cuneiform law collections, at least in the forms known to us, lacked prologues, and these apparently include the *Laws of Eshnunna*, which were earlier than the *Laws of Hammurapi*.[29] There is no hard evidence that the copy without a prologue reflects, despite its date, the earliest form of the *Laws*. This, however, was Finkelstein's conjecture:

[The prologue was] in all likelihood . . . an originally independent composition. It may be surmised that some time late in the reign of Hammurapi this separate royal

---

25. This was pointed out to me by Professor T. Jacobsen (letter of August 3, 1982), who stressed the similarities between the prologues to the *Laws of Hammurapi* (Meek, in *ANET*, pp. 164–65) and the *Laws of Lipit-Ishtar* (Kramer, in *ANET*, p. 159). See the detailed comparison by Paul, *Studies*, pp. 11–26.

26. Finkelstein, "Late Old Babylonian Copy," p. 48.

27. Ibid., p. 42.

28. Ibid.

29. See Paul, *Studies*, p. 11 n. 5. According to A. Goetze, the editor of the *Laws of Eshnunna*, "the 'preamble' contains in all probability little more than a date" (Goetze, *Laws*, p. 17).

hymn[30] was "fused" to the text of the laws proper as might be appropriate for monumental or display purposes, and that only henceforward did the entire composition enter the "canon" in its fullest form, under the title *inu Anum ṣirum* ["When august Anum"] (the first line of the prologue). But the text of the laws proper continued to circulate under more prosaic titles,

such as "The Decrees of Hammurapi" (*ṣimdat Hammurapi*) or "The Laws of Hammurapi" (*dīnāni ša Hammurapi*).[31]

The case is somewhat complicated by the discovery of an independent copy of a version of the historical inscription which constitutes the prologue.[32] This copy, from the Neo- or Late Babylonian period (first millennium B.C.E., probably the latter half), would seem at first blush to confirm the independence of the prologue, though one could argue that both this and the late Old Babylonian copy of the laws minus prologue were simply secondary, partial copies made for special purposes. The late copy is certainly not a reproduction of the version found on Hammurapi's stele; it differs from that version in a number of details, particularly in giving greater significance to the city of Nippur and the god Enlil than to Babylon and Marduk. R. Borger concluded that despite the lateness of this copy it reflects the oldest version of the prologue.[33] To Finkelstein these differences indicated that the late copy was "not just a variant text, but a text composed or adapted for a different time and place than the stela proper" and that "the 'prologue' was an adaptation of an already known Hammurapi hymn for the monumental purpose of the stela."[34]

If Finkelstein's conclusion is not inevitable,[35] it is not less plausible than the alternative that the *Laws* was originally issued with the prologue. Even

---

30. The historical inscription that constitutes the prologue is often described as a hymn because of its affinities with that genre; see Paul, *Studies*, p. 20.

31. Finkelstein, "Late Old Babylonian Copy," p. 42.

32. Wiseman, "Laws of Hammurapi Again." This copy includes those lines which Driver and Miles thought might have been composed to introduce the laws (ia, 27–49, and va, 14–24). Therefore, whatever else this copy may demonstrate, it cannot be used to support a conjecture that the prologue *minus* those passages was once an independent composition.

33. Borger, *BAL*, 2:7.

34. Finkelstein, "Late Old Babylonian Copy," p. 42 n. 5.

35. Cf. Hallo, "Cultic Setting," p. 121. In Hallo's view the originality of monuments as compared to related "canonical" texts (i.e., tablets transmitted in scribal schools) is the norm, rather than vice versa, and since Hammurapi's stele already contains the prologue, the combination of the prologue with the code would be original. This is not incompatible with Finkelstein's view. Hallo cites evidence suggesting that "even royal hymns seem to have originally graced stone steles, as was demonstrated for [another hymn of] Hammurapi by Sjöberg" (see Sjöberg, "Selbstpreis"); cf. Hallo, "Toward a History," p. 195 (the same is true of royal inscriptions). Nothing in Finkelstein's view rules out the possibility that the hymn on

this alternative would not rule out the suggestion of Driver and Miles that the prologue was modeled on or actually drew upon Hammurapi's earlier inscriptions. For the biblical critic, the discussion once again underlines the importance of considering the source criticism of ancient Near Eastern compositions without assuming that they represent texts with no prehistory of hands and redactors.

The *Sumerian King List*

A clearer case of the fusing of once independent compositions is the *Sumerian King List*.[36] In its fullest form, nearly four hundred lines long, this list contains two sections, a short introductory section listing the kings who ruled in southern Mesopotamia before the great flood, and a longer main section listing the kings who ruled after the flood.

Some copies of the list did not contain the antediluvian section.[37] T. Jacobsen and subsequent investigators have shown that this reflects the original form of the list, to which the antediluvian section was added secondarily.[38] Jacobsen showed this on the basis of the fullest manuscript of the list, WB 444. In this manuscript the antediluvian section displays a lexical-formulaic difference from the postdiluvian section. The postdiluvian section describes the changes of dynasties with the formula "City A was

---

the stele containing the code was adapted from another monumental hymn or historical inscription.

In the view of T. Jacobsen, the tradition of prefacing laws with a historical prologue indicates that the prologue was an integral part of the text, and that copies without it would have been for some secondary purpose. The differences between the prologue and the stele and the version on the LB/NB copy indicate that the former version was meant for the north of Hammurapi's realm (Sippar and Babylon), the latter, playing down Marduk, for the south (letter of August 3, 1982).

36. The text is translated by Jacobsen in *SKLJ* and by Oppenheim in *ANET*, pp. 265–66.

37. See Jacobsen, *SKLJ*, pp. 55–56; Kraus, "Zur Liste," p. 32; cf. Hallo, "Beginning and End," pp. 54–55. There are also three copies of the antediluvian section which were not attached to the main body of the list (WB 62, UCBC 9-1819 reverse, and Ni. 3195), but these all look like scribal exercise tablets or excerpts (see Jacobsen, *SKLJ*, p. 58; Kraus, "Zur Liste," p. 31; Finkelstein, "Antediluvian Kings," pp. 40–41, 45), and none was demonstrably based on a text consisting of only the antediluvian section. An unpublished tablet from Harmal contains both sections; see Finkelstein, "Antediluvian Kings," p. 45 n. 21. On the antediluvian kings, see now Lambert, "New Fragment," pp. 271–75. The tablet reconstituted by Lambert shows a longer change-of-dynasty formula than that restored by Jacobsen, *SKLJ*, p. 60 n. 113.

38. Jacobsen, *SKLJ*, pp. 55–64; Kraus, "Zur Liste," pp. 31–32; Finkelstein, "Antediluvian Kings"; Rowton, *JNES* 19:160–61.

smitten with weapons; its kingship was carried to city B."[39] The antediluvian section, on the other hand, uses the formula "City A was abandoned(?); its kingship was carried to city B."[40] From this difference Jacobsen reasoned as follows:

> The whole King List bears witness that its author was a man who was fond of formulas and used them with singular precision and consistency. It is inconceivable that a man of this type should have made the purposeless and totally unnecessary change from [one change-of-dynasty formula to another]. People with precise minds do not start before they have the exact formula to be used clearly in mind, and then they stick to it. They do not arbitrarily reject it when they get halfway, to evolve a different one. The existence of this change therefore points to a different hand.[41]

In this, Jacobsen's reasoning resembles that of biblical source critics[42]—but with this difference: he began with the fact that there are copies of the *Sumerian King List* which indeed lacked the section that he regards as secondary. This lends credibility to such reasoning even where the presumed original forms are not available.

Gilgamesh's Meeting with Utnapishtim

Our final cuneiform example comes from the *Gilgamesh Epic.*[43] In the eleventh tablet of the late Standard Babylonian version of this epic (ca. 1250; see Chapter 1, n. 81), Utnapishtim, the survivor of the flood, tells Gilgamesh of the deluge and the events that led to his own survival. Utnapishtim's narrative occupies 188 of the tablet's 307 lines, the rest of which describe Gilgamesh's encounter with Utnapishtim (continued from Tablet X) and his return journey to Uruk. There is no question about where the flood

---

39. (City) A^{ki} ^{giš}tukul ba-an-sìg nam-lugal-bi (city) B^{ki}-šè ba-túm; Jacobsen, *SKLJ*, pp. 29–30, 61.

40. City A^{ki} ba-šub-bé-en nam-lugal-bi (city) B^{ki}-šè ba-túm. The exact meaning of the verb šub here is problematic; see Jacobsen, *SKLJ*, pp. 61–62 n. 116; Finkelstein, "Antediluvian Kings," pp. 41–42; "abandoned" is the translation of Kramer, *Sumerians*, p. 328. This verb is also used in the antediluvian section of the Harmal fragment; see Finkelstein, "Antediluvian Kings," p. 42. The other manuscripts of this section use verbs which are used in the texts containing only the postdiluvian section; see ibid., and Kraus, p. 31 (ba-gul, "was destroyed," as in ms. Su₂); Lambert, "New Fragment," p. 273 (bala-bi ba-kúr, etc. "its term was altered, etc.", in partial agreement with mss. Ps and S). Perhaps these formulations represent secondary harmonizations of the antediluvian tradition to the postdiluvian.

41. See Jacobsen, *SKLJ*, pp. 62–63.

42. Cf. Carpenter and Harford-Battersby, *Hexateuch*, 2:125.

43. The epic was cited as an example by Gordon, *Ugaritic Literature*, pp. 6–7.

narrative in this tablet comes from. It is based on the *Atrahasis Epic*, which is attested in copies from the Old Babylonian period (first part of the second millennium B.C.E.) on. This epic narrated the early history of mankind from the events leading to man's creation down through the deluge and its aftermath.[44] That this is the source is clear from the following considerations: (1) In the *Atrahasis Epic* the flood is an integral part of the plot, and it was already part of that epic in the Old Babylonian period. In *Gilgamesh* the story is only incidental to the main theme and was apparently added to the epic only in its late version (see above, Chapter 1). (2) Certain lines in the two accounts are virtually identical, and they are therefore textually related. (3) In *Gilgamesh* XI, Utnapishtim opens his account with a list of gods and their offices which appears at the beginning of the Old Babylonian version of the *Atrahasis Epic*. The list is tailored to the events narrated at the beginning of *Atrahasis* but fits the flood story imperfectly; it clearly belongs originally to *Atrahasis*, not *Gilgamesh*. (4) Finally—and this is the giveaway—although the *Gilgamesh Epic* calls the survivor of the flood Utnapishtim, once it calls him Atrahasis (XI, 187), the name he bears throughout the *Atrahasis Epic*.[45]

While Utnapishtim's account of the flood is thus from the *Atrahasis Epic*, the rest of the Utnapishtim section (*GE* X, iv–vi and the rest of XI, that is, ll. 1–14 and 193–307) is from the hand of the writer who produced the late version of the *Gilgamesh Epic*. We thus have the advantage of knowing at the outset that the Utnapishtim section is composed of material from diverse hands, and we know which portions of the tablet come from each set of hands. A comparison of the flood account in *Gilgamesh* with that in *Atrahasis* can help show whether and to what extent the source (*Atrahasis*) retained its original features when incorporated in *Gilgamesh* or was modified in the process. A comparison of the flood section of *Gilgamesh* XI to the rest of the tablet (and the epic as a whole) can help show whether or to what extent such original features distinguish the incorporated material from its new context or were modified to harmonize the incorporated material with its new context.

We are partly handicapped in this endeavor by the likelihood that we do not have the version of *Atrahasis* which the editor of *Gilgamesh* drew on. The best-preserved version of the *Atrahasis* flood story is the Old Babylonian version. Since little more than scraps of its later versions remain, the Old Babylonian text must serve as the main basis of comparison with the *Gilgamesh* version. But enough is known of the later versions of *Atrahasis* to show that at least some details of the *Gilgamesh* version are based on them and are not the work of the editor of *Gilgamesh*. For

---

44. See Lambert-Millard.
45. See *EGE*, pp. 216–17, for details.

example, as we noted in Chapter 1, the formula for introducing direct speech in the flood section of *Gilgamesh* XI is found in late copies of the *Atrahasis* flood story, not earlier ones.[46] Not enough is known of the later versions of *Atrahasis* to characterize their relationship to *Gilgamesh* XI in detail. All that can be said at present is that some details of the *Gilgamesh* flood story are based on recensions or versions of *Atrahasis* which differ from the Old Babylonian version known to us.[47] We cannot confidently credit differences in the *Gilgamesh* flood story to an editor of *Gilgamesh* (instead of an editor of *Atrahasis*) unless there is a particular reason for doing so.

Keeping these reservations in mind, it is still likely that the editor of *Gilgamesh* did revise the text of the flood story to some extent. In the flood story the name of the survivor has been changed (except in l. 187) to Utnapishtim, the name by which he had been known throughout the *Gilgamesh Epic* since the Old Babylonian version (see Gilg. Me. iv, 6, 13; *GE* IX, i, 6; X, ii, 16; XI, 1–2, 8, 193–95, 202, etc.).[48] The fact that the flood story is told in the first person by Utnapishtim in *Gilgamesh*, unlike the third-person narrative in *Atrahasis*, fits the story into the plot of *Gilgamesh*, where Gilgamesh meets with Utnapishtim and hears the story from him firsthand in response to his inquiry about how Utnapishtim became immortal.[49] Since the sun-god Shamash had played no real role in the *Atrahasis* flood story but is an important character in *Gilgamesh*, his abrupt introduction in XI, 86[50] may be due to the editor of *Gilgamesh*. Unlike the *Atrahasis* version, which shows the reason for the gods' decision to bring the flood, *GE* XI gives none, apparently because this is irrelevant to its purpose of explaining how Utnapishtim became immortal.[51]

---

46. See ibid., pp. 217–18, for this and other examples, and see below, pp. 162–63.

47. Lambert-Millard, p. 15.

48. The Old Babylonian version apparently uses a slightly different form of the name, Utanaishtim (Gilg. Me. iv, 6, 13); this is often emended to Utanapishtim. The *Gilgamesh Epic*'s preference for this name is probably due to the fact that *napištim* (and perhaps *naʾištim*) means "life," the theme of *Gilgamesh*. See further, *EGE*, pp. 229–30.

49. This change of person is also found in a fragment of the flood story from Ras Shamra, where Atrahasis is the narrator (see Lambert-Millard, pp. 131–33; this fragment is probably not part of either *Atrahasis* or *Gilgamesh*; see *EGE*, p. 215 n. 5). The redactor of *Gilgamesh* XI did not necessarily have to rely on a precedent for so simple and appropriate a shift, but since *Gilgamesh* XI shares another detail with the Ras Shamra fragment (see *EGE*, p. 217 and n. 13), the latter could reflect a Mesopotamian text tradition lying behind the *Gilgamesh* version.

Whenever the shift to first person was made, however, a trace of the original third-person formulation remained in *GE* XI, 37. See Chapter 1, p. 47.

50. Noted by F. Böhl, *RLA* 3:370. In *Atrahasis*, Enki/Ea plays a role given here to Shamash (OB *Atr.* III, i, 36; *Atr.* W, 5).

51. Matouš, "Zur Neuern," p. 12. *Ar.Or.* 35:12.

On the stylistic level, *Gilgamesh* XI introduces two scenes with one of the *Gilgamesh Epic*'s frequent leitmotifs, "With the first glow of dawn" (*mimmû šēri ina namāri*, ll. 48, 96). Several episodes in *Gilgamesh* begin with this phrase,[52] which does not appear in *Atrahasis* and may in fact be unique to the *Gilgamesh Epic*.

In contrast to these changes whereby the flood account was apparently revised by the editor who incorporated it in the *Gilgamesh Epic*, a number of stylistic differences remain which reflect the flood story's original independence of *Gilgamesh*.

a. The first difference is lexical. In Utnapishtim's account of the flood, his wife is called his *sinništu*, literally "woman" (ll. 191, 194), while in the rest of the tablet she is termed his *marḫītu*, "spouse" (ll. 202, 205, 209, 258). Since both terms refer to the same woman in *Gilgamesh* XI and each is restricted to a separate component of the tablet, the differences clearly represent the vocabulary of the original components in this particular tablet. Unfortunately, all passages in *Atrahasis* which might have referred to the survivor's wife are missing, and we cannot document the inference that *sinništu* was taken from *Atrahasis*.[53] The *Akkadisches Handwörterbuch* does not cite examples of *sinništu* used with the meaning "wife" in other literary texts,[54] but it cites several examples from Neo-Assyrian nonliterary texts.[55] Since the examples are limited to first-millennium texts, we may infer that the word was taken into *Gilgamesh* XI from a late version of *Atrahasis*.

Although the flood and nonflood sections of *Gilgamesh* XI are thus distinguished from each other by the terms each prefers to use for wife, these preferences are only ad hoc; they are not parts of distinctive vocabularies consistently preferred by the larger sources (*Atrahasis* and *Gilgamesh*) from which these two sections, respectively, come. Within *GE* XI, *sinništu* is used for wife only in the section taken over from *Atrahasis*, but it also appears elsewhere in the late version of *Gilgamesh* in passages that obviously are not from *Atrahasis* (*GE* IX, ii, 13, 15). And although only *marḫītu* is used for wife in that part of *Gilgamesh* XI written by a writer of *Gilgamesh*, elsewhere the epic uses other terms for wife.[56]

b. The second difference, a formulaic one, was mentioned in Chapter 1. Outside the flood narrative, the Utnapishtim section (*GE* X, iv–vi, and Tablet XI) consistently uses a single formula for introducing speeches, "A

---

52. *GE* VIII, i, 1; ii, 23; iii, 8; v, 45; see, further, *EGE*, pp. 9 n. 25 and 231 n. 49.

53. In OB *Atr*. I, 276, 300 the word used for wife is *aššatu*.

54. The only other examples cited in *AHw*, p. 1047d, *sub* 5d, are from *GE* IX, ii, 13, 15.

55. *AHw*, p. 1047c, *sub* 4c.

56. *sinništu*, as noted; *ḫīrtu*, I, ii, 17, 28; *aššatu*, VI, 9; *marḫītu* is also used in Gilg. Me. iii, 13.

said to him/her, to B" (A *ana šâšu/šâšima izzakkar(a) ana* B). According to F. Sonneck, this formula is unique to *Gilgamesh*, but it is found in the Old Babylonian version as well as the late version.[57] In fact, it is used in the Old Babylonian forerunner of *Gilgamesh* X, which describes the events leading up to Gilgamesh's meeting with Utnapishtim.[58] It was therefore presumably taken over from the Old Babylonian version. In the flood narrative, on the other hand, a different formula is consistently used: "A opened his mouth to speak, saying to B" (A *pâšu īpušamma iqabbi izzakkara ana* B).[59] According to Sonneck, this particular formula is found only in late texts.[60] Here, then, we have two different formulas, each restricted to one of the component parts of the Utnapishtim section and clearly reflecting the vocabulary of the components in this pericope. In this case we have an added advantage in that the sources from which these formulas were taken over are preserved. Fragments of the late version of the flood section of *Atrahasis* employ the formula used in the flood section of *Gilgamesh* XI[61] (the parallel passages in the Old Babylonian version of *Atrahasis* use older formulas).[62] The formula used in the rest of *Gilgamesh* XI is the only one used in the Old Babylonian forerunner of the Utnapishtim section.[63]

In this case, too, some of the preferences are only ad hoc and do not extend throughout the larger sources from which these parts come. Although one of the formulas is unique to *Gilgamesh*, elsewhere in *Gilgamesh* one sometimes finds the formula which in Tablet XI is restricted to the flood story.[64] On the other hand, late *Atrahasis* texts sometimes use other formulas for introducing speeches, in one case even within the flood narrative.[65] Here too, then, the formulaic difference is restricted to the Utnapishtim section, and the formulas are not exclusive and characteristic features of the larger sources by which one could identify a particular source if and when it should appear elsewhere.

c. The third difference between the flood section and the rest of *GE* XI is stylistic in the broadest sense of the word, and in this case the difference is one of degree rather than kind. Repetitiousness and homogeneity of

---

57. *GE* XI, 1, 8, 202, 205, 209, 219, 222, 229, 234, 258, 263, 277, 302. Cf. Sonneck, "Einführung" p. 228 (no. 8).

58. *Gilg. Me.* i, 9; ii, 14; iv, 4, 7, 14; *Gilg. Mi.* iii, 2, 11; iv, 6.

59. *GE* XI, 36, 37, 174, 177.

60. Sonneck, "Einführung," pp. 227 (no. 3), 234.

61. *Atr.* S, ii, 8; iv, 21–22, 29–30 (different word order); U obv. 13–14; W, 11–12; x rev. ii, [1], 14, 44 (different word order).

62. OB *Atr.* III, vi, 11–12, 16–17; see Sonneck, "Einführung," 226–27 (no. 1).

63. See nn. 57 and 58.

64. E.g., *GE* I, iii, 1, 13.

65. Lambert-Millard, pp. 122–23, l. 4.

wording are well-known features of epic style.[66] Akkadian and Sumerian epics, like others, are filled with proposals and their execution, messages and their delivery, repeated speeches, identical introductions to successive episodes, and instructions conveyed through third parties followed by their transmission and execution, all repeated in virtually identical terms. The late version of *Gilgamesh*, far more than its Old Babylonian forerunner, is characterized by this kind of style. An outstanding case is found in the tenth tablet of the late version, which describes Gilgamesh's separate encounters with a barmaid, Utnapishtim's boatman, and finally Utnapishtim. The barmaid and Utnapishtim spot the approaching Gilgamesh from afar, and the thoughts of each are introduced in identical terms.[67] Although each encounter begins with unique actions and ends with unique advice, all three contain the same long dialogue in which Gilgamesh is presumably asked who he is (to judge from his answer in X, i, 31ff.) and why he appears so worn and sad, and in response he describes his achievements, his adventures with Enkidu, Enkidu's death, and his own fear of dying. In the first two encounters, Gilgamesh asks for directions to Utnapishtim in identical terms. The meeting with Gilgamesh's boatman includes instructions which Gilgamesh follows to the letter.[68]

When we come to Utnapishtim's account of the flood in Tablet XI, based on *Atrahasis*, this homogenized, repetitive style appears only sporadically and in short passages. The leitmotif "with the first glow of dawn" introduces two sections (XI, 48, 96), as do "when the seventh day arrived" (ll. 128, 145) and "as soon as (the deity so-and-so) arrived" (ll. 162, 170). Several passages have series of lines with identical beginnings and/or ends: "Three šar . . ." (ll. 65–67), "Whatever I had . . . I laded upon her" (ll. 80–83), "Mount Niṣir held the ship fast, allowing no motion; one day, a second day, Mount Niṣir (etc.)" (ll. 141–44), "The gods" (used as subject, ll. 159–61, with the same verb and object in two of the three lines), "instead of your bringing the deluge, would that . . . had risen up to diminish mankind" (ll. 183–86).[69] But the only sequence of identical actions identically described is the releasing of the birds (ll. 146–54), and only once is there a sequence of instruction followed by exact execution (ll. 86–90, 93, the stated time for boarding the ship, and Utnapishtim's doing so). Most telling, there is no coordination at all between Ea's instructions about the ship and its passengers and the actual building and loading (ll. 27–31, 50–85) and no

66. For Sumerian epics, see Kramer, "Sumerian Epic Literature," pp. 832–33; for Akkadian epics, see Hecker, *Untersuchungen*, esp. chap. 3; Cooper, "Symmetry" and "Gilgamesh"; *EGE*, pp. 100–103.

67. *GE* X, i, 10–12; iv, 12–14. The section that would have contained a similar passage about Urshanabi is missing. See, further, *EGE*, pp. 81–99, esp. 95–99.

68. *GE* X, iii, 40–46.

69. Note also the two cases of assimilation described in *EGE*, pp. 200–221.

descriptions of Utnapishtim's carrying out the ruse in which Ea instructed him (ll. 38–47). Only the last two lines of Ea's speech are later repeated, in the passage about boarding the ship (ll. 87, 90), but there they are spoken by Shamash, and not to the audience for whom they were originally intended (note the second-person plural dative suffix in l. 47 and its absence in ll. 87 and 90).

But as soon as the flood story is over, *GE* XI reverts to large-scale repetition and homogeneity of wording. Four examples appear in rapid succession: Utnapishtim's instructions to his wife to bake wafers and her compliance (ll. 211–14); the aging of the wafers and Utnapishtim's account of this to Gilgamesh (ll. 215–18, 225–28); Utnapishtim's instructions to Urshanabi and the latter's compliance (ll. 239–55); and the speeches of Utnapishtim's wife and Utnapishtim about a consolation prize for Gilgamesh (ll. 259–60, 264–65). Utnapishtim introduces his description of the rejuvenating plant with the same couplet with which he introduced the flood story: "I will reveal (to you), O Gilgamesh, a hidden matter, and a secret of the gods I will tell you" (ll. 9–10, 266–67). The nonflood portion of *GE* XI was thus written in the style characteristic of the late version of the *Gilgamesh Epic*, which rarely missed an opportunity to homogenize related passages,[70] while little was done to revise the flood story so that it would conform more completely to that style.

Here again the style displayed in the nonflood sections of *GE* XI cannot be said to be distinctive of *Gilgamesh* as against *Atrahasis* on the whole. *Atrahasis* is filled with repetition and homogenization. Only in its version of the flood, so far as we can tell, does this style appear but minimally. For example, its account of the building of the boat goes far beyond anything Atrahasis could have been told by Enki.[71] This kind of deviation from the normal homogenized style of *Atrahasis* is reflected in the minimal repetitiousness of the *Gilgamesh* flood story. But since this style is otherwise the rule in *Atrahasis*, one could not use repetition and homogenization for assigning other passages to the author of *Gilgamesh*, nor their absence for assigning other passages to the author of *Atrahasis*. Within *GE* XI, however, there is a clear quantitative divergence in the pursuit of this style, and along with the use of different words for wife and a different formula for introducing speeches, this is another indication that the flood account found in *GE* XI was not extensively revised when it was incorporated in the epic.

---

70. An exception is found in *GE* X, iv, 1–8, where there is no description of Gilgamesh's compliance with Urshanabi's instructions. In I, iii, 25–39, the hunter's compliance does not match his father's advice exactly (ll. 14–24). Note also *GE* I, vi, 16, in comparison with v, 39.

71. Although the text of the instructions and their execution is extensively damaged in the OB version, one can see that the latter (OB *Atr.* III, ii, and iii) is far longer than the former (OB *Atr.* III, i, 22–33). The later versions are also incomplete at these points.

It retained several features of its original style even though these differed from the style of its new locus in Gilgamesh.

Despite this, the flood story in *GE* XI displays verbal and thematic ties with the rest of Utnapishtim section which lend a degree of artistic unity to the tablet as a whole. Ea's command that Utnapishtim "seek life" (*šeʾi napšati*, XI, 25) echoes Gilgamesh's own quest and that which he attributes to Utnapishtim (*balāṭam šeʾû/buʾû/erēšu/saḫāru*, "seek/seek/ask for/pursue life," *GE* I, i, 39; XI, 7, 198, 203; *Gilg. Me.* i, 8; iii, 2), as well as Utnapishtim's own name ("He found(?) Life"). Utnapishtim's name is also echoed paronomastically in Enlil's angry complaint that "a life escaped" (*ūṣi napišti*, XI, 173). The theme of revealing the gods' secret to Utnapishtim (ll. 186–87) is echoed twice as the latter reveals secrets of the gods to Gilgamesh (ll. 9–10, 266–67). Twice crying is described with the formula "tears running down the side of his/my nose" (ll. 137, 291). Week-long sequences figure both in the flood account (ll. 127–29, 142–45) and in Gilgamesh's slumber afterward (ll. 199–208). Two of these items are already attested in pre-*Gilgamesh* flood accounts: the week-long duration of the flood in the Sumerian *Deluge* (l. 203) and the phrase *ūṣi napištim* in the Old Babylonian *Atrahasis* III, vi, 9. The other passages just cited from the *Gilgamesh* flood story are not attested in known texts of *Atrahasis* (the late version of the *Atrahasis* flood story survives, however, only in brief fragments). While this leaves open the possibility that these lines were composed by the editor of *Gilgamesh* for the very purpose of creating literary links between the components of Tablet XI, this does not seem to be the case. These links are mostly not verbatim,[72] whereas verbatim repetition of motifs and formulas is the hallmark of the late version of *Gilgamesh* outside the flood story.[73] The verbal and thematic links between the components of *Gilgamesh* XI seem to be due not to the free hand of the editor but to the vocabulary and motifs shared by many Akkadian epic texts, not just *Gilgamesh* and *Atrahasis*,[74] and to the fact that the flood story was relevant to *Gilgamesh* precisely because it shared a theme with *Gilgamesh* (seeking and obtaining life).

72. An exception is "tears running down the side of his/my nose," which is not so far attested outside of *Gilgamesh* and could therefore represent the editor conforming one of the passages to the other. Another exception is "with the first glow of dawn"; see above, n. 52.

73. Allowing for slight variation. See Hecker, *Untersuchungen*, pp. 157ff.

74. A number of the elements shared by both components of *GE* XI are also known elsewhere. On the "secret of the gods" (*pirišti ilāni*), see examples listed in *AHw*, p. 867b, c; on the seven-day motif, see *EGE*, p. 9 nn. 23, 24, and Tigay, *šabûaᶜ*, cols. 471–72; on *balāṭam šeʾû*, see the examples cited in *CAD* B, p. 48b; *AHw*, p. 1223d *sub* (11); on *ūṣi napištim*, cf. *šuṣû napišti*, etc., cited in *CAD* A₂, p. 375a. See also von Soden, "Hymnisch-epische Dialekt"; Hecker, *Untersuchungen*, chap. 6.

This is a situation which merits the attention of biblical scholars. Thematic and verbal links between parts of biblical pericopes have been cited as an argument for their original unity or at least their free recasting by the final editor/author. How, it is implicitly asked, could such marks of unity emerge from the "mechanical" combination of independent sources? The links between the components of *Gilgamesh* XI suggest a response to this challenge. Despite features unique to particular sources, either in individual pericopes or throughout these sources, biblical narratives still shared many common items of vocabulary,[75] style,[76] and motifs[77] which could appear in several versions of the same episode or in similar episodes. Given similar subject matter, two Israelite authors working independently of each other were quite likely to produce accounts that resembled each other to some extent. Similarities between the two creation stories in Genesis or between the stories about Moses' youth in Exodus 2[78] are therefore no more surprising and no more indicative of common authorship or free recasting than similarities between Genesis 2–3 and Psalm 104 or similarities between the framework of Job and both the patriarchal narratives and Ugaritic epics.[79]

To sum up the evidence of *GE* XI: three separate stylistic peculiarities join in distinguishing the flood story from the rest of the Utnapishtim pericope. Although two of these peculiarities do appear in other pericopes within *Gilgamesh*, outside the Utnapishtim pericope their use appears to be random. Only within the Utnapishtim pericope is there a consistent pattern in which all three peculiarities appear only in the flood story while their counterparts appear only in the nonflood section which precedes and follows it.

75. Note that J and E are similar enough as to be sometimes indistinguishable from each other (Gunkel, *Legends*, pp. 133–34). On the connections of Deuteronomic phraseology with that of earlier sources, see Weinfeld, *Deuteronomy*, p. i f. and, for details, his Appendix A. For random examples of vocabulary shared by two or more sources, see *BDB* s.v. *bll*, *gzl*, *ykl*, *krt*, *npš* (denominative verb), *ʿšh*, *rdp*, *šqh*.

76. See, e.g., the discussion of comments by Woods and Carpenter, below, pp. 171–72. Note also the use of alliteration in J (Gen. 2:22–23, 24; 3:22; 12:1–3; Exod. 15:9), P (Gen. 9:6), and H (Lev. 19:3–4, 9), and the use of chiasmus in J (names of characters in Gen. 3:9–17 and 4:1–5), in Gen. 14:13, 24, and in P (Gen. 1:27a; 7:11b; 9:6; for legal passages in P see Lund, *AJSL* 46:114–19).

77. Thus both J and P share the themes of matriarchal barrenness (Gen. 11:30, J; 16:1a, P), the eclipse of the eldest son by a younger son (25:23, J; 28:1–9, P; in E: 21:9–12) and measure-for-measure punishment (6:11–13, P; 11:4, 8, 9, J).

78. Cassuto, *From Adam*, pp. 59–61; idem, *Exodus*, p. 15.

79. The following words and phrases in Psalm 104 are paralleled in Genesis 2–3: *yašqû*, *mašqeh* (vv. 11, 13), *ḥayĕtô śādāy* (11), *ʿôp haššāmayim* (12), *maṣmîaḥ* . . . *ʿēśeb* (14), *ʿēśeb laʿăbōdat hāʾādām* (14), *yāṣartā* (26), *ʾel ʿăpārām yĕšûbûn* (29), *rûaḥ*, *ʾădāmâ* (30). For similarities between Job and both the patriarchal narratives and the Ugaritic epics, see Sarna, *JBL* 76:13–25; Tur-Sinai, *Job*, p. 5; Hurvitz, *HTR* 67:31 n. 50.

Conflation in Talmudic Literature

In Chapter 2 we noted that the juxtaposition of passages from Exodus
and Deuteronomy created certain vocabulary contrasts in the conflate passages of the Samaritan Pentateuch. The same phenomenon is observable in
Talmudic literature. Texts compiled from diverse sources still preserve the
original stylistic differences of those sources. This is due to the seriousness
with which the maxim "a man must quote in the very words of his teacher"
(*ʾādām ḥayyāb lômar bilĕšôn rabbô, m. Ed.* 1:3) was taken. When paragraphs in the Mishna incorporated the teachings of different authorities,
those authorities' original wording was often preserved faithfully even where
it resulted in inconsistent terminology within a paragraph. Indeed, this very
maxim is invoked in *m. Ed.* 1:3 to account for disparate terminology:

Hillel says: "One *hîn* of drawn water renders the immersion-pool unfit." ([The
biblical measure *hîn* is used instead of its normal Mishnaic equivalent, three *qabs*]
because a man must quote in the very words of his teacher.) And Shammai says:
"Nine *qabs*."[80]

The maxim here explains the Mishna's reluctance to rephrase Hillel's
statement in conformity with its standard terminology (that used by
Shammai) despite the resultant inconsistency. Starting from explicit cases
such as this one, J. N. Epstein argued that variant terms for the same thing
in successive clauses of the Mishna pointed to different sources (authorities)
even in cases where different authorities are not explicitly named. Examples
include the sequence *ᶜôśê zĕkûkît . . . zaggāgîn* for "glassmakers" (*m. Kelim*
8:9) and *kad . . . ḥābît* for "jug" (*m. B. Qam* 3:1, etc.).[81]

There is an interesting case of an accidental interpolation in the Mishna
which is distinguished by a unique lexical item. The opening sentence in
m. Taᶜan. 4:3 has long been recognized as a late interpolation in the text.
The sentence, beginning "the men of the lay division used to fast four days
a week (*šābûaᶜ*)," is absent from some manuscripts and from the Mishna of
the Palestinian Talmud.[82] J. Kafiḥ pointed out that the passage is actually
part of Maimonides' commentary on the Mishna and was accidentally
transferred from the Hebrew translation of the commentary into the Mishna
itself.[83] This is the only passage in literature of the Talmudic period where

---

80. See the commentary of S. Adeni, *mĕleʾket šĕlōmōh*, ad loc.
81. Epstein, *Prolegomena*, pp. 234–40. The examples cited here are discussed in ibid.,
pp. 236–38. While the conclusion is plausible, Epstein's argumentation in these two cases is
hard to follow.
82. See Albeck, *Šiššâ*, pp. 341–42; Malter, *Taanit*, p. 121 n. on l. 2.
83. Kafiḥ, *Sēder Môᶜēd*, p. 225. This error was facilitated by the format of the commentary: each paragraph of the Mishna was followed directly by Maimonides' comment (see

the Sabbatical week is called *šābûa*^c, a usage found otherwise only in post-Talmudic literature (including Maimonides[84]). Elsewhere in Talmudic literature (including the same chapter of the Mishna, *Ta^can.* 4:7) the term for Sabbatical week is *šabbāt*.[85]

At the other extreme, an entire tractate in the Palestinian Talmud, Tractate *Nĕzîqîn*, has been shown by S. Lieberman to have been edited independently of the rest of the Palestinian Talmud.[86] Whereas the rest of the Palestinian Talmud was edited in Tiberias, Lieberman showed that Tractate *Nĕzîqîn* differs from it in content, style, and terminology (e.g., *māhû*, "how is it?" vs. *hêk ^căbîdā*^ɔ "how would (such a case) happen?") and, most important, in the names of its dominant amoraim, who were located in Caesaria. The unique style and terminology of this tractate are a function of its different provenance.

Supplementation in Talmudic and Related Literature

Apart from the examples examined thus far, which are based on texts that a redactor pieced together by combining preexistent materials, vocabulary differences also appear in texts where later hands have supplemented a text with new matter. In Chapter 4, A. Rofé argued that the Masoretic Text of Joshua 20 consists of a base-text written in the language of P and a series of supplements (absent in the Septuagint) written in Deuteronomic language. The same phenomenon can be illustrated in other texts. We have already had occasion to refer to the *Passover Haggadah* and the views of Rab and Samuel on how to begin the narrative (above, Chapter 2, pp. 84–85). The text of Samuel's version which was fixed in the Middle Ages begins:

We were pharaoh's slaves in Egypt, and the Lord our God brought us forth from there with a mighty hand and an outstretched arm. And if the Holy One, blessed be He, had not brought our forefathers forth from Egypt, then we, our children, and our children's children would still be enslaved to Pharaoh in Egypt.[87]

Maimonides' introduction, trans. by Kafiḥ, *Sēder Zĕrā^cîm*, p. 26). Other examples of such errors are cited by Epstein, *Prolegomena*, pp. 1275–76.

84. See Maimonides' letter to R. Samuel ibn Tibbon (Sonne, "Maimonides' Letter," p. 332) and, further, Tigay, "Jewish Week," p. 114* n. 27.

85. See Tigay, "Jewish Week," pp. 112*–15*.

86. S. Lieberman, *The Talmud of Caesaria*; idem, *Siphre Zutta*, pp. 125–36. For a brief English summary of the argument, see Rabinowitz, "Talmud, Jerusalem," col. 773.

87. Glatzer, *Haggadah*, p. 22. For variants, insignificant for present purposes, see Kasher, *Hagadah*, pp. 13–14, 100. The complex history of the growth of the *Haggadah* is graphically illustrated in the polychrome edition of J. Freedman, *Polychrome* (our passage is cited in p. 24). For discussion, see Kasher, *Hagadah*, and E. D. Goldschmidt, *Haggadah*.

The first sentence is an inexact citation of Deut. 6:21; the second is part of a supplement to the text from an uncertain date in the Talmudic or Geonic period. The biblical statement refers to God as "YHWH our God," while the rabbinic supplement uses the exclusively postbiblical "the Holy one, blessed be He." The biblical statement speaks of slaves ($^c\bar{a}b\bar{a}d\hat{\imath}m$), while the second uses the exclusively postbiblical $m\check{e}\check{s}\hat{u}^cb\bar{a}d\hat{\imath}n$, "enslaved."

The redaction criticism of the Babylonian Talmud also employs stylistic indicators among its criteria for identifying later additions to the statements of early sages or to the text of the Talmud itself. These criteria include verbosity, distinctive vocabulary, and post-Talmudic linguistic forms.[88] S. Friedman points out that elements identified as late on the basis of such criteria are sometimes actually absent in manuscripts.[89]

Ad Hoc Differences and Systematic Differences

In the discussion above we have observed texts (*Gilgamesh* XI and the Samaritan version of Exodus 18) in which stylistic differences between sources were only ad hoc. They applied only within the pericopes under discussion but did not constitute unique differences that could be used to identify those sources wherever else they might appear. Such cases provide a reminder of something which is often overlooked. From the vocabulary lists published in handbooks of Pentateuchal criticism, one often gets the impression—not always intended—that the vocabulary said to be typical of the individual sources is exclusive to them and an unfailing indication of the source of a passage in which it appears. The examples just mentioned of ad hoc characteristics remind us that this need not always be so, and an examination of some specimens of Pentateuchal source criticism shows how such an assumption can sometimes seem arbitrary. R. Pfeiffer stated that in Num. 10:33 and 14:44 the word *běrît*, "of the covenant," was added after $^{\cdot a}r\hat{o}n$, "ark," by a Deuteronomic redactor ("R^D").[90] Presumably Pfeiffer based this statement on observations such as that in *BDB* that $^{\cdot a}r\hat{o}n$ is combined with *běrît* largely in D or passages under D's influence.[91] Earlier critics had been more cautious on this phrase. Thus S. R. Driver, while recognizing the frequency of this designation in Deuteronomic passages, held open the possibility that "in view of Num. 10:33; 14:44, it

---

88. S. Friedman, *Critical Study*, pp. 303–5, nos. 4, 8, 9.
89. Ibid., p. 308.
90. Pfeiffer, *Introduction*, p. 285.
91. *BDB*, p. 75, s.v. ʾrwn, 3–4; cf. S. R. Driver, *Deuteronomy*, pp. 122–24. For lists of supposed Deuteronomic modifications in the earlier books of the Pentateuch, see idem, *Exodus*, p. xviii; Woods, "Hexateuch," p. 367.

[might] be too much to maintain that it actually originated with [Deut.]"
and listed *bĕrît* among Deuteronomic words which may have been suggested
to the author by JE.[92] In M. Weinfeld's study of Deuteronomy, identification of the Ark as "the Ark of the Covenant" is not mentioned as part of
the Deuteronomic phraseology at all, presumably a result of Weinfeld's
methodological position:

> The main characteristic of deuteronomic phraseology is not the employment of new
> idioms and expressions, because many of these could be found in the earlier sources
> and especially in the Elohistic source. Indeed, it would be nonsense to say that all of
> a sudden in the seventh century a new vocabulary and new expressions were
> created. Language grows in an organic and natural way and is not created
> artificially. . . . What makes a phrase deuteronomic is not its mere occurrence in
> Deuteronomy, but its meaning within the framework of deuteronomic theology.
> Neutral phrases . . . although they occur in Deuteronomy very frequently, are part
> and parcel of the common Hebrew vocabulary and cannot be considered specifically
> deuteronomic phrases. . . . In no case can the occurrence of such phrases be used as
> evidence of deuteronomic origin. Only those recurrent phrases that express the
> essence of the theology of Deuteronomy can be considered "deuteronomic."[93]

Another example stems from a well-known feature of P's style, its "tendency to symmetry and similarity of phraseology in describing similar
events."[94] Carpenter described this characteristic thus: "Every description is
precise, and when once the proper form of words has been selected, it is
unfailingly reproduced on the next occasion."[95] From this general characteristic critics have inferred that in Gen. 6:7 and 7:23—verses which on the
whole belong to J—the *lists* of animals (to be) destroyed in the flood must
be redactorial interpolations in the style of P.[96] In fact, however, R. Busis
has shown that within the flood story the lists of animals appearing in J
passages are relatively more uniform than those appearing in P[97] and that
in the case of these lists Carpenter's description could be applied to J's style

---

92. S. R. Driver, *Deuteronomy*, pp. 122–24, lxxviii–lxxix, no. 8; cf. *BDB*, p. 75, s.v.
ʾrwn, 3–4.
93. Weinfeld, *Deuteronomy*, pp. 1–3.
94. Woods, "Hexateuch," p. 369.
95. Carpenter and Harford-Battersby, *Hexateuch*, 2:125.
96. E.g., Skinner, *Genesis*, pp. 151, 154–55; Gunkel, *Genesis*, pp. 61, 63.
97. J: Gen. 6:7; 7:23 (animals destroyed by flood); 7:2–3; 7:8 (animals taken aboard ark);
8:20 (animals sacrificed); P: 6:20; 7:14 (animals taken aboard ark); 7:21 (animals destroyed by
flood); 8:1 (animals on ark); 8:17, 19; 9:10 (animals that exit ark). My comments on the
analysis of the flood story are based on an unpublished seminar paper written by my student,
Richard Busis, in 1977.

with greater ease than to that of P.[98] In other words, what is typical of P's style elsewhere is in this case absent from P and in fact characteristic of J. The stylistic argument for the influence of P in Gen. 6:7 and 7:23 is thus undermined.

Our discussion thus amounts to only a partial endorsement of the stylistic criterion of source criticism. It shows that vocabulary, formulaic, and stylistic contrasts within a single context do sometimes result from the combination of once separate elements, each bearing its own characteristics, and can help disentangle the components of that context. But in some of these cases the contrasts are limited to a single context and do not extend to other contexts. This implies that some authors did not strive for unvarying consistency of style and expression throughout their work and that when the works of two such authors are combined we would not be able to use the contrasts in any single context to identify the larger works from which the components of that context were drawn. It remains to be seen whether and to what extent this is true of the Pentateuchal sources. If it is true to any extent, it could help us understand why the stylistic criteria by themselves were never enough to make possible a complete source analysis of the Torah.

The examples we have reviewed also bear on the attitudes of redactors toward the wording of their sources. That there were redactors who showed great deference toward their sources, as presumed by Pentateuchal criticism, is clear from the Samaritan Pentateuch, in which we can also see the unevenness that results from such deference (see Chapter 2). Such deference is especially prevalent among Jewish and Christian (e.g., Tatian) redactors of sacred texts. But other redactors, such as the successive redactors of the *Gilgamesh Epic*, showed a greater willingness to revise the wording of their sources, and thereby produced smoother compositions. Clearly, different redactors had different aims and different attitudes toward their source material, and even the same redactor may have varied his practice in different places.[99] As we noted at the end of Chapter 1, the unevenness within the Torah shows its redactors to have been largely of the first type. But even redactors who revised their sources extensively left some traces of the original wording, and where those traces occur in telltale combinations with each other or in association with other signs of compositeness, they can help guide the critic in identifying the components.[100]

---

98. Busis (see n. 97, above) also notes that no P verse can serve as an exact model for 6:7 and 7:23; in the flood story the three types of animal mentioned in these verses are never mentioned alone, in the same order or language, in P.

99. As is clear from Longstaff's discussion of Tatian; see, T.R.W. Longstaff, *Evidence*, pp. 10–42.

100. An example of "stylistic" and vocabulary differences resulting from conflation appears in the Greek translation of 1 Samuel 17–18 as it is presented in LXX[A]. As Tov notes, this

manuscript supplies a translation of the passages absent from the OG version contained in LXX^B, but the vocabulary of the additional verses is distinct from that used in the verses present in LXX^B (see above, Chapter 3, n. 2, and the examples cited by Driver, *Notes*, p. 140, and Wellhausen, *Text*, p. 104).

6

Assimilation in Biblical Narratives

YAIR ZAKOVITCH

Editor's Note

A noteworthy feature of biblical literature is the recurrence of strikingly similar stories about a single individual or different individuals. While it should not be forgotten that experiences do repeat themselves in the lives of individuals and nations,* the nature of the similarities between certain biblical narratives suggests a literary relationship between them. Usually it is suggested that a single event came to be described in different ways by different circles of traditionists, thus producing doublets of the sort we have seen in Chapters 2 and 3.† In a smaller number of cases, however, the reverse is presumed: two separate but *somewhat* similar events have come to resemble each other more in the course of transmission.‡ In the present chapter Yair Zakovitch shows that such assimilation has demonstrably taken place in secondary versions of certain biblical traditions, as shown by readings in extrabiblical paraphrases and allusions, in ancient translations and manuscripts of the Bible, and in later biblical retellings of earlier

---

* The story of the discovery of the Dead Sea Scrolls in 1947 is remarkably similar to the report about a nearly identical discovery in the eighth century; see Yadin, *Message*, pp. 22, 75–77. Note also the uncanny similarities between the circumstances surrounding the assassinations of Abraham Lincoln and John F. Kennedy (Duncan, *Strange but True*, pp. 45–47; ref. courtesy of Eytan and Hillel Tigay).

† See Stanton, "Gospels," p. 249.

‡ See, e.g., Moore, *Judges*, pp. 417–18, and Kaufmann, *Judges*, p. 281, on Judges 19 and Genesis 19; cf. also the works cited by Ishida, *Royal Dynasties*, p. 37 n. 58, p. 44 n. 99, and p. 60 n. 25.

stories.** At times the secondary, assimilating material is not entirely consistent with the original material, and editors try, with differing degrees of
success, to deal with this problem. On the strength of these documented
cases of assimilation, Zakovitch suggests that several other passages in the
Bible contain elements due to this phenomenon.

** For cases of assimilation in cuneiform literature, see *EGE*, pp. 81–103, 107, 128, 170–74.

•   •   •   •

The Phenomenon of Assimilation

When certain characters play similar roles in the history and culture of
a nation or undergo similar experiences, it sometimes happens that traditions about them become assimilated to each other. Literary motifs may
migrate from one character to another. Thus we find similar stories told
about Abraham and his son Isaac (the wife-sister stories, Gen. 12:10–20; 20;
26:1–11) and about the prophets Elijah and Elisha (e.g., the story of the
resurrection of a child, 1 Kings 17:17–24; 2 Kings 4:8–37). An affinity
is also found between the Moses and Elijah stories (compare the two
theophanies at Horeb, Exod. 33:17–23 and its parallel in 1 Kings 19), as
well as between the Moses and Joshua stories (e.g., Exod. 3:5; Josh. 5:15).
The similarity between parallel traditions may cover a whole story, as in
the first two examples mentioned above, or be limited to a segment of a
story, as in the second two examples. In each case we may ask whether the
similarity is the result of the influence of one tradition on the other and, if
so, which borrowed from the other.[1] However, sometimes we cannot speak
of borrowing, but rather of a similarity that was present in both stories
from the outset and derived ultimately from a common source, the treasury
of motifs from the well-known folk tradition. These different possibilities
are not mutually exclusive. At times we find an original similarity which
has been secondarily augmented with borrowed motifs. Such a phenomenon
may be termed *assimilation*. It arises when a traditionist or editor increases
the affinity of stories already similar in themselves by adding to one of
them material borrowed from the parallel tradition or composed by him
under the influence of the parallel tradition.
In this chapter we deal with this phenomenon of assimilation. To demonstrate the existence of assimilation, we begin with cases that can be documented because we have texts of both the earlier, less similar versions and

1. The chronological order of a character's appearance on the stage of history has no
bearing on the consideration of the direction of influence. *Stories* about Elisha, for example,
may be older than those dealing with Elijah, or vice versa.

the later, assimilated versions. These examples are drawn from biblical stories that were assimilated in later, *extrabiblical paraphrases* of the traditions and allusions to them, and from cases where assimilating details have been added in *ancient translations* of the Bible, in biblical *manuscripts*, and in *stories told twice* in the Bible itself (in the Former Prophets and Chronicles or elsewhere), in which the later version was made more similar to another, parallel biblical story. (Although we follow these four headings for simplicity, these stages are not watertight, since some cases of assimilation took place in more than one stage of the same tradition.) Finally, once the existence of assimilation has been demonstrated, we turn to certain problematic texts in the Bible in which we suggest that the present form of the text is the result of assimilation, and where, by the methods of biblical literary criticism, we seek to reconstruct the original form of a story which preceded its assimilation to another, partly similar, biblical story.

Assimilation in Extrabiblical Paraphrases

One of the hallmarks of rabbinic exegesis was its attentiveness to similarity of details between different passages, a sensitivity which was formalized in the recognition of inference from analogy (*gĕzērâ šāwâ*) as a hermeneutic method. The treatment of a detail in the story of Samuel illustrates nicely how such attentiveness on the part of other readers of the Bible contributed to assimilation. In 1 Sam. 1:11, Hannah had sworn to dedicate the son she prayed for to the Lord for life, adding that "no razor shall touch his head" (*ûmôrâ lō' yaᵃleh ᶜal rō'šô*). No explanation for this detail is given in the Masoretic Text of Samuel, but the similarity to the story of Samson is obvious. There the angel had told Samson's mother that "no razor shall touch his head (*ûmôrâ lō' yaᵃleh ᶜal rō'šô*), for the boy shall be a nazirite to God from the womb on" (Judg. 13:5; cf. the nazirite rules in Num. 6:5). The identical detail in the regimens prescribed for Samuel and Samson (the word *môrâ*, "razor," appears only in these two stories in the Bible) led the late-second-century sage R. Nehorai to conclude that "just as the reference to the razor in connection with Samson means (that he was to be) a nazirite, so does the reference to a razor in connection with Samuel mean (that he was to be) a nazirite" (*m. Nazir* 9:5). The reasoning stated explicitly in the Mishna is clearly implicit in Ben Sira's description of Samuel as "a nazirite of YHWH in the prophetical office" (Ecclus. 46:23), as well as in the LXX translation of 1 Sam. 1:11, which adds yet another nazirite prohibition before the promise that no razor would touch Samuel's head: "he shall drink no wine or strong drink" (*kaì oînon kaì méthysma ou píetai*; cf. Num. 6:3; Judg. 13:4, 7, 14). Finally, the recognition of Samuel's nazirite dedication penetrated the Hebrew text in a manuscript of Samuel from Qumran (4QSam^a), which adds at the end of 1 Sam. 1:22: "[and I shall de]dicate him as a nazirite forever, all the days of [his life] ([*wnt*]*tyhw nzyr* ^{c}*d* ^{c}*wlm kl ymy* [*hyyw*])."[2]

Another example of assimilation in an extrabiblical paraphrase is found in Josephus's account of Manoah's sacrifice to the angel who foretold the birth of Samson (Judg. 13:15–20). Details in the story as it is told in Judges are reminiscent of details in the story of Abraham's hospitality to the angels who foretold that Sarah (barren, like Manoah's wife) would give birth (Gen. 18:1–15), in the story of Elijah's fiery ascent to heaven (2 Kings 2:11), and especially, as we shall see below, in the story of Gideon's sacrifice to the angel who charged him with his mission (Judg. 6:11–24). In Josephus's retelling of the story, despite considerable abridgement, a number of details have been added which increase the similarities to these stories or make them more explicit.[3] This may be seen from the following comparison of the texts (the added details are italicized):

Judges 13	*Josephus*, Ant., 5.8.3.	*Source of addition*
[19]Manoah took the kid and the meal offering	§282 . . . And so, Manoah having killed a kid, *and bidden his wife*	Gen. 18:6–7 (tele-scoped)Abraham hastened into the tent

2. See Cross, "New Qumran Fragment," esp. p. 18 n. 5. See also Josephus, *Ant.* 5.10.3, sec. 347. Hertzberg, *I & II Samuel*, p. 25, believes that the MT already was influenced by the story of Samson.

Although the MT of Samuel is generally considered inferior to the LXX and the texts of Samuel from Qumran, we have here a clear example of the MT's superiority: there is no way to explain an omission of the details in question from the MT. On the other hand, it is natural to explain the additions of the LXX and 4QSam^a as a result of the assimilation process. Moreover, in 4QSam^a we also find other midrash-like additions, such as the story of the Ammonite oppression of the Transjordanian tribes published by Cross, "Ammonite Oppression"; see Rofé, "Acts of Nahash."

The process of assimilation in this story continued for a long time. In the Judeo-Spanish romance on Hannah's vow, "Mi señora de hora en hora," we find a promise of the birth of Samuel, the words of which are borrowed from the story of Samson's birth: "He will not drink any wine, / . . . / No razor will touch his head, / He will grow his locks, / He will be the judge of his tribe" (Attias, *Romancero Sefaradi*, p. 174; see the editor's comment in n. 1 there). [On the rabbinic use of analogy in exegesis and refusal to insert the resultant interpretation in the biblical text, see above, p. 62 n. 25—Ed.]

3. It is interesting that Josephus does not tell the story of Gideon's sacrifice. Perhaps it was his custom to *avoid* telling parallel or similar stories about heroes who play the same role in the nation's history—a practice opposite to that we are studying here. For example, Josephus does not relate the story of the resurrection of the child in the Elisha cycle, only in the Elijah cycle. In Joshua he does not tell of the captain of the Lord's army who orders Joshua, "Take off your shoes. The place where you are standing is holy" (Josh. 5:13), words which duplicate God's instruction to Moses (Exod. 3:5). He also does not tell the story about Isaac and Rebekah and Abimelek, which duplicates the story already told about Abraham and Sarah and Abimelek.

to Sarah and said,
"Quick . . . make cakes!"
Then Abraham ran to
the herd, took a calf
. . . and gave it to a
servant-boy, who has-
to cook it   tened to prepare it.
and offered them up on   when all was ready, *the*   Judg. 6:20The angel of
the rock to the Lord,   *angel ordered them to*   God said to him, "Take
set out the loaves and   the meat and the un-
the meat upon the rock   leavened bread, put
them on yonder rock,
without the vessels   and spill out the
broth." He did so.

and a marvelous thing
happened, while Manoah
and his wife looked on.

That done, he with   21The angel of the
the   Lord held out the
rod which he held   staff that he carried,
touched the meat   and touched the meat
and the unleavened
bread with its tip.
20As the flames leaped   and, a fire blazing out,   A fire sprang up from
up from the altar toward   the rock
the sky,

it was consumed, along   and consumed the meat
with the bread[4]   and the unleavened
bread.
the angel of the Lord   while the angel,
in the flames   borne   on the smoke
of the altar,   *as on a chariot,*   2 Kings 2:11 . . . a fiery
chariot with fiery
horses suddenly appear-
ed . . . and Elijah went
ascended,   ascending *into heaven*   up to heaven in a
whirlwind.

while Manoah and his   was plainly seen
wife looked on . . .   by them.

---

4. Similarly in *Bib. Ant.* 42:9: "The angel stretched out his hand and touched it [the sacrifice] with the tip of his staff, and a fire came forth from the rock and consumed the burnt offerings and sacrifices."

As we shall argue below, much of the similarity between the biblical accounts of the sacrifices of Gideon and Manoah is itself due to assimilation of the latter to the former.[5]

Assimilation in the Ancient Translations of the Bible

The books of Esther and Daniel have much material in common, dealing as they both do with Jews connected with the royal court of the Persian Empire.[6] The targum of Esther sometimes increases this similarity by adding details borrowed from Daniel. Thus Est. 1:7, "wine was served in golden vessels," is rendered "and he [Ahasuerus] ordered that they be given to drink from the golden vessels *from the Temple, which his father, the wicked Nebuchadnezzar, had brought from Jerusalem.*" This detail follows Dan. 5:2: "He [Belshazzar] ordered that the golden and silver vessels, which his father Nebuchadnezzar had taken out of the sanctuary at Jerusalem, be brought so that the king and his nobles, his consorts and his concubines, might drink from them." Est. 3:2 states that "the king's attendants at court all bowed down to Haman and did obeisance, for so the king had commanded; but Mordecai did not bow to him or do obeisance." The targum of this verse expands it significantly: "So the king's attendants at court all bowed down *to the statue he set up there* and did obeisance to Haman, for so the king had commanded; but Mordecai did not bow down *to the statue* or do obeisance to Haman." This expansion was written, of course, under the influence of Daniel 3, where Daniel's companions refuse to bow down to the statue erected by Nebuchadnezzar.

Assimilation in Biblical Manuscripts

An example of assimilation in a biblical manuscript, 4QSam[a], was mentioned above, in the section on extrabiblical paraphrases.

---

5. [A fine example of assimilation in a medieval aggadic work is found in *Sefer Hayashar*, where it is the *śāṭān* who instigates the trial of Abraham in Genesis 22. The account clearly assimilates Genesis 22 to Job 1–2. The original similarity between the two stories was the idea of men whose fear of God was tested by God, with the test endangering the lives of their children. See the text in L. Goldschmidt, *Sepher hajaschar*, pp. 74–75, and the English summary in Ginzberg, *Legends*, 1:272–73. That the process of assimilating these two stories began earlier than *Sefer Hayashar* is clear from the comments of Ginzberg, ibid., 5:248–49 nn. 227–28, who notes that the *śāṭān* and/or the *bĕnê hā⁾ᵉlōhîm* serve as instigators already in Jub. 17:15ff., *Gen. R.* 55:4, and *b. Sanh.* 89b.—Ed.]

6. See L. A. Rosenthal, "Josephgeschichte"; idem, "Nochmals."

Assimilation in Repetitions of Stories in the Bible

At times assimilation is found within the Masoretic Text of the Bible itself, in later repetitions of or allusions to one of two similar stories. The stories of Abraham's purchase of the cave of Machpelah in Hebron (Gen. 23:8–20) and of David's purchase of land in Jerusalem (2 Sam. 24:21–24) are very similar.[7] In both a gentile landowner is ready to give his plot of land and even more for free, but the Israelite leader insists on paying its full market price, and in both the final price paid is reported (Gen. 23:11, 13, 15; 2 Sam. 24:22–24). The Chronicler, aware of the similarities, increased them in his version of the story about Jerusalem (1 Chron. 21:22–25) by conforming the terminology to that of the Hebron story: the term for full price is changed from *mĕḥîr* (2 Sam. 24:24) to *kesep mālēʾ*, as in Gen. 23:9, and the verb *qānâ*, "buy," is replaced twice by *nātan* (the verb used several times in Gen. 23) in the senses "sell" (1 Chron. 21:22) and "pay" (v. 24; *qānâ* remains once, in v. 24; in Gen. 23:18 a derivative of *qānâ* is used once).

Further Cases of Assimilation

The examples reviewed above constitute documentary evidence for the phenomenon of assimilation. They illustrate a process which could underlie parts of the Masoretic Text. In what follows we suggest that assimilation is indeed responsible for the present form of a number of biblical narratives which contain intrusive elements or which seem suspiciously similar to other biblical texts.

The Illness of Hezekiah[8]

In the story of Hezekiah's illness in 2 Kings 20:1–11, verse 7 seems intrusive. In verse 5, Isaiah had conveyed God's promise to heal Hezekiah, adding that "on the third day you shall go up to the House of the Lord." In verse 7 we read: "Then Isaiah said, 'Get a cake of figs.' And they got one, and they applied it to the rash, and he recovered (*wayyeḥî*)." But in verse 8,

---

7. For more similarities between Abraham and David, see Clements, *Abraham and David*, pp. 47–60. For the polemic tendency of these stories and their parallels, see Zakovitch, "Purpose of Narrations."

8. The following discussion revises Zakovitch, "II Kings 20:7—Isaiah 38:21–22" (Hebrew). See also Talmon, "Textual Study," pp. 328–32.

Hezekiah asks, "What is the sign that the Lord will heal me and that I shall go up to the House of the Lord on the third day?" and Isaiah proceeds to give him a sign (vv. 9–11). In other words, verses 8–11 respond to verse 5 and assume that Hezekiah had not yet recovered, although verse 7 said that he had.

One way of resolving this inconsistency is to construe verse 7 as merely anticipating Hezekiah's recovery. This is the way the text reads in the LXX and Peshitta translations in Kings and in the parallel Hebrew text in Isa. 38:21. In these three versions the verb "and they got one" (*wayyiqĕḥû*) is absent, and all the other verbs are futures, yielding a reading that does not contradict the following verses: "Let them take a cake of figs and apply it to the rash, and he will recover (*wĕyeḥî*)." However, several reasons prevent us from accepting this reading:[9]

1. It makes the verse anomalous among biblical traditions concerning prophetic healing. In all other such traditions the effect of the treatment is virtually immediate and is never a promise for the future. In the Elisha stories, the story about the healing of the water in Jericho (2 Kings 2:19–21) and about the healing of the stew (4:38–41) are quite similar to the Hezekiah episode. In both stories Elisha instructs others to "get" (*qĕḥû*, *ûqĕḥû*) something for him (a new bowl, some meal [2:20; 4:41]),[10] as does Isaiah in the Masoretic Text of 2 Kings 20:7. Compliance with Elisha's orders is recorded with the same verb in 2:20 (*wayyiqĕḥû*, "and they got") and in the Vulgate of 4:41 (*tulissent*, "they got"),[11] exactly as in the Masoretic Text of 2 Kings 20:7. The reading of the versions and Isa. 38:21, which omit "and they got one," would leave our verse anomalous among such stories.

Furthermore, the inconsistency between verses 7 and 8 is not the only difficulty caused by verse 7, and the following points must also be considered.

2. The opening verses of the story do not mention the nature of Hezekiah's illness; what mattered was that the illness seemed mortal. The sudden naming of the illness in verse 7 as *šĕḥîn*, "skin disease," "rash," comes late and seems artificial (note also that *šĕḥîn* is nowhere described as a mortal illness in the Bible).

3. Biblical traditions concerning the appeal to a prophet for medical assistance fall into two clear types: (a) consulting an oracle in order to learn whether the person will live or die; this is the case with Jeroboam's

9. This reading was accepted by Burney, *Notes*, pp. 348–49.
10. In several mss. and in the ancient translations, the reading in 4:41 is also *qĕḥû*. The imperative *qĕḥû* appears once more in the Elisha cycle, in 3:15, *qĕḥû lî mĕnaggēn*, "get (lit. take) me a musician."
11. In the MT, immediate compliance with Elisha's orders is implicit even without "they took."

wife, Ahaziah's emissaries, and Hazael (1 Kings 14:1–18; 2 Kings 1:2–16; 8:7–15); (b) asking a prophet to cure the disease, as in the curing of Naaman's skin disease (ṣāraʿat, 2 Kings 5:1–19) and the parallel stories about the resurrection of a child (1 Kings 17:17–24; 2 Kings 4:8–37). Our story is anomalous in that it combines an oracular response foretelling recovery—the dominant element in the narrative—with the actual healing by the prophet (v. 7).

These points lead to the conclusion that verse 7 is not only contradictory to verse 8 but is also opposed to the general character of the story. Indeed, the parallel verse in Isaiah 38 and the Qumran text 1QIsᵃ indicate that the verse is a late addition in Isaiah.[12] In Isaiah 38 the equivalent of 1 Kings 20:7–8 appears not in the middle of the narrative but at its end, in Isa. 38:21–22 (the text varies slightly; see below).[13] In the Qumran scroll these verses did not appear in the original text but were added by another scribe in the space left at the end of the line, continuing into the left margin of the column.[14] Paleographic[15] and linguistic[16] considerations make it clear that it was a later hand which added verses 21–22 to the scroll.[17] The fact that the contradictory and intrusive element of the fig-plaster was not present in the original version of the story in Isaiah suggests that this version may have been derived from an older version of the story in Kings which likewise lacked this element.[18]

The addition of this verse to the original version of the story also demands an explanation. We suggest that the verse was added to enhance Isaiah's similarity to Elisha. Apparently, the interpolator, who was aware

12. In Isaiah 38 the verses in question were added after the psalm, which was added to the story of Hezekiah's illness in this version (compare the interpolated prayers of Hannah [1 Sam. 2:1–10], Jonah [Jonah 2:3–10], and Daniel [Dan. 9:4–20]).

13. The short version of our story in 2 Chron. 32:24 cannot help us in our discussion; cf. Talmon, "Textual Study," pp. 328–29.

14. See Burrows, *Dead Sea Scrolls of St. Mark's Monastery*, 1:Plate XXXII.

15. Burrows, "Variant Readings," p. 32.

16. E. Y. Kutscher, *Language*, pp. 444–45. Another bit of linguistic evidence for the lateness of the added verses in Isaiah is the use of the verb wĕyimrĕḥû, "and let them anoint, rub," in place of wayyāśîmû, "and they put," which is used in 2 Kings 20:7. mārah is common in postbiblical Hebrew, but is a hapax legomenon in the Bible.

17. Note also that the Peshitta to Isaiah 38 reverses the order of verses 21–22. In his commentary on Isaiah, Kimchi held that these verses really belong after verse 6. Luzzatto, on the other hand, recognized them as a later addition to the story taken, he thought, from the Book of the Annals of the Kings of Judah and Israel (Luzzatto, *Il Profeta Isaia*, pp. 441–43). F. Feldmann, too, held that Isa. 38:21–22 is a secondary addition, not a section that was accidentally omitted from the story and then added at its end (Feldmann, *Isaias*, p. 455).

18. Isaiah 37–39 is a secondary edition of the parallel material in 2 Kings. See S. R. Driver, *ILOT*, pp. 226–27. Driver remarks that the edition of Isaiah is shorter and simpler than the original edition. In addition, in his opinion the historiographical nature of the traditions fits Kings more than it fits the book of Isaiah.

of the similarity between Isaiah, the prophet who promises the future recovery of the king, and Elisha, the healing prophet,[19] was (perhaps unconsciously) interested in attributing to him therapeutic powers like Elisha's. He therefore diagnosed Hezekiah's disease as *šĕḥîn*, a skin affliction similar to Naaman's *ṣāraᶜat* (*šĕḥîn* is an actual sign of *ṣāraᶜat* in Lev. 13:18–20) which Elisha cured.[20] The addition was molded in the above-mentioned pattern of the Elisha stories ("get . . . and they got . . .").

The interpolation of verse 7 in the story in 1 Kings 20 created the inconsistencies to which we have referred. Nothing was done to smooth out these inconsistencies in the Masoretic Text of Kings, but in other texts copyists and translators tried to do so in various ways. One approach was to revise verse 7 so as to refer only to the future. This was done in at least one Hebrew version of Kings—the one on which Isa. 38:21 was based—and is reflected in the LXX and Peshitta of Kings, as noted above. When copyists of Isaiah sought to bring the text of Isaiah into line with the interpolated text of Kings, they followed a second approach (though the first, reflected in their *Vorlage*, would have sufficed) by inserting the verse at the end of the story, where it does not contradict the following verse or interrupt the connection between Isaiah's promise and the sign he gives to confirm the promise. The text of Isaiah actually reflects yet a third attempt to smooth out the inconsistency between verses 7 and 8. In Isa. 38:22— Isaiah's version of verse 8[21]—the verse reads: "What is the sign that I shall go up to the House of the Lord?" This reading, which avoids repeating the first half of Hezekiah's question, "What is the sign *that the Lord will heal me*?" (1 Kings 20:8a), resolves the contradiction by having Hezekiah ask only about his going up to the Temple and not about his healing; in this way his question is not inconsistent with the fact that he was already cured. If this is the intention behind the formulation of verse 22, then Isa. 38:21–22 reflects three different efforts to resolve the contradiction, each rendering the others superfluous: (a) the placement of both verses and (b) the formulation of verse 21 postpone the healing, and (c) the formulation of verse 22 restricts Hezekiah's question to going up to the Temple, taking his recovery for granted. 1QIs[a] thus reflects both stages in the development of the story of the curing of Hezekiah. The original text of the scroll bears witness to

---

19. The rabbis also noted the similarity between 2 Kings 20:7 and the Elisha cycle. See, e.g., Epstein and Melamed, *Mekhilta d'Rabbi Šimᶜon b. Jochai*, p. 104, ll. 4–14, and parallels.

20. The fig-cake plaster was apparently chosen as a treatment because of a reputation as an effective remedy. Figs are mentioned in a medical context in two veterinary texts from Ugarit, C. H. Gordon, *Ugaritic Textbook*, nos. 55:28 and 56:33.

21. Note that the version of the story in Isaiah was originally shorter than that in Kings and lacked verse 8—part of the original story—as well as verse 7. When 2 Kings 20:7 was interpolated in Isaiah, part of verse 8 was brought along as well.

the text of Isaiah before the process of assimilation took place. The secondary interpolation written in the margin by a later copyist bears witness to the assimilation process. The awkward placing of these verses in the Masoretic Text (of Isaiah), too, testifies to their secondary nature.

Thus we may sum up the development of the story of the healing of Hezekiah as going through the following stages:[22]

1. *1 Kings 20:1-6, 8-11*, reflected in abridged form in 1QIs[a] 38:1-8, minus the later addition of verses 21-22.
2. *1 Kings 20:1-11*, with verse 7 (ending *wayyeḥî*, "and he recovered") assimilating the story to those about Elisha.
3. Three attempts to resolve the inconsistency created by the addition of verse 7:
   a. A Hebrew text of 1 Kings 20, reflected in Isa. 38:21 and the LXX and Peshitta versions of 1 Kings 20, where *wyḥy*, "and he recovered," is construed as *wĕyeḥî*, "and he will recover."
   b. A version in which *kî yirpā³ YHWH lî*, "that the Lord will heal me," is omitted from verse 8, reflected in Isa. 38:22.
   c. Isa. 38:1-8, 21-22, reflected in the MT and 1QIs[a] with the later addition of verses 21-22 (both versions reading *wĕyimrĕḥû*, "and let them anoint, rub," instead of *wayyāśîmû*, "and they put").

THE RAPE OF DINAH

Recognition of assimilation helps explain the serious critical problems of Genesis 34. Since the days of A. Dillmann and J. Wellhausen, most scholars have endeavored to solve the difficulties by separating the chapter into two separate documents.[23] However, scholars have never arrived at complete agreement as to the precise definition of the documents presumably to be identified in the chapter. A. Kuenen's method of solving the difficulties differed in that he claimed the existence of only one story, to which postexilic interpolations were added.[24] A few scholars opposed the documentary solution. J. Pedersen tried to solve the literary problems by historical and anthropological considerations.[25] E. Nielsen showed that some of the so-called difficulties which first prompted the source analysis are artificial.[26] E. A. Speiser, too, concluded that there was no valid reason

22. For another stage, including Isa. 38:9-20, see Talmon, "Textual Study," p. 329.
23. Dillmann, *Genesis,* pp. 371-75; Wellhausen, *Composition des Hexateuchs* (3d ed.), pp. 314-25. See also Gunkel, *Genesis*, pp. 369-71; Skinner, *Genesis*, pp. 417-18.
24. Kuenen, *Gesammelte Abhandlungen*, pp. 255-77.
25. Pedersen, *Israel* I-II: 521-23, n. 1 to p. 291.
26. Nielsen, *Shechem*, pp. 242-59.

for assuming the chapter to be conflate,[27] and M. Sternberg's literary analysis took the story's unity for granted.[28]

In our view, the opponents of the documentary solution, especially Nielsen, by recognizing the narrator's literary skill and psychological insight, have shown persuasively that many of the inconsistencies presumed by this solution are indeed artificial. But there remain a number of details that do not seem compatible with a view that the present form of Genesis 34 is entirely from a single writer. These details have to do with the characterization of Shechem's conduct with Dinah and the identity of those who attacked the city of Shechem:

1. The sequence of actions at the beginning of the story is difficult: Shechem lay with the girl and ravished her (v. 2), and only afterward became infatuated with her and sought to persuade her (v. 3).

2. The anachronism "he had committed what the Israelites hold to be an outrage, an intolerable thing" (*kî nĕbālâ ʿāśâ bĕyiśrāʾēl,* v. 7) presupposes the existence of the *people* of Israel in a story dealing with Jacob and his children (that Israel in this idiom refers to the people and not to Jacob is clear from Deut. 22:21; Josh. 7:15; Judg. 20:6, 10; Jer. 29:23).

3. Two references to the "defiling" of Dinah are syntactically awkward in their contexts: *wayyaʿᵃnû bĕnê yaʿᵃqōb ʾet šĕkem wĕʾet hᵃmôr ʾābîw bĕmirmâ wayĕddabēru ᵊašer ṭimmēʾ ʾet dînâ ᵊᵃhōtām,* literally: "The sons of Jacob answered Shechem and Hamor his father with guile, and they spoke, because (?) he defiled their sister Dinah" (v. 13; even if ᵊašer means "because" here, the right place for the clause it introduces would be after "with guile," not after [the otiose] "and they spoke"); *bĕnê yaʿᵃqōb bāʾû ʿal hahᵃlālîm wayyābozzû hāʿîr ᵊašer ṭimmĕʾû ᵊᵃhōtām,* literally: "The sons of Jacob came upon the slain and plundered the city (singular), because (?) they defiled their sister" (v. 27). Moreover, in verse 13 only Shechem is accused of defiling Dinah, but here the whole city is said to have done it. Interestingly enough, those who advocate a documentary analysis of the chapter cannot find a place for these clauses in either of the two reconstructed documents but consider them glosses or editorial additions.[29]

4. There is a real tension within verses 25–31 over which of the brothers attacked the city of Shechem. According to verses 25–26, Simeon and Levi alone attack the city, whereas in verses 27–29 all the brothers plunder it; but then, in verses 30–31 Jacob rebukes only Simeon and Levi for the deed. Just as verses 30–31 seem unaware of verses 27–29, so does verse 27 seem unaware of verses 25–26: once we have read that Simeon and Levi took Dinah and departed (v. 26), we would expect to read that "Jacob's

27. Speiser, *Genesis,* p. 267.
28. Sternberg, "Delicate Balance."
29. Skinner, *Genesis,* p. 417, n. *; Gunkel, *Genesis,* p. 374, sec. 6.

other sons" plundered the city, not simply "Jacob's sons," as if all were included. Indeed, the statement at the end of verse 26 that Simeon and Levi went away seems to imply that they did nothing else to the city after retrieving Dinah.

The first three of these difficulties involve the idea that Dinah was raped, and within the inconsistent verses which constitute the fourth item, the idea of Dinah's rape is connected with the identification of two of her full brothers, Simeon and Levi, as the attackers of Shechem, and the consequent limitation of the other brothers' role to plundering. These two themes do not amount to a full alternative version of the Dinah-Shechem affair, but rather to a series of interpolations which modify an original story. These are: 2b, 5, 7a$_2$b, the end of 13a (*wayĕdabbērû*) + 13b, 17, parts of 25a, 26b, 27, 30, and 31.[30]

The following translation of the story, with the interpolations printed in italics, shows how smoothly the story reads without the interpolations.[31]

[1]Now Dinah, the daughter whom Leah had borne to Jacob, went out to visit the daughters of the land. [2]Shechem son of Hamor the Hivite, chief of the country, saw her, *and took her and lay with her and raped*[32] *her*. [3]He loved Dinah daughter of Jacob wholeheartedly and, being in love with the maiden, he sought to persuade her. [4]So Shechem said to his father Hamor, "Get me this girl as a wife." [5]*Jacob heard that he had defiled his daughter Dinah, but since his sons were in the field with his cattle, Jacob kept silent until they came home.* [6]Then Shechem's father Hamor came out to Jacob to speak to him. [7]Meanwhile Jacob's sons came in from the field, *having heard. The men were distressed and very angry because he had committed what the Israelites hold to be an outrage by lying with Jacob's daughter— a thing not to be done.* [8]And Hamor spoke to them, saying, "My son Shechem longs for your daughter. Please give her to him in marriage. [9]Intermarry with us: give your daughters to us, and take our daughters for yourselves. [10]You will dwell among us, and the land will be open before you; settle, move about, and acquire holdings in it." [11]Then Shechem said to her father and brothers, "Do me this favor, and I will pay whatever you tell me. [12]Ask of me a bride-price ever so high, and I will pay what you tell me; only give me the maiden for a wife. [13]But Jacob's sons answered Shechem and Hamor his father with guile, *and they spoke, because(?) he defiled their sister Dinah.*[33] [14]They said to them, "We cannot do this thing, to give our sister to a man who is uncircumcised, for that is a disgrace among us. [15]Only on

---

30. Verses 17 and 26b belong with the rape verses because they presume that Dinah is still in Shechem's house, which means that he did seize her.

31. The translation is based on the *NJV*, with modifications toward literalism when necessary to emphasize points in the discussion.

32. ʿinnâ, lit. "to afflict, humble," means to rape; see Deut. 22:24, 29; Judg. 20:5; Lam. 5:11; Ezek. 22:11, "they have raped their sisters, their fathers' daughters," clearly shows the influence of 2 Samuel 13.

33. On the syntax of this clause, see the discussion on p. 186.

this condition will we agree with you: that you will be like us in that every male among you is circumcised. [16]Then we will give our daughters to you and take your daughters to ourselves; and we will dwell among you and become as one kindred. [17]*But if you will not listen to us and become circumcised, we will take our daughter and go.* [18]Their words pleased Hamor and Hamor's son Shechem. [19]And the youth lost no time in doing the thing, for he wanted Jacob's daughter. Now he was the most respected in his father's house. [20]So Hamor and his son Shechem went to the gate of their city and spoke to their fellow townsmen, saying, [21]"These people are our friends; let them settle in the land and move about in it, for the land is large enough for them; we will take their daughters to ourselves as wives and give our daughters to them. [22]But only on this condition will the men agree with us to dwell among us and be as one kindred: that all our males become circumcised as they are circumcised. [23]Would not their cattle and substance and all their beasts be ours? Let us agree with them, that they may dwell among us." [24]All the fighting men in his city heeded Hamor and his son Shechem, and all males, all the fighting men in his city, were circumcised. [25]On the third day, when they were in pain, *two of* Jacob's sons, *Simeon and Levi*, brothers of Dinah, took each his sword, came upon the city unmolested, slew all the males, [26]they put to the sword Hamor and his son Shechem, *took Dinah out of Shechem's house, and went away.* [27]*The sons of Jacob came upon the slain*[34] *and plundered the city, because(?) they defiled their sister.*[35] [28]They seized their flocks and herds and asses, what was inside the city and what was in the countryside; [29]all their wealth, all their children, and their wives they captured, and they plundered everything[36] in the city.[37] [30]*Jacob said to Simeon and Levi: "You have brought trouble on me, making me odious among the inhabitants of the land, the Canaanites and the Perizzites; my men are few in number, so that if they unite against me and attack me, I and my house will be destroyed."* [31]*But they answered: "Should our sister be treated like a whore?"*

Minus the interpolations, this story tells of Shechem's innocent attraction to Dinah and Jacob's sons' treacherous exploitation of the situation in order to plunder the city. That Shechem had raped Dinah is neither mentioned nor even hinted at by either party in the course of the negotiations between the families. It seems that the rape element was added because the editor assumed that the brothers must have had a justifiable motive for their deceit and cruelty; what the motive was he inferred from the analogous story in 2 Samuel 13, as we shall see. The intention to justify the brothers'

34. We have no reason to emend *ḥᵃlālîm*, "slain," to *ḥōlîm*, "sick, wounded" (thus Gunkel, *Genesis*, pp. 370, 378).

35. See n. 33.

36. The *wāw* of *wĕʔēt* is a result of dittography; read *ʔet* with the Samaritan and the Syriac.

37. Reading *bāʕîr*, "in the city," with the Syriac, as against MT's *babbāyit*, "in the house." LXX and OL conflate both readings *bāʕîr ûbabbāyit*, "in the city and in the house."

behavior is clear in the references to the rape in verse 13b, which stands immediately after the reference to the deceit, and verse 27b, which follows the slaughter and plundering. Limiting the killing to two brothers has the effect of further minimizing the guilt of the others by presenting them as only plunderers. This limitation is also unexpected, for until verse 25 all the brothers act together, and they collectively give the deceitful reply to Shechem in verse 13a. (The selection of Simeon and Levi for the main role was logical, since they were full brothers to Dinah; the choice of these two may have been influenced by Gen. 49:5–7; see below.)

The idea that Dinah's full brothers acted in response to the rape of their sister seems to have been derived from the analogy of Absalom's murder of Amnon for Amnon's rape of Absalom's full sister, Tamar, in 2 Samuel 13. That the interpolations in Genesis 34 constitute an assimilation to the Absalom-Tamar story would account for a number of remarkable similarities between the two stories. Even our reconstructed original version of Genesis 34 has a number of similarities to 2 Samuel 13, and these would have been the basis for the assimilation:

1. Both stories deal with love directed toward the daughter of a Hebrew leader, the only daughter of each leader known by her name.

2. In both stories the man who falls in love with the girl is a prince.

3. In both stories the girl's brother(s) kills the man who falls in love with her.

4. In both stories the lovers meet their death after they place their trust in their future killers and assume that all is well between the two parties: Shechem expects Dinah to be given to him and Amnon drinks wine at Absalom's party (2 Sam. 13:26–29).

An editor who recalled these similarities between the stories would presumably have noticed one glaring omission in the putative original version of Genesis 34: an explicit and plausible motive for the killing of Shechem and his people. 2 Samuel 13 supplied such a motive by having the suitor rape the girl and by making the killing an act of revenge by the girl's full brother. In fact, 2 Samuel 13 is more logical than Genesis 34. 2 Sam. 13:1–2 tell of Amnon's infatuation with Tamar, and verse 13 tells of her attempt to convince him to ask her father for permission to marry her (v. 13); only afterward is the rape reported. In Genesis 34, by contrast, the report of the rape precedes the report of Shechem's love for Dinah and his offer of marriage.

In carrying out the assimilation, the editor of Genesis 34 hewed closely to the phraseology of 2 Samuel 13. Note the following:

Genesis 34	*2 Samuel 13*
(a) *wayyiškab ʾōtāh wayĕʿannehā*	*wayĕʿannehā wayyiškab ʾōtāh*
"he lay with her and ravished her" (v. 2)	"he ravished her and lay with her" (v. 14)

(Note the inversion of word order, which is very common in biblical passages that allude to other biblical passages.)[38]

(b) *kĕšāmĕ⁽ām wayyit⁽aṣṣĕbû hā⁾ᵃnāšîm*
wayyiḥar lāhem mĕ⁾ōd
"when they heard, they were distressed and very angry" (v. 7).

wĕhammelek dāwid šama⁽
wayyiḥar lô mĕ⁾ōd
"when King David heard . . . he was very angry" (v. 21).

(c) *kî nĕbālâ ⁽āśâ bĕyiśrā⁾ēl . . .*
wĕkēn lō⁾ yē⁽āśeh
"he had committed what the Israelites hold to be an outrage . . . a thing not to be done (v. 7)

kî lō⁾ yē⁽āśeh kēn bĕyiśrā⁾ēl
⁾al ta⁽ᵃśēh ⁾et hannĕbālâ hazzō⁾t
"For such a thing is not done in Israel. Do not commit this outrage" (v. 12; cf. v. 13: *kĕ⁾aḥad hannĕbālîm bĕyiśrā⁾ēl*, "like any of the scoundrels in Israel")

(The verse in Genesis is another allusion with inversion of word order.)

These similar phrases are not unique to these two stories, and they do not by themselves constitute proof of literary dependence. It is the entire pattern of similarities, several of which are intrusive elements in Genesis 34 or are associated with intrusive elements there, but which fit naturally in 2 Samuel 13, which suggests that their presence in Genesis 34 is due to an assimilation of that chapter to 2 Samuel 13.

A word must be said about the relationship between Genesis 34 and the "blessing" of Simeon and Levi in Gen. 49:5–7. That "blessing" reads as follows:

⁵Simeon and Levi are brothers; their weapons are tools of violence.
⁶Let my soul not enter their council, or my being be joined to their company. For in their anger they slew men (lit. a man) and in their wantonness they hamstrung oxen (lit. an ox).
⁷Cursed be their anger, so fierce, and their wrath, so harsh. I will divide them in Jacob, scatter them in Israel.

In our view these verses do not refer to the events of Genesis 34. There is nothing in these verses themselves which suggests a connection with those events,[39] and the statement that the brothers hamstrung an ox seems to refer to something different.[40]

38. See Zeidel, "Parallels"; Weiss, "Chiasmus."
39. There are a few similarities between the two passages, as noted below, and on the basis of these, postbiblical writers assimilated the two further. See, e.g., *Tg. Pseudo-Jonathan* to Gen. 49:6; *Testament of Levi* 6:6–7; *Gen. R.* 98:5.
40. "In their wantonness they hamstrung an ox" seems to refer to cruelty for its own sake, whereas in Genesis 34 all the brothers took the animals (flocks, cattle, asses) as booty. The versions and the rabbis resolved the inconsistency by taking Gen. 49:6 to refer to a wall (*šûr*) rather than an ox (*šôr*; see *Tg. Onqelos*, Symmachus, Vg., and *Leqaḥ Tob*, ad loc.).
Hamstringing work animals is not found elsewhere in the Bible. Hamstringing of war-horses is mentioned in Josh. 11:6, 9; 2 Sam. 8:4; 18:4.

In their present context in Jacob's blessing, these verses serve, along with verses 3-4, to explain why the rights of primogeniture were taken from Reuben, Simeon, and Levi and transferred to the next in line, Judah. But we accept the view that before these verses were embedded into the variegated material of "Jacob's blessing" the original speaker in them was God, and that the meaning of the threatened punishment (v. 6a) was that God will not be present in the cultic assemblies of the tribes of Simeon and Levi.[41] According to this assumption, this saying was originally an oracle intended to supply a theological explanation for the fact that the tribe of Simeon was assimilated to Judah and that the tribe of Levi had no land of its own. Their common fate was explained by their common negative character, "their weapons are tools of violence," and they were thus included in one oracle.

There are, of course, some undeniable similarities between these verses and Genesis 34: both refer to acts of violence[42] committed by sons of Jacob, specifically to killings committed in anger, and both deal with Simeon and Levi together (nowhere else in the entire Bible do these two sons of Jacob act in concert). In our view it was Genesis 49:5-7 which suggested to the editor of Genesis 34 that the sons of Jacob who committed the killings described in the original version of that story were not all the sons but only Simeon and Levi, and that they did so out of anger. These secondary elements in Genesis 34 thus represent an assimilation to Gen. 49:5-7, just as the rape theme represents an assimilation to 2 Samuel 13.

In summarizing this long and complicated example we should clarify several points: the addition to Genesis 34, which justifies the brothers' behavior as a vengeful reaction to their sister's rape and blames only two of them for taking revenge, borrows from a story that was similar to the original story. The author of the addition was also influenced by the oracle concerning Simeon and Levi which became an element in the Blessing of Jacob and explains the transfer of rights of the firstborn to Judah. Significantly, 2 Samuel 13, the literary source of the addition in Genesis 34, is a link in the narrative of the succession to David's throne, which presents the reasons why Amnon and Absalom (and later, in 1 Kings 1, Adonijah) did not succeed their father. The story of Genesis 34 in its present form thus also contains an element which explains the transfer of the rights of the

---

41. Zobel, *Stämmesspruch und Geschichte*, p. 8; Kittel, *Die Stämmesspruche Israels*, p. 13.

42. *ḥāmās*, "violence," used in Gen. 49:5, is often associated with *mirmâ*, "deceit," used in 34:13 (see Isa. 53:9; Zeph. 1:9) and functions as a synonym of *dām, dāmîm*, "blood" shed unjustly (note the parallelism in Judg. 9:24; Jer. 51:35; Joel 4:19; Hab. 2:8, 17; and the variants in Ezek. 9:9 [see *BHK*]). Note also the reference to "sword(s)" in Gen. 34:25 (*ḥereb*) and 49:5 (*mĕkērōtēhem*; for this meaning, see Dillmann, *Genesis*, p. 453). Levi is known for readiness to use the sword; note the use by the tribe of Levi, Exod. 32:26-29.

firstborn from Simeon and Levi to Judah, just as the following chapter contains an element explaining the deposition of Reuben (35:22).

THE SACRIFICES OF GIDEON AND MANOAH[43]

Our final example brings us back to a story mentioned earlier in this study, Manoah's sacrifice to the angel. We saw how Josephus's version of this episode supplemented the biblical account with details drawn from other episodes, including Gideon's sacrifice to an angel. Josephus's borrowing from the Gideon story was, in fact, the culmination of a process that began in the biblical version of Manoah's sacrifice (Judg. 13). This version too contains details that were added to it secondarily under the influence of the Gideon story, which has a similar function in biblical historiography. Here too the identification of the intrusive elements which disturb the natural continuity of the story enables us to discover the process of assimilation.

The account of the angel's visit to Gideon (Judg. 6:11–24), which constitutes one of the introductions to the Gideon cycle,[44] and the story of Samson's birth (Judg. 13), which stands at the beginning of his biography, are very similar to one another.[45] Note the following points:

1. Both stories stand at the beginning of the biographies and describe the angel's message concerning the future mission of the hero.

2. The appearance of God's angel is expressed in strikingly similar terms: *wayyērāʾ ʾēlāyw malʾak YHWH wayyōʾmer ʾēlāyw*, "The angel of the Lord appeared to Gideon and said to him" (Judg. 6:12), and *wayyērāʾ malʾak YHWH ʾel hāʾiššâ wayyōʾmer ʾēleyha*, "The angel of the Lord appeared to the woman and said to her" (13:3). This phrase appears only once again in the Bible, in Exod. 3:2: *wayyērāʾ malʾak YHWH ʾēlāyw bĕlabbat ʾēš*, "The angel of the Lord appeared to him (Moses) in a blazing fire."

43. The following discussion is based on Zakovitch, "Sacrifice," revised in Zakovitch, *Life of Samson*, pp. 33, 54–69 (both in Hebrew).

44. The story in Judg. 6:11–24 is an independent story which is not connected to the stories preceding and following it. It is a parallel tradition to the following story (vv. 25–32), since both of them deal with the beginning of the cult of YHWH at Ophrah. The first tells about the building of an altar and the foundation of the cult after the appearance of an angel there; the second tells about a cultic reform—ending the Baal cult in Ophrah and building an altar for the worship of the God of Israel. While the first is mainly an etiological-cultic story, the second emphasizes the change of the hero's name, an etiological etymological story.

45. Many scholars have dealt with the similarity of these two stories, but most did this from the point of view of the history of religion rather than the literary relationship between the stories. See, e.g., Kittel, *Studien*, pp. 97–158; S. A. Cook, "Theophanies."

3. The promise that the hero will save Israel is common to both introductions: *wĕhôšaʿtā ʾet yiśrāʾēl mikkap midyān*, "And you will deliver Israel from the hand of the Midianites" (6:14); *wĕhûʾ yāḥēl lĕhôšîaʿ ʾet yiśrāʾēl miyyad pĕlištîm*, "He will begin to deliver Israel from the hand of the Philistines" (13:5).

4. In both introductions there is a request that the angel stay and eat: "Please do not leave this place until I come back to you and bring out my offering and place it before you" (6:18); "Let us detain you and prepare a kid for you" (13:15).

5. The angel's reply expressing his willingness to wait (6:18) corresponds to a willingness to wait but not eat (13:16).

6. In both stories a kid is served (6:13; 13:15).

7. The sacrifice in both stories is offered upon a rock (*ṣûr*, 6:21 [*selaʿ* in v. 20]; 13:19), though the angel does not eat of it (6:20; 13:19).

8. After the offering the angel disappears (6:21; 13:20).

9. The fears of both Gideon and Manoah at having seen a supernatural being are calmed, Gideon's by the angel and Manoah's by his wife (6:22–23; 13:22–23).

These similarities are so numerous and at times so close that they can hardly be coincidental. They suggest a direct relationship between the stories and raise two questions: the direction of the relationship (i.e., which story was the source from which the second borrowed) and the motivation for the borrowing. Two factors lead to the conclusion that it was the story of Manoah's sacrifice that borrowed from that about Gideon:

1. The story about Gideon's sacrifice reads smoothly and does not suggest any serious difficulties in its composition, but the description of Manoah's meeting with the angel and his sacrifice does not read smoothly. Two of the verses dealing with his sacrifice seem unaware of the verses immediately preceding them. Manoah's promise in verse 17 to honor the angel when his words come true seems to ignore verses 15–16, in which he has already offered to honor the angel on the spot with the kid. Verse 21, "The angel of the Lord did not appear again to Manoah and his wife; then Manoah knew that he was the angel of the Lord," is hardly consistent with the preceding account of the sacrifice (vv. 19–20): had Manoah seen the angel going up in the flame, he would have already realized that this was a supernatural being and would not have required additional proof of that from the fact that the angel never appeared again. Minus the verses of which the text seems unaware (vv. 15–16, 19–20), the narrative would not only read more smoothly, it would also conform to a pattern known elsewhere: Manoah's asking the angel's name (v. 17), the angel's refusal to divulge it (v. 18), and Manoah's fear (vv. 20–21) is a sequence very similar to that in Gen. 32:30–31:

Jacob said, "Tell me, I pray, your name." He [the "man"/divine being] replied: "Why do you ask my name?" But he gave him his blessing there. Jacob called the place Peniel because he said, "I have seen God face to face and my life is spared."

We thus conclude that in the original story of Judges 13, verses 15–16 and 19–20, which deal with the sacrifice, were not present. It follows that the clause referring to the sacrifice in Manoah's wife's reply to her frightened husband (v. 23) is also secondary. The full text of her reply reads: "If the Lord had wanted to kill us, *He would not have accepted a burnt offering and meal offering from our hands, and* then He would not have let us hear all this." The original text of the reply must have read: "If the Lord had wanted to kill us, then He would not have let us hear all this," referring to the promise about the birth of their future child. Indeed, the clause (italicized above) stating that God would not have accepted the couple's offerings is syntactically awkward, for as part of the apodosis in an "if . . . then . . . (*lû* / *lôᵓ* . . . *kāᶜēt* / *kî ᶜattâ* . . .) hypothetical sentence it should appear after "then," with the rest of the apodosis, and not before it.[46] This strengthens our contention that in the apodosis only the final clause (beginning with "then") is original, with the first clause (italicized above) having been added along with verses 15–16, 19–20.

2. The sacrifice motif is an organic and essential element in the story of Gideon, an etiological story which constitutes the *hieròs lógos* of the altar "YHWH-Shalom" (6:24). The import of Samson's birth story is quite different. It tells of the birth of a child to a barren woman, following the appearance of God's angel and his promise. Here the sacrifice element is entirely foreign to the character of the story.[47] Furthermore, the Israelite cult is extraneous to the Samson stories and is not mentioned again in the whole cycle. In the Gideon story, on the other hand, the cult plays an important role, not only in the story about the altar "YHWH-Shalom," but also in the parallel story concerning the destruction of the Baal altar and its replacement by an altar of YHWH (6:25–32) and in the tradition about the setting up of the ephod in Ophrah (8:24–27).

---

46. This is true even in hypothetical sentences where the apodosis has more than one clause, as in our verse; cf. Isa. 8:23 (where 1QIsᵃ reads *lû* for MT's *lōᵓ*); Num. 22:33 (reading *lûlê*, as understood by the versions, for MT's *ᵓûlay*).

47. Cook (see n. 45, above), who is interested in the two stories as documents for the study of comparative religion, finds two different elements in the story of Manoah: the interest of the first is the mother's barrenness, and the second deals with the sacrifice followed by the theophany and the sanctification of the site. But he does not speak about any difficulties in chap. 13 or find any direct relationship with chap. 13. Both the tradition about Gideon's offering and that about Manoah's burnt offering are, for Cook, local, independent traditions, one from Ophrah and the other from the cultic site between Zorah and Eshtaol. Cook's idea that Samson's mother went to prostrate herself on the grave of a relative (Manoah, supposedly the eponym of the family Manahat Dan) finds no support in the story.

Among the verses added to the story of the angelic visit to Samson's parents we should apparently include the end of the angel's promise to Manoah's wife: "And he will begin to deliver Israel from the hand of the Philistines" (13:5b), a verse indicated above (p. 193) as being among the similarities to the Gideon story. These words of the angel are not cited by Manoah's wife in her report to her husband.[48] The angel's words to Gideon and their parallel in the story of Manoah's sacrifice are the only two places in Judges where a promise is made by God to one of the deliverers (or his mother) concerning his future role in the deliverance of Israel from the hands of the enemy. Furthermore, the phrase *hôšîa‌ᶜ mikkap*, "deliver from the hand(s) of," is not found elsewhere in Judges except in 6:14. The synonymous expression *hôšîa‌ᶜ miyyad* also appears only in relation to Gideon (8:22) and Samson (13:5).

These are the only passages in the story of Manoah's sacrifice which there are grounds for considering secondary. They do not include every one of the features shared by the two stories. Features 1, 2, and 9 (pp. 192, 193) are organic elements of the original story of Manoah. They constitute introductions to the stories of Israelite deliverers in which an angel appears and announces the hero's future mission, after which the recipients of the announcement are terrified at the appearance of the supernatural being and have to be calmed. These original similarities between the stories were the catalyst for the later, secondary assimilation which made the stories much more similar to each other. The editor's motive for this assimilation was apparently a desire to introduce theophanic elements into the Samson story in order to make it as impressive as the Gideon story and to prove that it really was God who stood behind the promise to Manoah's wife.

The phenomenon of assimilation is, as we have endeavored to show, a creative force which left its impression both on extrabiblical literature, which retells the biblical stories, and on stories in the Bible itself. To reveal this phenomenon in extrabiblical paraphrases, in translations, and in biblical manuscripts is very easy. It is also relatively easy to discover this process in biblical examples in which two versions of one story have been preserved, when one version has been assimilated to another story, while the other has not. Most frequently, however, the earlier version of a story has not been preserved in the Bible, and we have only a secondary, assimilated version of the story, along with the story to which it has been assimilated. Such cases are the most difficult ones in which to identify assimilation, and we can identify the secondary stratum in them only with

48. The other differences between the angel's words and their citation by the woman may be explained on literary-psychological grounds (see *Num. R.* 10:5 [ed. Wilna, p. 37 (73), col. b]), but there is no explanation for her omission of verse 5b; why should she hide this wonderful news from her husband?

the aid of our philological-critical sense, by spotting difficulties, contradictions, and duplications that can be correlated with details in the other story and explained as secondary additions added to further assimilate two stories which were already somewhat similar even before any interpolations. The fact that we can document cases of assimilation in extrabiblical literature and elsewhere makes such an explanation of similarities between stories plausible.

7

The Chronicler's Use of Chronology as Illuminated by Neo-Assyrian Royal Inscriptions

MORDECHAI COGAN

Editor's Note

The historical orientation of biblical literature often brings questions of chronology to the fore. In certain cases, owing to the fantastic character of the figures, their conformity to numerical patterns, or their incompatibility with other data, scholars have surmised that the chronology has been shaped or adjusted in order to make a point.* In the present chapter, Mordechai Cogan shows that this has demonstrably taken place in Assyrian royal inscriptions, where events which took place later than Esarhaddon's accession year are dated to that year in order to emphasize his devotion to the project in question. On the strength of this demonstration, Cogan argues that certain dates in Chronicles which place events earlier in a king's reign than is stated or implied in Kings, or earlier than seems possible, are not authentic variant traditions. They are tendentious dates given by the Chronicler in order to emphasize those kings' alacritous solicitude for God's temple. A related literary rather than historical use of chronology is found in the dating of events to "the third year," or assigning them a three-year duration.†

* See, e.g., Sarna, *Understanding Genesis*, pp. 81–85, on the patriarchal chronologies.
† Cf. Zakovitch, "*For Three.*"

● ● ● ●

The core of this study was presented at the Seventh World Congress of Jewish Studies in Jerusalem, August 1977, and appeared in Hebrew in *Zion* 45 (1980): 165–72. Material from that article is used here with permission.

Chronology in Chronicles

The reliability of the historical record in the book of Chronicles concerning the era of the Israelite monarchy, especially as regards those items which parallel the record in the book of Kings, is an issue on which biblical historians are divided. Roughly defined, two distinct and somewhat polar positions have been taken. According to the first, information appearing in Chronicles which differs or adds to that in Kings is considered to be the literary product of the Chronicler's unique historiography. According to the second, the Chronicler's additional material derives from sources not utilized by the editors of Kings; even so, each separate item must be evaluated before allowing its admissibility as historical evidence. While the first position, for the most part, dismisses the Chronicler as a contemporary witness to events in preexilic Israel, the second allows for utilization of material from Chronicles in historical reconstruction.[1]

One aspect of this scholarly debate will occupy us here: chronology. The date in 2 Chron. 29:3 illustrates vividly the issues under discussion. It is reported that "in the first year of his reign, in the first month" King Hezekiah reopened and reinforced the doors of the Temple closed by his father, Ahaz, the opening move in the countrywide cleansing of cultic installations in Judah. This date does not appear in the parallel account in 2 Kings 18:4, where Hezekiah's cultic reforms are summarily listed. As expected, scholarly assessment of the Chronicles date divides along the lines of the two positions outlined above. For M. Noth, the date is a free addition by the Chronicler, one of many, to the text which derived ultimately from Kings, its intention being to underscore Hezekiah's early piety.[2] For E. R. Thiele, on the other hand, it is a key building block in his reconstruction of the chronology of the eighth-seventh centuries B.C.E. in which he sets Hezekiah's accession in 715 B.C.E.[3]

Resolution of such differences of opinion seems unattainable by further inner-biblical investigation. It is appropriate, therefore, to turn our attention to the contemporary corpus of Mesopotamian historical literature, which in its techniques of composition and edition shows itself to be analogous to biblical historical writing.[4] We propose to examine a case in which chronology was enlisted to serve historiographic ends. Intentional alteration of

---

1. For a useful survey of these positions and bibliography, see Liver, "History and Historiography," pp. 221–33, and Welten, *Geschichte*, pp. 1–6.

2. See Noth, *Überlieferungsgeschichtliche Studien*, pp. 157–58.

3. See Thiele, *Mysterious Numbers*, pp. 150–52, and cf. Myers, *II Chronicles*, p. 170, and Tadmor, "Hezekiah," col. 97. Jepsen refers to both approaches in his work, but leaves the issue undecided; see Jepsen and Hanhart, *Untersuchungen*, p. 31 n. 33.

4. J. Lewy pointed to the Babylonian chronistic tradition as evidence against the claim that "Israelite and Judaean annalists worked differently than the(ir) Babylonian" counterparts. See Lewy, *Chronologie*, pp. 7–10.

regnal dates in the inscriptions of the Neo-Babylonian monarch Nabonidus has been studied by H. Tadmor.[5] Here we shall observe an example of pseudo-dating in a Neo-Assyrian text particularly relevant to issues in Chronicles. By bringing this example, it is in no way implied that a genetic relationship exists between the literatures of Assyria and Israel; rather, the analogous phenomenon is typologically suggestive.

Esarhaddon's *Babylon Inscription*

Among the royal inscriptions of the Neo-Assyrian period, the so-called *Babylon Inscription of Esarhaddon*[6] is perhaps better known to biblicists than others because of several of its motifs which are reminiscent of biblical prophecy: Marduk, Babylon's chief deity, became angry at his city and decreed its desolation for seventy years. But before this harsh punishment had run its full course, the god relented and, by reversing the cuneiform numbers, literally turned this lengthy period into eleven years.[7] Furthermore, a causal relationship between the moral behavior and piety of the residents of Babylon and the response of the gods informs the opening episodes of this composition, which surveys Babylon's fortunes from the days of Sennacherib on the eve of the city's destruction to those of Esarhaddon and its handsome rebuilding.[8]

---

5. See Tadmor, "Inscriptions of Nabunaid," pp. 351–58.

6. The cuneiform text in transliteration and translation is presented by Borger, *Asarhaddon*, pp. 10–29. The English translation in Luckenbill, *Ancient Records*, 2:242–64, is dated in several key episodes and is in need of revision.

7. 70 *šanāti minût nidûtišu išṭurma*
rēmēnû ᵈMarduk surriš libbašu inūḫma
eliš ana šapliš ušbalkitma
ana 11 šanāti ašābšu iqbi
   Seventy years, the reckoning of its destruction which he had inscribed,
   the merciful god Marduk, as soon as his heart had calmed down,
   reversed the order (of the signs) (lit. "exchanged upper and lower"),
   and ordered its resettlement after eleven years.
(See Borger, *Asarhaddon*, p. 15, Episode 10, Fassung A.) This interpretation of the amnesty granted Babylon was facilitated by the handy numerical play on the cuneiform signs. The number 70 written ⟨𐎟 (i.e., 60 + 10) was reversed to 11, which is written 𐎟⟨ (i.e., 10 + 1). See the comment by Borger, *Asarhaddon*, loc. cit. "Upper and lower" (*eliš u šapliš*: AN.TA and KI.TA) appear as grammatical terms in Akkadian and have their semantic correspondents in the postbiblical accentual terms *milʿêl* and *milraʿ*, as pointed out by Shaffer, *Or.* 38:435 n. 4.

8. The most recent consideration of the theological significance of this composition and its relevance to biblical thought is by Roberts, "Myth *versus* History."

The text of the *Babylon Inscription* appears in eight recensions, and in a recent study[9] we have shown that these recensions are not likely to have been contemporaneous. By comparing the information concerning the stages of construction at Babylon both within the various recensions and with parallel descriptions in chronicle texts, a sequence is suggested according to which a detailed recension containing information about late stages in the construction is compositionally posterior to a recension that relates only the early stages. What is most astonishing is that the colophons of all recensions, early as well as late, bear the same date: *šanat rēš šarrūti Aššur-aḫu-iddina šar māt Aššur*, "the accession year of Esarhaddon, king of Assyria."[10] Thus, according to this colophon date, the inscriptions themselves and the events they describe are attributed to Esarhaddon's accession year. But from what we know about this time period, this date is inconceivable. The events which surrounded Esarhaddon's rise to the throne—the assassination of Sennacherib and the civil war waged against Esarhaddon by rival brothers—marked his *rēš šarrūti* as one of much turmoil,[11] hardly a time for construction at Babylon on the scale described in our inscription, even on the limited scale described in the earliest recension, G.[12] In fact, the major historical prism of Esarhaddon reports that "in the month of Adar, a propitious month, on the 8th day, the day of the *eššešu*-festival of the god Nabu . . . I (Esarhaddon) joyfully sat on my father's throne." Since accession years ended on the last day of Adar, this means that Esarhaddon's *rēš šarrūti* could not have lasted more than twenty-two days![13]

---

9. See Cogan, "Omens and Ideology," pp. 85–87.

10. See Borger, *Asarhaddon*, p. 29. *šanat rēš šarrūti*, "accession year," is the Akkadian term for the incomplete year extending from the king's ascending the throne until the next New Year's Day, after which the "first year" of his reign began. Its biblical equivalent is *šěnat molkô* (2 Kings 25:27) and not *rēʾšît malkût* or *rēʾšît mamlěkût/mamleket* (Jer. 26:1; 27:1), as recognized by some, e.g., Bright, *Jeremiah*, p. 169, and misinterpreted by others, e.g., Sarna, "Zedekiah's Emancipation," p. 149. See, too, Tadmor, *rēʾšît malkût*, col. 313.

11. See Borger, *Asarhaddon*, pp. 40–45, Nin. A, Episode 2; cf. Luckenbill, *Ancient Records*, pp. 200–203.

12. See Borger, *Asarhaddon*, p. 19, note to Episode 18, and Cogan, "Omens and Ideology," pp. 85–87.

13. See Borger, *Asarhaddon*, p. 45, ll. I 87–II 2. The *Babylonian Chronicle* for 681/80 B.C.E. reads: "20 Tebet. Sennacherib king of Assyria was killed by his son in a revolt. Sennacherib had reigned 23 years in Assyria. From 20 Tebet until 2 Adar there was a revolt in Assyria. On 8(?) Adar Esarhaddon his son took the throne of Assyria." The signs for the date of accession are partially broken and they are now read as 18(?) by Grayson, *Assyrian and Babylonian Chronicles*, p. 82, note to Chronicle 1, iii, 38. Given these facts, the month name in the colophon of recension G of the *Babylon Inscription* must be considered erroneous: *Iyar šanat rēš šarrūti*. G. Frame's recent suggestion (*RA* 76:157 n. 5) to take *rēš šarrūti* here as meaning the first regnal year or generally the early part of the reign is not acceptable to us; it would upset the common understanding of the intent of colophon dating: to record the exact date of the copy at hand. The date in recension G cannot be correct; it is further evidence for "date

The date in the *Babylon Inscription* is obviously a pseudo-date, and in an inscription we suspect was reedited several times over a span of five to six years the utilization of this pseudo-date would seem to have been purposeful. It is not hard to suggest the rationale behind this antedating. The *Babylon Inscription*, focusing as it does on the tragedies that had overtaken Babylon, sought to rationalize the city's destruction by Sennacherib and to set the contending parties in Assyria and Babylonia on a conciliatory course.[14] The *rēš šarrūti* date served as testimony to Esarhaddon's early concern for Babylon. It was as if to say: From his very first days on the throne, the Assyrian monarch, encouraged and supported by the god Marduk, turned to the affairs of his lord's city, "the city (from which) the gods supervise the fate (of mankind)."[15] As the inscription was revised over the years, all progress on the reconstruction of Babylon which had taken place in the intervening years was similarly credited to the accession year.

With this extrabiblical case of pseudo-dating in hand, we return to our initial point of departure to examine three narratives in the book of Chronicles which exhibit a similar use of pseudo-dating.

Hezekiah's Reform

2 Chron. 29:3 relates that "in the first year of his reign, in the first month, he (i.e., Hezekiah) opened the doors of the House of the Lord and strengthened them."[16] This act signaled the start of an extensive rehabilitation of the Temple and its service, which concluded with the celebration of

---

tampering" in the colophons of the *Babylon Inscription*. Or might it represent an alternate tradition on the accession of Esarhaddon, two months later than the one recorded in the Chronicle? Cf. now Owen and Watanabe, *Or.Ant.* 22:37–38 n. 3. If indeed a discrepancy exists as to the date of Esarhaddon's accession, it would not be an isolated occurrence in late Assyrian texts. For an example from the reign of Ashurbanipal, see Cogan, "Ashurbanipal Prism F," pp. 98–99.

14. This was treated in Cogan, *Imperialism*, pp. 12–13.

15. *ālum masnaqti ilāni* (from the text published by Millard, "Some Esarhaddon Fragments," p. 118, Episode 35b). This unique expression, pointing to the centrality of Babylon in the divine sphere, appears only in recension E of the *Babylon Inscription* and is one of the markers of the inscription's Babylonian provenance. See further in Cogan, "Omens and Ideology," pp. 82–84.

16. Cf. also 2 Chron. 29:7. The matter of the locked doors of the Temple's Main Hall is an instructive example of midrashic expansion which typifies the Chronicler's work. 2 Kings 16:18 seems to have served as the source, albeit an oblique one, for information that Ahaz had made architectural alterations to the Temple building. Also from 2 Kings 18:16 it might be possible to deduce that Hezekiah had refitted the doors of the Temple prior to his own stripping of their precious overlay. Several of Ahaz's alterations were the direct result of an urgent need to meet the heavy tribute payment due Tiglath-pileser III, apparently after the

the Passover by all Israel in a festive mood unlike anything the capital had seen since the days of Solomon.[17] A countrywide cleansing of the cult followed (31:1).

The parallel account in 2 Kings 18:4 is much shorter than the one in Chronicles. It knows nothing of Hezekiah's Temple activities, but does contain a report of his reform:

It was he who abolished the high-places, and broke the sacred pillars and cut down the sacred trees, and crushed the bronze serpent that Moses had made; for until those very days Israelites were offering sacrifices to it. It was called Nehushtan.

The offensive Nehushtan, associated with Moses and the desert traditions (cf. Num. 21:9), is passed over in Chronicles;[18] at the same time, a date is introduced at the head of the narrative.

All attempts at coordinating the date in 2 Chron. 29:3 with the calendar of Hezekiah's reign have run into difficulties and have unnecessarily complicated the chronology of the late eighth century. For example, if the first year of Hezekiah is set at 727/26 (cf. 2 Kings 18:1), prior to the Assyrian conquest of the Kingdom of Israel, it is hard to imagine the circumstances under which an invitation to participate in the celebrations in Jerusalem would be addressed to the residents of that kingdom and under which they would be designated as "the remnant who escaped out of the hands of the kings of Assyria" (2 Chron. 30:6). If, on the other hand, the date 715 is preferred for Hezekiah's accession, one is forced to assume, as is J. M. Myers, that the invitation to the Israelite residents of the province of Samaria was received while Assyrian authorities were engaged in events outside the area.[19] M. Vogelstein's unique solution to the date problem posits the introduction by Hezekiah of a new calendar, marking the start of his "reform era."[20]

Assyrian king's intervention on Judah's behalf in 734–732. There is no reason for associating these changes with the introduction of foreign cults into Jerusalem. See Cogan, "Ahaz Altar," pp. 119–24. On the Chronicler's midrash in 2 Chronicles 29 and its intent, see Williamson, *Israel*, pp. 115, 119–25, and Japhet, *Ideology*, p. 184.

17. The participation of residents of northern Israel—the territory of the former Israelite kingdom and subsequently the Assyrian province of Samaria—cannot be historically verified. The item does point, however, to the unique approach to the question of the unity of the people of Israel in Chronicles. See the discussion of Williamson, *Israel*, pp. 88–140, and Japhet, *Ideology*, pp. 228–77.

18. No reference to the Neshushtan is to be found in 2 Chronicles; it was likely not repeated from 2 Kings 18:4 so as to avoid linking Moses in any way with an Israelite fetish. Cf. the remarks of Rudolph, *Chronikbücher*, p. 305.

19. Myers, *II Chronicles*, p. 170; idem, *I Chronicles*, p. xx.

20. Vogelstein, *Biblical Chronology*, pp. 2–4; idem, *Fertile Soil*, pp. 72–74. Vogelstein's supposed "reform era" dating encompassed the difficult date "the fourteenth year of Hezekiah" in 2 Kings 18:14.

But such attempts do not dissuade us from viewing the Chronicles date as a pseudo-date, attributing no chronological significance to "the first year of his reign, in the first month." This was simply the Chronicler's way of saying: The pious Hezekiah concerned himself with Temple affairs from his very first day on the throne.[21]

Josiah's Reform

The story of King Josiah's reform and its chronology as related by the Chronicler differs considerably from the parallel account in 2 Kings 22–23. In 2 Kings 22:1, Josiah comes to the throne at eight years of age; he begins his reform eighteen years later (22:3). At first this encompassed only repairs to the Temple, but after the discovery of the Torah book, the king initiated a purge of idolatry throughout his kingdom, which he extended into Samaria as well.[22] In Chronicles the order of events differs. Josiah ascends the throne at the age of eight (2 Chron. 34:1). At age sixteen, "while he was still a youth, he began to seek the God of David his ancestor" (34:3). At age twenty, he undertook the reform of the cult (34:3). Six more years were to pass until Temple restorations were begun, during which the Torah book was discovered (34:8). In sum, Chronicles has added the element of Josiah's piety at age sixteen, reversed the order of the Temple restorations plus the discovery of the Torah book and the cultic reform, and antedated the latter by six years.

The rationality of the Chronicler's account has made it attractive to some scholars, and for this reason it has been preferred to 2 Kings 22–23.[23] F. M. Cross and D. N. Freedman, for example, thought it possible to coordinate the dates in 2 Chronicles 34 and those of political upheavals within the Assyrian empire which followed the death of King Ashurbanipal. In their view, Josiah undertook a series of actions in 632, 628, and 622 which culminated in Judah's release from political and religious vassaldom.[24] Even though the suggested coordination has been upset by the fixing of

21. Note the fitness of the choice of the "first month," Nisan; it was the month of the Passover festival, the season of cultic renewal. Cf. the remarks of Michaeli, *Chroniques*, ad loc.

22. The detailed story of the reform in Kings (2 Kings 23:4–20) reports the Temple as the main arena of activity, with the city of Jerusalem and its suburbs certainly not neglected. Only at a later stage did the reformers move into Samaria (vv. 15–20). By contrast, the literary phrase "Judah and Jerusalem" sums up all that is said about the geographical limits of the reform in 2 Chron. 34:3b–5.

23. See, e.g., Smirin, *Josiah*, p. 62; Liver, "Josiah," cols. 418–20; Myers, *II Chronicles*, p. 205; Bright, *History*, p. 318; Reviv, "History of Judah," pp. 201–2.

24. See Cross and Freedman, "Josiah's Revolt," pp. 56–58.

Ashurbanipal's death in 627,[25] there are still some who hold the account in 2 Chronicles 34 "to be more reasonable."[26]

It is not necessary to enter here into a detailed analysis of both the Kings and Chronicles traditions, for even if we were to grant that a reform carried out in stages as posited by Chronicles as compared with one completed in under a year as presented in 2 Kings[27] is a historically plausible reconstruction, the chronology in 2 Chronicles 34 would still be suspect. The neat progression of events and its very rationality raise the suspicion that the Chronicler has ordered his data to conform to his conceptions of royal piety. Its effect is to have Josiah undertake the reform as soon as he was able to act on his own. Because he was a minor when he succeeded to the throne, Josiah would certainly have been under regent's tutelage for the first period of his rule (likely the tutelage of the *ʿam hāʾāreṣ*, the People of the Land, who had overseen the restoration of order after Amon's assassination[28]). On his own initiative he began to seek the Lord at the age of sixteen. The sequel to this devotion took place when Josiah reached his majority at age twenty, the traditional age for military enlistment:[29] Josiah took over the reins of government and, as his very first act, purged the *entire* land of Israel of *all* idolatry (34:6–7). Note that this action needed no prompting from any circle or from any book (the Torah book was not to be discovered for six more years). The pious king knew from previous exposure to the Lord since age sixteen what was pleasing to Him. By age twenty-six—the age at which Kings has the whole reform take place and six years into Josiah's majority—there was nothing left to do but repair the Temple and learn of the Torah book, whose demands Josiah had already fulfilled.[30] The schematic nature of the Chronicler's chronology and its his-

---

25. Oates, "Assyrian Chronology," pp. 135–59.

26. So, e.g., Bright, *History*, p. 317 n. 23.

27. Several manuscripts of the LXX to 2 Kings 22:3 add "the seventh month" or "the eighth month" to the date "the eighteenth year." See Montgomery and Gehman, *Kings*, p. 257, ad loc. These LXX interpolations simply highlight a fact implicit in Kings: all of Josiah's reform program was executed within the short period from New Year's until Passover; cf. 22:3 and 23:23.

28. The scholarly issue of the constituency of the People of the Land and its active role in Judean politics was treated by Ishida, " 'The People of the Land.' "

29. Cf. Num. 1:3; 26:2; 1 Chron. 27:23; 25:5.

30. J. Tigay called my attention to an incongruity in the text created by antedating the reform, for now that the reform precedes the discovery of the Torah book, the sudden recognition of guilt which the book prompts is pointless: the sins mentioned by the book had been abolished six years earlier. Whereas 2 Chron. 34:21, like 2 Kings 22:13, ascribes the guilt to "our ancestors," under Kings' chronology of the reform this is a sin continuing up to the present, as implied by 2 Kings 22:16–17. Chronicles' chronology, however, implies that the sin has been rooted out, which leaves Chronicles' retention of this passage (in 2 Chron. 34:24–25) purposeless. In fact, in Chronicles Josiah purges no further sins from Judah after the Torah

toriographic underpinnings are readily discernible: they are designed to show the earliness and self-motivation of the king's piety.[31]

David's Transfer of the Ark to Jerusalem

The exploits of King David provide us with our third example of chronological restructuring in Chronicles, and this emerges from a comparison of the placement assigned to certain narratives in 2 Samuel and 1 Chronicles. They include the following episodes:

2 Samuel	1 Chronicles
1. Anointment of David as king over all Israel (5:1–5)	1. Anointment of David as king over all Israel (11:1–3)
2. Capture of Jebusite Jerusalem and its settlement (5:6–10)	2. Capture of Jebusite Jerusalem and its settlement (11:4–9) [David's heroes (11:10–47); Volunteers at Ziklag and Hebron (12)[32]]
	6A. Transfer of the Ark to Jerusalem: Stage 1 (13)
3. Construction of a royal palace (5:11–12)	3. Construction of a royal palace (14:1–2)

---

book is discovered. 2 Chron. 34:33, if not a recap, implies at most further mopping up of stray divergent cults (cf. Galling, *Chronik, Esra, Nehemia*, p. 176), although the verse seems to add nothing to what is said in verses 6–7.

31. It is of more than passing interest to recall here the laudation heaped on Esarhaddon in a tablet copy of a monumental inscription (Borger, *Asarhaddon*, pp. 79–85), summarizing the king's good works at Ashur and Babylon:

Obv. 32. [*šarru ša ultu*] *ṣeḫerišu adi rabîšu bēlūssunu puqqūma qurussunu dallu*

33. *šarru* [*ša*] *ina ūmē palîšu ilāni rabûti ana ešret māḫāzīšunu salīmu iršû iškunu tayartu . . .*

36. *išippu mubbib ṣalam ilāni rabûti bānû bīt Aššur ēpiš Esagil u Babili*

[King, who from] his youth until his maturity, has revered their (the gods') lordship and has proclaimed their valor.

King, during whose rule the great gods became reconciled with the sanctuaries of their temples and undertook a return . . .

the purification priest, who cleanses the statues of the great gods, restores the Temple of Ashur, rebuilds (the temple) Esagil and Babylon.

Is this example of youthful piety followed by royal beneficence evidence for a common *topos*, one which appears in Israelite literature in the Chronicler's depiction of Josiah?

32. For the suggestion that the introduction of this material at this point in the narrative is the Chronicler's way of enlarging the list of David's supporters in his bid for the throne, see Williamson, "We Are Yours," pp. 164–76. For a comparative study of the double list of David's heroes and the additional data in Chronicles, see Mazar, "Military Élite."

4. David's family (5:13–16)   4. David's family (14:3–7)
5. Sundry battles with the Philistines   5. Sundry battles with the Philistines
   (5:17–25)   (14:8–17)
6. Transfer of the Ark to Jerusalem (6)[33]   6B. Transfer of the Ark to Jerusalem:
                                               Stage 2 (15–16)

This is not the place for a full-scale historical analysis of the events comprising David's early rule in Jerusalem; suffice it to say that the collocation of events as presented in 2 Samuel does not a priori command our confidence any more than does that in 1 Chronicles.[34] What is relevant to the discussion here is that the Chronicler saw fit to rearrange the episodes in his telling of the story. Such rearrangement does not occasion surprise; it is an editorial procedure not unfamiliar in history writing, one which has been documented in Assyrian historical texts in particular.[35] At times, the Ninevite scribes followed a geographical order of presentation; at others, they lumped incidents together on an associative basis. Strict chronology was not a necessary principle in their presentation of history. In our case, the biblical Chronicler moved the ill-fated first attempt to transfer the Ark from its position in 2 Samuel, where it follows the construction of David's palace, and conspicuously placed it after the unit on Jerusalem's capture, prior to the construction of the palace. The second half of the episode was left in its original end position. To demonstrate David's piety, it was sufficient to indicate that he had tried to move the Ark to Jerusalem immediately after its conquest and that his failure to complete the move was due to an act of God. The Chronicler did not assign a date to David's attempt, as he did in the other instances studied above; he simply reordered his data to obtain the desired message: Care for the Jerusalem cult precedes one's personal desires and ambition. Unattended during Saul's reign, the Ark is

---

33. The independence of the narrative concerning the Lord's Ark in Philistine hands in 1 Samuel 4—7:1 from 2 Samuel 6 is convincingly argued by Miller and Roberts, *Hand of the Lord*, pp. 22–26.

34. Mazar recognized that 2 Samuel 5–6 is a composite editorial unit and that "there is no reason to assume that" the events of the history of Jerusalem as presented in these chapters "are of necessity chronologically linked to each other." See Mazar, "David's Reign," pp. 235–44.

S. Japhet brought no supporting evidence for her claim that the order of events in 2 Samuel 2–5 bears a "strong stamp of political logic" and is "unanimously accepted as historical." See Japhet, "Conquest and Settlement," p. 208 n. 12. Mazar's arguments to the contrary were not considered.

35. The standard introduction to the study of the Assyrian texts remains Olmstead, *Assyrian Historiography* (1916), although many of the basic scribal practices were already clear to C. P. Tiele, *Babylonische-Assyrische Geschichte* (1886), 1:27–33. For a recent survey of the formal types in this literature, see Grayson, "Assyria and Babylonia."

taken up by David to his new capital as the first royal act. David's exemplary behavior set the standard by which all future monarchs would be measured.[36]

"Three Years" as a Typological Period

Before concluding this study of pseudo-dating in Chronicles, it might be useful to point out two other instances in which dates accompanying narratives seem to be of merely literary character. Both are parts of episodes found only in Chronicles, and because they are unparalleled in Kings, the episodes are suspect of being the creations of the Chronicler. 2 Chron. 11:7 states that "for three years" Rehoboam enjoyed the support of those priests who had relocated to Judah after the rupture with the North. 2 Chron. 17:7 states that Jehoshaphat commissioned royal officers to enforce the Law in the cities of Judah "in the third year of his reign." These dates are probably typological; the number three indicates, as it so often does, the end point or the completion of a short span of time.[37] That the Chronicler did not take such numbers seriously is shown by his deletion of such a date from a story he took over from 1 Kings 22, correctly sensing that it had no chronological significance. The "three years" of peace between Israel and Aram-Damascus which preceded the battle of Ramoth-Gilead (1 Kings 22:1) was replaced by "toward the end of his reign" (lit. "at the end of years," 2 Chron. 18:2); fitted out with a new "date" and a new context, the Chronicler's telling of the story directs attention to Jehoshaphat's senility as an explanation for his forsaking the Lord.[38]

36. The miscellaneous addition in LXX at 1 Kings 2:35 has been shown to be a "carefully constructed piece" which expands on the theme of Solomon's "wisdom in completing the Lord's house before he built his own. . . ." See Gooding, *Relics*, pp. 7–12. The author of the addition unmistakably considered Solomon to be one who passed muster by the Chronicler's criterion of royal piety.

37. See Pope, "Number," pp. 564–65; and Zakovitch, "*For Three*," pp. 1–40, esp. pp. 18–20.

38. Williamson, *1 and 2 Chronicles*, observed "the juxtaposition of varying episodes" in the chronological framework of 2 Chronicles 17–21 (p. 278), but then missed the mark by stating that "the Chronicler may have thought that for the first two years of his reign Jehoshaphat was merely a co-regent with the ailing Asa," the third year being "the beginning of his own effective rule" (p. 282).

Had the judicial reform been cultic in nature, it could have been assigned the primary position in the list of Jehoshaphat's accomplishments, i.e., dated to "the first year." Note that the Chronicler did begin this listing with the statement "He was exceedingly loyal to the ways of the Lord; and he even removed the high places and the sacred poles from Judah" (17:6). And then he continued: "In the third year. . . ."

That ancient historiographers used such figures as literary devices is clear from elsewhere in the ancient Near East.[39] The following example from the Neo-Assyrian corpus illustrates the point. In a dedicatory inscription to the Nergal Temple in Cutha by Ashurbanipal (K 2631+), the efforts of the king to release the cult objects captured 1,635 years earlier during the Elamite raids into Babylonia are a central theme.[40] The narration skips over the early Assyrian moves against Elam, which are known to us from the Ashurbanipal annals, and proceeds immediately to a description of the major battles that led to the fall of Susa. A comparison of the annals and K 2631+ shows verbal congruence between the two inscriptions in many passages, and so it is likely that the same *Vorlage* served the scribes/authors of both. But unlike the annals author who integrated the Elamite wars into the overall chronological scheme of Ashurbanipal's reign, the author of K 2631+ chose an independent course: he concentrated solely on the Elamite wars, which he numbered "my first campaign" and "my second campaign." Then in the summation he wrote:

> *ištēnit šattu māt Elam aṣbat*
> *ina šanītu šattu šanītu uḫalliqši*
> *šalultum ša . . . [. . .]*[41]
> The first year I captured Elam;
> in the second year, I destroyed it a second time;
> the third time. . . .

The typological number three was pressed into service to describe the climax of the Elamite campaigns: *šalultum*, "the third time," Ashurbanipal delivered the "knock-out punch" to Elam.[42]

As we compare the dates and order of events in ancient texts, either with the sources of those texts or with other information about the events themselves, we observe that dates and order were on occasion used as literary devices rather than precise historical data. Chronologies were malleable. One cannot but conclude, on the basis of the cases examined above,

---

39. For an example of the use of "three years" in Babylonian historical writing, see Tadmor, "Inscriptions of Nabunaid," pp. 353–54. See, too, the comments of Loewenstamm, "Seven-Day Unit," pp. 131–33 (reprint, pp. 205–6).

40. See Streck, *Assurbanipal*, 2:176–89.

41. Ibid., 2:184, rev. 8–9; cf. also 2:175, K 1364, rev. 9, where the parallel *šalšiānu*, "for the third time," appears.

42. The synthesis by Grayson, "Chronology," honestly admits that a new source study of the Elamite campaigns is needed.

that the Chronicler as a chronographer did not follow present-day standards. Modern biblical historians would do well if they studied the ancient Chronicler's work not only as a theological statement based on history—the focus of most major investigations during the last two decades—but also as an example of historiographic writing which mirrors the canons of ancient Near Eastern literature.[43]

43. For examples of antedating in Hellenistic chronography, see Bickerman, "Notes"; for a study of chronology, esp. "symmetrical" chronology, put to the service of historiography, see Cohen, *Book of Tradition by Abraham Ibn Daud*, pp. 189–222.

8

The Literary History of the Book of Jeremiah in the Light of Its Textual History

EMANUEL TOV

Editor's Note

In its simplest form the critical view that biblical texts have not reached us in their original form means that they have undergone revision (reformulation, expansion, less often abridgement). This view has often been applied to prophetic literature. Whether the revision involved conforming old prophecies to the subsequent course of events, or ascribing later ideas to earlier prophets, is debated; but even the view which denies that there were changes of substance agrees that "the prophetic literature has not reached us in its primary state."* A case in point is the book of Jeremiah. The Septuagint text of that book is shorter than the Masoretic Text and arranged differently. A Hebrew fragment agreeing with the Septuagint was found at Qumran, confirming that the short version is based on a Hebrew *Vorlage*. In the present chapter, Emanuel Tov, building

---

* Kaufmann, *Religion*, pp. 349–50.

An earlier version of this chapter appeared as "Some Aspects of the Textual and Literary History of the Book of Jeremiah," in P.-M. Bogaert (ed.), *Le livre de Jérémie*, containing the papers read in Leuven during the "Journées bibliques," August 1980. Material from that paper is reproduced here by permission.

on his own and others' demonstrations that the shorter text is earlier,† proceeds to compare the longer version to the shorter one and to describe the nature of the revision and the techniques of the editor who produced it. At certain points the editor's activity has left the kind of awkwardness which would suggest tampering even if we did not have the documentary evidence to prove it. The work of the editor was of a literary character, not merely scribal, and the evidence thus bears on the literary-critical as well as the text-critical study of the book. But although there are major as well as minor changes, including new material and changes in content, Tov concludes that the revision was not radical and did not significantly distort the message of Jeremiah.

† As was the case with the LXX of 1 Samuel 17–18, Robertson Smith (*OTJC*, pp. 103–6) took for granted that the LXX of Jeremiah reflected a more original text than did the MT, and he cited Jeremiah as an example of editorial activity which supported biblical criticism. Here too the priority of the text reflected in LXX must first be demonstrated before literary-critical conclusions can be based on it.

•   •   •   •

The Two Editions of Jeremiah

The LXX of Jeremiah often differs from the Masoretic Text of that book in major details. It is shorter than the Masoretic Text by one-seventh,[1] and it differs from the Masoretic Text in its arrangement of the material.[2] Since the LXX's translation technique in Jeremiah is relatively literal where the two texts overlap,[3] it is unlikely that the LXX translator would have abridged his Hebrew *Vorlage*. This implies that the brevity of the LXX reflects that of its Hebrew *Vorlage*, in other words, that it reflects a short Hebrew text.[4]

The existence of a shorter Hebrew text of Jeremiah has been confirmed by the discovery of fragments of such a text at Qumran, 4QJer[b] (containing parts of chapters 9–10, 43, and 50).[5] This manuscript, dated by Cross to the

1. See Min, *Minuses and Pluses*.
2. This situation is most clearly visible in the different location of the oracles against the foreign nations. In the MT they constitute chapters 46–51, but in the LXX they follow 25:13 and are arranged in a different order, See further below, p. 217.
3. For a description of the translation technique of the LXX of Jeremiah, see Min. *Minuses and Pluses*, and, more briefly, Scholz, *Masorethische Text*, and Giesebrecht, *Jeremia*, pp. xix–xxxiv.
4. For this reasoning, see above, Chapter 3, pp. 100–101 and, with reference to Jeremiah, Tov, "Exegetical Notes," pp. 73–74.
5. The text was provisionally published by Janzen, *Studies in the Text of Jeremiah* (1973), pp. 181–84; imprecisions are to be corrected in the official publication and in the forthcoming *Hebrew University Bible*. The other fragments of Jeremiah from Qumran (2QJer

Hasmonean period,[6] differs significantly in its contents from the Masoretic Text. In fact, 4QJer[b] resembles the LXX of Jeremiah in the two major features in which the reconstructed *Vorlage*[7] of that translation differs from the Masoretic Text, namely, the arrangement of the text and its shortness compared to the Masoretic Text. Although the fragments are small, the recognition of these two main characteristics is beyond doubt.[8] 4QJer[b] shares seven minuses with the LXX, two of which are long[9] and five short (mainly names).[10] In addition, the LXX has three minuses which are definitely not shared with 4QJer[b],[11] as well as ten short minuses that cannot be compared with 4QJer[b], since only a small section of the reconstructed lines of the scroll has been preserved. The reconstructed text of the scroll also agrees with the LXX (against the MT) in the *sequence* of the verses in chapter 10, where the verses appear in the order 1–5a, 9, 5b, 11–12.

At the same time, it is clear that 4QJer[b] is not *identical* with the reconstructed *Vorlage* of the LXX. In addition to the three LXX minuses not shared with the scroll (mentioned just above), the scroll agrees with the Masoretic Text against the LXX in five details,[12] and it also contains some unique readings found in neither the LXX nor the Masoretic Text.[13] While 4QJer[b] is thus not identical to the *Vorlage* of the LXX, the existence of such a short and differently ordered Hebrew version of Jeremiah, coupled with the fact that the translator of Jeremiah was relatively literal and not likely to have made such changes himself, confirms the conjecture that the LXX of Jeremiah must be based on a short Hebrew *Vorlage*, similar to 4QJer[b].[14]

---

and 4QJer[a,c]) are textually close to the MT, as are the other ancient versions (Pesh, Tg, Vg). See Tov, "Some Aspects," pp. 145–47.

6. See Cross, "Evolution," in Cross and Talmon, *Qumran*, pp. 308 and 316 n. 8.

7. On the problems connected with the reconstruction of the Hebrew *Vorlage* of the LXX to Jeremiah, see Tov, "Exegetical Notes," and *Text-Critical*, chap. 3.

8. The following discussion is indebted to Min, who investigated 4QJer[b] in detail, particularly in comparison with the LXX.

9. 10:6–8, 10.

10. 43:4–5, "Son of Kareah"; 43:5, "from all the countries to which they had been scattered"; 43:6, "chief of the guards" (*rab ṭabbāḥîm*); 43:6, "son of Shaphan."

11. 43:7, "land"; 43:9, "in mortar in the brick structure which" (*bammeleṭ bammalbēn ᵓašer*); 50:4, "declares the Lord."

12. 10:2 MT = 4Q, "way"; LXX, "ways";
43:7 MT = 4Q, "land"; LXX omits;
43:9 MT = 4Q, "take in your hand"; LXX, "take for yourself";
43:9 MT = 4Q, "Judean men"; LXX, "men of Judah";
50:4 MT = 4Q, "declares the Lord"; LXX omits.

13. 10:15 MT = LXX, "their visitation"; 4Q, "I visited them";
43:5 MT, "in the land Judah"; 4Q, "[in the la]nd [Egyp]t"?; LXX, "in the land."
42:9 MT, "in mortar in the brick structure which"; LXX omits; 4Q has a longer text than MT, as shown by calculations of space.

14. Janzen, *Studies*, and earlier in his dissertation of the same title; Tov, "L'incidence"; idem, "Exegetical Notes"; earlier studies are mentioned by Min.

The question of whether the shorter or the longer version of Jeremiah is the earlier of the two has been discussed on a number of occasions by J. G. Janzen, Y.-J. Min, and the present writer.[15] Pursuing partly identical and partly different lines of argument, which cannot be repeated here, each of us has concluded that the shorter version is earlier and the longer one is later. It has been suggested further, especially by the present writer and by P.-M. Bogaert,[16] that the common text of the LXX and 4QJer[b], that is, the short version, does not reflect a different *text* of Jeremiah but an earlier *edition* of that book (*edition I*; by the same token, the MT is called *edition II*).[17] The two editions differed from each other not only in length but also, as noted, in the arrangement of the material. The first, short edition was expanded to the form now found in edition II during one of the stages of the literary growth of the book. Edition II contains many pluses over against edition I, not only in words, phrases, and sentences but also in complete sections, the largest of which are 33:14–26 and 39:4–13. For the sake of clarity it should be added that the date of the textual *witnesses* of the first edition does not bear on the date of the edition itself, because presumably edition I was written long before the time of the LXX, and it was not destroyed even when edition II was created on the basis of edition I. It was still known in the second century B.C.E. in Egypt, when it served as the *Vorlage* for the LXX translation, and was present (along with manuscripts close to the second edition) at Qumran[18] in the Hasmonean manuscript 4QJer[b].

If this description of the relationship between the texts is correct, we can now proceed to describe the nature of edition II, and especially the principles guiding its editor, beyond the earlier studies of Janzen and Min. The description that follows is based on the premise that the Hebrew *Vorlage* of the LXX as well as 4QJer[b] represent different texts of an early edition of Jeremiah which was expanded by the editor of the Masoretic Text into edition II.

---

15. See the previous note.

16. Tov, "L'incidence"; idem, "Exegetical Notes"; Bogaert, "De Baruch à Jérémie," and idem, "Mécanismes," pp. 168–73, 222–38.

17. We use the terms *edition/editor* and *text/scribe* to describe different stages in the development of the book as well as the persons involved. *Editions* belong to the stages of the growth of the book, up to and including its final formulation, and they involve major changes, additions, and transpositions; the writers who produced them are termed *editors*. The *textual* transmission, performed by *scribes* for each edition, starts *after* that edition was completed. Scribes involved in this process did insert changes into the text, but to a much smaller degree than editors did.

18. See n. 5.

The Nature of the Added Layer of Edition II
(the Masoretic Text)

The first question that comes to mind is why editor II chose to reedit Jeremiah rather than other books. This question, however, can hardly be discussed, since we lack manuscript evidence with regard to the other books. Possibly other biblical books have been rewritten in a similar way, but the unrevised editions simply have not been preserved, so that the very fact and extent of that rewriting is not known. (The question arises, for example, with regard to the LXX of Ezekiel, which is somewhat shorter than the Masoretic Text of that book.) We are therefore justified in disregarding this issue, concentrating on Jeremiah only.

The second issue is the liberty which editor II took when inserting his own words and thoughts in a book that was transmitted under the name of the prophet Jeremiah. This issue also should not preoccupy us, because most biblical books were rewritten, edited, and reedited in this way. Pseudepigraphal authorship and revision were common practice in antiquity.[19] Among other things, it should be noted that editor II did not distort significantly the message of the prophet as handed down to him. True, he added a great deal and changed a lot, but as a rule these changes were not radical. Furthermore, editor II did not rewrite a scroll that contained only authentic Jeremianic utterances, but he found the *Deuteronomistic* edition of Jeremiah's sayings and biography so that much of what he added was based on an already edited book.[20]

We shall now review the main aspects of the additions and changes of edition II. It should be remarked in passing that edition II is sometimes shorter than edition I (in other words, the LXX sometimes has a plus over against the Masoretic Text),[21] but these relatively few instances may be disregarded in the overall description of edition II. The background of this situation is that both 4QJer[b] and the Hebrew *Vorlage* of the LXX developed from an earlier form of edition I and that editor II rewrote a text which was very similar to edition I, but not identical with it. The resultant sequence of texts is represented in a diagram (stemma) in Figure 1.

---

19. Cf. M. Smith, "Pseudepigraphy," pp. 200ff.
20. See p. 220, below, and n. 28.
21. For the data, see Janzen, *Studies*, pp. 63–65, and Min, *Minuses and Pluses*. It is not likely that editor II omitted these details, as they resemble typologically similar details that were added in edition II.

FIGURE 1

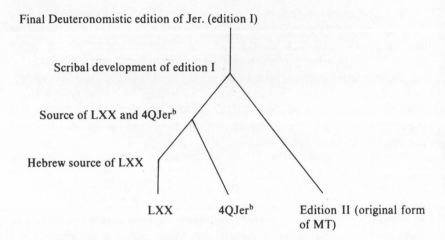

Final Deuteronomistic edition of Jer. (edition I)

Scribal development of edition I

Source of LXX and 4QJer^b

Hebrew source of LXX

LXX   4QJer^b   Edition II (original form of MT)

Editor II rewrote, reedited, and, in a way, revised a text almost identical with edition I, even though edition II does not reflect a *consistent* rewriting of the previous edition. Revisional activity in literary compositions bears a very personal and subjective character, and this should be borne in mind when the additions of edition II are analyzed.

The anonymous author of edition II was not a scribe, as we are not dealing with scribal phenomena, but he was an editor who produced one of the stages of the literary growth of the book. He had access to genuine Jeremianic material not included in edition I (see p. 223), he rearranged sections of the book (p. 217), and he also added new material (pp. 219–24). This activity took place in writing, that is, editor II revised in writing an edition that was known to him in a written form. The assumption of an oral edition I seems very unlikely because edition II often inserts new elements neatly between the words found in edition I. Furthermore, in view of the story in chapter 36, no oral base should be presumed at all.

Since editor II was not consistent, the inconsistency of his rewriting cannot be taken as an argument against our working hypothesis. In fact, very few revisions are consistent—in the biblical realm only "inconsistent" revisers are known, such as the Deuteronomistic reviser of Joshua through 2 Kings and Jeremiah, the "Elohist" in the Psalms, the Lucianic reviser of the LXX, and, on a different level, the Samaritan Pentateuch.[22]

22. The inconsistency of the Deuteronomistic reviser of Joshua through 2 Kings and Jeremiah reveals itself in the discrepancy between the proto-Deuteronomistic composition and the Deuteronomistic layer, and further in the amount of intervention differing from one

Editorial Aspects

Editor II took the liberty of adding and changing many minor details and a few major ones. These changes are visible in (1) text arrangement; (2) the addition of headings to prophecies; (3) repetition of sections; (4) addition of new verses and sections; (5) addition of new details; and (6) changes in content.

TEXT ARRANGEMENT

There are but few differences between the two editions in text arrangement, and in those cases it cannot be determined whether editor II found these differences in his *Vorlage* or whether he made the changes himself. The main difference between the two editions consists of the place of the oracles against the foreign nations. In this case the location in edition II (chaps. 46–51 in the MT) is clearly inferior to that of edition I (after 25:13 in the LXX),[23] so that edition I probably contains the original tradition while the Masoretic Text contains a revised text.

Further differences are found in chapters 10 (where 4QJer[b] concurs with the LXX; see above, p. 213), 23 (in the LXX vv. 7–8 occur after v. 40), and 31 (vv. 35–37 occur in the LXX as 37, 35, 36).

---

section to the other. Similarly, the "Elohist" in the Psalms did not replace all occurrences of YHWH. The Lucianic reviser was not consistent in his vocabulary, linguistic changes, or the amount of intervention. In the Samaritan Pentateuch, the so-called harmonizing readings are not inserted consistently.

23. This argument is based especially on the MT of 25:13, which refers to the punishment of Babylon as "everything written in *this* book which Jeremiah prophesied against all the peoples" (*ʾašer nibbāʾ yirměyāhû ʿal kol haggôyim*). In the setting of the MT this passage makes little sense, as the prophecy on Babylon does not follow immediately, but rather in chapters 50–51. In the LXX, on the other hand, this verse is followed immediately by the collection of prophecies against the nations. Furthermore, in the reconstructed *Vorlage* of the LXX, *ʾašer nibbāʾ*, etc., is not a relative clause, as in the MT, but forms the introduction to the collection of oracles, identical with 46:1 in the MT. An additional argument for the setting of the oracles against the nations *within* chapter 25 is the oracle in 25:15ff. which immediately follows these oracles in the LXX. This oracle on the drinking from the "cup of wrath" by the nations forms an appropriate conclusion for the collection of oracles, while in the MT that oracle is not connected with its context.

It is hard to determine why the collection of oracles was removed in the MT from its proper place to the end of the book (chap. 52 was added later). Editor II may have placed the collection at the end of the book because it formed a large *separate* collection or because he harbored doubts with regard to its authenticity.

ADDITION OF HEADINGS TO PROPHECIES

Editor II added several headings to prophecies which in edition I had no heading at all; he also expanded existing short headings:[24]

2:1-2. The word of the Lord came to me, saying, Go proclaim to Jerusalem.

7:1-2. (The word which came to Jeremiah from the Lord: Stand at the gate of the house of the Lord, and there proclaim this word:) Hear the word of the Lord, all you of Judah (who enter these gates to worship the Lord).

The added information in this last heading derives from v. 10 and the parallel passage in chap. 26.

16:1. The word of the Lord came to me.

27:1. At the beginning of the reign of King Jehoiakim son of Josiah of Judah, this word came to Jeremiah from the Lord.

This last heading is added wrongly, for the chapter itself speaks of Zedekiah; cf. vv. 3, 12, and 28:1ff. The added heading erroneously repeats that of the previous chapter, 26:1.[25]

47:1. (The word of the Lord that came to the prophet Jeremiah) concerning the Philistines, (before Pharaoh conquered Gaza).[26]

One of the added headings is connected with the different sequence of chapters in edition II: after the prophecies against the foreign nations had

---

24. When the additions are quoted along with their larger contexts, parentheses are used for the added matter. When the additions supplement pronouns which were implicit in verbs, the pronouns are placed in brackets. For additions that are presented without any context, no parentheses are used. The Hebrew text (reconstructed from the LXX where necessary) of passages quoted here can be found in Tov, "Some Aspects." The English translations follow NJV as much as possible.

25. It is not impossible that the original text of edition II referred to the *rēʾšît* of the reign of Zedekiah, just as in 28:1 (where this element was not found in edition I), and that the text was corrupted on a scribal level. In any event, from the point of view of method it is very questionable to correct individual words in 27:1 (as in *BHS*), since those corrections do not solve the problems of meaning (except for one detail) of 26:1 and 27:1, or of the absence of the verse in the LXX.

26. There is no consistency in the addition of headings in the prophecies against the nations. Indeed, some "historical" headings are found in editions I and II in the prophecies against Egypt (46:1, 13), Kedar (49:28-33), and Elam (49:34-39), but other prophecies have no heading at all in editions I and II: Moab (48), Ammon (49:1-6), Edom (49:7-27), Babel (50-51). On the whole, neither in this nor in other details should consistency be expected.

been separated from their natural context (after 25:13, as in the LXX) and had been placed in edition II as chapters 46–51, they needed a new heading, hence:

46:1. The word of the Lord to the prophet Jeremiah concerning the nations.

For further examples of added or expanded headings, see pp. 221–22.

REPETITION OF SECTIONS

In edition I, several sections of two or more verses occur twice, for example, 6:22–24 = 50:41–43; 10:12–16 = 51:15–19; 23:19–20 = 30:23–24; 49:18–21 = 50:44–46. This repetition may have originated with the prophet himself, who applied certain prophecies to more than one situation, either orally or in writing, or it may have derived from editor I. In any event, editor II found an edition in which a few sections occurred twice and perhaps for this reason felt at liberty to continue this practice. The following sections are duplicated in edition II (and not in edition I): 6:13–15 (duplicated in 8:10b–12); 15:13–14 (duplicated in 17:3–4); 46:27–28 (duplicated in 30:10–11); 49:22 (duplicated in 48:40b, 41b).

ADDITION OF NEW VERSES AND SECTIONS

Editor II added a substantial number of new verses, both in prose and in poetry, which derive from all three major strata recognized in the book.[27] Some of these are presumably authentic utterances of the prophet (stratum A), others belong to the historical-biographical stratum of the book (stratum B, by Baruch?), and still others, written in Deuteronomistic diction (stratum C), were probably composed by editor II himself.[28]

Let us turn first to the presumably authentic sayings of the prophet, stratum A. Here editor II added some original Jeremianic verses and passages. It should, however, be noted that we do not know why this Jeremianic material had not previously entered edition I and why or how it was preserved. We hasten to add that one should not doubt the originality of these verses (see below on 33:14–26, and see also n. 33) just because they

27. So-called double readings in the MT (such as *mišpĕḥôt mamlĕkôt* in 1:15, where LXX has *mišpĕḥôt* only) are not included in the discussion, since by definition they developed at a late stage, viz., that of the textual transmission. Their number is not large, and they always involve parallel elements.
28. For a summary of the research, see Lipinski, "Jeremiah."

were lacking in edition I. Authentic material probably continued to circulate among the prophet's followers even after edition I was completed. For a possible parallel, see the authentic traditions relating to 1 and 2 Kings contained in the books of Chronicles.

The most remarkable addition of this kind is the prophecy in 33:14–26 on the ṣemaḥ ṣĕdāqâ ("true branch") and the durability of the covenant. Although this section has often been denied to Jeremiah because it is absent from the LXX and may have been added secondarily on the basis of 23:5–6 and 31:35–37,[29] there is no sound reason for this skepticism. On the contrary, in addition to 33:14–16, 25–26, which resemble the aforementioned passages, there are several Jeremianic expressions in this section reminiscent of other passages in the book,[30] and the argument that these elements reflect a glossator's imitation is artificial. The burden of proof is on those who deny the section to the prophet in whose name it has been transmitted.

Other sections added in poetry are 17:1–2; 30:15 (cf. vv. 12b, 14b$_2$); and 51:44b–49a.[31]

The largest addition in the stratum B material is 39:4–13. Verses 4–10 add data derived from 2 Kings 25:4–7, 9–12 (= Jer. 52:7–11, 13–16) before that section was added as an appendix to Jeremiah (chap. 52). At the same time, it provides new data in verses 11–13, in which Nebuchadrezzar commands Nebuzaradan about Jeremiah.

Of special interest are the Deuteronomistic additions in edition II. Edition I already contained a Deuteronomistic layer, which probably derived from editor I himself. This Deuteronomistic rewriting was rather extensive, especially in chapters 7, 11, 19, and 21, but it changed the basic message of the prophet only slightly. The assumption of a Deuteronomistic stratum in Jeremiah (stratum C) is widespread among scholars, but normally it is not realized that this stratum in Jeremiah is composed of two layers. The larger part of the Deuteronomistic stratum is found in edition I, but editor II added many Deuteronomistic phrases (see p. 233) and also complete sections that abound with Deuteronomistic phraseology such as 11:7–8; 29:16–20, and sections of chap. 27 (vv. 7, 13–14a, 17). Editor II may have been one of the last members of that ill-defined "Deuteronomistic school," or else he simply imitated its style.

29. See Rudolph, *Jeremia*, pp. 199–201; Skinner, *Prophecy and Religion*, p. 310. For a discussion of the whole issue, see esp. Janzen, *Studies*, pp. 122–23.

30. "The good thing" (v. 14), cf. 29:10; "the house of Israel (. . .) and the house of Judah" (v. 14), cf. 3:18; 13:11; 31:27; 31:31; "in those days and at that time" (v. 15), cf. 50:4, 20.

31. 10:6–8, 10 (lacking in the LXX and 4QJer^b), on the other hand, may be secondary. The main topic of the chapter is a derogation of the idols, and therefore verses 6–8, 10, are contextually out of place as they extol the God of Israel (if these verses were added secondarily, they resemble the "doxologies" which have also been added elsewhere in the Bible). See further Bogaert, "Mécanismes."

ADDITION OF NEW DETAILS

When analyzing the nature of the added elements, one must pay attention to the amount of "new information" contained in them. Many of the added elements somehow derive from the context, but others contain such data as cannot have derived from the context. It is the latter that we term *new details*. These show that editor II must have had access to Jeremianic material that had not entered edition I, as demonstrated by the data mentioned in the previous section with reference to stratum A. In this section further examples are given, consisting of a few words only. First, some examples from the prose sections of the book.

25:1. The word which came to Jeremiah concerning all the people of Judah, in the fourth year of king Jehoiakim son of Josiah of Judah, (which was the first year of Nebuchadrezzar king of Babylon).

Here editor II has added a synchronism such as is found often in the historical books.

25:20. all the mixed peoples; (all the kings of the land of Uz).

25:25. (all the kings of Zimri) and all the kings of Elam.

25:26. . . . all the royal lands which are on the earth. (And last of all, the king of Sheshach shall drink.)

This last addition remedies the absence of the king of Babylon in the list of kings and nations that are to drink from the "cup of wrath" (vv. 15–17). He is added here in edition II, though in the "atbash" code of secret writing ($\check{s}\check{s}k = bbl$).[32] Likewise, *zmry*, lacking in edition I, if corrected to *zmky*, may be an "atbash" form for Elam (^cylm). The phrase mentioning Uz in verse 20 is lacking in edition I.

27:19–22. [19]For thus said the Lord (of Hosts concerning the columns, the tank, the stands and) concerning the rest of the vessels (which remain in this city), [20]which (Nebuchadnezzar) the king of Babylon did not take when he exiled Jeconiah (son of Jehoiakim, king of Judah) from Jerusalem (to Babylon, with all the nobles of Judah and Jerusalem—[21]thus said the Lord of Hosts, the God of Israel, concerning the vessels remaining in the House of the Lord, in the royal palace of Judah and in Jerusalem): [22]They shall be brought to Babylon (and there they shall remain until I

---

32. In the "atbash" system of secret writing, an *aleph* represents a *tav* and vice versa, a *beth* represents a *s(h)in* and vice versa, etc. See esp. Sasson, "Wordplay in the OT," *IDBS*, p. 969.

take note of them)—declares the Lord—(and bring them up and restore them to this place).

The additions in 27:19–22 stress that the Temple vessels which will be carried off to Babylon will subsequently be returned to Jerusalem. This idea is not consistent with the spirit of the surrounding verses, which deal with false prophets and not with the fate of the Temple vessels. Even if this were not the case, it is nevertheless anticlimactic to mention immediately after the threat to the vessels that ultimately they will be returned to Jerusalem. Nevertheless, from his point of view, editor II felt that he could not leave the words of Jeremiah without correction. (For the realization of both the threat and the promise, see Dan. 5:2–3 and Ezra 1:7, 11; 6:5).

It should further be noted that in this section edition II speaks of two groups of vessels which were left in Jerusalem after Jechoniah's exile and which were to be carried away to Babylon. Of these vessels, "the vessels left in the house of the Lord" are also mentioned in edition I, in 52:17, but the "vessels in the house of the king" are not mentioned there. On the other hand, in 52:13 Nebuzaradan is said to have burnt "the house of the king," and as it is known that Nebuchadrezzar took vessels from "the house of the Lord" before it was burnt, he probably acted similarly with regard to the vessels found in "the house of the king."

29:21. Thus said the Lord (of Hosts, the God of Israel) concerning Ahab (son of Kolaiah) and Zedekiah (son of Maaseiah, who prophesy falsely in my name).

The patronymics of the two false prophets are not mentioned elsewhere.

36:22. the king was sitting in the winter house (in the ninth month).

36:26. . . . to arrest Baruch (the scribe) and Jeremiah (the prophet).

36:32. So Jeremiah got another scroll, (and gave it to Baruch son of Neriah the scribe).

Only in edition II is Baruch explicitly called "the scribe."[33]

---

33. Since Baruch is not known from other books of the Bible, it is of interest to mention a recently published bulla with the inscription *lbrkyhw bn nryhw hspr*, "belonging to Berechyahu son of Neriyahu the scribe." The title "scribe" is applied to Baruch only in edition II of Jeremiah (36:26, 32), not in edition I. The bulla confirms that Baruch actually bore the title. Although editor II could have simply inferred this from Jeremiah 36, it is equally possible that he learned this from authentic traditions about Jeremiah's life. For the bulla, see Avigad, "Baruch the Scribe."

37:17. Zedekiah (the king) sent for him and took him and questioned him (in his palace) secretly.

It is not stated elsewhere in the context that the meeting took place "in his palace."

38:1. Shephatiah son of Mattan, Gedaliah son of Pashhur, Jucal son of Shelemiah (and Pashhur son of Malchiah) heard.

Pashhur the son of Malchiah is known from 21:1, but here he is not mentioned in edition I.

38:7. Ebed-melech the Ethiopian, (a eunuch), heard.

Only here is Ebed-melech called "eunuch."

38:12. And [he] said, (Ebed-melech the Ethiopian to Jeremiah), "Put [them] (the worn cloths and rags under your armpits), inside the ropes."

It is noteworthy that the word for armpits, *ʾaṣṣilôt*, does not occur in this form elsewhere in the Bible (cf., however, *ʾaṣṣîlê* in Ezek. 13:18 and possibly also *ʾaṣṣîlâ* in Ezek. 41:8; the word is further known from rabbinic Hebrew, [*ʾaṣṣîl*, elbow] and Syriac [*yaṣîlāʾ*, elbow]).

There exist similar additions in the *poetry* sections, but the notion of "new details" in poetry differs from such additions in prose. For the prose, examples were given of details that provide new *factual* information, but little such information is contained in the additions in poetry. For these, other criteria must be applied. It seems to us that a "new detail" in the poetry sections is the addition of any detail that conceivably could have derived from the prophet himself. It must be remembered that the poetry sections in the book (stratum A), as opposed to the biographical stratum (B) and the Deuteronomistic stratum (C), are ascribed by all scholars to the prophet himself; therefore any detail added in stratum A may ultimately go back to an authentic tradition, but there can be no certainty in these matters. Some examples follow:

1:18. I make you this day a fortified city, (and an iron pillar), and bronze walls.

2:2. I accounted to your favor the devotion of your youth, your love as a bride—how you followed me (in the wilderness, in a land not sown).

5:15. Lo, I am bringing against you, O House of Israel, a nation from afar—declares the Lord; (an enduring nation, an ancient nation).

13:17. For if you will not give heed, my inmost self must weep because of your arrogance (and copiously shed tears), and my eye must stream with tears.

14:3. They found no water; they returned, their vessels empty (they are shamed and humiliated, they cover their heads).

31:30. But everyone shall die for his own sins; (every person) who[ever] eats sour grapes, his teeth shall be blunted.

31:35. Thus said the Lord, who established the sun for light by day, (the laws of) the moon and stars for light by night.

31:40. (And the entire Valley of the Corpses and Ashes), and all the fields.

46:5. Why (have I seen) they are dismayed, yielding ground.

46:18. As I live—declares (the King), the Lord (of Hosts is his name).

CHANGES IN CONTENT

Editor II sometimes reformulated the text of edition I, often changing its content:

	LXX	*MT*
29:25.		Thus saith the Lord of Hosts, the God of Israel:
	I did not send you in my name to	Because you sent letters in your own name to all the people in Jerusalem, to the priest
	Zephaniah son of Maaseiah the priest saying . . .	Zephaniah son of Maaseiah the priest and to the rest of the priests saying . . .
35:18.		And to the family of the Rechabites Jeremiah said:
	Therefore, thus said the Lord:	Thus said the Lord of Hosts, the God of Israel:
	Because the sons of Jonadab the son of Rechab have obeyed the charge of their father to do as their	Because you have obeyed the charge of Jonadab your father and have kept all his commandments and done all that
	father enjoined them.	he enjoined you.
36:32.	So Baruch got another scroll	So Jeremiah got another scroll and gave it to the scribe Baruch

	son of Neriah
and wrote in it.	and he wrote in it.

38:9.		O lord, king,
	You have acted wickedly	those men have acted wickedly
	in what you have done	in all they did
		to the prophet Jeremiah;
		they have put him down in the pit,
	to kill this man by starvation.	to die there of starvation.

Editor II mitigates the previous edition's direct accusation against the king for trying to kill the prophet.

44:11–12.	I am going to set my face	I am going to set my face
		against you for punishment,
	to cut off all	to cut off all
		of Judah. I will take
	the remnant	the remnant
		of Judah who turned their faces
	in Egypt.	toward the land of Egypt.

Clarification

An important aspect of editor II's work was the attempt to clarify passages which apparently struck him as insufficiently clear. He seems to have read the book as an exegete and then revised the text, clarifying details in the context, making explicit what was implicit, and stressing ideas already found in the book, either in the immediate context or in remote contexts. In any event, one should note that this editor added but few new ideas.

When inserting the new elements between the existing words of edition I, editor II often created syntactic difficulties disturbing the flow of the Hebrew sentence, as in the following examples.

36:6. and read the scroll (that you wrote at my dictation—the words of the Lord—) to the people.

41:1. and they ate together there (at Mizpah).

41:2. struck down Gedaliah (son of Ahikam son of Shaphan with the sword and killed him) whom the king of Babylon had put in charge of the land.

41:3. and all the Judeans who were with him (with Gedaliah) in Mizpah.

41:7. he slaughtered them (Ishmael son of Nethaniah) [and threw their bodies] (in)to a cistern, (he and the men who were with him).

In other instances, the additions actually contradict the immediate or remote context:[34]

1:3. and in the days of King Jehoiakim son of Josiah of Judah, until the (end of the) eleventh year of King Zedekiah son of Josiah of Judah, until Jerusalem went into exile in the fifth month.

In this addition, the added word *tōm* (end), referring to the lower limit of the prophet's ministry at the "end" of the eleventh year of Zedekiah, contradicts the mention of "the fifth month" of that year, also mentioned in 52:5ff. = 2 Kings 25:2ff.

27:1. [The title of this chapter contradicts the content of the chapter itself; cf. p. 218.]

27:7. [See below, p. 236.]

28:1. And it occurred (in that year, early in the reign of) Zedekiah [was] King of Judah in the fourth year in the fifth month (LXX: And it occurred in the fourth year of Zedekiah King of Judah in the fifth month).

The sequence of the elements is different in edition I, but it is clear which elements are lacking. The added words contradict the chronological indication found in the continuation of the verse.

29:16–20. [There is a large addition in edition II.]

The greatest contextual difficulty caused by the insertion is that the verse before the insert (v. 15) has its direct continuation in verse 21 and that verses 16–20 have no connection at all with that verse. The added section was inserted in a section that deals with other matters, although the connecting link can still be recognized. The verses before and after the addition turn to the exiles, while the added section itself speaks of the people in Jerusalem, even though it is addressed to the exiles. In verses 1–24, the prophet asks the exiles to acquiesce in their situation and to start a new life. At the same time, in the added section he informs the exiles that the people left behind in Jerusalem shall perish. The added section and the

---

34. For further inconsistencies, see n. 23 (on 25:15ff.), pp. 221–22 (on 27:19–22), n. 31 (on 10:6–8, 10), and p. 233 (on 28:16; 29:32).

surrounding verses thus speak of different matters, but yet are connected: The exiles are urged to obey the Lord, since their brothers in Jerusalem, who did not obey, will be punished (v. 20). A further connection between the old and new material is the mentioning of prophets in both.

We now turn to the elucidating aspects of the editorial activity of editor II.

HOMOGENIZING ADDITIONS

The most conspicuous feature of edition II is its homogenizing filling in of details that are mentioned elsewhere in the context.[35] Editor II probably wanted to make the book of Jeremiah as *explicit* as possible, and he therefore filled in details that were *implicit* in edition I.

PERSONAL NAMES

Among the homogenizing additions, the filling in of personal names is the most manifest; indeed, this feature characterizes edition II as a whole. The picture emerging from the evidence is that editor II was in the habit of mentioning personal names in their full form, that is, including the name of the father, sometimes also the grandfather, the title ("king" or "prophet"), and so on. These additions occur mainly in the prose sections; there are few personal names in the poetry sections. The following examples are chosen at random:

21:2, etc. (Nebuchadrezzar) the king of Babylon.

28:4, etc. Jeconiah (son of Jehoiakim king of Judah).

28:5, etc. Jeremiah (the prophet) answered Hananiah (the prophet).

36:8, etc. Baruch (son of Neriah) did just as Jeremiah (the prophet) had instructed him.

40:9, etc. Gedaliah (son of Ahikam son of Shaphan) = 2 Kings 25:24 MT and LXX.

52:16, etc. (Nebuzaradan) the chief of the guards = 2 Kings 25:12 MT and LXX.

---

35. [For a similar phenomenon see *EGE*, pp. 81–82, 100–103. See also above, Chapter 4, n. 26.—Ed.]

The full evidence for the filling in and addition of names in edition II is provided in the studies of J. G. Janzen (his Appendix A) and Y.-J. Min. The picture emerging from these lists is that the data must be analyzed not only for the book as a whole but also for individual literary units. For example, one notes that editor I mentioned the full name or title of the person when he was introduced for the first time in a given unit, but in all or most subsequent references he referred to him in a shortened form. In this manner editor I follows the practice of biblical narrative.[36] Editor II, on the other hand, filled in the details of the full formula in many (sometimes: most or all) occurrences of the name.

A good example of this procedure is the name "Ishmael son of Nethaniah son of Elishama," thus introduced in its full form in edition I in the beginning of chapter 41 (v. 1), but shortened in that edition to "Ishmael" in the following verses (2, 6, 7, 8, 9 bis, 10, 11, 13, 15, 16, 18). Editor II left the short name in some verses, but expanded it to "Ishmael son of Nethaniah" in verses 2, 6, 7, 9, 11, 15, 16, 18). Furthermore, he added the short name in verses 3, 10, and 14 and the expanded name in verse 12.

Likewise, in edition I Johanan is introduced in chapter 41 as "Johanan son of Kareah" (41:11), but the next verses refer to him as "Johanan" only (13, 14, 16). In edition II, on the other hand, he is presented in all four verses with the long form.

Similar filling in is visible for Gedaliah, whose name is often expanded to "Gedaliah son of Ahikam (son of Shaphan)" (40:6, 7, 9, 11, 14, 16; 41:1, 2, 6, 18), and for Jeconiah, expanded to "Jeconiah son of Jehoiakim king of Judah" (27:20; 28:4), and so on.

When the names in editions I and II are compared, some interesting details come to light. In edition I, Jeremiah is usually referred to by his name only; surprisingly, the fuller description, "Jeremiah the prophet," occurs but four times in this edition (42:2; 43:6; 45:1; 51:59). In edition II the title is frequently added to Jeremiah's name (twenty-seven times in all), but the filling in is systematic only in chapters 28–29. In these two chapters the prophet is called "Jeremiah the prophet" consistently in edition II (eight times) and also once "Jeremiah the Anathotite" (29:27).[37]

---

36. Cf. the examples gathered by Cross, "Ammonite Oppression," p. 111.

37. The status of chapters 27–29 must be discussed separately. In their present form these chapters manifest some clearly unique features which have recently been summarized by Sarna "The Abortive Insurrection in Zedekiah's Day (Jer. 27–29)," esp. p. 92. Sarna expresses the view, which had been suggested earlier, that this section "must once have circulated separately" (ibid.). This suggestion may be somewhat farfetched, but it must be admitted that the evidence (mainly relating to the form of names) displays a scribal tradition that sets the section off against the remainder of the book. However, the status of these chapters does not bear on the issue under investigation, because the special features of these chapters were inserted before or during the completion of edition I and they were left intact in edition II. On the other hand,

Edition I of chapter 38 speaks often of "the king," who according to the context of chapter 37 can only be Zedekiah. Edition II added this name in several verses (38:5, 9, 14, 15, 16, 17, 19, 24).

"The king of Babylon" is mentioned often in edition I in this general fashion, but his identity is made explicit in edition II through the addition of "Nebuchadrezzar." In fact, the name Nebuchadrezzar occurs but rarely in edition I, mainly in editorial introductions to chapters, so that the prophet himself probably mentioned this name seldom if at all.

CONTEXTUAL ADDITIONS

With his extremely formalistic approach, editor II often did not leave much to the imagination when he added details in one verse in order to make it identical with another verse in the immediate context. This homogenizing approach, visible especially in the prose sections, is known from the Samaritan Pentateuch[38] and from some of its antecedents among the Qumran manuscripts.

13:5. (I went) and buried it at Perath.

Cf. 13:4, and go at once to Perath and bury it there.

13:7b. and found (the loincloth) [it] ruined.

Cf. 13:7a, and took the loincloth.

18:6b. Just like clay in the hands of the potter, so are you in my hands, (O House of Israel).

Cf. 18:6a, O House of Israel, can I not deal with you like this potter.

36:15b. And Baruch read it (to them).

Cf. 36:15a, and read it to us.

40:6. and stayed (with him) among the people.

Cf. 40:5, stay with him among the people.

---

the disproportionately large number of additions of the phrase "the prophet" in edition II could point to a separate circulation of chapters 27–29 in their present form, that is, as edition II. This, however, is an unnecessary assumption, since these chapters provide more occasion than the remainder of the book for the addition of this phrase as they speak of Jeremiah's encounter with the false prophets. Accordingly, if chapters 27–29 circulated separately, this occurred *before* edition II, and the frequent addition of the phrase "the prophet" occurred as *part of* edition II.

38. One is reminded of the words of F. M. Cross, who ascribed the MT of Jeremiah to the "Palestinian" local recension of which the Samaritan Pentateuch is a prominent representative. See Cross, "Evolution," pp. 308–9.

46:6. In the north by (the river) Euphrates.

Cf. 46:2, which was at the river Euphrates near Carchemish.

27:16. The vessels of the House of the Lord shall be brought back from Babylon (shortly).

Cf. 28:3 (below).

28:11. So will I break the yoke of (Nebuchadnezzar) the king of Babylon (in two years).

Cf. 28:3, In two years, I will restore to this place all the vessels of the House of the Lord which Nebuchadnezzar the king of Babylon took from this place and brought to Babylon.

28:14. that they may serve (Nebuchadnezzar) the king of Babylon—(and serve him they shall! I have even given the wild beasts to him).

Cf. 27:6, I have given . . . to my servant Nebuchadnezzar the king of Babylon, I even give him the wild beasts to serve him.

44:1. living in Migdol, Tahpanhes, (and Noph), and in the land of Pathros.

Cf. 46:14, Declare (in Egypt, proclaim) in Migdol, proclaim in Noph and Tahpanhes.

Cf. also 2:16, Those, too, in Noph and Tahpanhes will lay bare your head.

CONTEXTUAL CLARIFICATIONS

Editor II often added clarifying words or phrases explaining a matter that, in his view, was not clear in the context. For example, the original text of 28:16–17 (edition I) was very short and therefore impressive: "'You shall die this year'; and he died in the seventh month." Editor II, however, added the reason for the verdict and furthermore made it clear that the phrase "in the seventh month" refers to "the same year." Edition II thus reads: "'You shall die this year (for you have urged disloyalty to the Lord)'; and (the prophet Hananiah) [he] died (that year), in the seventh month.

Similar additions were made throughout the book:

27:5. It is I who made the earth, (and the men and beasts who are on the earth).

27:8. The nation or kingdom that (does not serve him—Nebuchadnezzar king of Babylon—and that) does not put its neck under the yoke of the king of Babylon.

27:16–17. . . . Give no heed to the words of your prophets who prophesy to you . . . for they prophesy falsely to you. (Give them no heed. Serve the king of Babylon, and live! Otherwise this city shall become a ruin).

28:3. In two years, I will restore to this place (all) the vessels of the House of the Lord (which Nebuchadnezzar king of Babylon took from this place and brought to Babylon).

28:15. And Jeremiah (the prophet) said to Hananiah (the prophet, "Listen, Hananiah!), The Lord did not send you. . . ."

29:6. Take wives and beget sons and daughters; and take wives for your sons, and give your daughters to husbands, (that they may bear sons and daughters). Multiply (there), do not decrease.

41:1. In the eleventh month Ishmael . . . came to Gedaliah (son of Ahikam) at Mizpah; and they ate there together (at Mizpah).

41:6. Ishmael (son of Nethaniah) went out (from Mizpah) to meet them, weeping as he walked. (As he met them), he said (to them), "Come to Gedaliah (son of Ahikam)."

41:7. When they came inside the town, (Ishmael son of Nethaniah) [he] slaughtered them [and threw their bodies] in(to) a cistern, (he and the men with him).

41:13–14. When all the people held by Ishmael saw Johanan (son of Kareah) and (all) the army officers with him (they were glad; all the people whom Ishmael had carried off from Mizpah turned back), and [they] went over to Johanan (son of Kareah).

42:9. and said to them: "Thus said the Lord, (the God of Israel, to whom you sent me to present your supplication before him)."
Cf. v. 2, Grant our plea, and pray for us to the Lord your God. . . .

Among these clarifying additions, one meets many added names (cf. the amplified names mentioned above, pp. 227–29):

1:11. The word of the Lord came to me: "What do you see, (Jeremiah)?" I replied: "A branch of an almond tree (I see)."

36:4. So Jeremiah called Baruch son of Neriah; and (Baruch) [he] wrote down at Jeremiah's dictation all the words which the Lord had spoken.

Other names are amplified from pronouns in edition I:

35:12. The word of the Lord came to Jeremiah (LXX: to me).

37:21. gave instructions to lodge Jeremiah (LXX: him).

52:8. and they overtook Zedekiah (LXX: him = 2 Kings 25:5).

Clarifying amplifications like these are found especially in the prose sections. A few similar elements are found in the poetry sections, but these cannot be evaluated well because they may also have derived from an authentic Jeremianic tradition (above, p. 223).

Edition I contained several formulaic expressions, especially at the beginning and end of prophetic utterances (*ně'ūm YHWH*, declares the Lord; *kōh 'āmar YHWH*, thus said the Lord, etc.). These formulas were often added in edition II, so that this edition presents a fuller use of these formulas than edition I. For example, *ně'ūm YHWH*, which occurs 109 times in both editions I and II, occurs an additional 65 times in edition II only. The same applies to *kōh 'āmar YHWH*.

18:11. And now, say (I pray) to the men of Judah and the inhabitants of Jerusalem (saying: Thus said the Lord:) I am devising disaster for you.

27:11. But the nation which puts its neck under the yoke of the king of Babylon, and serves him, will be left by me on its own soil (—declares the Lord—) to till it and dwell on it.

29:9. For they prophesy falsely to you in my name; I did not send them (—declares the Lord).

29:11. (For I am mindful of the plans) I have made concerning you (declares the Lord)—plans for your welfare.

31:37. (Thus said the Lord) If the heavens above could be measured. . . .

The same is true of *lē'mōr* (saying), *'ēlay* (to me), etc. after verbs of speaking, and of *ṣěbā'ôt* (Hosts) in various combinations:

1:4. The word of the Lord came to me (saying). . . .

3:1. (Saying): If a man divorces his wife. . . .

5:20. Proclaim this to the House of Jacob (saying). . . .

1:17. Arise and speak (to them). . . .

13:1. Thus the Lord said (to me): Go buy yourself a loincloth.

17:19. Thus said the Lord (to me): Go and stand in the People's Gate.

6:6. For thus said the Lord (of Hosts). . . .

7:3. Thus said the Lord (of Hosts), God of Israel. . . .

The latter formula is of particular interest because the full formula occurs thirty-two times in edition II, but never in edition I.

Of special interest are some formulaic Deuteronomistic expressions added in edition II (cf. p. 220).[39] For example:

7:13. and though I spoke to you (persistently), you would not listen.
[35:15 is similar; cf. Bright, "Date," no. 1.]

13:10. This wicked people who refuse to heed my bidding (who follow the willfulness of their own hearts).
[Cf. Bright, "Date," no. 6.]

19:9. because of the desperate straits to which they will be reduced by their enemies (who seek their life).
[Similarly 34:20; 38:16; cf. Bright, "Date," no. 11.]

21:12. Else my wrath will break forth like fire and burn, with none to quench it (because of your wicked acts).
[Cf. Bright, "Date," no. 14.]

23:16. Do not listen to the words of the prophets (who prophesy to you).
[Cf. Bright, "Date," no. 15.]

25:3. From the thirteenth year . . . I have spoken to you persistently, (but you would not listen).
[Cf. Bright, "Date," no. 46.]

25:7. But you would not listen to me (declares the Lord; you vexed me with what your hands made, to your own hurt).
[Cf. Bright, "Date," no. 2.]

32:19. to repay every man according to his ways, (and with the proper fruit of his deeds).
[Cf. Bright, "Date," no. 14.]

43:5. the entire remnant of Judah who had returned (from all the countries to which they had been scattered).
[Cf. Bright, "Date," no. 31.]

In addition, note the use of a Deuteronomic idiom in 28:16: "You shall die this year (for you have urged disloyalty [*dibbartā sārâ*] to the Lord)." The same expression, *dibbēr sārâ*, occurs in edition II in 29:32 and elsewhere in the Bible only in Deut. 13:6. Interestingly enough, while the phrase in Deuteronomy refers to a prophet who incites to the worship of "other Gods" (Deut. 13:3, "let us follow other Gods"), the prophets mentioned in Jeremiah prophesy in the name of the God of Israel.

39. For a descriptive list of the vocabulary of the Deuteronomistic stratum (the C stratum) in the book, see Bright, "Date," pp. 30–35.

Some Further Characteristics of Edition II

PECULIAR WORDS AND EXPRESSIONS

Edition II contains some words and expressions that within Jeremiah are characteristic of that edition only. One example was given on p. 232 ("Thus said the Lord of Hosts, God of Israel"), and further examples follow:

1. Nebuchadnezzar is known as "God's servant" only in edition II:[40]

25:9. I am going to send for (all) the peoples of the north (declares the Lord—and for my servant Nebuchadrezzar king of Babylon), and bring them against this land.

27:6. I herewith deliver (all these) lands to king Nebuchadnezzar of Babylon, to serve him [*lĕᶜobdô*] (MT: *ᶜabdî* my servant); I even give him the wild beasts.

43:10. I am sending for (my servant) king Nebuchadrezzar of Babylon. . . .

2. The idea that he who serves Nebuchadnezzar will enjoy a long life is not found in edition I. The reward of long life is known elsewhere, though in different contexts, from the sixth commandment, from Deuteronomistic phraseology, and from Amos 5:4, 6.[41]

27:12. LXX: put your necks and serve the king of Babylon.
      MT: put your necks under the yoke of the king of Babylon; serve him and his people and live.

27:17. give them no heed. Serve the king of Babylon and live. . . .

3. The word *dešen*, "fatness, fat ashes," occurs within Jeremiah only in edition II:

31:14. I will give the priests their fill (of fatness).

31:40. (And the entire Valley of Corpses and Ashes [*dešen*]) and all the fields. . . .

4. The special meaning of *ᶜam hāᵓāreṣ* in the Bible has long been recognized. In Jeremiah this phrase occurs only in 34:19 (for this purpose 52:25 may be disregarded, because chapter 52 has been transferred from 2 Kings 24–25 as an appendix to Jeremiah [note Jer. 51:64]).

---

40. For a full discussion of this issue, see Tov, "Exegetical Notes," pp. 83–84, and Bogaert, "Mécanismes."

41. For the idea of longevity in the Bible and the ancient Near East, see Weinfeld, *Deuteronomy*, pp. 257, 308–9; Malamat, *Israel in Biblical Times*, pp. 295–306.

34:19. and (all) the people (of the land) (*wĕ[kol]* *ᶜam* [*hā ᵓāreṣ*]).

5. Within the Bible the term *rabbê* (*ham*)*melek*, "the king's commanders," occurs only in edition II of Jeremiah:

39:13. . . . and Nergal-sarezer the Rab-mag, and all the comanders of the king of Babylon (*rabbê melek bābel*).

41:1. Ishmael son of Nethaniah son of Elishama, who was of royal descent (and one of the king's commanders [*wĕrabbê hammelek*])[42] came with ten men. . . .

The component *rab* used in this phrase is probably parallel to the other terms compounded with *rab* that are mentioned in 39:13. Note that the phrase is absent from 2 Kings 25:25, which is otherwise identical with Jer. 41:1.

RESUMPTIVE REPETITION ("Wiederaufnahme")

Of the literary techniques of editor II, at least one is manifest. From time to time, when editor II inserted several new elements, and when he feared that the idea of the original text might be lost because of the insertion, he *repeated* the lead phrase or its approximate contents. A similar technique termed *Wiederaufnahme* or "resumptive repetition" has been recognized in the redaction of biblical books.[43] Note, for example, Jer. 27:21 (see text, on p. 221): After the long additions in verses 19 and 20, editor II felt the need to repeat the introductory formula of the prophecy as well as the object of the prophecy:

[19]For thus said the Lord (of Hosts . . . [21]Thus said the Lord of Hosts, the God of Israel, concerning the vessels. . . .)

Another example of resumptive repetition is:

28:3-4. [3]In two years, I will restore to this place (all) the vessels of the House of the Lord (which Nebuchadnezzar king of Babylon took from this place and brought

---

42. This reconstruction is based on the assumption that *apò génous toũ basiléos* ("from the offspring of the king") represents, *mizzeraᶜ hammᵉlûkâ*, "from the offspring of the kingship" (cf. the LXX of 26[33]:1).

43. Cf. Kuhl, "Wiederaufnahme"; Seeligmann, "Hebräische Erzählung," pp. 314–24. For the terminology and further bibliography, see Talmon, "Textual study," p. 395 n. 174. [And see above, pp. 48–49.—Ed.]

to Babylon). [4]And Jeconiah (son of Jehoiakim king of Judah) and (all) the Judean exiles (who went to Babylon, I will bring back to this place—declares the Lord).

In this example, the repetition of "I will bring back to this place" (cf. v. 3a) was needed after the long additions in verses 3b–4a.

41:2-3. [2]Then Ishmael (son of Nethaniah) and the ten men who (were) with him arose and struck down Gedaliah (son of Ahikam son of Shaphan with the sword and killed him), whom the king of Babylon had put in charge of the land, [3]and all the Judeans who were with him (with Gedaliah) in Mizpah and the Chaldeans who were stationed there (the soldiers, Ishmael struck down).

Since in this passage the object of the verb *wayyakkû*, "struck down" (v. 2) was greatly expanded, editor II repeated the subject and the verb at the end of the sentence in verse 3.

41:10. Ishmael carried off (all the rest of the people who were in Mizpah), the daughters of the king, all the people left in Mizpah over whom (Nebuzaradan) the chief of the guards, had appointed Gedaliah son of Ahikam (and Ishmael son of Nethaniah carried them off) and set out to cross over to the Ammonites.

As in the preceding example, after the object was expanded editor II repeated the verb and its subject.

The Postexilic Date of Edition II

There are indications of the exilic date of some of the passages in edition I (e.g., 8:3; 9:15; 16:13; 16:15; 30:10–11). Other passages may even be postexilic (esp. 25:11; 29:10), but no certainty can be had. At the same time there are indications of the postexilic date of edition II:

25:14. For they too shall be enslaved by many nations and great kings; and I will requite them according to their acts and according to their conduct.

27:7. All nations shall serve him, his son and his grandson—until the turn of his own land comes, when many nations and great kings shall subjugate him.

Both the above verses, added in edition II, foreshadow the fall of the Babylonian empire and were probably added as *vaticinia ex eventu*.[44]

---

44. For a full discussion of 27:9, see Tov, "Exegetical Notes," pp. 84–85.

Two final examples:

27:19–22. [See above, pp. 221–22[45]]

29:6. Take wives and beget sons and daughters; and take wives for your sons, and give your daughters to husbands, (that they may bear sons and daughters). Multiply (there), do not decrease.

Through the addition the prophet refers to an exile that would last for three generations, but it is not certain that this was indeed intended by the addition.

The reader is referred, furthermore, to the articles of Bogaert and Lust[46] for the appearance in edition II of details that show that some time had lapsed between the composition of editions I and II.

The above description shows that editor II inserted many minor and major changes in Jeremiah, both in the editing and rearranging of the material and in its clarification. As an editor he rearranged the text, added headings to prophecies, repeated sections, added new material, and inserted some changes in content. In the clarification of the text, he added homogenizing details (especially in personal names) and clarified details in the context. The sources for his additions are the context, his own imagination, but also genuine Jeremianic material which somehow found its way into edition II. The additions were inserted neatly in between the elements of edition I, and sometimes the editor added so many elements that after them he had to repeat the last words that had preceded them (resumptive repetition). In other cases, however, the secondary character of the insertion is still visible from its formulation or content. All these changes were inserted during the final stage of the growth of the book and as such they must be treated within literary rather than textual criticism.

---

45. The addition mentions, among other things, the return from the exile and thus betrays its late origin. For a similar addition, see 29:14, and on a different level, 40:12. On these additions, see the discussion of Lust, "'Gathering and Return.'"

46. Bogaert, "Mécanismes," pp. 236–37, referring to the postexilic emphasis on the priests in edition II in 33:14–26; 27:16, 19. For Lust, see n. 45.

Summary and Conclusions

JEFFREY H. TIGAY

The preceding chapters have shown that many of the central hypotheses of biblical criticism are realistic. They do not prove that these hypotheses are correct, but they show that the processes of literary development which critics inferred from clues within biblical literature are real phenomena, attested in the history of literature from ancient times down to our own. This conclusion is based on case studies of texts whose earlier stages are known and do not have to be hypothetically reconstructed; it is based, in other words, on *empirical models*. In Chapter 1 we saw how the *Gilgamesh Epic* illustrates the growth of a composite but integrated hero epic from several previously unconnected tales about the hero and others, and how the content and wording of the epic were revised over the centuries, at first rather freely but later with less and less allowance for changes. In Chapters 2 and 3 we saw the growth of conflate narratives and other types of compositions in the textual traditions of the Hebrew Bible and postbiblical literature. In the Appendix we shall see a conflate narrative in the textual tradition of the Gospels. In these examples, different versions of an episode were spliced or woven together into a single running narrative, with the resultant texts sometimes retaining enough inconsistencies to suggest their composite origins. In Chapter 4 we saw how a composite text could be produced by supplementation instead of conflation, with the resultant text again retaining inconsistencies that point to its composite origin. Chapter 5 focuses on one type of inconsistency, the "stylistic" ones. Vocabulary, formulaic, and stylistic differences between the original components of a composite text often survive redaction and remain as traces of the text's variegated background. In Chapter 6 we saw several examples of assimilation in which stories similar to each other were made even more similar by the addition of details from one of them to the other, again producing in some cases inconsistencies that point to editorial activity. In Chapter 7 we saw cases of the molding of chronology to express ideology rather than historical fact, once again sometimes at the cost of consistency. And in Chapter 8 we saw the extensive revision of a prophetic book, sometimes producing telltale rough spots in the text, but ultimately not significantly distorting the prophet's own message.

Most of the studies in this volume have dealt with the source and redaction criticism of narratives. Far more remains to be said in these areas, but extrabiblical analogues could also be studied with reference to critical questions about other genres and other disciplines. For example, studies of the development of individual Mesopotamian liturgical texts and the evolution of Mesopotamian liturgical genres have a bearing on aspects of biblical psalms criticism.[1] For the form-critical study of biblical law, a recently published Aramaic administrative decree, inscribed on stone and formulated in the "he who" pattern,[2] provides important West Semitic evidence for the view that the relative form in biblical law had its origin in proclamations and decrees.[3] Both the *Temple Scroll* and cuneiform law collections have been used in studies discussing the redaction of biblical law collections.[4]

Cases that tend to confirm established hypotheses of biblical criticism occupy center stage in this volume, but here and there we have seen analogues which may suggest different explanations of certain problems. In Chapter 4, Alexander Rofé argues that the case of Joshua 20 supports the supplementary hypothesis instead of the documentary hypothesis. In Chapter 6, Yair Zakovitch suggests that assimilation explains the critical problems of Genesis 34 better than the documentary hypothesis does. Certainly the possibility exists that in other cases, too, analogues may suggest explanations better than those currently preferred by critics. The aim of the present volume is not to foreclose any options but to encourage those who study the evolution of biblical literature to approach this necessarily hypothetical task with the perspective and experience offered by empirical case histories.

The value of such a perspective is not limited to the light it sheds on the prehistory of biblical books, for it also reminds us of something which classical criticism often neglected: the product of the redactor is a literary work that should be studied in its own right. The analytical work of the nineteenth century inevitably diverted scholarly attention from the final product, which came to be felt as a barrier hampering the critics' view of

---

1. See Tigay, "Some Aspects," pp. 372–78.
2. Caquot, "Inscription."
3. Yaron, "Forms," pp. 150–53; idem, *Laws of Eshnunna*, pp. 67–68; see also Sonsino, *Motive Clauses*, pp. 21–22, 34, 36.
4. Kaufman, "Temple Scroll"; Weinfeld, *Deuteronomy*, pp. 148–57.

the pristine sources.[5] This disinterest in the final product is being remedied today by redaction criticism,[6] which takes the source analysis as an indispensable starting point and proceeds to study the contribution of the redactor.[7] This approach dovetails with the study of empirical models, for these have the effect of highlighting the work of redactors. Since the sources of empirical models are available, the critic is free to concentrate on comparing them with the final product. To cite one example, S. N. Kramer, whose study of the Sumerian sources of the Akkadian *Gilgamesh Epic* first made serious comparison of the epic and its sources possible, undertook the comparison to discover "in what manner and to what extent the creators of the [Akkadian] epic utilized their Sumerian sources."[8] He concluded from the comparison that the Akkadian epic was not slavishly copied from its sources but so thoroughly modified the sources as to constitute a new creation.[9] It was this new creation, and not its sources, that Kramer described as "the most significant literary creation of the whole of ancient Mesopotamia."[10] In such cases we can understand and evaluate redactors' achievements in a way that was never possible when scholars were unaware of the sources or when their efforts were devoted mainly to identifying and reconstructing the sources. Such examples encourage and, more important, inform the biblical scholar's recognition of redaction as a literarily significant undertaking.

5. For the same deficiency among the Homeric "analysts," see Whitman, *Homer*, p. 1.

6. See, e.g., Greenberg, *Understanding Exodus*, pp. 1–8; idem, "Thematic Unity"; idem, "Redaction"; and Friedman, "Sacred History." Cf. Alter, *Art*, pp. 10, 19–20. For similar appreciation of the artistry of the *Iliad*, even if composite, see Whitman, *Homer*, p. 14.

7. See Wharton, "Redaction Criticism." The differing perspectives that underlie these contrasting attitudes to redactors' creativity are visible in reviews of Wolkstein's edition of Sumerian myths about Inanna (see our Introduction, p. 18). From the historical perspective of a Sumerologist, the story created by Wolkstein "is hers, not the Sumerians', for she has violated the culture that produced the texts in which Inanna appears. . . . [The original character of the texts about Inanna] is lost . . . when [they] are arbitrarily cut and pasted together in deference to modern tastes" (Michalowski, "Sumer for Moderns"). From the ahistorical perspective of a modern free-lance writer, "any attempt to make a story live again has to impose something of the storyteller's own will upon it, and the distortions that may result from Wolkstein's shaping of the fragmentary myths seem less important than the gains realized by having Inanna restored to life" (Bancroft, "Tales").

8. Kramer, "Epic of Gilgameš," p. 13.

9. Ibid., p. 18.

10. Kramer, *History*, pp. 180–81.

Appendix:
Tatian's *Diatessaron* and the Analysis of the Pentateuch

GEORGE FOOT MOORE

Editor's Note

One of the pioneering efforts to demonstrate the verisimilitude of the
documentary hypothesis on the basis of an extrabiblical analogue was
G. F. Moore's "Tatian's Diatessaron and the Analysis of the Pentateuch,"
published in 1890.* Moore's method in analyzing the *Diatessaron* by comparing it to its sources was exemplary, and in many respects this study has
never been surpassed. Although the *Diatessaron*'s relatively late date left its
aptness for Pentateuchal criticism open to question, we can now see that
Tatian used a method that was practiced when the biblical books were still
being formed and has continued in use down to modern times. Since we
have referred to Moore's study often, it is reprinted here for the convenience of the reader.†

* *JBL* 9 (1890): 201–15.

† For further information on the *Diatessaron*, see Hill's translation of the Arabic version;
Stenning, "Diatessaron"; Longstaff, *Evidence*, pp. 10–42; Metzger, *Early Versions*, pp. 10–36.

•   •   •   •

[201] THE GREAT majority of modern Old Testament scholars regard the
Pentateuch as a composite work. An author, who according to the prevail-
ing hypothesis, lived after the rebuilding of Jerusalem, set himself to write
the history of his people from the earliest times at least to the death of

Joshua, with special attention to the history of religion and the origin of the sacred institutions and customs. His sources were not original, but were the writings of others, who, at different times and from different points of view, had attempted the same task before him. A modern literary man in such a case would have digested these earlier narratives, formed his own conception of the progress of the history, and his own judgment of its several moments, made his own plan, and written the whole story over, from his own point of view and in his own fashion. The author of the Pentateuch—to call him a "redactor" arises from and gives rise to a misapprehension of his aim—went to work in a very different way. He cut up and pieced together his sources in such a way as to make a single continuous narrative. Where he found parallel accounts of the same event, his procedure was determined by circumstances. If they were too diverse to be combined, he treated them as accounts of different events, and incorporated both, usually in different places. If they were substantially identical, he used one and dropped the other. In the greater number of cases, however, he wove them ingeniously together, so as to preserve every detail which was found in either of them, and yet avoid striking repetitions. What he adds *de suo* consists chiefly of those modifications of phrase or of fact which were necessary to fit and cement his fragments together, or of matter substantially from one of his sources, which for some reason was impracticable in its original shape. Thus out of three or four histories he makes one [202] continuous history of the origins of the Israelitish people and its religion—a composite *Tora*.

It is not infrequently urged against this theory that such a way of making a book is unheard of. Such a "crazy patch-work," as an American scholar lately called the analysis, is without a parallel in literature.‡ The layman who knows nothing of Oriental literature takes this assertion for a self-evident fact, and of itself sufficient to stamp the theories of the critics as not only false, but absurd. This easy method with critics, however effective with the common man, especially when spiced with a little sarcasm, has one serious defect; its premise is false. Literature furnishes examples enough of every procedure which criticism ascribes to the author of the Pentateuch. I wish here to direct special attention to one work, which offers a most striking and complete parallel to the hypothesis of composition from documents, and which is therefore most instructive to the critic of the Pentateuch—the Diatessaron of Tatian.

This harmony of the Gospels was made after the middle of the second century, whether in Syriac or Greek, scholars are not agreed. The internal evidence seems to me to favor the former alternative. It was for several

‡ [See introduction, n. 4—Ed.]

generations the Gospel of a large part of the Syrian church, and is quoted simply as such. The Doctrine of Addai, a work, in its present form, of the fourth century, carries its use back to the apostolic age, assuming that it was the original form in which the church in Edessa received the Gospel. After the beginning of the fifth century, however, there came a change. Rabbula, Bishop of Edessa (411–435), ordered that the churches of his diocese should be supplied with copies of the Separate Gospels, and that they should be read. A few years later, Theodoret, Bishop of Cyrrhus (423–457), found the Diatessaron in use in two hundred churches in his diocese—one in four of the whole number. He sequestered them, and replaced them by copies of the Gospels of the Four Evangelists. These names are not without significance. They are the opposite of "Composite Gospel," the common name for the Diatessaron. The title of Matthew in the Curetonian fragments, which puzzled Cureton, and of which Bernstein proposed a wholly untenable explanation, expresses this contrast; it is "The Separate Gospel, Matthew." The Arabic translation, made by a Nestorian scholar in the eleventh century, shows that the Composite Gospel maintained itself to a much later time in private, if not in ecclesiastical use.

[203] Until recently this Harmony of the Gospels has been known only from the much altered and interpolated Latin Harmony of which Victor of Capua discovered a copy in the sixth century, and from a commentary on it by Ephraim the Syrian, which is preserved in Armenian, and was published in 1836 (in Latin translation in 1876). From these sources Zahn, in 1881, reconstructed the Diatessaron with what, under the circumstances, must be regarded as conspicuous success. It has long been known that an Arabic harmony bearing the name of Tatian existed in the Vatican Library. A specimen of it was printed by Lagarde, from a copy by Ciasca, in 1886. In 1888, Ciasca edited the whole from two MSS—the Vatican Codex Arab. XIV, and a manuscript lately acquired by the Museum Borgianum. That in its structure—not in the text, as we shall see hereafter—this translation represents the long-lost Diatessaron, there is no reason to doubt. We are now able, therefore, to study its composition in a way which, from the nature of his materials, we could not so well do in Zahn's reconstruction.

The author proposed to himself to make out of the four Gospels a single continuous narrative of the doings and teachings of Jesus, a life of Christ in the words of the evangelists. His sources divided themselves into two groups, John and the Synoptics. The latter so often presented identical parallels, that, to avoid repetition, extensive omissions were necessary. In the Fourth Gospel the parallels to the Synoptics are so few that almost the whole Gospel could be incorporated in his work. A count shows that of John ca. 847 verses out of 880 are found in the Diatessaron, or over 96 percent. Of Matthew, on the other hand, ca. 821 verses out of 1071, or 76.5 percent; of Mark, 340 out of 678, or a fraction over 50 percent; and of

Luke, 761 out of 1151, or 66.2 percent. The chief difficulty in combining John with the other three Gospels was, of course, chronological. Zahn finds that the author disposed the *Hauptmassen* of his material in conformity to the scheme of the Fourth Gospel. I do not feel sure that this was the case. It seems to me, on the contrary, that he follows substantially the order of Matthew, and brings in the various journeys and feasts of John as best he can. This is, however, not a question of primary importance for my present purpose. The disposition of this earliest Life of Christ has an interest of its own, and I have made an analytical table of contents by means of which it can readily be compared with other harmonies and with modern Lives [204] of Christ; but I am here concerned only with the composition of the work.

Where the author found in one of the Gospels matter not contained in any of the others, as is the case with the greater part of the Gospel of John, he had only to find the appropriate place to bring it in; a problem of disposition purely. In this he was guided partly by the order of the Gospel itself; partly by similarity of situation or of content to passages in the other Gospels.

Where he had two accounts of the same event which were so diverse that they could not be combined, he placed them side by side. Thus, the narratives of the birth of Jesus in Matthew and Luke present insuperable difficulties to the harmonist. Tatian gives Luke's account complete, including the adoration of the shepherds, the presentation in the Temple, and the return to Nazareth (ii. 1–39); then, with the words "After this," he introduces the account of the appearance and adoration of the Magi, the flight into Egypt, and the return and establishment in Nazareth, from Matthew (ii. 1–23). It would be impossible to set the two narratives in a light in which the conflict between them would appear more glaring. At the end of chapter ɪ Joseph and Mary, with the child, return to their home in Nazareth; in the first words of chapter ɪɪ, we read that *after this* Magi came from the East to Jerusalem seeking the new-born King of the Jews; they are directed to Bethlehem, journey thither and do homage to him, and go their way. Joseph, still in Bethlehem, is warned in a dream of Herod's purpose, escapes to Egypt, and only after the death of Herod, and because he is afraid to return to his home in Judea, takes up his abode in Nazareth. The case is the more noteworthy, because the author might have removed the most striking contradiction by ending his extract from Luke at verse 38 instead of verse 39. That he did not do so is evidence of the conscientiousness with which he used his sources. The example is instructive for the Old Testament critic. We are often told that if the Redactor of the Pentateuch had found in his sources irreconcilable contradictions of this sort, he would not have left them unreconciled; but would, by conformation or by omission, have given unity to his narrative. The inference is, that the contradictions which we find are all in our own imagination. The premise and inference are groundless. The author of the Pentateuch put Gen. ii. 4–iii. alongside of Gen. i, as little concerned about the difficulty of reconciling the order of creation in the two pieces as Tatian when he **[205]** put the visit of the Magi after the return of the holy family to Nazareth. He meant above everything else to embody in his work all that his sources gave him. The same aim, with the same results, can be seen in Ibn Hisham's Life of Mohammed, which excellently illustrates the growth of a book by supplement.

Where, on the other hand, the accounts which he found in his sources were not in themselves conflicting, but were set in a different connection, or ascribed to a different time in Jesus' ministry, our author does not, like many modern harmonists, think that the same thing was done twice, but makes his choice. The cleansing of the Temple is put by John in the earliest, by the Synoptics in the last, period of Jesus' public work. Tatian follows the latter, though he uses the account of John as largely as that of Matthew in relating the transaction. So in regard to the healing of the blind man at Jericho, where there is a difference among the Synoptics as to whether the miracle took place when Jesus was entering or leaving the city, and whether there was one blind man or two, the author treats the question with more freedom than many modern scholars, who are disposed to find here two distinct miracles.

Where two reports agree in substance, but differ in detail, our author's principle is to embody in his harmony all that is given by his sources. An interesting example is the Sermon on the Mount, in chapters viii–x. Matthew, as the fuller report, is naturally his principal source, but he makes a place for all that is peculiar to Luke. The Beatitudes are given, with the exception of the last, just as they stand in Matthew; but they are followed by the Woes, which in Luke form the pendant to them; and so throughout. The author has, however, not merely combined the reports of Matthew and Luke; he has also incorporated in his Sermon on the Mount a number of sayings of Jesus which are found in the Gospels in other connections. Thus the saying, "With what measure ye mete it shall be measured to you again," which in Matthew and Luke is connected with the warning "Judge not that ye be not judged," brings to mind the passage in Mark where the same proverbial expression has a different application, "Take heed what ye hear, for with what measure ye mete it shall be measured to you; and more shall be given to you. I say unto those who hear: He that hath, to him shall be given, and he that hath not, from him shall be taken away what he might have." Thus the bringing together of sayings on the same subject, or containing the same figure, **[206]** of which the longer discourses of Jesus in the Synoptics supply abundant examples, is here carried a step further.[1]

---

1. Observe also how in chapter xlvi, Luke xxii. 35–38 is interpolated in the Johannean Farewell Discourse, between John xiv. 31 a and b.

Two or more parallel accounts of the same event are usually interwoven with great ingenuity, and often still greater intricacy, so as to preserve every detail found in any one of the sources, and yet avoid repetitions and hard transitions. As an illustration, take the storm on the Sea of Galilee and the scene following with the demoniac, Mark iv. 35 ff., with the parallels in Matthew and Luke.[2]

Mr 4 35a Lu 8 22b Mr 4 36a	And he said to them that day at evening,' Let us go over to the other side of the lake.' And he sent away the multitude.'
Lu 8 22a Mr 4 36b Mt 8 24a	And Jesus embarked in the boat, he and his disciples;' and there were with them other boats.' And there arose in the sea a
Lu 8 23b	great commotion of tempest and wind,' and the boat was near
Mr 4 38a	being swamped by the immense waves.' But Jesus was asleep
Mt 8 25	on a cushion in the stern of the boat.' And his disciples came and woke him, and said to him, Master, save us; behold,
Lu 8 24b	we perish.' And he arose, and rebuked the winds and the
Mr 4 39b–41a	raging of the water,' and said to the sea, Be still, and be thou rebuked. And the wind was still, and there was a great calm. 40 And he said to them, Why are ye so fearful? Why
Lu 8 25b–27a	have ye no faith? And they feared with a mighty fear,' and were amazed; and said one to another, Seest thou who this is, who commands even the winds and the waves and the sea, and they obey him? 26 And they went on, and came to the country of the Gadarenes, which is over against Galilee. 27 And
Mr 5 2b	when he went out of the boat to land,' there met him from
Lu 8 27b	among the tombs' a man in whom was a devil of long time; and he ware no clothes, nor lived in a house, but among the
Mr 5 3b 4a	tombs.' And no man was able to bind him with chains; for as often as he was bound with chains and fetters, he broke the
Lu 8 29b	chains, and severed the fetters,' and he was driven by the devil
Mr 5 4b 5a	into the desert;' and no man was able to tame him. 5 And all the time, by night and day, he was among the tombs and in the
Mt 8 28b Mr 5 5b–7a	mountains, [207] 'and no man could pass by that way.' And he cried and cut himself with stones. 6 And when he saw Jesus from afar, he ran and fell down before him, 7 and cried with a
Lu 8 28b	loud voice,' What have we to do with thee, Jesus, Son of the
Mr 5 7b	Most High God?' I adjure thee by God that thou torment me
Lu 8 29a–33a	not.' And Jesus commanded the unclean spirit to come out of the man. And he had been a long time in bondage to it.

2. This passage is given in a literal translation. In the second example, The Baptism of Jesus, I have followed the English version as closely as possible, in order to illustrate the effect of such composition in the familiar words of the Gospels.

30 And Jesus asked him, What is thy name? He answered him, Legion; because many devils had entered into him. 31 And they besought of him that he would not command them to depart into the abyss. 32 And there was there a herd of many swine, feeding on the mountain; and the devils besought of him that he would give them leave to enter into the swine. And he gave them leave. 33 And the devils went out of the man, and entered into the swine, etc.

This is not an unfair illustration of the method of the author. Where there are four sources, as, for example, in the narrative of the baptism and temptation of Jesus, the interweaving is still more complex.

Mt 3 13
Lu 3 23
Jo 1 29–31

Then cometh Jesus from Galilee to Jordan unto John, to be baptized of him.' And Jesus was about thirty years of age, and was supposed to be the son of Joseph.' And John seeth Jesus coming unto him, and saith, Behold the Lamb of God which taketh away the sin of the world. 30 This is he of whom I said, After me cometh a man which is preferred before me, for he was before me. 31 And I knew him not; but that he should be made manifest to Israel, therefore am I come baptiz-

Mt 3 14f

ing with water.' And John forbade him, saying, I have need to be baptized of thee, and comest thou to me? 15 Jesus answer- ing said unto him, Suffer it to be so now; for thus it becometh

Lu 3 21a
Mt 3 16b

us to fulfil all righteousness. Then he suffered him.' And when all the people were baptized, Jesus also was baptized.' And he went up straightway out of the water, and the heavens were

Lu 3 22a
Mt 3 17
Jo 1 32–34

opened unto him.' And the Holy Ghost descended upon him in the likeness of a dove;' and lo, a voice from heaven, saying, This is my beloved Son, in whom I am well pleased.' And John bare record, saying, I saw the Spirit descending from heaven, like **[208]** a dove, and it abode upon him. 33 And I knew him not; but he that sent me to baptize with water, the same said unto me, Upon whom thou shalt see the Spirit descending and remaining on him, the same is he which baptizeth with the Holy Ghost. 34 And I saw and bare record that this is the Son

Lu 4 1a
Mr 1 12
Mr 1 13b
Mt 4 2a
Lu 4 2b
Mt 4 2b–7

of God.' And Jesus, being full of the Holy Ghost, returned from Jordan.' And immediately the Spirit driveth him into the wilderness' to be tempted of Satan; and he was with the wild beasts.' And he fasted forty days and forty nights,' and in those days he did eat nothing;' and he was afterward ahungered. 3 And the tempter came to him, and said, If thou be the Son of God, command that these stones be made bread. 4 But he answered and said, It is written, Man shall not live by bread alone, but by every word that proceedeth out of the mouth of

God. 5 Then the devil taketh him up into the Holy City, and setteth him on a pinnacle of the temple, 6 and saith unto him, If thou be the Son of God, cast thyself down; for it is written, He shall give his angels charge concerning thee, and in their hands they shall bear thee up, lest at any time thou dash thy foot against a stone. 7 Jesus said unto him, It is written again, Thou shalt not tempt the Lord thy God.' And the devil took him up into a high mountain, and showed unto him all the kingdoms of the world and the glory of them in a moment of time. 6 And the devil said unto him, All this power will I give thee, and the glory of it, for that is delivered unto me, and to whomsoever I will I give it. 7 If thou therefore wilt worship me, all shall be thine, etc.

Lu 4 5-7

The most hair-splitting analysis of the Pentateuch seems sober in comparison with this Composite Gospel. It is, to use Prof. Mead's figure, a patch-work, crazier than the wildest dreams of the critics. And yet I think no one will read it, especially in a Semitic language, without feeling that the author has succeeded beyond what we should have thought possible in making a unity of it.

It must be borne in mind, too, that this patch-work was made, not of indifferent historical writings, but of the sacred books of the Christian church; that it was meant to take the place of the Gospels; that it accomplished its end so successfully that it almost completely superseded the separate Gospels in the public use of a considerable part of **[209]** the Syrian church; that it was apparently only under influences from without that it was banished from the use of these churches in the fifth century. Aphraates and Ephraim are acquainted, indeed, with the separate Gospels; but it is certainly within the bounds of possibility that, if the Syrian church had been left to itself, without constant contact with the greater church to the West, the knowledge of the separate Gospels might in the end have been lost, even among the learned. The parallel to the history of the Pentateuch would then have been complete.

The way in which the author treats his sources deserves somewhat more detailed notice. I have incidentally referred above to the extensive omissions. These amount to more than one fourth of the whole; if we take the Synoptics alone, to about one third. Most of the omitted matter is from the parallels in the Synoptic Gospels; and the author has taken great pains that no fact, no detail in the relation of a fact, should be lost. The one conspicuous omission which is not of this sort is already remarked upon by the fathers. Tatian excluded both the genealogies of Jesus. Whatever may have led him to omit these documents, the fact is a striking testimony to the freedom of his attitude toward the sources. If they had had for him strictly canonical authority, it is not likely that he would have ventured to suppress them in a book intended for church use.

The Gospels do not present the events of Jesus' life in the same order. Not only has John a scheme of his own, but the order of Matthew differs from that of Luke. A connected narrative can only be made by the freest transposition. We find this on every page of the Diatessaron. Luke iv. 1 f. 5–7, e.g., is in chap. iv; 13–22ᵃ in v (14ᵇ, 15 also in vii); 23–30 in xvii; 42ᵇ, 43 in vii; 44, 31–41 in vi. The conversation with Nicodemus is carried over with the account of the cleansing of the Temple which precedes it to the last period of Jesus' ministry, and so on. Not only are passages transposed as wholes, to bring them into connection with other parallels in other Gospels, but in working together the details of the parallel narratives of any given doing of Jesus, or the reports of any saying, the most complicated transposition of verses, fragments of verses, and single phrases is constantly necessary. There is another cause of transposition, of which I will speak later; namely, the use of words or verses taken from their original connection to form the bridge be-[210] tween different sources or passages where the transition would otherwise be too hard.

The author has added nothing which was not contained in his sources, and has changed them as little as possible. Yet he was frequently compelled, in order to make a passable connection or transition, to supply or omit an explicit subject, to substitute different particles of transition, and sometimes to make the connection in his own words. Thus, in a case already referred to, he joins Matt. ii. 1 to Luke ii. 39 by substituting for the words "Now when Jesus was born in Bethlehem of Judea in the days of Herod the King," simply, "After this." Mark iii. 14 relates the choice of twelve disciples. After Luke vi. 13 ff. it could only find a place by making it read, "These twelve he chose," etc., by which means it is made to resume the preceding, instead of introducing, as it does in the original, the list of the twelve. Matt. xii. 32 ff. is made possible alongside of Mark iii. 28 ff., by prefacing it with the words, "He said again." Such cases are very common. A joint is often made, as I have said above, by taking a verse or a phrase quite out of its original connection, or by cutting through one of his sources in such a way as to make the last words serve as a transition to something different from what originally followed. Thus Luke iv. 38 tells us that Jesus, on going out of the synagogue, went into Simon's house, where Simon's mother-in-law lay ill of a fever, etc. The author puts in here the calling of Matthew, and makes it fit thus: "And when Jesus went out of the synagogue,' he saw a man whose name was Matthew, sitting among the publicans; and he said to him, Follow me, and he arose, and followed him. 'And Jesus came into the house of Simon and Andrew, with James and John. 'And Simon's mother-in-law was ill," etc. (Luke iv. 38ᵃ, Matt. ix. 9ᵇ, Mark i. 29, Luke iv. 38ᵇf.). In Luke vi. 27 we read, "I say unto you which hear, Love your enemies, do good to them that hate you," etc. The introductory phrase is used by Tatian to connect Luke vi. 24–27 with Matt. v. 13, so that it runs, "I say unto you which hear, Ye are the salt of the earth," etc. In such ways a reasonably smooth connection is made between passages originally wholly unrelated to one another. It should be said that this is, in one way, much easier to do in a Semitic language than it would be in English or in Greek. A similar harmony of the Greek Gospels would involve far more extensive changes in grammatical structure, in order to fit the bits together. But in [211] Syriac, where a simple paratactic structure is the rule, the members of what would in Greek be a complex sentence stand side by side, each complete in itself, and the sentence may be divided after almost any of its clauses without destroying it.

There is one thing in which the Arabic Diatessaron which we have in our hands differs notably from the Pentateuch. The sources from which the composite narrative is made up are distinguished by diacritical signs—M for Matthew, R for Mark, Q for Luke, H for John. In the Borgian manuscript these signs are generally lacking, so that the text runs on unbroken. The prologue, however, shows that it is derived from a copy which had these signs. In the Vatican MS they are employed throughout, though often erroneously. Ciasca is of the opinion that the original had no such signs, but that they have been added by later hands. This seems to me very unlikely. It would be a work of the greatest difficulty, and of no practical utility, to add these signs to a text originally devoid of them, and attain even a tolerable degree of correctness. On the other hand, it is very natural that they should be dropped by later copyists as useless. I am inclined to think, therefore, that the author distinguished his sources by such signs in the original composition of the Diatessaron. If this be true, does it not outweigh all the analogies we have observed to the composition of the Pentateuch? Must we not say that we have indeed dismemberment, rearrangement, but no real composition, so long as every fragment bears the name of its own Gospel? As to the latter point, any one can easily convince himself that the Diatessaron is meant to read smoothly, with grammatical and psychological connection, right over these divisions; and in the public reading of the book in church it is not to be supposed that the sense was broken, every half dozen words sometimes, by the names of the Evangelists. The diacritical signs are there for the use of the learned, not for practical purposes. For the church, therefore, it was a composite work, as truly as the Pentateuch. But why are the signs there at all, if the author designed a real Composite Gospel? Any one who is familiar with Moslem tradition will be at no loss for the answer. It is the ᵓ*Isnād*. The tradition of the life and sayings of Jesus went back to certain men who had a personal knowledge of the things they handed down,—Matthew, Peter, John,—or otherwise stood at the source of Christian tradition, as Paul. The second and third Gospels were traced, in this interest, to Peter and Paul. Tatian, therefore, names [212] his sources, precisely because the whole weight rests on their names; just as Ibn Hisham, in his Life of Mohammed, gives us in all cases the names of the persons from whom and through whom a given relation has come to him. The case was wholly different with the Pentateuch. The analogy of the whole historical literature of the Old Testament gives us the right to assume that the sources which the compiler wove together were anonymous. Even if the name of the author of any one of these sources, or of all of them, had been known, however, he stood in no such relation to the facts he narrated as one of the companions of the Prophet to Moslem tradition, or one of the evangelists to the Christian tradition of the life of Jesus. The compiler of the Pentateuch, therefore, had no reason to distinguish by name the sources from which he made up his history, even if he was in a position to do so. The same consideration may explain why Tatian keeps closer to his sources than the author of the Pentateuch. It is a fair question, however, whether the original Diatessaron followed them as exclusively as the text we have. The latter has been systematically revised after the Syrian Church Bible, and *exotica* once contained in it may have been removed in that process. In fact, it can be shown with much probability that this is the case.

I have touched here on another point in resemblance between the Diatessaron and the Pentateuch. Both were, at a time long subsequent to their origin, subjected to a thorough recension of the text. The original Syriac text of the Diatessaron no doubt resembled the so-called Curetonian, more than the Peshitto, whatever view we take of the relation of the one to the other. The Syriac from which our Arabic was translated in the eleventh century was substantially the Peshitto. I say substantially, for there are a considerable number of readings which differ from that version, without showing any definite resemblance to any other type of Syriac text. I have not collated Ciasca's text with the Peshitto, except in a few passages; but in my reading of it for the purpose of investigating the composition of the book I have incidentally remarked several variants. In Mark vii. 26, e.g. the Syrophoenician woman is said to be from Emesa. Matt. xvii. 25, in answer to Jesus' question from whom the kings of the earth take tribute, reads: "Simon said to him, From the strangers. Jesus said to him, Then the sons are free. Simon said to him, Yes. Jesus said to him, Do thou also give to them, as a stranger; and, lest it make them trouble, go to the sea," etc. Matt. xxiii. 34 reads: **[213]** "Therefore behold I, the wisdom of God, send unto you prophets," etc.[3] I do not reckon the many places where the text has been slightly modified in favor of a better connection, or where a conflation, perhaps unintentional, has taken place. After making allowance for these, there still remain variations from the common Peshitto text, such as those given above.

3. But Matt. xxiv. 8, "haec omnia initium sunt *inundationum*" (p. 73), is Ciasca's error. The Arabic has *dolorum*.

Every Old Testament scholar who examines the Diatessaron will doubt-less ask himself the question: If this Composite Gospel had come down to us as the Pentateuch has, without diacritical signs to distinguish one source from another, the original sources themselves having been lost, should we be able, by the methods which we have applied to the Pentateuch, to decompose it, and to reconstitute its elements? We could not fail to dis-cover its composite character by the same marks by which we recognize this in the case of the Pentateuch. No matter how closely parallel the sources, no matter how ingenious the mosaic, the lack of homogeneousness in conception will appear. The narrative does not go straight to its end, but doubles on itself; there are incongruities, if not contradictions; doublets, joints, and seams; in short, all the signs by which we can in literary com-position distinguish a patch-work from whole cloth. I have called attention to the conflict in which the two narratives of the infancy stand. The same thing may be observed in other instances. Thus, in chap. xviii we read, from Mark vi. 20, that Herod feared John, knowing him to be a pure and holy man; and watched over him, and heard much from him, and did it, and obeyed him willingly. In the very next words, however, from Matthew, we learn that he wished to kill him, and was only restrained by fear of the people; and then again, from Mark, that when Herodias demanded John's head, Herod was very sorry. In the same chapter we have, Mark vi. 16, Herod said to his servants, "This is John the Baptist, whom I beheaded; he is risen from the dead," and a little later, Luke ix. 9, "Herod said, John I have beheaded, but who is this, of whom I hear these things?" In chap. xii at the beginning, we read, from Matt., "Jesus embarked in the boat, and crossed over and came to his own city"; but in the next words, from Luke viii. 38, we are still in the country of the Gadarenes: "And the man out of whom he had cast the demons asked that he might remain with him," etc. Instances could be mul-[214]tiplied almost indefinitely. Of a different kind are cases like this, from chap. iv. Matt. iii. 13, Jesus comes to John to be baptized, 14, but John forbids him. In the Diatessaron, Luke iii. 23, John i. 29-31 are wedged in between these two verses of Matthew, with the con-sequence that the words "But John forbade him" have no connection with the preceding. Examples of doublets are also numerous. The *Vox clamantis* is given in chap. iii from Matthew, and in iv from John. The call of the first disciples by the sea is told twice, with verbal parallels: "I will make you fishers of men" (chap. v), and, "Henceforth you shall catch men unto life" (chap. vi—observe the added words). Overlapping is common, as, e.g., in chap. xxix near the beginning, Luke xviii. 30 and Mark x. 30[b]. An example where substantially the same thing is told three times is in the beginning of chap. xxxix, the words of Jesus about the anointing in Bethany. But it is especially in the account of the appearances of the angels to the women after the resurrection, and the appearances of the risen Lord, that the unwillingness to omit anything has led to a confusing multiplication of details, in which the composite character is most plainly seen.

There is not, as far as I see, any one of the phenomena on which we rely in the Pentateuch to prove the composite character of a text, which is not abundantly illustrated in the Diatessaron. And the indirect demonstration which this fact gives of the correctness of our method is complete. That some of these phenomena could in individual cases be explained in some other way, or, if need were, explained away, does not affect this in the least. One simple hypothesis explains them all; and the correctness of this hypothesis receives the strongest support from the actual case before us, in which we see that the same phenomena have arisen from composition.

Whether we should be able to analyze the Composite Gospel with as much success as we have had in the Pentateuch, is another question. We may answer confidently, that we should not. If we had the Diatessaron in Greek, we should be able to take out the portions which belong to the Fourth Gospel almost as completely and surely as we can P in the Pentateuch. But the remainder would be more stubborn. No doubt we should observe differences, such as the Kingdom of Heaven and the Kingdom of God; no doubt we should note characteristic expressions, such as the ever recurring "straightway" of Mark; we should discover differences of conception as well **[215]** as of language. But we should lack any such external criteria as we have in the relation of J E or D or P to the history and the prophets. The Gospels are the product of one age, of one circle; they have a common basis of evangelic tradition; and their relation to one another is a problem which criticism has not satisfactorily solved, even with the separate Gospels to work on. The problem is more like that of the composition of one of the chief sources of the Pentateuch—say P or D—than that of the primary analysis, but is even more complex. Something, no doubt, would be possible; but the irresolvable remainder would be very large. Analysis cannot do everything. That it has done as much as it has in the Old Testament is due to the peculiarly favorable circumstances under which the problem is there presented. The Homeric scholar, the critic set down to a Composite Gospel like this, has a task with which far less can be done. In the Pentateuch itself there is a limit, and it may be narrower than we think. But even if what can with reasonable certainty be established by the analysis were far less than we believe it to be, it would not alter the fact that the Pentateuch is a composite work, any more than our inability to resolve the Synoptic element in the Diatessaron would prove that that work was not composite.

In conclusion, I repeat that a thorough study of this book will be very profitable to Old Testament critics and to their opponents. For an answer to a good many of the common arguments against the analysis, it will be sufficient, as I have tried to show, to refer to Tatian.[4]

4. A convenient synopsis of the contents of the Arabic Diatessaron and of Ephraim's Commentary is to be found in Hemphill, S., *The Diatessaron of Tatian*, London. 1888. An appendix subjoins the *capita* of the Latin Harmony, from Ranke's *Codex Fuldensis*.

Abbreviations: Scholarly Literature and Ancient Texts

Scholarly Literature

AASOR	Annual of the American Schools of Oriental Research
AB	Anchor Bible
Act. Ant.	*Acta Antiqua Academiae Scientiarum Hungaricae*
AfO	*Archiv für Orientforschung*
AHw	von Soden, *Akkadisches Handwörterbuch*
AJA	*American Journal of Archaeology*
AJBI	*Annual of the Japanese Biblical Institute*
AJSL	*American Journal of Semitic Languages and Literatures*
AJSR	*Association for Jewish Studies Review*
ANEH	Hallo and Simpson, *The Ancient Near East: A History*
ANET	Pritchard, ed., *Ancient Near Eastern Texts Relating to the Old Testament*, 3d. ed.
An.Or.	Analecta Orientalia
An.St.	*Anatolian Studies*
AOAT	Alter Orient und Altes Testament
APB	Albright, *The Archaeology of Palestine and the Bible*
Ar.Or.	*Archiv Orientální*
AS	Assyriological Studies
ATD	Das Alte Testament Deutsch
AV	Anniversary Volume (used for Festschriften)
BA	*The Biblical Archaeologist*
BAL	Borger, *Babylonisch-Assyrische Lesestücke*
BASOR	*Bulletin of the American Schools of Oriental Research*
BDB	Brown, Driver, and Briggs, *Hebrew and English Lexicon of the Old Testament*
BETL	Bibliotheca Ephemeridum Theologicarum Lovaniensium

Bi.Or.	*Bibliotheca Orientalis*
BZAW	Beihefte zur Zeitschrift für die Alttestamentliche Wissenschaft
CAD	Gelb et al., *The Assyrian Dictionary of the Oriental Institute of the University of Chicago* (each volume is cited by the letter(s) of the alphabet it covers, thus *CAD* B, *CAD* M$_2$, etc.)
CB	Cambridge Bible
CBQ	*Catholic Biblical Quarterly*
CRRAI	*Compte rendu de la Rencontre Assyriologique Internationale*
CT	*Cuneiform Texts from Babylonian Tablets in the British Museum*
DJD	Discoveries in the Judaean Desert (of Jordan)
EGE	Tigay, *The Evolution of the Gilgamesh Epic*
EI	*Eretz-Israel*
EJ	C. Roth, ed., *Encyclopaedia Judaica*
EM	E. L. Sukenik et al., eds., *Enṣîqlôpedyâ Miqrāʾît*
ETL	*Ephemerides Theologicae Lovanienses*
FSAC	Albright, *From the Stone Age to Christianity*
GAG	von Soden, *Grundriss der Akkadischen Grammatik*
GETh.	Thompson, *The Epic of Gilgamesh. Text, Transliteration, and Notes*
GKC	Cowley, *Gesenius' Hebrew Grammar*
GSL	Garelli, ed., *Gilgameš et sa légende*
HAT	Handbuch zum Alten Testament
HDB	Hastings, ed., *A Dictionary of the Bible*
HSM	Harvard Semitic Monographs
HUCA	*Hebrew Union College Annual*
ICC	International Critical Commentary
IDB	Buttrick, ed., *The Interpreter's Dictionary of the Bible*
IDBS	Crim, ed., *The Interpreter's Dictionary of the Bible. Supplementary Volume*
IEJ	*Israel Exploration Journal*
ILOT	Driver, *Introduction to the Literature of the Old Testament*

IOSCS	International Organization for Septuagint and Cognate Studies
JANES	*Journal of the Ancient Near Eastern Society of Columbia University*
JAOS	*Journal of the American Oriental Society*
JBL	*Journal of Biblical Literature*
JCS	*Journal of Cuneiform Studies*
JNES	*Journal of Near Eastern Studies*
JSS	*Journal of Semitic Studies*
JTS	*Journal of Theological Studies*
KEHAT	Kurzgefasstes exegetisches Handbuch zum Alten Testament
Lambert-Millard	Lambert and Millard, *Atra-ḫasīs*
LCL	Loeb Classical Library
LUÅ	Lunds Universitets Årsskrift
MIO	*Mitteilungen des Instituts für Orientforschung*
MVAG	Mitteilungen der Vorderasiatischen (or: Vorderasiatisch-Aegyptischen) Gesellschaft
NCB	New Century Bible Commentary
NJV	Jewish Publication Society of America, *The Torah, The Prophets,* and *The Writings*
OIP	Oriental Institute Publications
Or.	*Orientalia* (all references to New Series)
OTI	Eissfeldt, *The Old Testament: An Introduction*
OTJC	W. Robertson Smith, *The Old Testament in the Jewish Church*
OTL	Old Testament Library
OTS	*Oudtestamentische Studiën*
PBS	Publications of the Babylonian Section, University Museum, University of Pennsylvania
RA	*Revue d'assyriologie et d'archéologie orientale*
RB	*Revue biblique*
RIDA	*Revue internationale des droits de l'antiquité*

RLA	Ebeling and Meissner et al., *Reallexikon der Assyriologie*
SAKI	Thureau-Dangin, *Die sumerischen und akkadischen Königsinschriften*
SBLMS	The Society of Biblical Literature Monograph Series
SKLJ	Jacobsen, ed., *The Sumerian King List*
SVT	Supplements to Vetus Testamentum
TLZ	*Theologische Literaturzeitung*
UET	Ur Excavations, Texts
VAB	Vorderasiatische Bibliothek
VT	*Vetus Testamentum*
WHJP	*The World History of the Jewish People*
WMANT	Wissenschaftliche Monographien zum Alten und Neuen Testament
YNER	Yale Near Eastern Researches
YOR	Yale Oriental Series, Researches
ZA	*Zeitschrift für Assyriologie* (volumes cited according to consecutive numeration from *ZA* 1 [1886], without shifting to New Series numbers employed since *ZA* 35 = *ZA* N.F. 1)
ZAW	*Zeitschrift für die Alttestamentliche Wissenschaft*

Ancient Texts

Biblical Texts and Versions

BHK	Kittel, ed., *Biblia Hebraica*
BHS	Elliger and Rudolph, eds., *Biblia Hebraica Stuttgartensia*
LXX	Septuagint (ed. Rahlfs; Eng. trans. in *The Septuagint . . .*)
LXX^A	Codex Alexandrinus of the Septuagint
LXX^B	Codex Vaticanus of the Septuagint

MG	*Miqrā²ôt Gĕdôlôt*
MT	Masoretic Text

OG	The Old Greek translation
OL	The Old Latin translation
OT	Old Testament

Pesh	Peshitta

Q (1Q, 4Q, etc.)	Qumran. The numeral preceding Q indicates the cave in which a particular ms. was found; sigla following the Q indicate the content of the ms. (e.g., 4QJer[b] = the second copy [b] of Jeremiah from Qumran cave 4). For full listings and bibliography, see Fitzmyer, *Dead Sea Scrolls*; Sanders, "Palestinian Manuscripts."

SP	Samaritan Pentateuch (critical edition by von Gall; edition with MT in parallel column by A. and R. Sadaqa)

Tg	Targum

Vg	Vulgate

POSTBIBLICAL AND RABBINIC LITERATURE

b.	*Babylonian Talmud*
Ber.	Tractate *Bĕrākôt*
Bib. Ant.	Pseudo-Philo, *Biblical Antiquities*
B. Meṣ.	Tractate *Bābā Mĕṣî^cā²*
B. Qam.	Tractate *Bābā Qammā²*

Ed.	Tractate *Edûyôt*
Erub.	Tractate *^cErûbîn*

Gen. R.	*Genesis (Bĕrē²šît) Rabbâ* (cited from ed. Theodor and Albeck)

Ḥul.	Tractate *Ḥûllîn*

Jos(ephus),
   Ant.   Josephus, *Antiquities of the Jews* (cited from ed.
          Thackeray)

   Lev. R.   *Leviticus* (*Wayyiqrā*ʾ) *Rabbâ* (cited from ed.
          Margulies)

   m.   Mishna
   Mak.   Tractate *Makkôt*
   Meg.   Tractate *Měgîllâ*

   Num. R.   *Numbers* (*Běmidbar*) *Rabbâ* (cited from *Sēfer Midrāš
          Rabbâ*, Vilna)

   Pes.   Tractate *Pěsāḥîm*

   Sanh.   Tractate *Sanhedrîn*
   Soṭa   Tractate *Sôṭâ*

   t.   *Tôseftā*ʾ
   Taᶜan.   Tractate *Taᶜănît*

   y.   *Jerusalem* (*Palestinian*) *Talmud*

Cuneiform Literature

   Anzû   *The Myth of Anzû*; citations from *ANET*, pp. 111–13,
          514–16.
   Atr.   *The Atrahasis Epic*, ed. Lambert-Millard; references to
          the Old Babylonian version are preceded by "OB";
          for citations such as "Atr. S." see manuscript
          symbols in Lambert-Millard, pp. 40–41.

   Deluge   "The Sumerian Flood Story," ed. Civil, in Lambert-
          Millard, pp. 138–45, 167–72; older trans. by Kramer
          in *ANET*, pp. 42–44.
   DG   *The Death of Gilgamesh* (see Chapter 1, n. 40).

   En. El.   *Enuma Elish*, ed. Labat, *Le Poème babylonien*; trans-
          lation in *ANET*, pp. 60–72, 501–3.

   GA   *Gilgamesh and Agga* (see Chapter 1, n. 47).

GBH	*Gilgamesh and the Bull of Heaven* (see Chapter 1, n. 39).
GE	The late, standard Babylonian ("canonical") version of the *Gilgamesh Epic*, cited from *GETh.* except where noted otherwise (for additional texts, see Borger, *Handbuch* I and II, s.v. Thompson, EG); translation in *ANET*, pp. 72–99, 503–7.
GEN	*Gilgamesh, Enkidu, and the Netherworld* (see Chapter 1, n. 44).
Gilgamesh	The *Gilgamesh Epic*, irrespective of version.
Gilg. Me.	Meissner, MVAG 7; *ANET*, pp. 89–90.
Gilg. Mi.	Lambert and Millard, *CT* 46, 16; ed. Millard, *Iraq*, 26:99–105; *ANET*, p. 507.
Gilg. O. I.	Oriental Institute fragment; Bauer, *JNES* 16:254–62; *ANET*, pp. 504–5.
Gilg. P.	Pennsylvania tablet; Langdon, PBS 10(3); ed. Jastrow and Clay, YOR 4(3), pp. 62–86; *GETh.*, pp. 20–24; *ANET*, pp. 76–78.
Gilg. Y.	Yale tablet; ed. Jastrow and Clay, YOR 4(3), pp. 87–102; *GETh.*, pp. 25–29; *ANET*, pp. 78–81.
GLL	*Gilgamesh and the Land of the Living* (see Chapter 1, n. 38).
LH	*The Laws of Hammurapi*, ed. Driver and Miles, *Babylonian Laws*, 2.
SKL	*The Sumerian King List.*
VTE	*The Vassal Treaties of Esarhaddon.*

Works Cited

Adeni, Solomon bar Joshua. *Mĕleʾket Šĕlōmōh.* In *Mišnāyôt,* Vilna edition. Repr. with additions, in 13 vols.: Jerusalem: *Ḥayyê-ʿôlām,* 1975.

Agnon, S. Y. *Šîrâ* (in Hebrew). Jerusalem–Tel Aviv: Schocken, 1971.

Albeck, H. *Šiššâ Sidrê Mišnâ.* Vol. 2. *Sēder Môʿēd.* Jerusalem: Bialik Institute; Tel Aviv: Dvir, 1958.

Albright, W. F. *Archaeology, Historical Analogy, and Early Biblical Tradition.* Baton Rouge: Louisiana State University Press, 1966.

————. *The Archaeology of Palestine and the Bible.* Cambridge, Mass.: American Schools of Oriental Research, 1974.

————. *From the Stone Age to Christianity.* 2d ed. Garden City, N.Y.: Doubleday, 1957.

————. *The Proto-Sinaitic Inscriptions and Their Decipherment.* Harvard Theological Studies 22. Cambridge, Mass.: Harvard University Press; London: Oxford University Press, 1969.

————. "Some Canaanite-Phoenician Sources of Israel's Wisdom." Pp. 1–15 in *Wisdom in Israel and in the Ancient Near East.* SVT 3. Leiden: Brill, 1955.

————. "Some Oriental Glosses on the Homeric Problem." *AJA* 54 (1950): 162–76.

Allegro, J. M. "Further Messianic References in Qumran Literature." *JBL* 75 (1956): 182–87.

Allegro, J. M. with the collaboration of A. A. Anderson. *Qumran Cave 4: I (4Q158–4Q186).* DJD 5. Oxford: Clarendon, 1968.

Alster, B. *Dumuzi's Dream.* Mesopotamia: Copenhagen Studies in Assyriology, 1. Copenhagen: Akademisk Forlag, 1972.

Alt, A. *Essays on Old Testament History and Religion.* Garden City, N.Y.: Doubleday, 1967.

Alter, R. *The Art of Biblical Narrative.* New York: Basic Books, 1981.

Arnaud, M. D. "La bibliothèque d'un devin syrien à Meskéné-Emar (Syrie)." *Comptes rendus des séances de l'Académie des Inscriptions et Belles-Lettres.* 1980, pp. 375–88.

Astruc, J. *Conjectures sur les mémoires originaux dont il paroit que Moyse s'est servi pour composer le livre de la Genèse.* Brussels, 1753.

Attias, M. *Romancero Sefaradi.* Jerusalem: Kiryat Sefer, 1961.

Avigad, N. "Baruch the Scribe and Jerahmeel the King's Son." *IEJ* 28 (1978): 52–56.

Baillet, M. "Le texte samaritaine de l'Exode dans les manuscrits de Qumran." Pp. 363–81 in *Hommages à André Duppont-Sommer*. Paris: Libraire d'Amérique et d'Orient, Adrien-Maissonneuve, 1971.

Baillet, M., Milik, J. T., and de Vaux, R., eds. *Les 'Petites Grottes' de Qumran*. 2 vols. DJD 3. Oxford: Clarendon, 1962.

Bancroft, C. "Tales of a 4,000-year-old Sumerian goddess." Review of Wolkstein and Kramer, *Inanna*. . . . In *Philadelphia Inquirer*, December 25, 1983, Section L, p. 5.

Barthélemy, D. *Les devanciers d'Aquila*. SVT 10. Leiden: Brill, 1963.

_____. "La qualité du Texte Massorétique de Samuel," in Tov, ed., *Texts of Samuel*, pp. 1–44.

Barthélemy, D., and Milik, J. T., eds. *Qumran Cave I*. DJD 1. Oxford: Clarendon, 1955.

Bauer, T. "Ein viertes altbabylonisches Fragment des Gilgameš-Epos." *JNES* 16 (1957): 254–62.

Beck, F. A. G. *Greek Education 450–350 B.C.* New York: Barnes & Noble, 1964.

Bendavid, A. *Parallels in the Bible* (in Hebrew). Jerusalem: Carta, 1972.

Bentzen, A. *Introduction to the Old Testament*. 2 vols. 2d ed. Copenhagen: Gad, 1952.

Berlin, A. "Ethnopoetry and the Enmerkar Epics." *JAOS* 103 (1983): 17–24.

Bialik, H. N., and Rawnitzki, Y. H. *Sēfer hā-ʾAggādâ*. 3d ed. Tel Aviv: Dvir, 1960.

Bickerman, E. J. *Four Strange Books of the Bible*. New York: Schocken, 1967.

_____. "Notes on Seleucid and Parthian Chronology." *Berytus* 8 (1944): 73–83.

_____. *Studies in Jewish and Christian History (Part One)*. Arbeiten zur Geschichte des Antiken Judentums und des Urchristentums 9. Leiden: Brill, 1976.

Biggs, R. D. "The Abū-Ṣalābīkh Tablets." *JCS* 20 (1966): 73–88.

_____. "The Ebla Tablets. An Interim Perspective." *BA* 43 (1980): 76–87.

_____. *Inscriptions from Tell Abū Ṣalābīkh*. OIP 99. Chicago and London: University of Chicago Press, 1974.

Bing, J. D. "Gilgamesh and Lugalbanda in the Fara Period." *JANES* 9 (1977): 1–4.

Böhl, F. M. Th. deL. "Gilgameš. B. Nach akkadischen Texten." *RLA* 3:364–72.

Boer, P. A. H. de. "I Samuel XVII. Notes on the Text and the Ancient Versions." *OTS* 1 (1942): 79–103.

Bogaert, P.-M. "De Baruch à Jérémie, les deux rédactions conservées du livre de Jérémie." Pp. 168–73 in Bogaert, ed., *Le livre de Jérémie*.

_____. "Les mécanismes rédactionnels en Jér 10, 1–16 (LXX et TM) et la signification des suppléments." Pp. 222–38 in Bogaert, ed., *Le livre de Jérémie*.

Bogaert, P.-M., *Le livre de Jérémie. Le prophète et son milieu, les oracles et leur transmission*. BETL 54. Leuven: Leuven University Press, 1981.

Boling, R. G. "'Synonymous' Parallelism in the Psalms." *JSS* 5 (1960): 221–55.

Borger, R. *Babylonisch-Assyrische Lesestücke*. 3 vols. Rome: Pontifical Biblical Institute, 1963.

_____. *Handbuch der Keilschriftliteratur*. 3 vols. Berlin: de Gruyter, 1967–75.

_____. *Die Inschriften Asarhaddons Königs von Assyrien*. AfO Beiheft 9. Graz, 1956.

Bright, J. "The Date of the Prose Sermons of Jeremiah." *JBL* 70 (1951): 15–35.

_____. *A History of Israel*. 3d ed. Philadelphia: Westminster, 1981.

_____. *Jeremiah*. AB 21. Garden City, N.Y.: Doubleday, 1965.

Brin, G. "The Bible as Reflected in the Temple Scroll." *Shnaton* 4 (1980): 182–225 (Hebrew; Eng. summary, pp. xvii–xviii).

Brown, F., Driver, S. R., and Briggs, C. A. *A Hebrew and English Lexicon of the Old Testament*. Oxford: Clarendon, 1959.

Budde, K. *Die Bücher Richter und Samuel: Ihre Quellen und ihr Aufbau*. Giessen: Ricker, 1890.

Burney, C. F. *The Book of Judges, with Introduction and Critical Notes*. Repr. New York: KTAV, 1970.

_____. *Notes on the Hebrew Text of the Book of Kings*. Repr. New York: KTAV, 1970.

Burrows, M., ed. *The Dead Sea Scrolls of St. Mark's Monastery*. Vol. 1. New Haven: American Schools of Oriental Research, 1950.

_____. "Variant Readings in the Isaiah Manuscript." *BASOR* 111 (1948): 16–24; *BASOR* 113 (1949): 24–32.

Busis, R. "An Application of the Documentary Hypothesis to the Flood Story." Seminar Paper, University of Pennsylvania, 1977.

Buttrick, G. A., et al., eds. *The Interpreter's Dictionary of the Bible*. 4 vols. Nashville: Abingdon, 1962.

Caquot, A. "Une inscription Araméene d'epoque Assyrienne." Pp. 9–16 in *Hommages à André Dupont-Sommer*. Paris: Librairie d'Amérique et d'Orient, Adrien-Maissonneuve, 1971.

Carpenter, J. E., and Harford-Battersby, G. *The Composition of the Hexateuch*. London: Longmans, Green, 1902.

_____. *The Hexateuch*. 2 vols. London: Longmans, Green, 1900.

Cassuto, U. M. D. *Biblical and Oriental Studies*. 2 vols. Translated by I. Abrahams. Jerusalem: Magnes, 1973–75.

_____. *A Commentary on the Book of Exodus* (in Hebrew). 3d ed. Jerusalem: Magnes, 1959.

_____. *A Commentary on the Book of Genesis*. (Part 1) *From Adam to Noah* (in Hebrew). 3d. ed. Jerusalem: Magnes, 1959.

_____. *The Documentary Hypothesis and the Composition of the Pentateuch*. Translated by I. Abrahams. Jerusalem: Magnes, 1961.

_____. *The Goddess Anath* (Hebrew). Jerusalem: Bialik Institute and Waʾad Hallashon Haʾivrit, 1953.

———. "*ḥᵃnôk.*" *EM* 3:203–4.

Civil, M. "The Sumerian Flood Story." In Lambert-Millard, pp. 138–45, 167–72.

Clark, W. M. "The Patriarchal Traditions. Section 2, The Biblical Traditions." Pp. 120–48 in J. H. Hayes and J. M. Miller, eds., *Israelite and Judaean History*. OTL. Philadelphia: Westminster, 1972.

Clements, R. *Abraham and David*. Studies in Biblical Theology, Second Series, 5. London: SCM Press, 1967.

Cogan, M. "The Ahaz Altar. On the Problem of Assyrian Cults in Judah" (Hebrew). Pp. 119–24 in *Proceedings of the Sixth World Congress of Jewish Studies*. Vol. 1. Jerusalem: World Union of Jewish Studies, 1977.

———. "Ashurbanipal Prism F: Notes on Scribal Techniques and Editorial Procedures." *JCS* 29 (1977): 97–107.

———. *Imperialism and Religion*. SBLMS 19. Missoula, Mont.: Scholars Press, 1974.

———. "Omens and Ideology in the Babylon Inscription of Esarhaddon." Pp. 76–87 in H. Tadmor and M. Weinfeld, eds., *History, Historiography, and Interpretation: Studies in Biblical and Cuneiform Literatures*. The Hebrew University of Jerusalem, Papers of the Institute of Advanced Studies. Jerusalem: Magnes, 1983.

———. "Tendentious Chronology in the Book of Chronicles" (in Hebrew). *Zion* 45 (1980): 165–72.

Cogan, M., and Tadmor, H. "Gyges and Ashurbanipal. A Study in Literary Transmission." *Or.* 46 (1977): 65–85.

Cohen, G. D. *Sefer Ha-Qabbalah (The Book of Tradition) by Abraham Ibn Daud*. Philadelphia: Jewish Publication Society of America, 1967.

Conroy, C. "Hebrew Epic: Historical Notes and Critical Reflections." *Biblica* 61 (1980): 1–30.

Cook, S. A. "The Theophanies of Gideon and Manoah." *JTS* 28 (1927): 368–83.

Cooke, G. A. *The Book of Joshua*. CB. Cambridge: University Press, 1918.

Cooper, J. S. "Gilgamesh Dreams of Enkidu: The Evolution and Dilution of Narrative." Pp. 39–44 in M. deJ. Ellis, ed., *Essays on the Ancient Near East in Memory of Jacob Joel Finkelstein*. Memoirs of the Connecticut Academy of Arts and Sciences 19 (December 1977). Hamden, Conn.: Archon, 1977.

———. "Heilige Hochzeit. B. Archäologisch." *RLA* 4:259–69.

———. "Symmetry and Repetition in Akkadian Narrative." *JAOS* 97 (1977): 508–12.

Cowley, A. E., ed. *Gesenius' Hebrew Grammar*. Oxford: Clarendon, 1910.

Crim, K. et al., eds. *The Interpreter's Dictionary of the Bible. Supplementary Volume*. Nashville: Abingdon, 1976.

Cross, F. M., Jr. "The Ammonite Oppression of the Tribes of Gad and Reuben: Missing Verses from 1 Samuel 11 found in 4QSamuel[a]." Pp. 105–19 in E. Tov, ed., *The Hebrew and Greek Texts of Samuel*. 1980 Proceedings IOSCS-Vienna. Jerusalem: Academon, 1980; repr. pp. 148–58 in H. Tadmor and M. Weinfeld, eds., *History, Historiography, and Interpretation: Studies in Biblical and Cuneiform Literatures.* The Hebrew University of Jerusalem, Papers of the Institute of Advanced Studies. Jerusalem: Magnes, 1983. (Citations are from the latter version.)

_____. *The Ancient Library of Qumran and Modern Biblical Studies.* 2d ed. Garden City, N.Y.: Doubleday Anchor, 1961.

_____. *Canaanite Myth and Hebrew Epic.* Cambridge, Mass.: Harvard University Press, 1973.

_____. "The Contribution of the Qumran Discoveries to the Study of the Biblical Text." *IEJ* 16 (1966): 81–95 (repr., with original pagination preserved, in Cross and Talmon, eds., *Qumran*, pp. 278–92).

_____. "The Epic Traditions of Early Israel: Epic Narrative and the Reconstruction of Early Israelite Institutions." Pp. 13–39 in R. E. Friedman, ed., *The Poet and the Historian: Essays in Literary and Historical Biblical Criticism.* Harvard Semitic Studies 26. Chico, Calif.: Scholars Press, 1983.

_____. "The Evolution of a Theory of Local Texts." Pp. 108–26 in R. A. Kraft, ed., *1972 Proceedings of IOSCS Pseudepigrapha.* Septuagint and Cognate Studies 2. Missoula, Mont.: Society of Biblical Literature, 1972 (repr. in Cross and Talmon, eds., *Qumran*, pp. 306–20).

_____. "The History of the Biblical Text in the Light of the Discoveries in the Judaean Desert." *HTR* 57 (1964): 281–99 (repr., with original pagination preserved, in Cross and Talmon, eds., *Qumran*, pp. 177–95).

_____. "A New Qumran Fragment Related to the Original Hebrew Underlying the Septuagint." *BASOR* 132 (1953): 15–26.

_____. "The Origin and Early Evolution of the Alphabet." *EI* 8 (1967) 8*–24*.

Cross, F. M., Jr., ed. *Scrolls from the Wilderness of the Dead Sea.* Washington, D.C.: Smithsonian Institution; Cambridge, Mass.: American Schools of Oriental Research, 1965.

Cross, F. M., and Freedman, D. N. "Josiah's Revolt Against Assyria." *JNES* 12 (1953): 56–58.

Cross, F. M., and Talmon, S., eds. *Qumran and the History of the Biblical Text.* Cambridge, Mass.: Harvard University Press, 1975.

David, M. "Die Bestimmungen über die Asylstädte in Josua XX—ein Beitrag zur Geschichte des biblischen Asylrecht." *OTS* 9 (1951): 30–48.

Davison, J. A. "The Transmission of the Text." Pp. 215–33 in *A Companion to Homer*, edited by A. J. B. Wace and F. H. Stubbings. New York: Macmillan, 1974.

Demsky, A. "A Proto-Canaanite Abecedary Dating from the Period of the Judges and Its Implications for the History of the Alphabet." *Tel Aviv* 4 (1977): 14–27.

Dijk, J. J. A. van. "L'hymne à Marduk avec intercession pour le roi Abī'ešuḫ." *MIO* 12 (1966): 57–74.

Dillmann, A. *Die Bücher Numeri, Deuteronomium, und Josua.* 2d ed. (first by Dillmann). KEHAT 13. Leipzig: Hirzel, 1886.

————. *Die Genesis.* 6th ed. (fourth by Dillmann). KEHAT 11 Leipzig: Hirzel, 1892 (Eng. trans. *Genesis Critically and Exegetically Expounded,* trans. W. B. Stevenson, 2 vols. [Edinburgh: T. & T. Clark, 1897]).

Dinur, B. "The Religious Character of the Cities of Refuge and the Ceremony of Granting Asylum in Them" (in Hebrew). *EI* 3 (1954): 135–46 (Eng. summary, pp. viii–ix).

Dorsch, T. S. *Julius Caesar.* The Arden Edition of the Works of William Shakespeare. Cambridge, Mass.: Harvard University Press, 1958.

Driver, G. R. *The Judaean Scrolls. The Problem and a Solution.* Oxford: Blackwell, 1965.

Driver, G. R., and Miles, J. C. *The Babylonian Laws.* 2 vols. Oxford: Clarendon, 1952–55.

Driver, S. R. *The Book of Exodus.* CB. Cambridge: University Press, 1911.

————. *A Critical and Exegetical Commentary on Deuteronomy.* 3d ed. ICC. Edinburgh: T. & T. Clark, 1902.

————. *An Introduction to the Literature of the Old Testament.* New York: Meridian, 1956.

————. *Notes on the Hebrew Text and the Topography of the Books of Samuel.* 2d ed. Oxford: Clarendon, 1913.

Duncan, D. *Strange but True. 22 Amazing Stories.* New York: Scholastic Book Services, 1973.

Ebeling, E., and Meissner, B. et al. *Reallexikon der Assyriologie.* Berlin and Leipzig: de Gruyter, 1932.

Edzard, D. O. "The Early Dynastic Period," "The Third Dynasty of Ur—Its Empire and Its Successor States," and "The Old Babylonian Period." Chaps. 2, 4, and 5, pp. 52–90 and 133–231 in J. Bottéro et al., eds., *The Near East: The Early Civilizations.* Delacorte World History 2. New York: Delacorte, 1967.

————. "Enmebaragesi, contemporain de Gilgameš." In *GSL,* p. 57.

————. "Enmebaragesi von Kiš." *ZA* 53 (1959): 9–26.

————. "Mesopotamien. Die Mythologie der Sumerer und Akkader." Pp. 17–141 in H. W. Haussig, *Wörterbuch der Mythologie.* Band I. *Götter und Mythen in Vorderen Orient.* Stuttgart: Ernst Klett, 1965.

————. *Die "zweite Zwischenzeit" Babyloniens.* Wiesbaden: Harrassowitz, 1957.

Ehrlich, A. B. *Miqrâ Ki-Pheschutô* (in Hebrew). 3 vols. 1899–1901. Repr. New York: KTAV, 1969.

Ehrman, A., ed. *The Talmud with English Translation and Commentary.* Jerusalem and Tel Aviv: El-ᶜAm-Hozaᵓa Leor Israel, 1965–.

Eichhorn, J. G. *Einleitung ins Alte Testament.* 2d ed. Leipzig, 1787.

Eichler, B. L. "'Please Say That You Are My Sister': Nuzi and Biblical Studies." *Shnaton* 3 (1978–79): 108–15 (Hebrew; English summary, p. xiv).

Eissfeldt, O. *The Old Testament: An Introduction.* Translated by P. R. Ackroyd. New York: Harper & Row, 1965.

Elliger, K., and Rudolph, W. *Biblia Hebraica Stuttgartensia.* Stuttgart: Deutsche Bibelstiftung, 1966–77.

Ellis, R. S. *Foundation Deposits in Ancient Mesopotamia*. YNER 2. New Haven: Yale University Press, 1968.

Engnell, I. *The Call of Isaiah: An Exegetical and Comparative Study*. Uppsala Universitets Årsskrift 1949: 4. Uppsala: Lundequistska; Leipzig: Harrassowitz, 1949.

_____. "Methodological Aspects of Old Testament Study." Pp. 13–30 in *Congress Volume*. Oxford, 1959. SVT 7. Leiden: Brill, 1960.

_____. *A Rigid Scrutiny*. Nashville, Tenn.: Vanderbilt University Press, 1969.

Epstein, J. N. *Māvôɔ lĕnûsaḥ hammišnâ*. 2 vols. 2d ed. Jerusalem: Magnes; Tel Aviv: Dvir, 1964.

_____. *Prolegomena ad Litteras Amoraiticas*. Jerusalem: Magnes; Tel Aviv: Dvir, 1962.

Epstein, J. N., and Melamed, E. Z. *Mekhilta d'Rabbi Šimᶜon b. Jochai*. Jerusalem: Mekize Nirdamim, 1955.

Erman, A. *The Literature of the Ancient Egyptians*. London: Methuen, 1927.

Falkenstein, A. "La cité-temple sumérienne." *Cahiers d'histoire Mondiale* 1 (1954): 784–814.

_____. "Gilgameš. A. Nach sumerischen Texten." *RLA* 3:357–63.

_____. "Gilgameš-Epos. 1. Der sumerische Gilgameš-Zyklus." Cols. 803–7 in *Kindler's Literatur Lexikon*. Vol. 3. Zurich: Kindler, 1967.

_____. "Sumerische religiöse Texte, 2. Ein Šulgi-Lied." *ZA* 50 (1952): 61–91.

_____. "Zu den Inschriftenfunden der Grabung in Uruk-Warka 1960–1961." *Baghdader Mitteilungen* 2 (1963): 1–82.

_____. "Zur Chronologie der sumerischen Literatur." *CRRAI* 2 (1951): 12–27.

Feldmann, F. *Das Buch Isaias*. Exegetisches Handbuch zum Alten Testament 14. Münster: Aschendorffschen Verlagsbuchhandlung, 1925–26.

Finkelstein, J. J. "The Antediluvian Kings: A University of California Tablet." *JCS* 17 (1963): 39–51.

_____. "A Late Old Babylonian Copy of the Laws of Hammurapi." *JCS* 21 (1967; published 1969): 39–48.

Finley, M. *The World of Odysseus*. 2d ed. New York: Penguin, 1982.

Fitzmyer, J. A. *The Dead Sea Scrolls: Major Publications and Tools for Study*. Sources for Biblical Study 8. Missoula, Mont.: Scholars Press and Society of Biblical Literature, 1977.

Fohrer, G. *Introduction to the Old Testament*. Translated by David E. Green. Nashville: Abingdon, 1968.

Frame, G. "Another Babylonian Eponym." *RA* 76 (1982): 157–66.

Frankena, R. "The Vassal Treaties of Esarhaddon and the Dating of Deuteronomy." *OTS* 14 (1965): 122–54.

Freedman, D. N. "Pentateuch." *IDB* 3:711–27.

_____. *Pottery, Poetry, and Prophecy*. Winona Lake, Ind.: Eisenbrauns, 1980.

Freedman, J. *Polychrome Historical Haggadah for Passover*. Springfield, Mass.: Jacob Freedman Liturgy Research Foundation, 1974.

Fretheim, T. E. "Source Criticism." *IDBS*, pp. 838–39.

Friedman, R. E., ed. *The Creation of Sacred Literature.* University of California Publications, Near Eastern Studies, 22. Berkeley: University of California Press, 1981.

———. "Sacred History and Theology: The Redaction of the Torah." Pp. 25–34 in Friedman, ed., *Creation of Sacred Literature.*

Friedman, S. *A Critical Study of Yevamot X with a Methodological Introduction* (Hebrew, with English summary). Jerusalem and New York: Jewish Theological Seminary of America, 1978. Originally published in *Texts and Studies.* Analecta Judaica 1, ed. H. Z. Dimitrovsky (New York: Jewish Theological Seminary of America, 1977), pp. 275–441.

Friedrich, J. "Churritische Märchen und Sagen in hethitischer Sprache." *ZA* 49 (1950): 213–55.

Frye, R. M. "The Synoptic Problems and Analogies in Other Literatures." Pp. 261–302 in W. O. Walker, *The Relationships Among the Gospels: An Interdisciplinary Dialogue.* San Antonio, Tex.: Trinity University Press, 1978.

Gadd, C. J., and Kramer, S. N. *Literary and Religious Texts.* UET 6(1). London: British Museum, 1963.

Gall, A. F. von. *Der Hebräische Pentateuch der Samaritaner.* 5 vols. Giessen: Töpelmann, 1914–18. Repr. in 1 vol., 1966.

Galling, K. *Die Bücher Chronik, Esra, Nehemia.* ATD. Göttingen: Vandenhoeck & Ruprecht, 1954.

Gandz, S. "Oral Tradition in the Bible." Pp. 248–69 in *Jewish Studies in Memory of George A. Kohut,* edited by S. W. Baron and A. Marx. New York: Alexander Kohut Memorial Foundation, 1935.

Garelli, P., ed. *Gilgameš et sa légende.* CRRAI 7, Cahiers du Groupe François-Thureau-Dangin 1. Paris: Imprimerie Nationale and Librarie C. Klincksieck, 1960.

Garitte, G., ed. *Traités d'Hippolyte sur David et Goliath, sur le Cantique des Cantiques et sur l'Antéchrist.* 2 vols. Corpus Scriptorum christianorum orientalium 263–64. Scriptores Iberici, t. 15–16. Louvain: Sécretariat du Corpus Scriptorum christianorum orientalium, 1965.

Gaster, M. *The Samaritans.* London: British Academy, 1925.

Gehman, H. S. "Exegetical Methods Employed by the Greek Translator of I Samuel." *JAOS* 70 (1950): 292–96.

Gelb, I. J. et al., eds. *The Assyrian Dictionary of the Oriental Institute of the University of Chicago.* Chicago: Oriental Institute; Glückstadt, Ger.: J. J. Augustin, 1956.

Gerleman, G. *Synoptic Studies in the Old Testament.* LUÅ N.F. Avd. 1, 44/5. Lund: Gleerup, 1948.

Giesebrecht, F. *Das Buch Jeremia.* HAT III, 2.1: Göttingen: Vandenhoeck & Ruprecht, 1894.

Gilula, M. "The Smiting of the First-Born—An Egyptian Myth?" *Tel Aviv* 4 (1977): 94–95.

Ginsberg, H. L., trans. "Ugaritic Myths, Epics, and Legends." In *ANET* pp. 129–55.

Ginzberg, L. *The Legends of the Jews.* 7 vols. Philadelphia: Jewish Publication Society of America, 1955.

Glatzer, N. N., ed. *The Passover Haggadah.* New York: Schocken, 1969.

Goedicke, H. *The Report of Wenamun.* Baltimore and London: Johns Hopkins University Press, 1975.

Goetze, A. *The Laws of Eshnunna.* AASOR 31. New Haven: Department of Antiquities of the Government of Iraq and the American Schools of Oriental Research, 1956.

Goldschmidt, (E.) D. *Maḥᵃzôr layyāmîm hannôrāʾîm.* 2 vols. Jerusalem: Koren, 1970.

Goldschmidt, E. D. *The Passover Haggadah. Its Sources and History* (in Hebrew). Jerusalem: Bialik Institute, 1960.

Goldschmidt, L. *Sepher hajaschar. Das Heldenbuch.* Berlin: Benjamin Harz, 1923.

Gooding, D. W. *Relics of Ancient Exegesis.* Cambridge: Cambridge University Press, 1976.

Gordis, R. *The Biblical Text in the Making: A Study of the Kethib-Qere.* Augmented edition with a Prolegomenon. New York: KTAV, 1971.

Gordon, C. H. "Homer and Bible." *HUCA* 26 (1955): 43–108.

———. *Ugaritic Literature.* Rome: Pontifical Biblical Institute, 1949.

———. *Ugaritic Textbook.* An.Or. 38. Rome: Pontifical Biblical Institute, 1965.

Gordon, E. I. "Mesilim and Mesannipadda—Are They Identical?" *BASOR* 132 (1953): 27–30.

Grafman, R. "Bringing Tiamat to Earth." *IEJ* 22 (1972): 47–49.

Gray, G. B. *A Critical and Exegetical Commentary on Numbers.* ICC. Edinburgh: T. & T. Clark, 1903.

Grayson, A. K., trans. "Akkadian Myths and Epics," in *ANET*, pp. 501–18; revisions of Speiser, "Akkadian Myths and Epics," in *ANET*, pp. 60–119.

———. "Assyria and Babylonia." *Or.* 49 (1980): 140–94.

———. *Assyrian and Babylonian Chronicles.* Texts from Cuneiform Sources 5. Locust Valley, N.Y.: J. J. Augustin, 1975.

———. "The Chronology of the Reign of Ashurbanipal." *ZA* 70 (1981): 227–45.

Greenberg, M. "Decalogue." *EJ* 5:1435–46.

———. "The Redaction of the Plague Narrative in Exodus." Pp. 243–52 in H. Goedicke, ed. *Near Eastern Studies in Honor of William Foxwell Albright.* Baltimore: Johns Hopkins University Press, 1971.

———. "Response to Roland de Vaux's 'Method in the Study of Early Hebrew History.'" Pp. 37–43 in *The Bible in Modern Scholarship*, edited by J. P. Hyatt. Nashville: Abingdon, 1965.

———. "The Stabilization of the Text of the Hebrew Bible, Reviewed in the Light of the Biblical Materials from the Judean Desert." *JAOS* 76 (1956): 157–67.

———. "The Thematic Unity of Exodus III–XI." Pp. 151–54 in *Fourth World Congress of Jewish Studies. Papers.* Vol. 1. Jerusalem: World Union of Jewish Studies, 1967.

———. *Understanding Exodus.* New York: Behrman House, 1969.

Gunkel, H. *Genesis*. 7th ed. Göttingen: Vandenhoeck & Ruprecht, 1966.

――――. *The Legends of Genesis: The Biblical Saga and History*. Translated by W. H. Carruth. Introduction by W. F. Albright. New York: Schocken, 1964.

Habel, N. C. *Literary Criticism of the Old Testament*. Philadelphia: Fortress Press, 1971.

Halevy, E. E. "The Composition of the Aggadah" (in Hebrew). *Keneset* 10 (1946–47): 41–58.

Halivni, D. Weiss. "Epistemological Bondage." Unpublished lecture delivered to the Association of Jewish Studies, December 18, 1978.

Hallo, W. W. "Beginning and End of the Sumerian King List in the Nippur Recension." *JCS* 17 (1963): 52–57.

――――. "The Coronation of Ur-Nammu." *JCS* 20 (1966): 133–41.

――――. "The Cultic Setting of Sumerian Poetry." CRRAI 17 (1970): 123–33.

――――. "The Date of the Fara Period: A Case Study in the Historiography of Early Mesopotamia." *Or.* 42 (1973): 228–38.

――――. "Letters, Prayers, and Letter-Prayers." Pp. 17–27 in *Proceedings of the Seventh World Congress of Jewish Studies. Studies in the Bible and the Ancient Near East*. Jerusalem: Perry Foundation for Biblical Research and World Union of Jewish Studies, 1981.

――――. "New Viewpoints on Cuneiform Literature." *IEJ* 12 (1962): 13–26.

――――. "Toward a History of Sumerian Literature." Pp. 181–203 in S. J. Lieberman, ed., *Studies . . . Jacobsen*.

Hallo, W. W., and Dijk, J. J. A. van. *The Exaltation of Inanna*. YNER 3. New Haven: Yale University Press, 1968.

Hallo, W. W., and Moran, W. L. "The First Tablet of the SB Recension of the Anzu Myth." *JCS* 31 (1979): 65–115.

Hallo, W. W., and Simpson, W. K. *The Ancient Near East: A History*. New York: Harcourt, Brace, Jovanovich, 1971.

Haran, M. "Behind the Scenes of History: Determining the Date of the Priestly Source." *JBL* 100 (1981): 321–33.

――――. "Methodological Observations on the Depiction of the Exodus Route in the Pentateuchal Sources." *EI* 10 (1971): 138–42 (Hebrew; English summary, p. xiii).

――――. "Scribal Workmanship in Biblical Times." *Tarbiz* 50 (1980–81): 66–87 (Hebrew with English summary).

――――. *Temples and Temple Service in Ancient Israel*. Oxford: Clarendon, 1978.

Harrison, R. K. *Introduction to the Old Testament*. Grand Rapids, Mich.: Eerdmans, 1969.

Hastings, J. *A Dictionary of the Bible*. 5 vols. Edinburgh: T. & T. Clark, 1898–1904.

Hayes, J. H., and Miller, J. M. *Israelite and Judaean History*. OTL. Philadelphia: Westminster, 1977.

Hecker, K. *Untersuchungen zur akkadischen Epik*. AOAT Sonderreihe 8. Kevelaer: Butzon & Bercker; Neukirchen-Vluyn: Neukirchener Verlag, 1974.

Heidel, A. *The Gilgamesh Epic and Old Testament Parallels.* 2d ed. Chicago: University of Chicago Press, 1963.

Heinemann, J. "On Bialik's Method with Talmudic Aggadah" (Hebrew). *Molad* 31 (no. 241; 1974): 83–92.

———. *Studies in Jewish Liturgy* (Hebrew). Edited by A. Shinan. Jerusalem: Magnes, 1981.

Hertzberg, H. W. *Die Bücher Josua, Richter, Ruth.* ATD, 9. Göttingen: Vandenhoeck & Ruprecht, 1953.

———. *I & II Samuel.* OTL. Philadelphia: Westminster, 1964.

Hirsch, E. D. *Validity in Interpretation.* New Haven: Yale University Press, 1967.

Hoffman, D. *Sēfer Dĕvārîm.* 2 vols. Tel Aviv: Nezach, 1959.

Hollenberg, J. *Der Charakter der Alexandrinischen Übersetzung des Buches Josua und ihr Textkritischer Werth.* Moers: Eckner, 1876.

Holmes, S. *Joshua: The Hebrew and Greek Texts.* Cambridge: University Press, 1914.

Homer. *The Odyssey: A New Verse Translation.* Translated by A. Cook. New York: Norton, 1967.

Hurvitz, A. "The Date of the Prose-Tale of Job Linguistically Reconsidered." *HTR* 67 (1974): 17–34.

———. *A Linguistic Study of the Relationship Between the Priestly Source and the Book of Ezekiel: A New Approach to an Old Problem.* Cahiers de la Revue Biblique 20. Paris: Gabalda, 1982.

Ishida, T. "'The People of the Land' and the Political Crises in Judah." *AJBI* 1 (1975): 23–38.

———. *The Royal Dynasties in Ancient Israel.* BZAW 142. Berlin and New York: de Gruyter, 1977.

Jacobsen, T. "Early Political Development in Mesopotamia." *ZA* 52 (1957): 91–140.

———. "Primitive Democracy in Ancient Mesopotamia." *JNES* 2 (1943): 159–72.

———. *The Sumerian King List.* AS 11. Chicago: University of Chicago Press, 1939.

———. *The Treasures of Darkness: A History of Mesopotamian Religion.* New Haven: Yale University Press, 1976.

Janzen, J. G. "Double Readings in the Text of Jeremiah." *HTR* 60 (1967): 433–47.

———. "Studies in the Text of Jeremiah." Ph.D. dissertation. Harvard University, 1965.

———. *Studies in the Text of Jeremiah.* HSM 6. Cambridge, Mass.: Harvard University Press, 1973.

Japhet, S. "Conquest and Settlement in Chronicles." *JBL* 98 (1979): 205–17.

———. *The Ideology of the Book of Chronicles and Its Place in Biblical Thought.* Jerusalem: Mosad Bialik, 1977 (Hebrew).

Jason, H. "The Story of David and Goliath: A Folk Epic?" *Biblica* 60 (1979): 36–70.

Jastrow, M. "Adam and Eve in Babylonian Literature." *AJSL* 15 (1899): 193–214.

———. "Adraḫasis and Parnapištim." *ZA* 13 (1898): 288–301.

———. "On the Composite Character of the Babylonian Creation Story." In C. Bezold, ed., *Orientalische Studien Theodor Nöldeke* 2:969–82. Gieszen: Töpelmann, 1906.

———. *The Religion of Babylonia and Assyria*. Boston: Ginn, 1898.

Jastrow, M., and Clay, A. T. *An Old Babylonian Version of the Gilgamesh Epic*. YOR 4(3). New Haven: Yale University Press, 1920.

Jepsen, A., and Hanhart, R. *Untersuchungen zur israelitisch-jüdischen Chronologie*. BZAW 88. Berlin, 1964.

Jewish Publication Society of America. *The Prophets*. 2d ed. Philadelphia: Jewish Publication Society of America, 1978.

———. *The Torah*. 2d ed. Philadelphia: Jewish Publication Society of America, 1967.

———. *The Writings*. Philadelphia: Jewish Publication Society of America, 1982.

Johnson, B. *Die Hexaplarische Rezension des 1 Samuelbuches der Septuaginta*. Studia Theologica Lundensia 22. Lund: Gleerup, 1963.

Kafiḥ, Y. *Mišnâ ᶜim pērûš Rabbênû Mōšeh ben Maymôn. Sēder Zĕrāᶜîm* and *Sēder Môᶜēd* (in one volume). Jerusalem: Mossad Harav Kook, 1976.

Kahle, P. *The Cairo Geniza*. London: British Academy, 1947.

———. "Untersuchungen zur Geschichte des Pentateuchtextes." In P. Kahle, *Opera Minora*. Leiden: Brill, 1956, pp. 3–37.

Kallai, Z. *The Tribes of Israel: A Study in the Historical Geography of the Bible* (in Hebrew). Jerusalem: Mosad Bialik (Bialik Institute), 1967.

Kasher, M. M. *Hagadah Shelemah*. 3d ed. Jerusalem: Torah Shelema Institute, 1967.

Kaufman, S. A. "The Temple Scroll and Higher Criticism." *HUCA* 53 (1982): 29–43.

Kaufmann, W. *Critique of Religion and Philosophy*. Garden City, N.Y.: Doubleday Anchor, 1961.

Kaufmann, Y. *The Book of Joshua* (in Hebrew). Jerusalem: Kiryat Sepher, 1959; 2d ed., 1963.

———. *The Book of Judges* (in Hebrew). Jerusalem: Kiryat Sepher, 1962.

———. *The Religion of Israel*. Translated and abridged by M. Greenberg. Chicago: University of Chicago Press, 1960.

———. *Tôlĕdôt hāʾemûnâ hayyisrĕʾēlît*. 4 vols. Jerusalem and Tel Aviv: Mosad Bialik and Dvir, 1955.

Kelly, B. H. "The Septuagint Translators of I Samuel and II Samuel 1:1–11:1." Dissertation. Princeton Theological Seminary, 1948.

Kiel, J. *The Book of Joshua* (in Hebrew). Jerusalem: Mossad Harav Kook, 1970.

Kirk, G. S. *Homer and the Epic*. Cambridge: Cambridge University Press, 1965.

Kitchen, K. A. *Ancient Orient and Old Testament*. Chicago: Inter-Varsity Press, 1966.

Kittel, H. J. *Die Stämmessprüche Israels*. Berlin, 1959.

Kittel, R. *Biblia Hebraica.* Edited by A. Alt and O. Eissfeldt. 15th ed. Stuttgart: Wurttembergische Bibelanstalt, 1968.

————. *Studien zur hebräische Archäologie und Religionsgeschichte.* Leipzig: Hinrichs, 1908.

Klein, J. "Šulgi and Gilgamesh: Two Brother-Peers (Šulgi O)." Pp. 271–92 in B. L. Eichler, ed., *Kramer Anniversary Volume: Cuneiform Studies in Honor of Samuel Noah Kramer.* AOAT 25. Kevelaer: Butzon & Bercker; Neukirchen-Vluyn: Neukirchener Verlag, 1976.

————. Review of Wilcke, *Das Lugalbandaepos.* In *JAOS* 91 (1971): 295–99.

Koch, K. *The Growth of the Biblical Tradition.* New York: Scribner's, 1969.

König, E. "Samaritan Pentateuch." *HDB* extra volume, pp. 68–72.

Komlosh, Y. *The Bible in the Light of the Aramaic Translations.* Tel Aviv: Bar Ilan University and Dvir, 1973 (Hebrew).

Komoróczy, G. "Akkadian Epic Poetry and Its Sumerian Sources." *Act.Ant.* 23 (1975): 41–63.

Kramer, S. N. "The Death of Gilgamesh." *BASOR* 94 (1944): 2–12.

————. "The Death of Ur-Nammu and His Descent to the Netherworld." *JCS* 21 (1967; published 1969): 104–22.

————. "The Epic of Gilgameš and Its Sumerian Sources: A Study in Literary Evolution." *JAOS* 64 (1944): 7–23, 83.

————. "Gilgameš: Some New Sumerian data." In *GSL*, pp. 59–68.

————. "Gilgamesh and Agga, with comments by Thorkild Jacobsen." *AJA* 53 (1949): 1–18.

————. "Gilgamesh and the Land of the Living." *JCS* 1 (1947): 3–46.

————. *History Begins at Sumer.* Garden City, N.Y.: Doubleday, 1959.

————. "New Literary Catalogue from Ur." *RA* 55 (1961): 169–76.

————. "The Oldest Literary Catalogue: A Sumerian List of Literary Compositions Compiled About 2000 B.C." *BASOR* 88 (1942): 10–19.

————. "Sumerian Epic Literature." Pp. 825–37 in *Atti del convegno internazionale sul tema: La poesia epica e la sua Formazione* (Roma, 28 marzo–3 aprile 1969). Academia Nazionale dei Lincei, Anno CCCLXVII-1970. Quaderno N. 39. Roma: Academia Nazionale dei Lincei, 1970.

————. *The Sumerians: Their History, Culture, and Character.* Chicago: University of Chicago Press, 1963.

Kramer, S. N., trans. "Sumerian Myths and Epic Tales," "Lipit-Ishtar Lawcode," "Sumerian Hymns," "Sumerian Lamentation," "Sumerian Sacred Marriage Texts," and "Sumerian Miscellaneous Texts." In *ANET*, pp. 37–59, 159–61, 573–86, 611–19, 637–45, 646–52.

Kraus, F. R. "Altmesopotamisches Lebensgefühl." *JNES* 19 (1960): 117–32.

————. "Zur Liste der älteren Könige von Babylonien." *ZA* 50 (1952): 29–60.

Krecher, J. "Glossen. A. In sumerischen und akkadischen Texten." *RLA* 3:431–40.

Kuenen, A. *Gesammelte Abhandlungen zur biblischen Wissenschaft.* Edited by K. Budde. Freiburg: Mohr, 1894.

————. *An Historico-Critical Inquiry into the Origin and Composition of the Hexateuch*. London: Macmillan, 1886.

————. *Historisch-kritische Einleitung in die Bücher des Alten Testaments*. Vol. 1, part 2. Leipzig: Reisland, 1890.

Kugel, J. L. *The Idea of Biblical Poetry*. New Haven and London: Yale University Press, 1981.

Kuhl, C. "Die 'Wiederaufnahme'—Ein literarkritisches Prinzip?" *ZAW* 64 (1952): 1–11.

Kutscher, E. Y. *The Language and Linguistic Background of the Isaiah Scroll* (Hebrew). Jerusalem: Magnes, 1959.

Kutscher, R. *Oh Angry Sea (a-ab-ba-hu-luh-ha). The History of a Sumerian Congregational Lament*. YNER 6. New Haven and London: Yale University Press, 1975.

Labat, R. *Le poème babylonien de la création*. Paris: Librarie d'Amérique et d'Orient, 1935.

Laessøe, J. "Literacy and Oral Tradition in Ancient Mesopotamia." Pp. 205–18 in *Studia Orientalia Ioanni Pedersen . . . Dicata*. Copenhagen: E. Munksgaard, 1953.

Lambert, W. G. "The Birdcall Text." *An.St.* 20 (1970): 111–17.

————. "Gilgameš in Religious, Historical and Omen Texts and the Historicity of Gilgameš." In *GSL*, pp. 39–56.

————. "A New Fragment from a List of Antediluvian Kings and Marduk's Chariot." Pp. 271–80 in M. A. Beek et al., eds., *Symbolae Biblicae et Mesopotamicae Francisco Mario Theodoro de Liagre Böhl Dedicatae*. Leiden: Brill, 1973.

————. "The Reign of Nebuchadnezzar I: A Turning Point in the History of Ancient Mesopotamian Religion." Pp. 3–13 in W. S. McCullough, ed., *The Seed of Wisdom*. Essays in Honour of T. J. Meek. Toronto: University of Toronto Press, 1964.

————. "The Theology of Death." Pp. 53–66 in B. Alster, ed., *Death in Mesopotamia*. CRRAI 26. Mesopotamia: Copenhagen Studies in Assyriology 8. Copenhagen: Akademisk Forlag, 1980.

Lambert, W. G., and Millard, A. R. *Atra-ḫasīs. The Babylonian Story of the Flood*, with "The Sumerian Flood Story," by M. Civil. Oxford: Clarendon, 1969.

————. *Babylonian Literary Texts*. *CT* 46. London: British Museum, 1965.

Landsberger, B. "Einleitung in das Gilgameš-Epos." In *GSL*, pp. 31–36.

Langdon, S. H. *The Epic of Gilgamesh*. PBS 10(3). Philadelphia: University Museum, 1917.

Lemaire, A. *Les écoles et la formation de la Bible dans l'ancien Israël*. Orbis biblicus et orientalis 39. Freiburg: Switz.: Editions Universitaires; Göttingen: Vandenhoeck & Ruprecht, 1981.

Lesky, A. *History of Greek Literature*. London: Methuen, 1966.

Letteris, M. *Sēfer Tôrâ, Něvîʾîm û-Kětûvîm*. New York: Hebrew Publishing Company, n.d.

Levi della Vida, G. "The Shiloah Inscription Reconsidered." Pp. 162–66 in *In Memoriam Paul Kahle*, edited by M. Black and G. Fohrer. BZAW 103. Berlin: A. Töpelmann, 1968.

Levine, B. A. "The Descriptive Tabernacle Texts in the Pentateuch." *JAOS* 85 (1965): 307–18.

————. "Priestly Writers." *IDBS*, pp. 683–87.

————. Review of Haran, *Temples*. In *JBL* 99 (1980): 448–51.

————. "The Temple Scroll: Aspects of Its Historical Provenance and Literary Character." *BASOR* 232 (1978): 5–23.

Lewis, I. M. "Literacy in a Nomadic Society: The Somali Case." Pp. 266–76 in *Literacy in Traditional Societies*, edited by J. Goody. Cambridge: Cambridge University Press, 1968.

Lewy, J. *Die Chronologie der Könige von Israel und Juda*. Giessen: Töpelmann, 1927.

Licht, J. "An Analysis of the Treatise of the Two Spirits in DSD." Pp. 87–100 in *Aspects of the Dead Sea Scrolls*. Scripta Hierosolymitana 4. Jerusalem: Magnes, 1958.

————. "Torah. The Five Books of the Torah" (Hebrew). *EM* 8:483–91.

Lieberman, S. *Hellenism in Jewish Palestine*. Texts and Studies of the Jewish Theological Seminary of America, vol. 18. New York: Jewish Theological Seminary of America, 1962.

————. *Siphre Zutta (The Midrash of Lydda). II The Talmud of Caesaria* (Hebrew). New York: Jewish Theological Seminary of America, 1968.

————. *The Talmud of Caesaria* (Hebrew). Supplement to *Tarbiz* 2/4. Jerusalem, 1931.

Lieberman, S. J., ed. *Sumerological Studies in Honor of Thorkild Jacobsen*. AS 20. Chicago: University of Chicago Press, 1976.

Limet, H. "Les chants épiques sumériens." *Revue Belge de Philologie et d'Histoire* 50 (1972): 3–23.

Lipinski, E. "Jeremiah." *EJ* 9:1345–59.

Liver, J. "History and Historiography in Chronicles." Pp. 221–33 in *Studies in Bible and Judean Desert Scrolls*. Jerusalem: Mosad Bialik, 1971.

————. "Josiah" (Hebrew). *EM* 3:417–24.

Loewenstamm, S. E. "The Seven-Day Unit in Ugaritic Epic Literature." *IEJ* 15 (1965): 122–33; repr. in Loewenstamm, *Comparative Studies in Biblical and Ancient Oriental Literatures*. AOAT 204. Kevelaer: Butzon & Bercker; Neukirchen-Vluyn: Neukirchener Verlag, 1980, pp. 192–207.

————. *The Tradition of the Exodus in Its Development* (Hebrew). Jerusalem: Magnes, 1965.

Longstaff, T. R. W. *Evidence of Conflation in Mark: A Study in the Synoptic Problem.* Society of Biblical Literature Dissertation Series 28. Missoula, Mont.: Scholars Press, 1977.

Lord, A. B. *The Singer of Tales.* New York: Atheneum, 1968.

Luckenbill, D. D. *Ancient Records of Assyria and Babylonia.* 2 vols. Chicago: University of Chicago Press, 1926–27.

Lund, N. W. "The Presence of Chiasmus in the Old Testament." *AJSL* 46 (1929–30): 104–26.

Lust, J. "'Gathering and Return' in Jeremiah and Ezekiel," pp. 119–42 in Bogaert, ed., *Le Livre de Jérémie.*

_____. "The Story of David and Goliath in Hebrew and Greek." *ETL* 59 (1983): 5–25.

Luzzatto, S. D. *Il Profeta Isaia.* Padova: Antonio Bianchi, 1867 (Hebrew and Italian).

McCarter, P. Kyle. *I Samuel.* AB 8. Garden City, N.Y.: Doubleday, 1980.

Malamat, A. *Israel in Biblical Times* (in Hebrew). Jerusalem: Mosad Bialik, 1983.

_____. "Longevity: Biblical Concepts and Some Ancient Near Eastern Parallels." CRRAI 28. *AfO Beiheft* 19 (1982): 215–24.

Malter, H. *The Treatise Taanit.* New York: American Academy for Jewish Research, 1930.

Margulies, M. *Midrash Wayyikra Rabbah.* 5 parts. Jerusalem: Ministry of Education and Culture of Israel and the Louis and Minnie Epstein Fund of the American Academy for Jewish Research, 1953 (Part 1); Ararat Publishing Society Ltd., London, 1954 (Part 2); Louis and Minnie Epstein Fund of the American Academy for Jewish Research, 1956–60 (Parts 3–5).

Martin, W. J. *Stylistic Criteria and the Analysis of the Pentateuch.* London: Tyndale, 1955.

Matouš, L. "Les rapports entre la version sumérienne et la version akkadienne de l'epopée de Gilgameš." In *GSL*, pp. 83–94.

_____. "Zu neueren Literatur über das Gilgameš-Epos." *Bi.Or.* 21 (1964): 3–10.

_____. "Zur Neuern Epischen Literatur in Alten Mesopotamien." *Ar.Or.* 35 (1967): 1–25.

Mazar, B. "David's Reign in Hebron and the Conquest of Jerusalem." Pp. 235–44 in *In the Time of Harvest: Essays in Honor of A. H. Silver,* edited by D. J. Silver. New York: Macmillan, 1963.

_____. "The Historical Background of the Book of Genesis." *JNES* 28 (1969): 73–83.

_____. "The Military Élite of King David." *VT* 13 (1963): 310–20.

Mead, C. M. "Tatian's Diatessaron and the Analysis of the Pentateuch: A Reply." *JBL* 10 (1891): 44–54.

Meek, T. J., trans. "The Code of Hammurabi." In *ANET*, pp. 163–80.

Meissner, B. "Ein altbabylonisches Fragment des Gilgamos-Epos." MVAG 7/1. Berlin: Peiser, 1902.

Melamed, E. Z. *Introduction to Talmudic Literature* (Hebrew). Jerusalem: Kiryat Sepher, 1961.

Mendenhall, G. E. "Biblical History in Transition." Pp. 27–58 in *The Bible and the Ancient Near East: Essays in Honor of William Foxwell Albright*, edited by G. E. Wright. Garden City, N.Y.: Doubleday Anchor, 1965.

Méritan, J. *La version grecqe des livres de Samuel*. Paris: Librairie orientale et américaine, 1898.

Metzger, B. M. *The Early Versions of the New Testament: Their Origin, Transmission, and Limitations*. Oxford: Clarendon, 1977.

Michaeli, F. *Les Livres des Chroniques, d'Esdras et de Néhémie*. Neuchâtel: Delachaux & Niestlé, 1967.

Michalowski, P. "Sumer for Moderns." Review of Wolkstein and Kramer, *Inanna.* . . . In *New York Times Book Review*, September 25, 1983, p. 31.

Milgrom, J. "Profane Slaughter and a Formulaic Key to the Composition of Deuteronomy." *HUCA* 47 (1976): 1–17.

―――. "Sancta Contagion and Altar/City Asylum." SVT 32 (1981): 278–310.

Millard, A. R. "Gilgamesh X: A New Fragment." *Iraq* 26 (1964): 99–105.

―――. "A New Babylonian 'Genesis' Story." *Tyndale Bulletin* 18 (1967): 3–18.

―――. "Some Esarhaddon Fragments Relating to the Restoration of Babylon." *AfO* 24 (1973): 117–19.

Miller, P. D., and Roberts, J. J. M. *The Hand of the Lord*. Baltimore: Johns Hopkins University Press, 1977.

Min, Y.-J. "The Minuses and Pluses of the LXX Translation of Jeremiah as Compared with the Masoretic Text: Their Classification and Possible Origins." Dissertation. Hebrew University, Jerusalem, 1977.

Miqrāʾôt Gĕdôlôt. New York: Pardes, 1951.

Montgomery, J. A., and Gehman, H. S. *A Critical and Exegetical Commentary on the Book of Kings*. ICC. Edinburgh: T. & T. Clark, 1951.

Moor, J. C. de. "Studies in the New Alphabetic Texts from Ras Shamra." *Ugarit-Forschungen* 1 (1969): 167–88.

Moore, C. A. *Daniel, Esther, and Jeremiah: The Additions*. AB 44. Garden City, N.Y.: Doubleday, 1979.

Moore, G. F. *A Critical and Exegetical Commentary on Judges*. Edinburgh: T. & T. Clark, 1895.

―――. "Tatian's Diatessaron and the Analysis of the Pentateuch." *JBL* 9 (1890): 201–15 (reprinted in Appendix above, pp. 243–56).

Mowinckel, S. *Prophecy and Tradition*. Oslo: I Komisjon Hos Jacob Dybwad, 1946.

Murray, G. *The Rise of the Greek Epic*. 4th ed. New York: Oxford University Press, 1960.

Myers, J. M. *I and II Chronicles*. 2 vols. AB 12–13. Garden City, N.Y.: Doubleday, 1965.

Naveh, J. *Early History of the Alphabet*. Jerusalem: Magnes; Leiden: Brill, 1982.

Nielsen, E. *Oral Tradition.* Studies in Biblical Theology 11. London: SCM, 1954.

———. *Shechem: A Traditio-Historical Investigation.* Copenhagen: Gad, 1955.

Nilsson, M. P. *Homer and Mycenae.* London: Methuen, 1933; repr. Philadelphia: University of Pennsylvania Press, 1972.

Nissen, H. J. "The City Wall of Uruk." Pp. 793–98 in *Man, Settlement, and Urbanism,* edited by P. J. Ucko, R. Tringham, and G. W. Dimbleby. London: Duckworth, Gerald, 1972.

North, C. R. "Pentateuchal Criticism." Pp. 48–83 in *The Old Testament and Modern Study,* edited by H. H. Rowley. London: Oxford University Press, 1961.

Noth, M. *A History of Pentateuchal Traditions.* Englewood Cliffs, N.J.: Prentice-Hall, 1972; repr. Chico, Calif.: Scholars Press, 1981.

———. "Noah, Daniel und Hiob in Ezechiel XIV." *VT* 1 (1951): 251–60.

———. *Überlieferungsgeschichtliche Studien.* Halle: M. Niemeyer, 1943.

———. Review of J. Hoftijzer, *Die Verheissungen an die drei Erzväter* (Leiden: Brill, 1956), in *VT* 7 (1957): 430–33.

Oates, J. "Assyrian Chronology." *Iraq* 27 (1965): 135–59.

Olmstead, A. T. E. *Assyrian Historiography.* Columbia, Mo.: University of Missouri, 1916.

———. "Source Study and the Biblical Text." *AJSL* 30 (1913): 1–35.

Oppenheim, A. L. *Ancient Mesopotamia: Portrait of a Dead Civilization.* Chicago: University of Chicago Press, 1964.

Oppenheim, A. L., trans. "Babylonian and Assyrian Historical Texts." In *ANET,* pp. 265–317, 556–67.

Owen, D. I., and Watanabe, K. "Eine Neubabylonische Gartenkaufurkunde mit Flüchen aus dem Akzessionjahr Asarhaddons." *Or.Ant.* 22 (1983): 37–47.

Paul, S. M. *Studies in the Book of the Covenant in the Light of Cuneiform and Biblical Law.* SVT 18. Leiden: Brill, 1970.

Pedersen, J. *Israel: Its Life and Culture.* Vols. I–II. London: Oxford University Press; Copenhagen: Branner og Korch, 1959.

Perles, F. *Analekten zur Textkritik des Alten Testaments.* Munich: Ackermann, 1895.

———. *Analekten zur Textkritik des Alten Testaments. Neue Folge.* Leipzig: G. Engel, 1922.

Peters, R. *Beiträge zur Text- und Literarkritik sowie zur Erklärung der Bücher Samuel.* Freiburg im Breisgau, 1899.

Pettinato, G. *The Archives of Ebla: An Empire Inscribed in Clay.* Garden City, N.Y.: Doubleday, 1981.

———. *Catalogo dei testi cuneiformi di Tell Mardikh-Ebla.* Istituto Universitario Orientali de Napoli. Seminario di Studi Asiatici. Series Major, 1. Materiali Epigrafici di Ebla, 1. Naples: 1979.

Pfeiffer, R. *Introduction to the Old Testament.* New York: Harper, 1948.

Ploeg, J. van der. "Le rôle de la tradition orale dans la transmission du texte de l'AT." *RB* 54 (1947): 5–41.

Polzin, R. *Late Biblical Hebrew: Toward an Historical Typology of Biblical Hebrew Prose.* HSM 12. Missoula, Mont.: Scholars Press, 1976.

Pope, M. H. *Job.* AB 15. 2d ed. Garden City, N.Y.: Doubleday, 1973.

———. "Number, Numbering, Numbers." *IDB* 3:561–67.

Porter, J. R. "Pre-Islamic Arabic Historical Traditions and the Early Historical Narratives of the Old Testament." *JBL* 77 (1968): 17–26.

Pritchard, J. B. *Ancient Near Eastern Texts Relating to the Old Testament.* 3d ed. Princeton: Princeton University Press, 1969.

Purvis, J. D. *The Samaritan Pentateuch and the Origin of the Samaritan Sect.* HSM 2. Cambridge, Mass.: Harvard University Press, 1968.

———. "Samaritans [2]. The Samaritan Version of the Torah" (Hebrew). *EM* 8:173–82.

Rabinowitz, L. I. "Talmud, Jerusalem," *EJ* 15:772–79.

Rad, G. von. *Genesis. A Commentary.* OTL. Philadelphia: Westminster, 1961.

———. *Old Testament Theology.* Vol. 1. New York and Evanston: Harper & Row, 1962.

———. *The Problem of the Hexateuch and Other Essays.* Translated by E. W. Trueman Dicken. New York: McGraw-Hill, 1966.

Rahlfs, A. *Septuaginta.* 2 vols. Stuttgart: Wurttembergische Bibelanstalt, 1962.

Rank, O. *The Myth of the Birth of the Hero and Other Writings.* Edited by P. Freund. New York: Vintage, 1959.

Rast, W. E. *Tradition History and the Old Testament.* Guides to Biblical Scholarship, Old Testament Series. Philadelphia: Fortress Press, 1972.

Redford, D. B. *A Study of the Biblical Story of Joseph (Genesis 37–50).* SVT 20. Leiden: Brill, 1970.

Reiner, E., trans. "Akkadian Treaties from Syria and Assyria." In *ANET*, pp. 531–41.

Renger, J. "Heilige Hochzeit. A. Philologisch." *RLA* 4:251–59.

Reviv, H. "The History of Judah from Hezekiah to Josiah." Pp. 193–204, 344–48 in A. Malamat and I. Eph‘al, eds., *The Age of the Monarchies: Political History. WHJP.* First Series: Ancient Times. Vol. 4, part 2. Jerusalem: Massada, 1979.

Reynolds, L. D., and Wilson, N. G. *Scribes and Scholars: A Guide to the Transmission of Greek and Latin Literature.* 2d ed. Oxford: Clarendon, 1978.

Roberts, B. J. *The Old Testament Text and Versions.* Cardiff: University of Wales, 1951.

Roberts, J. J. M. "Myth *versus* History." *CBQ* 38 (1976): 1–13.

Roche, O. I. A., ed. *The Jefferson Bible.* New York: Clarkson N. Potter, 1964.

Rofé, A. "The Acts of Nahash according to 4QSam^a." *IEJ* 32 (1982): 129–33.

———. *The Belief in Angels in Ancient Israel* (in Hebrew). 2 vols. Jerusalem: Makor, 1979.

———. *The Book of Balaam (Numbers 22:2–24:25)—A Study in Methods of Criticism and the History of Biblical Literature and Religion* (in Hebrew). Jerusalem: Simor, 1979.

————. "The End of the Book of Joshua According to the Septuagint." *Henoch* 4 (1982): 17–36.

————. "The Method of Historico-Literary Criticism Exemplified by Joshua 20" (in Hebrew). In Zakovitch and Rofé, eds., *Isac Leo Seeligmann Volume*, vol. 1. Jerusalem: Rubinstein, 1983.

————. *The Prophetical Stories* (in Hebrew). Jerusalem: Magnes, 1982.

————. Review of Weinfeld, *Deuteronomy and the Deuteronomic School*, in *Qiryat Sefer* 48 (1972–73): 83–89 (Hebrew; English trans. in *Christian News from Israel* 24 [1974]: 204–9).

Rosenthal, E. S. "Lĕšônôt Sôfĕrîm." Pp. 293–324 in *Yuval Shay: A Jubilee Volume Dedicated to S. Y. Agnon on the Occasion of His Seventieth Birthday*. Edited by B. Kurzweil. Ramat Gan, Israel: Bar Ilan University, 1958.

Rosenthal, F. "Die Parallelstellen in den Texten von Ugarit." *Or.* 8 (1939): 213–37.

Rosenthal, L. A. "Die Josephgeschichte mit den Büchern Ester und Daniel verglichen." *ZAW* 15 (1895): 278–84.

————. "Nochmals der Vergleich Ester-Joseph-Daniel." *ZAW* 17 (1897): 125–28.

Roth, C., ed. *Encyclopaedia Judaica*. 16 vols. Jerusalem: Keter, 1972.

Rowton, M. B. "The Date of the Sumerian King List." *JNES* 19 (1960): 156–62.

Rudolph, W. *Chronikbücher*. HAT, 1st series, Band 21. Tübingen: J. C. B. Mohr, 1955.

————. *Jeremia*. 2d ed. HAT, 1st series, Band 12. Tübingen: Mohr (Paul Siebeck), 1958.

Russo, J. A. "Is 'Oral' or 'Aural' Composition the Cause of Homer's Formulaic Style?" Pp. 31–54 in Stolz and Shannon, *Oral Literature and the Formula*.

Sadaqa, A. and R. *Jewish and Samaritan Version of the Pentateuch*. 5 parts. Tel Aviv: n.p., 1962–65 (parts 1–4); Holon, Israel: n.p., 1961 (part 5). Distributed by Rubin Mass, Jerusalem.

Sandars, N. K. *The Epic of Gilgamesh*. Baltimore: Penguin, 1960.

Sanders, J. A. "Palestinian Manuscripts, 1947–72." In Cross and Talmon, eds., *Qumran*, pp. 401–13.

————. *The Psalms Scroll of Qumran Cave 11* (11QPsᵃ). DJD 4. Oxford: Clarendon, 1965.

————. *Torah and Canon*. Philadelphia: Fortress Press, 1972.

Sarna, N. M. "The Abortive Insurrection in Zedekiah's Day (Jer. 27–29)." *EI* 14 (1978): 89–96.

————. "The Anticipatory Use of Information as a Literary Feature of the Genesis Narratives." Pp. 76–82 in Friedman, ed., *The Creation of Sacred Literature*.

————. "Epic Substratum in the Prose of Job." *JBL* 76 (1957): 13–25.

————. *Understanding Genesis*. New York: Jewish Theological Seminary and McGraw-Hill, 1966.

————. "Zedekiah's Emancipation of Slaves and the Sabbatical Year." Pp. 143–49 in H. A. Hoffner, Jr., ed., *Orient and Occident: Essays Presented to Cyrus H. Gordon on the Occasion of His Sixty-fifth Birthday*. AOAT 22. Kevelaer: Butzon & Bercker; Neukirchen-Vluyn: Neukirchener, 1973.

Sasson, J. M. "Wordplay in the OT." *IDBS*, pp. 968–70.

Schmid, J. "Septuagintageschichtliche Studien zum I. Samuelbuch." Dissertation. Breslau, 1941.

Scholz, A. *Der Masorethische Text und die LXX Übersetzung des Buches Jeremias.* Regensburg, 1875.

Schott, A. *Die Vergleiche in den akkadischen Königsinschriften.* MVAG 30(2). Leipzig: Hinrichs, 1926.

Seeligmann, I. L. "Aetiological Elements in Biblical Historiography" (Hebrew). *Zion* 26 (1961): 141–69; English summary, pp. i–ii.

_____. "Hebräische Erzählung und biblische Geschichtsschreibung." *TLZ* 18 (1962): 305–25.

_____. Review of K. Elliger, *Studien zum Habakuk-Kommentar vom Toten Meer.* In *Kirjath-Sepher* 30 (1954–55): 36–46.

Sēfer Midrāš Rabbâ. Vilna ed. Repr., in 2 vols. Jerusalem: Ortsel, 1961.

Segal, M. H. *The Pentateuch: Its Composition and Its Authorship, and Other Biblical Studies.* Jerusalem: Magnes, 1967.

The Septuagint Version of the Old Testament, with an English Translation; and with Various Readings and Critical Notes. London: Samuel Bagster, 1879; repr. Grand Rapids, Mich.: Zondervan, 1970.

Seters, J. van. *Abraham in History and Tradition.* New Haven and London: Yale University Press, 1975.

Shaffer, A. "The Sumerian Sources of Tablet XII of the Epic of Gilgameš." Dissertation. University of Pennsylvania, 1963.

_____. "TA ša kima A itenerrubu: A Study in Native Babylonian Philology." *Or.* 38 (1969): 433–46.

Shenkel, J. D. *Chronology and Recensional Development in the Greek Text of Kings.* HSM 1. Cambridge, Mass.: Harvard University Press, 1968.

Sheridan, E. R. "Introduction." Pp. 3–42 in Dickinson W. Adams, ed., *Jefferson's Extracts from the Gospels.* The Papers of Thomas Jefferson, Second Series. Princeton: Princeton University Press, 1983.

Shinan, A. *The Aggadah in the Aramaic Targums to the Pentateuch* (Hebrew). Jerusalem: Makor, 1979.

Simon, R. *Histoire critique du Vieux Testament* 1678 (2d ed. Rotterdam, 1685). English trans. *A Critical History of the Old Testament.* London, 1682.

Simpson, W. K., ed. *The Literature of Ancient Egypt.* New Haven and London: Yale University Press, 1973.

Sjöberg, A. "Ein Selbstpreis des Königs Hammurapi von Babylon." *ZA* 54 (1961): 51–70.

Skehan, P. W. "Exodus in the Samaritan Recension from Qumran." *JBL* 74 (1955): 182–87.

_____. "The Period of the Biblical Texts from Khirbet Qumran." *CBQ* 19 (1957): 435–40.

_____. "Qumran and the Present State of Old Testament Text Studies: The Masoretic Text." *JBL* 78 (1959): 21–25.

————. "The Scrolls and the Old Testament Text." Pp. 99–112 in D. N. Freedman and J. C. Greenfield, eds., *New Directions in Biblical Archaeology.* Garden City, N.Y.: Doubleday, 1971.

————. "Two Books on Qumran Studies." *CBQ* 21 (1959): 71–78.

Skinner, J. *A Critical and Exegetical Commentary on Genesis.* 2d ed. ICC. Edinburgh: T. & T. Clark, 1930.

————. *Prophecy and Religion.* Cambridge: University Press, 1963.

Smirin, S. *Josiah and His Age* (in Hebrew). Jerusalem: Mosad Bialik, 1952.

Smith, H. P. *A Critical and Exegetical Commentary on the Books of Samuel.* ICC. Edinburgh: T. & T. Clark, 1899.

Smith, M. "On the Differences Between the Culture of Israel and the Major Cultures of the Ancient Near East." *JANES* 5 (1973): 389–95.

————. *Palestinian Parties and Politics That Shaped the Old Testament.* New York and London: Columbia University Press, 1971.

————. "The Present State of Old Testament Studies." *JBL* 88 (1969): 19–35.

————. "Pseudepigraphy in the Israelite Literary Tradition." Pp. 191–215 in *Pseudepigrapha I.* Entretiens sur l'Antiquité Classique XVIII. Vandoevres-Geneva: Fondation Hardt, 1972.

Smith, W. Robertson. *The Old Testament in the Jewish Church.* New York: Appleton. 1st ed., 1881; 3d ed., 1892 (citations from 3d ed.).

Soden, W. von. *Akkadisches Handwörterbuch.* Wiesbaden: Harrassowitz, 1959–81.

————. *Grundriss der Akkadischen Grammatik.* An.Or. 33. Rome: Pontifical Biblical Institute, 1952.

————. "Der hymnisch-epische Dialekt des Akkadischen." *ZA* 40 (1931): 163–227; 41 (1933): 90–183.

————. Review of Kitchen, *Alter Orient und Altes Testament.* In *WdO* 4 (1967): 38–47.

————. "Sumer, Babylon, und Hethiter bis zur Mitte des zweiten Jahrtausends v.chr." Pp. 523–609 in G. Mann and A. Heuss, eds., *Propyläen Weltgeschichte* I. Berlin: Propyläen, 1961.

Soisalon-Soininen, I. *Die Infinitive in der Septuaginta.* Annales Academiae Scientiarum Fennicae, Ser. B Tom. 132, 1. Helsinki: Suomalainen Tiedeakatemia, 1965.

Sollamo, R. *Renderings of Hebrew Semiprepositions in the Septuagint.* Annales Academiae Scientiarum Fennicae, Dissertationes Humanarum Litterarum 19. Helsinki: Suomalainen Tiedeakatemia, 1979.

Sollberger, E. *Royal Inscriptions. Part 2.* UET 8. London: British Museum and University of Pennsylvania, 1965.

————. "The Tummal Inscription." *JCS* 16 (1962): 40–47.

Sonne, I. "Maimonides' Letter to Samuel ibn Tibbon" (Hebrew). *Tarbiz* 10 (1938–39): 135–54, 309–32.

Sonneck, F. "Die Einführung der direkten Rede in den epischen Texten." *ZA* 46 (1940): 225–35.

Sonsino, R. *Motive Clauses in Hebrew Law: Biblical Forms and Near Eastern*

Parallels. Society of Biblical Literature Dissertation Series 45. Chico, Calif.: Scholars Press, 1980.

Speiser, E. A., *Genesis.* AB 1. Garden City, N.Y.: Doubleday, 1964.

Speiser, E. A., trans. "Akkadian Myths and Epics." Revised by A. K. Grayson. In *ANET*, pp. 60–119.

Spiegel, S. "Introduction" to L. Ginzberg, *Legends of the Bible.* Philadelphia: Jewish Publication Society, 1966, pp. xi–xxxix; repr. in J. Goldin, ed., *The Jewish Expression.* New York: Bantam, 1970, pp. 134–62.

―――. *The Last Trial.* Translated by J. Goldin. Philadelphia: Jewish Publication Society, 1967.

―――. "Noah, Daniel, and Job." Pp. 305–55 in A. Marx et al., eds., *Louis Ginzberg Jubilee Volume.* New York: American Academy for Jewish Research, 1945.

Stanton, V. H. "Gospels." In *HDB* 2:234–49.

Steinsaltz, A. *Masseket Bābāʾ Měṣîʿāʾ.* Jerusalem: Israel Institute for Talmudic Publications, 1981.

Stenning, J. F. "Diatessaron." *HDB* Extra Volume, pp. 451–61.

Sternberg, M. "Delicate Balance in the Story of the Rape of Dinah: Biblical Narrative and the Rhetoric of the Narrative Text" (Hebrew). *Ha-Sifrut* 4 (1973): 193–231.

Steuernagel, K. *Lehrbuch der Einleitung in das Alte Testament.* Tübingen: Mohr, 1912.

Stoebe, H. J. "Die Goliathperikope 1 Sam. XVII.1–XVIII.5 und die Textform der Septuaginta." *VT* 4 (1954): 397–413.

Stolz, B. A., and Shannon, R. S. *Oral Literature and the Formula.* Ann Arbor: Center for the Coordination of Ancient and Modern Studies, 1976.

Streck, M. *Assurbanipal und die letzen Assyrischen Könige.* 2 vols. VAB 7. Leipzig: J. C. Hinrichs, 1916.

Strugnell, J. "Notes en marge du Volume V des 'Discoveries in the Judaean Desert of Jordan.'" *RQ* 26 (1970): 163–276.

Sukenik, E. L. et al., eds. *ʾEnṣîqlôpedyâ Miqrāʾît (Encyclopaedia Biblica).* Jerusalem: Mosad Bialik, 1950–82.

Swete, H. B. *An Introduction to the Old Testament in Greek.* Cambridge: University Press, 1902. Repr. New York: KTAV, 1968.

Tadmor, H. "Hezekiah" (Hebrew). *EM* 3:95–99.

―――. "History and Ideology in the Assyrian Royal Inscriptions." Pp. 13–33 in *Assyrian Royal Inscriptions: New Horizons in Literary, Ideological, and Historical Analysis.* Orientis Antiqui Collectio, 17. Edited by F. M. Fales. Rome: Istituto per L'Oriente; Centro per le Antichità e la Storia dell'arte del Vicino Oriente, 1981.

―――. "The Inscriptions of Nabunaid: Historical Arrangement." Pp. 351–63 in *Studies in Honor of Benno Landsberger.* AS 16. Chicago: University of Chicago Press, 1965.

―――. *rēʾšît malkût.* *EM* 7:312–14.

Talmon, S. "Did There Exist a Biblical National Epic?" Pp. 41–61 in *Proceedings of the Seventh World Congress of Jewish Studies. Studies in the Bible and the Ancient Near East*. Jerusalem: Perry Foundation for Biblical Research and World Union of Jewish Studies, 1981.

———. "Conflate Readings." *IDBS*, pp. 170–73.

———. "Double Readings in the Masoretic Text." *Textus* 1 (1960): 144–84.

———. "The Old Testament Text." Pp. 159–99 in P. R. Ackroyd and C. F. Evans, eds., *Cambridge History of the Bible*. Vol. 1. Cambridge: Cambridge University Press, 1970. Repr. in Cross and Talmon, eds., *Qumran*, pp. 1–41.

———. "The Samaritan Pentateuch." *JJS* 2 (1951): 144–50.

———. "Synonymous Readings in the Textual Traditions of the Old Testament." Pp. 335–83 in C. Rabin, ed., *Studies in the Bible*. Scripta Hierosolymitana 8. Jerusalem: Magnes, 1961.

———. "The Textual Study of the Bible—A New Outlook." In Cross and Talmon, eds., *Qumran*, pp. 321–400.

Talmon, S., and Fishbane, M. "Aspects of the Literary Structure of the Book of Ezekiel." *Tarbiz* 42 (1972–73): 27–41 (Hebrew; English summary, pp. ii–iv).

Thackeray, H. St. J., ed. and trans. *Josephus*. LCL. Repr. Cambridge, Mass.: Harvard University Press, 1966. Vol. 5: *Jewish Antiquities*, Books V–VIII.

Thenius, O. *Die Bücher Samuels*. Leipzig, 1842.

Theodor, J., and Albeck, Ch. *Midrash Bereshit Rabba*. 3 vols. 2d corrected printing. Jerusalem: Wahrmann, 1965.

Thiele, E. R. *The Mysterious Numbers of the Hebrew Kings*. 2d ed. Grand Rapids, Mich.: W. B. Eerdmans, 1965.

Thompson, R. C. *The Epic of Gilgamesh: Text, Transliteration, and Notes*. Oxford: Clarendon, 1930.

Thompson, T. L. *The Historicity of the Patriarchal Narratives*. BZAW 133. Berlin and New York: de Gruyter, 1974.

Thompson, T. L., and Irvin, D. "The Joseph and Moses Narratives." Pp. 149–212 in Hayes and Miller, eds., *Israelite and Judaean History*.

Thomson, P. "The Four Gospels According to Thomas Jefferson." *Smithsonian* 14/6 (September 1983): 139–48.

Thureau-Dangin, F. "Notes Assyriologiques. XXIII. Un double de l'inscription d'Utu-ḫegal." *RA* 10 (1913): 98–100.

———. *Die Sumerischen und Akkadischen Königsinschriften*. VAB 1. Leipzig: Hinrichs, 1907.

Tiele, C. P. *Babylonische-Assyrische Geschichte*, 1. Gotha: F. A. Perthes, 1886.

Tigay, J. H. "An Empirical Basis for the Documentary Hypothesis." *JBL* 94 (1975): 329–42. Revised Hebrew version, "The Samaritan Pentateuch as an Empirical Model for Biblical Criticism." *Beth Mikra* 22 (1977): 348–61.

———. *The Evolution of the Gilgamesh Epic*. Philadelphia: University of Pennsylvania Press, 1982.

_____. "Literary-Critical Studies in the Gilgamesh Epic: An Assyriological Contribution to Biblical Literary Criticism." Dissertation. Yale University, 1971.

_____. "Notes on the Development of the Jewish Week." *H. L. Ginsberg Volume.* *EI* 14 (1978): 111*–121*.

_____. "On Some Aspects of Prayer in the Bible." *AJSR* 1 (1976): 363–79.

_____. *šābûaᶜ. EM* 7:468–79.

Toeg, A. *Lawgiving at Sinai.* Jerusalem: Magnes, 1977.

Tournay, R.-J. "Inscription d'Anam, roi d'Uruk et successeur de Gilgamesh." Pp. 453–57 in H. Goedicke, ed., *Near Eastern Studies in Honor of William Foxwell Albright.* Baltimore: Johns Hopkins University Press, 1971.

Tov, E. "Exegetical Notes on the Hebrew Vorlage of the LXX of Jeremiah 27(34)." *ZAW* 91 (1979): 73–93.

_____. *The Hebrew and Greek Texts of Samuel.* 1980 Proceedings, IOSCS-Vienna. Jerusalem: Academon, 1980.

_____. "L'incidence de la critique textuelle sur la critique littéraire dans le livre de Jérémie." *RB* 79 (1972): 189–99.

_____. "The 'Lucianic' Text of the Canonical and the Apocryphal Sections of Esther: A Rewritten Biblical Book." *Textus* 10 (1982): 1–25.

_____. "The Nature and Background of Harmonizations in Biblical MSS." *JSOT* 31 (1985): 3–29.

_____. "Old Testament Textual Criticism, Its Methods and Limitations." Pp. 207–21 in vol. 1 of Y. Avishur and J. Blau, eds., *Studies in Bible and the Ancient Near East Presented to Samuel E. Loewenstamm on His Seventieth Birthday.* 2 vols. Jerusalem: Rubinstein, 1978. English summary, vol. 2, pp. 212–13.

_____. "Pap. Giessen 13, 19, 22, 26: A Revision of the LXX?" *RB* 78 (1971): 355–83.

_____. "Septuagint. A. Contribution to OT Scholarship." *IDBS*, pp. 807–11.

_____. "Some Aspects of the Textual and Literary History of the Book of Jeremiah." Pp. 145–67 in Bogaert, ed., *Le livre de Jérémie.*

_____. "The 'Temple Scroll' and Old Testament Textual Criticism." *H. M. Orlinsky Volume. EI* 16 (1982): 100–111.

_____. *The Text-Critical Use of the Septuagint in Biblical Research.* Jerusalem Biblical Studies 3. Jerusalem: Simor, 1981.

Tsevat, M. "Common Sense and Hypothesis in Old Testament Study." *HUCA* 47 (1976): 217–30.

Tur-Sinai, N. H. *The Book of Job: A New Commentary.* Jerusalem: Kiryath Sepher, 1957.

Vaux, Roland de. *The Bible and the Ancient Near East.* Garden City, N.Y.: Doubleday, 1971.

Vööbus, A. "Diatessaron." *Encyclopaedia Britannica.* Chicago: Encyclopaedia Britannica Corp., 1966. Vol. 7:367–68.

Vogelstein, M. *Biblical Chronology.* Cincinnati: private printing, 1944.

_____. *Fertile Soil.* New York: American Press, 1957.

Vries, S. J. de. "David's Victory over the Philistine as Saga and as Legend." *JBL* 92 (1973): 23–36.

Waltke, B. K. "The Samaritan Pentateuch and the Text of the Old Testament." Pp. 212–39 in *New Perspectives on the Old Testament*, ed. J. B. Payne. Waco, Tex.: Word Books, 1970.

Warner, S. "The Alphabet. An Invention and Its Diffusion." *VT* 30 (1980): 81–90.

Weinfeld, M. *Deuteronomy and the Deuteronomic School.* Oxford: Clarendon, 1972.

_____. "Literary Creativity." Pp. 27–70, 286–92 in A. Malamat and I. Eph‿al, eds., *The Age of the Monarchies. WHJP.* First series: Ancient Times. Vol. 4 Pt. 2: The Age of the Monarchies: Culture and Society. Jerusalem: Massada, 1979.

_____. "Torah. Research on the Torah in Modern Times." *EM* 8:492–507.

Weingreen, J. *From Bible to Mishna: The Continuity of Tradition.* Manchester, Eng.: Manchester University Press, 1976.

Weippert, M. *The Settlement of the Israelite Tribes in Palestine.* Studies in Biblical Theology. Second Series, 21. Naperville, Ill.: Alec R. Allenson, 1971.

Weiss, R. *The Aramaic Targum of Job.* Tel Aviv: Chaim Rosenberg School for Jewish Studies, Tel-Aviv University, 1979.

_____. "Chiasmus in the Bible." *Beth Mikra* 7 (1962): 46–51 (Hebrew; expanded repr. in R. Weiss, *Studies*, pp. 259–73).

_____. Review of Allegro, *Qumran Cave 4:I.* In *Kirjath-Sepher* 45 (1970): 54–63 (in Hebrew; repr. in Weiss, *Studies*, pp. 319–34).

_____. *Studies in the Text and Language of the Bible* (Hebrew). Jerusalem: Magnes, 1981.

Wellek, R., and Warren, A. *Theory of Literature.* 3d ed. New York: Harcourt, Brace & World, 1956.

Wellhausen, J. *Die composition des Hexateuchs und der historischen Bücher des Alten Testaments.* 3d ed. Berlin: Reimer, 1899; 4th ed., repr. Berlin, 1963.

_____. *Prolegomena to the History of Ancient Israel.* New York: Meridian, 1957.

_____. *Der Text der Bücher Samuelis Untersucht.* Göttingen: Vandenhoeck & Ruprecht, 1871.

Welten, P. *Geschichte und Geschichtsdarstellung in den Chronikbücher.* WMANT 42. Neukirchen: Neukirchener Verlag, 1973.

Westenholz, J. G. Review of *EGE.* In *JAOS* 104 (1984): 370–72.

Wharton, J. A. "Redaction Criticism, OT." In *IDBS*, pp. 729–32.

Whitman, C. H. *Homer and the Heroic Tradition.* New York: Norton, 1965.

Widengren, G. *Literary and Psychological Aspects of the Hebrew Prophets.* Uppsala Universitets Årsskrift 1948:10. Uppsala: Lundequistska; Wiesbaden: Harrassowitz, 1948.

_____. "Oral Tradition and Written Literature Among the Hebrews in the Light of Arabic Evidence, With Special Regard to Prose Narratives." *Acta Orientalia* 23 (1959): 201–62.

Wilcke, C. "Formale Gesichtspunkte in der Sumerischen Literatur." Pp. 205–316 in S. J. Lieberman, ed., *Studies . . . Jacobsen.*

_____. *Das Lugalbandaepos.* Wiesbaden: Harrassowitz, 1969.

Williamson, H. G. M. *1 and 2 Chronicles.* NCB. Grand Rapids, Mich.: Eerdmans, 1982.

_____. *Israel in the Book of Chronicles.* Cambridge: Cambridge University Press, 1977.

_____. "We Are Yours, O David." *OTS* 21 (1981): 164–76.

Wilson, J., trans. "Egyptian Myths, Tales, and Mortuary Texts" and "Egyptian Texts." In *ANET*, pp. 3–36, 495.

Wiseman, D. J. "The Laws of Hammurabi Again." *JSS* 7 (1962): 161–72.

Witzel, P. J. "Noch einmal die sumerische Himmelsstier-Episode." Pp. 45–68 in *Keilschriftliche Miscellanea.* An.Or. 6. Rome: Pontifical Biblical Institute, 1933.

Wolkstein, D., and Kramer, S. N. *Inanna, Queen of Heaven and Earth: Her Stories and Hymns from Sumer.* New York: Harper & Row, 1983.

Woods, F. H. "Hexateuch." *HDB* 2:363–76.

_____. "The Light Thrown by the Septuagint Version on the Books of Samuel." Pp. 21–38 in *Studia Biblica* 1, *Essays in Biblical Archaeology and Criticism and Kindred Subjects.* Edited by S. R. Driver et al. Oxford: Clarendon, 1885.

Wright, G. E. "Deuteronomy. Introduction." Pp. 311–30 in *The Interpreter's Bible*, vol. 2. Edited by G. A. Buttrick. Nashville: Abingdon, 1953.

Wright, G. E., and Boling, R. *Joshua: A New Translation with Notes and Commentary.* AB 6. Garden City, N.Y.: Doubleday, 1982.

Yadin, Y. *The Message of the Scrolls.* New York: Simon & Schuster, 1969.

_____. "A Note on the Scenes Depicted on the ᶜAin-Samiya Cup." *IEJ* 21 (1971): 82–85.

_____. *The Temple Scroll* (in Hebrew). 3 vols. and supplement. Jerusalem: Israel Exploration Society, Institute of Archaeology of the Hebrew University, and The Shrine of the Book, 1977.

Yalon, H. *Pirqê Lāšôn.* Jerusalem: Mosad Bialik, 1971.

Yaron, R. "Forms in the Laws of Eshnunna." *RIDA* 9 (1963): 150–53.

_____. *The Laws of Eshnunna.* Jerusalem: Magnes, 1969.

Yeivin, S. "Additional Notes on the Date of the Book of Deuteronomy" (in Hebrew). *Beth Mikra* 22 (1977): 183–87.

Young, E. J. *An Introduction to the Old Testament.* Grand Rapids, Mich.: Eerdmans, 1964.

Zakovitch, Y. *"For Three—and for Four."* 2 vols. Jerusalem: Makor, 1979.

_____. "II Kings 20:7—Isaiah 38:21–22." *Beth Mikra* 17 (1972): 302–5.

_____. *The Life of Samson* (Hebrew). Jerusalem: Magnes, 1982.

————. "The Purpose of Narrations in Scripture Concerning Purchase of Possessions." *Beth Mikra* 24 (1979): 17–21 (Hebrew; English summary, p. 117).

————. "The Sacrifice of Gideon (Jud. 6:11–24) and the Sacrifice of Manoah (Jud. 13)." *Shnaton* 1 (1975): 151–54 (Hebrew; English summary, p. xxv).

Zakovitch, Y., and Rofé, A., eds. *Isac Leo Seeligmann Volume.* Jerusalem: Rubinstein, 1983– .

Zeidel, M. "Parallels Between the Book of Isaiah and the Book of Psalms." *Sinai* 38 (1956): 149–72, 229–40, 272–80, 333–55 (Hebrew).

Zimmern, H. *Sumerische Kultlieder aus altbabylonischer Zeit.* 2d series. Vorderasiatische Schriftdenkmäler der Königlichen Museen zu Berlin 10. Leipzig: Hinrichs, 1913.

Zipor, M. A. "The Ancient Versions of Samuel, Kings, and Chronicles: A Comparative Study of Their Translation Techniques for Terms of Realia." Dissertation. Bar Ilan University, Ramat Gan, 1979.

Zobel, H. J. *Stämmesspruch und Geschichte.* BZAW 95. Berlin: Töpelmann, 1965.

Zwettler, M. *The Oral Tradition of Classical Arabic Poetry: Its Character and Implications.* Columbus: Ohio State University Press, 1978.

Index

FOREIGN TERMS

I. HEBREW

II. ARAMAIC

VII. VERSIONS OF THE HEBREW BIBLE